The Purim
Anthology

99146

DATE DUE	BORROWER'S NAME	ROOM NUMBER

DEMCO

PHILIP GOODMAN

The Purim Anthology

The Jewish Publication Society

Philadelphia   New York   Jerusalem

5748/1988

Seventh impression, 1988
ISBN 0-8276-0022-4

 60

PRINTED IN THE UNITED STATES OF AMERICA

To My Wife

חנה

אשת חיל מי ימצא ורחוק מפנינים מכרה
משלי ל"א, י'.

CONTENTS

BOOK TWO

PURIM IN LITERATURE, ART AND MUSIC

BOOK THREE

PURIM FOR YOUNG PEOPLE

BOOK FOUR

PURIM JOY

BOOK FIVE

COMMEMORATION OF PURIM

MUSIC SUPPLEMENT

LIST OF ILLUSTRATIONS

PREFACE

PURIM assumes unusual significance in these post-war days. The many similarities between the position of the Jews in ancient Persia and that of the Jews in modern Europe are readily apparent. Modern antisemitism does not differ basically from the irrational hatred of Haman towards the Jews. Haman's defeat might have served as a warning to his later successors and modern counterparts. Notwithstanding the ever-present persecutions by new Hamans that arise in every generation, the Jewish people do not despair, for they have celebrated many Purims. Unfortunately, the time has not yet come to institute a new Purim in our generation, although Hitler and the Nazis have been defeated. The festival does not commemorate merely the downfall of the enemy but the deliverance of the people; and that full deliverance has not yet arrived.

Today Jews cherish the story of Esther for the message of faith and courage that it conveys. Purim comes as a ray of light and salvation, not only to the remnants of European Jewry, but to all persecuted minorities. The timely deliverance of the Jews from their Persian enemies and their vindication are celebrated as a time of *feasting and gladness, and sending portions one to another, and gifts to the poor* (Esther 9.22). The Jew gives expression to his joyful gratitude by aiding the needy. It is vital that, particularly in times of stress, the Jew should not lose his equilibrium and his sense of humor.

It is in the hope of presenting vividly the character and message of this festival and the manner of its observance that this book has been prepared. If it succeeds in conveying to its readers a feeling of optimism concerning the Jewish future, the editor will consider that his efforts have more than realized his hopes.

It is hoped that this collection will take its place alongside of the other holiday books, such as: *Sabbath, The Day of Delight*, by Abraham E. Millgram, and *Hanukkah, The Feast of Lights*, by Emily Solis-Cohen, both published by The Jewish Publication Society of America; and their counterparts in Hebrew — *Sefer ha-Shabbat* and the volumes of the *Moadim* series.

Although there are many bulletins and pamphlets that include Purim material, the publication of this book hardly needs justification, for there is no comprehensive Purim anthology available in any language.

In view of the paucity of material in certain areas, the compilation of this book would not have been possible without the original contributions of several collaborators to whom I herewith express my sincere gratitude. I feel privileged to have had their cooperation in this work.

Mrs. Rachel Wischnitzer, recognized authority on Jewish art, wrote the informative and revealing chapter on "The Esther Story in Art" and selected the illustrations for the book.

The noted musician, Prof. A. W. Binder, is responsible for the illuminating chapter on "Purim in Music" as well as the musical selections.

Another original article which reveals deep erudition is "The History of Purim Plays," by Dr. Jacob Shatzky.

Dr. Solomon Grayzel, author and Jewish historian, wrote "The Origin of Purim" in a popular style.

The fascinating article, "Tel Aviv — The City of Purim," was contributed by Dr. Mortimer J. Cohen.

"Purim Parties and Programs," by Libbie L. Braverman, educator and author, should be welcomed by parents, teachers and group leaders.

Mrs. Dvora Lapson, outstanding exponent of the Jewish dance, contributed "Purim Dances."

Jacob Sloan translated several selections from Hebrew and Yiddish literature.

In addition to those mentioned above, I am indebted to many friends whose willing assistance made possible the compilation of this book. Rabbi I. Edward Kiev, librarian of the Jewish Institute of Religion, generously made available to me many volumes of the Institute's library and called my attention to numerous others. Dr. Joshua Bloch, chief of the Jewish Division, New York Public Library, and his staff were most helpful. Dr. Jacob S. Golub, librarian-consultant of the Jewish Education Committee of New York, put at my disposal the library of which he is in charge. Dr. Jacob R. Marcus, professor of Jewish history at the Hebrew Union College, kindly gave me an extensive bibliography of sources not easily found. The popular humorist and Hebraist, Daniel Persky, furnished me with many newspaper clippings and other material.

Dr. Louis L. Kaplan, executive director of the Baltimore Board of Jewish Education; Dr. Abraham J. Feldman, president of the Central Conference of American Rabbis; and Dr. David de Sola Pool, rabbi of the Spanish and Portuguese Synagogue, were kind enough to review the manuscript and offered many constructive criticisms.

To Dr. Mortimer J. Cohen I am deeply obligated for his sincere and wholehearted interest and his zealous and ready cooperation in this work which were a great boon to me.

The encouragement and practical assistance of Dr. Maurice Jacobs, executive vice-president of The Jewish Publication Society of America, are largely responsible for the fruition of this work. Without his active interest, it might not have been possible.

To Dr. Solomon Grayzel, the Society's editor, I owe a

particular debt of gratitude. From the very inception of the idea of this volume until the final proofreading, he has been a continuous source of stimulation and guidance. His critical evaluation of the abundance of material originally submitted, of which this book is but a small portion, entitles him to share the credit for whatever merit my work has.

While acknowledging my immense obligations to all those who so kindly assisted in this labor, I assume full responsibility for whatever inadequacies may be found in this book.

PHILIP GOODMAN

New York, N. Y.
May 15, 1948.
יום שני להקמת מדינת ישראל.

ACKNOWLEDGMENTS

The compiler and publisher herewith express their sincere appreciation to the following authors and publishers who have kindly granted permission to use the material indicated:

ALFRED A. KNOPF, Inc., New York: "The Judgments of Reb Yozifel," from *The World of Sholom Aleichem*, by Maurice Samuel, 1943.

THE ALUMNI ASSOCIATION OF THE HEBREW UNION COLLEGE, Cincinnati: excerpt from *Studies, Addresses, and Personal Papers*, by K. Kohler, 1931.

The American Hebrew, New York: "An English Purim of Long Ago," by Gabriel Costa; "Purim in Cairo," by Herbert Friedenwald; and "The Last Purim Pageant," by Joel Blau.

AMERICAN JEWISH HISTORICAL SOCIETY, New York: "Purim Celebration of the Seixas Family, New York," from *Gershom Seixas Letters, 1813–1815*, by David de Sola Pool; and "Purim Association of New York," from *Myer S. Isaacs*, by I. S. Isaacs.

BEHRMAN HOUSE, Inc., New York: "The Song of Water," by Solomon ibn Gabirol, from *The Jewish Anthology*, by Edmond Fleg, translated by Maurice Samuel, 1933; "Reb Abraham" from *Hath Not A Jew*, by A. M. Klein, 1940; and "How Esther Became Queen," from *The Magic Flight, Jewish Tales and Legends*, by Joseph Gaer, 1926.

BLOCH PUBLISHING Co., New York: selections from *Pirke de Rabbi Eliezer*, translated and annotated, with introduction and indices, by Gerald Friedlander, 1916; "Purim," from *Mother Goose Rhymes for Jewish Children*, by Sara G. Levy, 1945; and "Blessing for Purim," from *Around the Year in Rhymes for the Jewish Child*, by Jessie E. Sampter, 1920.

BRUCE HUMPHRIES, INC., Boston: "For Purim," by Zalman Shneour, from *Gems of Hebrew Verse*, translated by Harry H. Fein, 1940.

CENTRAL CONFERENCE OF AMERICAN RABBIS, Cincinnati: "Reform Service for Purim," from *Union Prayer Book*, 1940; and *Megillah Ritual*, 1939.

THE CLARENDON PRESS, Oxford: selections from "Mishnah Megillah," from *The Mishnah*, translated from the Hebrew by Herbert Danby, 1933.

COLUMBIA UNIVERSITY PRESS, New York: "The History of Purim Parody in Jewish Literature," from *Parody in Jewish Literature*, by Israel Davidson, 1907.

CROWN PUBLISHERS, New York: "Two Dead Men," from *The Old Country*, by Sholom Aleichem, translated from the Yiddish by Julius and Frances Butwin. Copyright, 1946, by Crown Publishers. Reprinted by permission of Crown Publishers.

DOUBLEDAY & COMPANY, INC., New York: "Purim Gifts," from *The Bridal Canopy*, by S. J. Agnon, copyright, 1937, by Doubleday & Company, Inc.

THE DROPSIE COLLEGE FOR HEBREW AND COGNATE LEARNING, Philadelphia: "Mordecai — Man of Peace," from *The Book of Esther in the Light of History*, by Jacob Hoschander, 1923.

MRS. A. DROUIANOFF, Tel Aviv: excerpts from *Sefer ha-Bedihah veha-Hidud* by A. Drouianoff, Dvir, Tel Aviv, 1936.

DVIR, Tel Aviv: "Purim in Poland," from *Ba-Yamin ha-Haim*, by Mendele Moker Sefarim, 1929.

EDWARD GOLDSTON LTD., London: "Purim de Las Bombas," "Purim of Tiberias" and "Purim of Bandits," from *A Jewish Book of Days*, by Cecil Roth, 1931.

WALTER J. FISCHEL, Berkeley, California: "With Mordecai and Esther in Shushan."

FUNK AND WAGNALLS COMPANY, New York: "Purim of Shiraz," by M. Franco; "Curtain Purim," by Henry Malter; "Purim of the Poisoned Sword," by M. Franco, from *The Jewish Encyclopedia*, 1905.

THE FURROW PRESS, New York: "Tel Aviv," from *Children of the Emek*, by Libbie L. Braverman, 1937.

JULIUS H. GREENSTONE, Philadelphia: "Purim of Yom Tob Lipmann Heller," from *Jewish Feasts and Fasts*, by Julius H. Greenstone, 1945.

Hadoar, New York: "Purims of Tripoli," by A.R. Malachi.

HARVARD UNIVERSITY PRESS, Cambridge, Mass.: selections from *Josephus: Jewish Antiquities, Book XI*, translated by Ralph Marcus (*Loeb Classical Library*), 1937. Reprinted by permission of the publishers.

HEBREW PUBLISHING CO., New York: selections from *Code of Jewish Law*, translated by Hyman E. Goldin, 1927.

Hebrew Union College Annual, Cincinnati: 'Miracle of the Bomb,' from "Some Revolutionary Purims (1790–1801)," by Cecil Roth.

JEWISH EDUCATION COMMITTEE OF NEW YORK: "The Story of Purim," by Deborah Pessin; "The Magic Grogger," by Levin Kipnis; and "Merry Purim," by Levin Kipnis, from *The Festival of Purim, Jewish Life and Customs, Unit Six*, by Ben M. Edidin, 1943; and a dance by Dvora Lapson.

JEWISH NATIONAL FUND, Jerusalem: "Purim of Ibrahim Pasha," by Joseph Meyuhas, and "Purim Among the Yemenites," by Samuel ben Joseph, from *Programme for Purim*.

JEWISH TELEGRAPHIC AGENCY, INC., New York: "Nazis Banned Purim Observance," and "Esther Story Read in English Shelters."

The Jewish Quarterly Review, Philadelphia: 'Day of the Miracle,' by Hakam Ezra Reuben Dangoor, from "The History of the Jews in Basra," by David S. Sassoon.

Jüdische-Rundschau — The Jewish Review, Marburg-Lahn, Germany: "Purim 5706," by Leopold Neuhaus.

EDWARD E. KLEIN AND MABEL H. MEYER: excerpt from *It Happened in Chelm*.

M. LIPSON, Tel Aviv: selections from *Medor Dor*, by M. Lipson, Dorot, Tel Aviv and New York, 1938.

A. C. McCLURG & Co., Chicago: "Haman and Esther in

Poland," from *Jewish Tales*, by Leopold von Sacher Masoch, translated by H. L. Cohen, 1894.

MOSAD HARAB KUK PUBLISHING CO., Jerusalem: "Purim of Saragossa," from *Hagim u-Moadim* by Judah Leb ha-Kohen Fishman, 1944.

NATIONAL COUNCIL FOR JEWISH RELIGIOUS EDUCATION, London: "The Purim Guest," from *Dreams of Childhood*, by Hermann Schwab, translated by Joseph Leftwich, 5705.

THE NATIONAL WOMEN'S LEAGUE OF THE UNITED SYNAGOGUE OF AMERICA, New York: "How K'tonton Masqueraded on Purim," from *The Adventures of K'tonton*, by Sadie Rose Weilerstein, 1935; "What Shall She Be," from *The Singing Way*, by Sadie Rose Weilerstein, 1946; recipes for Hamantashen, Kreplah, Verenikes and Nahit, from *The Jewish Home Beautiful*, by Betty D. Greenberg and Althea O. Silverman, 1941.

NATIONAL YOUNG JUDAEA, New York: "Why I Like Purim," by Elma Ehrlich Levinger; and "Purim in Palestine," by Jessie E. Sampter, from *The Young Judaean*.

LOUIS I. NEWMAN, New York: selections from *The Hasidic Anthology*, selected, compiled and arranged by Louis I. Newman in collaboration with Samuel Spitz, Bloch Publishing Co., New York, 1934.

Opinion, New York: "Plum Jam Purim," by William Mordecai Kramer.

PALESTINE COMPOSERS AND AUTHORS ASSOCIATION, New York: some of the Hebrew songs.

DANIEL PERSKY, New York: "Purim in Minsk, White Russia," from *Likbod ha-Regel*, by Daniel Persky, 5707.

L. RABINOWITZ, Johannesburg, South Africa: "Purim of Castile."

The Reconstructionist, New York: "Purim in Persia, 1945," by Ralph M. Weisberger; and "Song of the Mask Vendor," by I. D. Minzberg.

SHARON BOOKS, Inc., New York: "Purim in Benghazi, North

Africa," from *Letters from the Desert*, by Moshe Mosenson, translated from the Hebrew by Hilda Auerbach, 1945.

THE SONCINO PRESS LTD., Hindhead, Surrey, England: selections from *Megillah*, by Maurice Simon, in *The Babylonian Talmud, Seder Mo'ed*, translated into English with notes, under the editorship of Rabbi Dr. I. Epstein, 1938; and "Esther," translated by Maurice Simon in *Midrash Rabbah*, translated under the editorship of Rabbi Dr. H. Freedman and Maurice Simon, 1939.

THE UNION OF AMERICAN HEBREW CONGREGATIONS, Cincinnati: "Commentary on Shulhan Aruk," by Moses Isserles, from *The Jew in the Medieval World*, by Jacob R. Marcus, 1938; "Esther Today," by Elma Ehrlich Levinger and "About Purim," by Miriam Myers, from *Jewish Festivals in the Religious School*, by Elma Ehrlich Levinger, 1923.

UNION OF SEPHARDIC CONGREGATIONS, New York: "The Banquet of Queen Esther," by Yehudah Halevi, from *Book of Prayers*, translated from the Hebrew by David de Sola Pool, 1941.

THE UNIVERSITY OF CHICAGO PRESS, Chicago: selections from "The Additions to the Book of Esther," from *The Apocrypha*, an American translation, by Edgar J. Goodspeed, 1938.

UNIVERSITY OF TORONTO PRESS, Toronto: "Purim in China," by Gabriel Brotier, from *Chinese Jews*, by William Charles White, 1942.

THE VIKING PRESS, INC., New York: "Hadassah Founded on Purim," from *Henrietta Szold: Life and Letters*, by Marvin Lowenthal, 1942.

THE
PURIM
ANTHOLOGY

BOOK ONE

The Story of Purim

Now it came to pass in the days
of Ahasuerus...

ESTHER 1. 1.

CHAPTER I

THE ORIGIN OF PURIM

Solomon Grayzel

THE festival of Purim derives from the biblical story of Esther, one of the most dramatic and best-told stories in all literature. Generations of Jews and Christians have retold it with undiminished interest. History itself has re-enacted it time and again; for Hamans have risen against the Jews and Mordecais have appeared to save them in many countries throughout the past two millennia. It is surprising, therefore, that the truth of the original story has in more recent times been called into question.

Almost everything about the story of Purim has been doubted. There are distinguished students of the Bible who assert that the events narrated in the story of Esther never happened, that the characters there mentioned never existed — not Esther, nor Mordecai, nor Haman, nor Vashti — that the story is merely a story and that the holiday was not Jewish in origin. These matters must be looked into before Purim can be discussed as historical fact.

The most obvious difficulty is that none of the names mentioned in the Scroll of Esther has been found in any of the records or inscriptions of Persia. Of course, the available information about ancient Persia is rather meager. Most of the documents and tablets of that period were destroyed in the course of the many wars which were fought in that part of the world. Alexander the Great himself, as early as about the year 340 before the Common Era, wrought a great deal of destruction in this respect. Nonetheless, many scholars argue, some mention of the event or of the people connected with it might have been found, and the fact that not a trace of the Purim story exists is highly damaging evidence. The origin of the Jewish festival must, therefore, they believe, be sought elsewhere than in the story itself.

The Esther story, in addition to lacking external corroboration, also presents certain internal difficulties. Neither Mordecai nor Esther are Jewish names. It is, in fact, obvious that the former derives from the god Marduk and the latter from the goddess Ishtar. At the same time, the story contains not a single mention of the name of God. It is apparently a secular story from beginning to end: the miraculous deliverance is achieved by purely human means; the revenge taken by the Jews and the rewards granted to Mordecai are equally human. Moreover, it is well known that as late as the time of the Maccabees the holiday of Purim was not observed as it was later. Centuries afterwards the rabbis still knew a tradition that their predecessors, the men of the Great Assembly, had refused to agree to Esther's and Mordecai's request for the holiday to be instituted as an everlasting memorial.[1] Finally, certain differences exist between the story of Esther as told in the Bible and the same story as told in the Greek translation known as the Septuagint. The very name of the day is different, the Septuagint calling it *Fruria* and omitting the verses which speak of the casting of lots whence the name *Purim* is derived.

Almost every Bible scholar during the past century has tried his hand at solving these seeming mysteries of the Book of Esther. They sought the solution in Jewish history and in non-Jewish history, among the stories of the ancient gods and among the literatures of Palestine's pagan neighbors. Heinrich Graetz, for example, the noted Jewish historian, himself given to higher criticism of the Bible, argued that the story was mostly invention. It had been written, he held, at the time of the Maccabean revolt against Antiochus of Syria, in order to fortify the spirit of the Jews in that hour of crisis by showing that God does not abandon His people.[2]

1. *ESTHER AND MORDECAI*   Painting
Aert de Gelder, 1685

Other critics displayed even more remarkable ingenuity in finding parallels, references and novel clues to the identification of the story's original motive, form, time and place.

A recent discussion of the subject deserves special attention, not only because it summarizes and refutes many previous theories, but also because it presents a rather plausible theory of its own. Dr. Julius Lewy, focusing his vast learning upon this little book, traces in it the transformation of a pagan myth into the Jewish holiday.[3] In the Persian city of Susa there had long lived a colony of Babylonians whose religion, still centering about their ancient gods, Marduk and Ishtar, differed from the religion of the victorious Persians. Naturally, the Babylonian Marduk worshippers (Mardukians) looked upon the Persian gods as hostile. In a manner not uncommon among pagans, the hostility was dramatized by personifying the various gods and telling the story of their conflict so as to permit one's favorite to come out victorious. Mordecai would thus seem to be the embodiment of the entire group of Mardukians. Esther obviously stands for Ishtar, especially in view of the adjective "the queen" usually appended to her name as it was attached to the name of the goddess Ishtar. Ishtar was represented as triumphing over the Elamite goddess Mashti (Vashti). In like manner, Haman represents the anti-Mardukians. Dr. Lewy points out that in the Greek story of Esther, Haman is not called the Agagite, but the Bugite or Bagaite, which is a legitimate characterization for a follower of the Persian god Mithra. This story, current among the Babylonian minority of Susa, must have been well known among another minority of the city, namely, the Jews. Actually, of course, no such story has come down to us; Dr. Lewy merely assumes that the form of a story supposedly current among the Mardukians had the essential elements of the story of Esther as we know it.

Stories about gods were told with special relish near the time when the seasons changed. The end of winter among the pagans of Persia was marked by a holiday, called Farvardigan, which fell on the fourteenth day of the twelfth month. As a holiday, it was marked by the exchange of gifts and much gaiety. Now, such holidays have a way of being adopted by minorities among the population. In the course of time, this holiday spread among the Jews of the Persian Empire. It was known in Palestine about the time of the Maccabean revolt (167 B.C.E.), though certainly not yet

officially recognized. Someone, whether in or out of Palestine, then modified the Mardukian story, giving it a Jewish coloring, in order to give justification to the widespread
festivities of the day.

Whether or not one accepts the involved, detective-like
reasoning which leads Dr. Lewy to the above conclusions or
adopts similar theories on the Book of Esther, the fact remains that the earliest mention of the feast of Purim dates
from only the second century B.C.E.[4] This time element is
important. Judah the Maccabee won his great victory over
the Syrian general Nicanor on the 13th of Adar in the year
161 and that day was declared a holiday.[5] This would never
have been done had the Fast of Esther, which traditionally
falls on that day, already been commonly observed. At
least in Palestine, Purim was evidently not yet universally
acknowledged, although the Purim day itself, under the
name of "the Day of Mordecai," was known. The early
Greek translation of the Book of Esther, made soon thereafter, concludes with the remark that the translation was the
work which a certain Lysimachus, son of Ptolemy of Jerusalem, completed in the fourth year of the reign of Ptolemy
and Cleopatra.[6] Historians have calculated that this could
have been either the year 177 B.C.E. or about the year 114
B.C.E. Even assuming the earlier date, which would place
the translation before the Maccabean revolt, we could only
say that the book had become sufficiently popular to merit
translation, not that the holiday was then already definitely
established.

The festival grew more important with every passing generation. It is clear that Purim was generally observed in
Palestine some time before the destruction of the Second
Temple. Priests officiating at the Temple service were required to leave their sacrificial duties and listen to the
reading of the Scroll.[7] About two generations after the

destruction, that is, about the middle of the second century of the Common Era, the famous Rabbi Meir is known to have followed the strict rules which had already become accepted regarding the reading of the Scroll of Esther.[8] A regulation from that period reflects the joyful attitude prevalent at the Purim season. Nevertheless, the rabbis of that age still remembered the doubts which their predecessors had expressed about considering the Scroll as sacred as other portions of the Holy Writings.[9]

Does all this lend countenance to the theory of the story's foreign origin and to the assumption that it has no historical foundation? Many traditionalist Jewish and Christian scholars have denied this and attempted to defend the historicity of the book. None has made a greater and more convincing effort to do so than the late Professor Jacob Hoschander, who published a book on the subject in 1923.[10] Delving deeply into the history of ancient Persia, and reasoning quite as learnedly and as tortuously as those who deny the story any basis in fact, Hoschander presents for his side at least as convincing an argument as do his opponents for theirs.

Hoschander concludes that the Persian king involved in the story was not Xerxes, who is generally assumed to have been the fickle king of the Esther story, but Artaxerxes II, who reigned almost a century later (403-358 B.C.E.). The latter's character, his love of wine, the events of his reign and the extent of his empire coincide with the description of the king in the Scroll. There is also good reason why the feast of his accession should have taken place in the third year of his kingship, as the first verse of the Scroll relates. The identification of the other names in the story seems to be more difficult. Vashti, which in Persian means "Beauty," might well have been the popular name of Artaxerxes' queen, Stateira, who was murdered in a palace intrigue. As to Esther, Mordecai and Haman, it is possible to explain their names but not to identify them with any known character in the extant Persian annals of that period. Dr. Hoschander, however, did not feel that this represented a serious flaw in his argument, since the official titles of such prominent people could have been altogether different from the names they bore in private life. Moreover, in view of our scant knowledge about the history of ancient Persia, our failure to identify these people cannot invalidate the story told by one who lived much nearer the events and was acquainted with the circumstantial details.

Far more important than the identification of the names is the discovery of the motives which underlay Haman's plot to exterminate the Jews. Dr. Hoschander, for example, does not believe that Mordecai's failure to bow before Haman could have been the cause of the cruel edict. He finds a deeper and, on the whole, more reasonable theory to account for the events. The Persian religion, with its belief in the eternal conflict between the force making for light (goodness) and that making for darkness (evil), possessed two qualities which brought it closer to Judaism than most religions of the ancient world: it emphasized ethics and it shunned images. Under the circumstances, Zoroastrians and Jews were favorably disposed toward each other. Most of the rest of the empire's population, however, was still steeped in image-worship. The result was a certain amount of religious disunity in Artaxerxes' vast population. Haman, probably of non-Zoroastrian origin, suggested the reintroduction of images and their compulsory worship. The Jews of the Empire not only objected to this "reformation," but actively opposed it; they did not "obey the laws of the king" and set a bad example to the dominant class of Zoroastrians. An example was, therefore, to be made of them. But before the plan could succeed, Haman fell from favor, due to a palace intrigue not uncommon in that day.

Plausible as such theories seem, are they really necessary? After all the erudite deductions have been considered, the simple, unadorned story which the Bible tells still seems the most reasonable and credible. This was not the only time in the eventful history of the Jews when an enemy plotted their destruction and all but succeeded in his plans; nor was this the only time when petty, purely human motives operated both against them and in their favor. The very fact that their deliverance is not attributed to God speaks for the credibility of the story as an actual, historical event. The story was told in Susa and spread to other parts of the empire, until it eventually reached Palestine. The dark days of Syrian persecution, during the pre-Maccabean period, afforded a favorable atmosphere for its spread. It soon became popular because it proved that, in the last moment, God intervenes to save His people and that He does so through human instruments. This actually happened in the case of the Maccabees. The subsequent loss of Jewish independence to Rome heightened the hopes for a human deliverer and thereby increased the popularity of the story of Esther. The Jews who lived in the midst of pagans, such as those of Egypt, Syria and Asia Minor, had an even more immediate reason for finding the story interesting. There was considerable anti-Jewish feeling in these countries. It was comforting for the Jews to be able to cite an instance — as a source of edification to themselves and as a warning to their neighbors — when a pagan enemy was so thoroughly discomfited.

The 14th of Adar coincided with a holiday period in the pagan calendar in western Asia. Haman may deliberately have chosen a holiday of this sort for the execution of his plans. The merry-making, half-inebriated rabble could the more easily be aroused to join in the slaughter of innocent people, especially if the latter were unprotected by the authorities and if loot were in prospect. Quite possibly, some Jews had participated in the fun and the gift-giving of the pagan holiday before the Haman incident. With the example of Christmas and New Year's festivities before us now, we can readily understand why the Jews of that day imitated their neighbors. They justified their actions after the incident, by pointing to the request included in the Book of Esther that her and Mordecai's victory be commemorated by rejoicing, exchanging of gifts and the giving of portions to the poor — the last probably a purely Jewish addition.

One may well imagine that the religious leaders of the Jewish people in Palestine did not like the growing popularity of the new holiday. They could not easily resign themselves to approving a book in which eating and drinking were encouraged but the name of God was not mentioned.[11] Nevertheless, there was no gainsaying the popular will. In time, the religious guides of the people yielded. They accepted the book into the Holy Writings, made its reading obligatory and gift-giving part of the celebration. For a long time, variations in the observance continued to exist. It is possible that in some Greek-speaking countries the book was read in Greek rather than in Hebrew. For some generations, there was uncertainty about the time of reading, whether at night, in the morning, or both.[12] The latest addition to the observance was the introduction of the Fast of Esther, on the day preceding Purim, which is not mentioned until gaonic times, that is, after the seventh century.[13]

The "beating of Haman" was probably an early feature of the reading of the Scroll in public. It may have been taken over from the pagan festivities, when the communal fool was crowned king for a day. Hanging Haman in effigy soon turned into a popular sport and on several occasions brought trouble to a Jewish community here and there. Cecil Roth has argued that it gave rise to the blood accusation which, in later centuries, so plagued the Jews of Europe.

Miracle plays were introduced later, as were also the Purim *Se'udah* (feast) and *Hamantashen* (cakes filled with a paste of honey-sweetened poppyseeds).

One of the incidents in the Purim story to which Christian Bible critics have always pointed with scorn is the "revenge" which the Jews took and the relish with which the Scroll speaks of so many thousands killed in Susa and so many more thousands in the provincial towns. They see in the narrative an expression of blood-lust. Apart from the obvious reflection that such a characterization applies with infinitely greater force to ancient and modern enemies of the Jews, the charge displays complete lack of imagination. What actually happened? Haman was an efficient executive. He laid his plans many months in advance; he promised compensation to his assistants; he put the matter in the hands of local authorities. Every town must have had a band of cutthroats ready for "the day," and a propaganda campaign to enlist volunteer rioters undoubtedly had been put in motion. These orders, having been given under the king's seal, could not be countermanded. Only later did Mordecai's edict arrive giving the Jews permission to defend themselves. Presumably, the police, fearing Mordecai, now risen to power, remained neutral. Many of the would-be rioters, caring only to be on the winning side, joined the Jewish defense forces — the Scroll (8.17) speaks of these as *Mityahadim*, that is, joining the Jews. It was too late to stop the riots, but there was no reason why the Jews, now armed and strengthened, should not beat them back. The numbers killed were comparatively small, and the Jews proudly refrained from looting.

The frequent bitterness of life in unfriendly diaspora lands made Purim increasingly meaningful to the Jewish people. Very early, they broadened its application and gave it universal meaning by connecting it with God's vow, as expressed in Exodus 17.14–16, to destroy Amalek, the prototype of cowardice and evil. It is therefore easy to understand why a rabbi, many centuries ago, declared that even after the arrival of the Messiah, Purim would survive as a holiday to be observed by all mankind.

CHAPTER II

SPECIAL PURIMS

JEWISH history bears testimony to the statement of the Haggadah that "not one alone has risen against us, but in every generation there are those who rise against us to destroy us; but the Holy One, blessed be He, rescues us from their hands." Purim commemorates but one of the many occasions when Israel was threatened with destruction and was saved as by a miracle. These deliverances were celebrated on their yearly anniversaries as festivals. Festivals were inaugurated not only to commemorate a timely release from tyrannical rulers, but also to celebrate an escape from such impending disasters as plagues, earthquakes and conflagrations.

The common element that emerges from each of these tragic historical episodes, so varied and yet so similar, is the inauguration and observance of a day of deliverance. These festive occasions, which were called "Purims" after their biblical prototype, emphasized the spiritual lesson of the original Purim, namely, that the hand of God guides the destiny of the Jewish people.

Private families often instituted the observance of a Purim to mark an escape from a danger that may have threatened the patriarch of the family or possibly the whole family. So personal were these festivals that Rabbi Jonathan ben Jacob of Fulda conceived it proper to name the 17th of Tammuz, the day on which his congregation was saved from an impending calamity, *Purim Sheli* (My Purim).

While the original Purim is observed universally, the special Purims, commemorating days of deliverance of a local Jewish community or of an individual Jewish family, have been kept only by the descendants of the members of that community or family.

In emulation of the original Purim, many communities and families observed their own Purims by dispensing charity to the poor. They engaged in no work, but spent the day in enjoyable pastimes. In the synagogue they recited special psalms and prayers, and insofar as possible they followed the traditional features of Purim. Descriptions of many of them are found in *Megillot* (scrolls) which parody the style of the Book of Esther and are read on the annual anniversaries of the historic days.

From these *Megillot* we can recapture something of the constant uncertainty and anxiety that possessed the minds of the Jews who faced troubled times of persecution and even death. And we can learn, too, how throughout the ages their profound faith in a benevolent Providence, who watched over and protected them, deeply permeated their lives.

Not all of the historical records of these Purims are complete or accurate, for, not enjoying universal observance, many ultimately fell into disuse as communities and families were scattered and disappeared. Sufficiently fascinating and, for the most part, authentic information exists that needs only to be retold to remind us that, no matter how bleak and dreary the present Jewish outlook may be, *relief and deliverance will arise to the Jews from another place* (Esther 4.14).

That these special Purims do not coincide in any instance with the Purim of the Bible may be attributed to the rabbinical injunction that one should not "mix joy with joy." It can be safely assumed that if, by chance, a day of deliver-

ance of a local community or of a family fell on the day of
the original Purim, its anniversary was advanced or postponed, or the new celebration was merged with the old.

The name Purim is usually preceded or followed by another word or phrase which identifies either the event itself
or the geographic location where the event took place that
gave rise to the holiday (Cairoan Purim, Purim of Saragossa). In the former category are found such unusual
appellations as Brigands' Purim, Plum Jam Purim, Earthquake Purim and even Purim of the Christians.

While Steinschneider, the famous bibliographer, records
only twenty-two Purims, the Jewish Encyclopedia twenty-
nine, and Zunz in his *Ha-Minhagim* forty, there may have
been as many as a hundred. Here are recorded a few of the
better known special Purims which, during the past centuries, have been and to some extent are still being observed
on various dates in different lands.

PURIM OF SHIRAZ[1]

M. FRANCO

On the second day of Heshvan, the Jews of Shiraz in Persia celebrate a festival called *Mo'ed Katan* (Little Feast).
On that day they do no work, exchange visits and salute
one another with the words, "Mo'ed Katan" and "Abu Al-
Hasan." According to a tradition which is substantiated by
an ancient Judaeo-Persian manuscript of uncertain date
(possibly written about 1400 or even as early as 1200), a
Jew named Abu Al-Hasan, who was both *Shohet* and butcher,
was accused of having sold *Terefah* meat on the eve of Rosh
Hashanah. The anger of the Jews was aroused against
the culprit, who immediately embraced Islam and accused
his former coreligionists of many crimes. The Mohamme-
dans gave the Jews their choice between death and conver-

sion to Islam; and all chose the latter alternative. One month afterwards Abu Al-Hasan died mysteriously, on the second day of Heshvan. A statement was found in his pocket declaring that the Jews were innocent of the charge he had brought against them. They were then permitted to return to Judaism; and in memory of the event the Purim of *Mo'ed Katan* was instituted.

PURIM OF CASTILE[2]

L. RABINOWITZ

The "villain" in the case of the Purim of Castile was a certain poor knight, Gonzalo Martinez de Oviedo, who had been promoted to high positions by Joseph Benveniste de Ecija, the Jewish favorite of Alfonso XI of Castile. Gonzalo Martinez eventually rose to the position of Grand Master of the Order of Alcantara, and in this position, being at the same time an especial favorite of the king, he began to show his intense hatred of the Jews. He exerted all his powers to oust the Jews from public positions, repaying his former benefactor with gross ingratitude, accusing him and his rival, Samuel ibn Wakar, of speculation and of waxing rich at the expense of their royal master.

The king believed the charges and Gonzalo was given full powers to proceed against the Jews in general. Thereupon he ordered the two favorites, with two brothers of Ibn Wakar and eight relatives of the families, to be arrested and their wealth confiscated. Joseph died in prison, Samuel on the rack. But true to his prototype (Haman), this was not sufficient for Gonzalo.

But it seemed contemptible in his eyes to lay hands on Mordecai alone; for they had made known to him the people of Mordecai; wherefore Haman sought to destroy all the Jews that were throughout the whole kingdom ... (Esther 3.6).

He found his opportunity of carrying this into effect very soon. In 1339, the Christian kings of Spain resolved to make a determined attack on the Mohammedan kingdom of Granada. This king appealed to Abulhassan, King of Morocco, for help, representing it as a religious war, and the latter readily assented to help, gathering a large army at the Straits of Gibraltar, under the command of his son Abumelik, with the avowed intention of attacking Castile and the Mohammedan kingdom of Andalusia.

Alfonso was totally unprepared for this sudden turning of the tables, and he appointed Gonzalo as Commander-in-Chief of the Castilian Army of Defense.

Money, however, was needed to carry on the war and, at a Council held at Madrid, Gonzalo suggested a plan amazing in its simplicity. Let the Jews be expelled and their money confiscated! Not only would this bring in a large sum but, since the Jews held many deeds of Christians, if these were confiscated and the debts annulled, the Christians, overflowing with heartfelt gratitude, would join the army and give their wholehearted support. Opposition to this plan was fortunately expressed by many, not least by the Archbishop of Toledo, on the grounds that it was more profitable to the king to ensure a continuous revenue from the Jews, and — a more honorable reason — because the Jews had been granted protection by the King of Castile, who should never break his word.

It is here that the "Mordecai" of this event comes prominently to the fore. Moses Abudiel had held a position at court and had been accused by Gonzalo, together with Joseph de Ecija and Samuel ibn Wakar, but had succeeded in maintaining himself in the king's favor by large gifts of money. In this position he heard of Gonzalo's machinations and did all within his power to frustrate his evil designs. But like Mordecai of old, he did not content himself with invoking earthly help alone, but sent messengers to all the communities of Castile instituting a public fast and exhorting the people to pour forth prayers and supplication to avert the designs of their arch-enemy.

Meanwhile, Gonzalo had marched against the enemy to the border of Castile, surprised and defeated the Moors, killing their leader Abumelik; and the threatened invasion collapsed. Gonzalo's influence and popularity increased enormously. Yet during all this campaign, he had not forgotten his design — indeed, it must have become a passion to him — of humiliating, destroying, or expelling the Jews of Castile. On his return he renewed his former suggestions, adding the new idea of reducing the Jews materially.

But, it was the pride that comes before its fall! "The feeble hand of a woman was the cause of his downfall." The king had become infatuated with the beautiful Leonora de Guzman, to whom he was more faithful than to the queen, and so enthralled was he with her that her slightest wish was law. She hated Gonzalo and determined to weaken his influence; she pointed out to the king that Gonzalo was preaching sedition against him. The king was incredulous, but invited Gonzalo to appear immediately before him in Madrid. To the dismay of the king, he refused to come, and it was found that he was occupied with nothing less than treason against the king, having entered into communication with the King of Portugal and even with his recent enemy, the Arabic King of Granada, and had induced the entire Order of the Knights of Alcantara, and the citizens of the villages and towns belonging to them, to unite with him.

What his purpose was in taking this mad step can only be surmised. Spanish historians suggest that he actually aimed at becoming king, or right-hand man to the king. Be that as it may, this foolish attempt at rebellion was the be-

ginning of the end. Gonzalo entrenched himself in the fortress of Valencia de Alcantara, and Alfonso in person led his
nobles against him to besiege the fortress. Gonzalo, des-
perately stopping at nothing to achieve his purpose, ordered
his soldiers to shoot at the person of the king, and one of the
king's attendants was mortally wounded.

This was further than his knights would go. A number of
them forsook their master, surrendered themselves and the
fortress to the king, and Gonzalo was forced to yield. He
was condemned to death as a traitor and burnt alive at the
stake, and his fortune was confiscated.

Thence the story continues like the biblical prototype.
The communities of Castile instituted a second Purim in the
same month as the first, that is, Adar. Moses Abudiel was
again taken into the favor of the king who, as a matter of
fact, was extremely inconsistent in the bestowal of his favors,
and from this time till the day of his death (1360) Alfonso
XI, who had during his reign issued some vexatious decrees
against the Jews at the request of the Cortes, acted justly
towards them, refusing to hearken to the proposals of the
enemies of the Jews, and even abolished the decree prohibiting them to acquire landed property, one of the most important and harmful of the decrees passed against the Jews.

PURIM OF SARAGOSSA[3]

JUDAH LEB HA-KOHEN FISHMAN

Until recently there were some families in Jerusalem that
used to celebrate a sort of "Second Purim" on certain days
of the year as a memorial of ancient events. The events
themselves had taken place not in Palestine but in the Diaspora. According to what is related in the scroll composed
to record this event, the city of Saragossa was at that time

(5188–1428) the capital of the kingdom of Aragon. It was the king's custom to visit the Street of the Jews from time to time, and the latter would go out to meet him with decorated Torah scrolls borne in wooden cabinets, as is the practice of the Sephardim to this day. In the course of time, many began to doubt the wisdom of this practice, wondering whether there was not some sacrilege in the carrying about of Torah scrolls. The Jews of Saragossa, therefore, decided to go out to meet the king, carrying only empty wooden cabinets. But a Jew who had been converted revealed their decision to the king, and the latter decided to visit the Street of the Jews and to clear up this matter without giving them prior notice. During the course of that night, however, the sextons of the synagogues were informed in a dream from on high that they must return the Torah scrolls to the cabinets — and thus the informer was shamed. The 17th of Shebat, the day on which this event occurred, was instituted as a second Purim to be observed by coming generations in Saragossa; and the Sephardim in Jerusalem, certainly a branch of the families in Saragossa, were accustomed until recently to celebrate the Purim of Saragossa every year according to the law, by declaring a work-holiday, reading the scroll and holding a feast and celebration in every home. The Scroll of Saragossa is written on parchment and is to be found in the hands of the Sephardim of Saragossa in Jerusalem. It was published in a special edition in the year 5634 (1874).

PURIM DE LAS BOMBAS[4]

CECIL ROTH

In 1578, Sebastian, the young king of Portugal, fired with crusading zeal, had espoused the cause of a pretender to the throne and landed on the coast of Morocco. He was, how-

ever, overwhelmingly defeated at the "Battle of the Three
Kings"near Alcazir Kebir, where the flower of the Portuguese
nobility was destroyed. It is on record that those who fell
into the hands of the compassionate Jews, whose fathers they
had so ruthlessly persecuted and expelled, now considered
themselves fortunate in the extreme: for they received at
their hands only the kindest and most considerate treatment. Nevertheless, the local communities realized the
danger in which they would have been, had the result of
the battle been otherwise, and instituted a local festival to
be celebrated each year on the anniversary of their escape
(Elul 1). At Tangier this is called the *Purim de las Bombas*
(Purim of the Bombs); at Tetuan, the *Purim de los Chris-
tianos* (Purim of the Christians).

PURIM FETTMILCH[5]

David Philipson

The guilds in Frankfort were always very strong. They
had a particular animosity against the Jews, and were continually laboring to effect their expulsion from the city. Not
succeeding in this, an attack on the Jewish quarter was determined upon. The leader was a baker, Vincent Fettmilch.
On August 22, 1614, the attack was made. The Jews, having
been warned, did not quietly wait for the attack, but made
preparations to resist. They procured arms, removed their
wives and children to the cemetery for refuge, locked the
gates that led into their street and barricaded the gate upon
which the attack was expected. They then proceeded to the
synagogue and prayed and fasted. While assembled there,
they heard the blows upon the gates and the angry cries of
the mob. In terror they poured out of the synagogue, men

2. *RIOT IN THE GHETTO, LED BY VINCENT FETTMILCH*

M. Merian

Engraving

and youths taking up arms to defend themselves. The mob, foiled by the barricade of the gate, broke into the street through a house which stood next to the gate. A bitter fight of eight hours followed; two Jews and one Christian were killed, and many wounded. The Jews, few in number, were gradually overcome. Then began a fearful scene of plunder and destruction. The mob rushed into the houses. They had proceeded about half way through the streets, when a band of armed citizens appeared and drove them out. The Jews, thoroughly frightened, hastened to seek refuge in their cemetery, situated at the end of the *Gasse*, in which they had placed their wives and children. They were advised by the town council to leave the city, since it could not protect them. On the next day, they did this, and for one year and a half they remained away from the city and lived in the neighboring towns. In the meantime, order had been restored, and steps were taken looking to the return of the Jews. The leaders of the mob, Fettmilch and six others, were beheaded. On the very day this took place, February 28, 1616, the Jews returned. Their return was celebrated with music. When they arrived in front of the *Gasse*, they were formed into a circle and the new *Stättigkeit*, drawn up by the imperial commissioners, was read to them. The town council having shown itself so powerless to guard them, the protection of the Jews reverted to the emperor; they once again became his private property. After their return into their "street," a large shield was placed upon each of the three gates, upon which was painted the imperial eagle with the inscription, "Under the protection of His Roman Imperial Majesty and the August Empire." Strange to say, the Christian population was compelled by imperial mandate to pay the Jews 175,919 florins indemnity for the loss they had sustained. In memory of these events, the Jewish congregation of Frankfurt annually celebrated two events, the 19th of Adar, as a fast day commemorative of their departure from the city, and the 20th as a holiday, called Purim Fettmilch, in memory of their return.

CURTAIN PURIM[6]

HENRY MALTER

Purim Fürhang (Curtain Purim) was enjoined on his family by Hanok ben Moses Altschul of Prague, to be observed by it annually on the 22nd of Tebet in remembrance of his deliverance from the hands of a tyrant. In 1623, damask curtains were stolen from the palace of the governor, Prince Lichtenstein, during his absence from Prague. In compliance with an order from the custodian of the palace, an announcement was made in all the synagogues of Prague that any one having the stolen goods in his possession should turn them over to the sexton. Thereupon a Jew, Joseph ben Jekuthiel Thein, delivered the curtains to Altschul, at that time sexton of the Meisel Synagogue, Prague, stating that he had bought them from two soldiers. Vice-Governor Count Rudolph Waldstein, who was in charge of the affairs of the provincial government, demanded that the buyer be named and delivered to him for punishment; but as the congregational statutes forbade the naming of receivers of stolen goods who voluntarily had given them up, the sexton refused and, in consequence, was thrown into prison, an order being issued to hang him on the following day.

To save his life, Altschul, with the permission of the president of the congregation, revealed the name of the buyer, whereupon Altschul was set free and Joseph Thein was sentenced to the gallows in his stead. All the efforts of influential Jews to effect his release proved futile, but finally through the efforts of a prominent Christian and upon the intercession of the city councilors, Count Waldstein released the prisoner on the condition that the congregation pay a fine of 10,000 florins. In order to humiliate the Jews, he further ordered that this money, divided into ten equal parts, be paid in silver coin and carried in linen bags by ten prominent Jews escorted by soldiers through the streets of Prague to the city hall.

Altschul recorded the event in a scroll entitled *Megillat Pure ha-Kela'im* (Scroll of the Purim of the Curtains), and made it obligatory upon all his descendants to read the scroll annually on the 22nd of Tebet, on which day Thein was liberated, and to observe the day by "feasting and giving thanks to God for his salvation." The event was made the subject of a novel by Matthias Kisch.

PURIM OF YOM TOB LIPMANN HELLER[7]

Julius H. Greenstone

The most characteristic family Purim is that enjoined on the descendants of Yom Tob Lipmann Heller, who was chief rabbi of Prague in 1627. Forced to preside at the meeting which had to apportion the heavy taxes imposed upon the Jewish community because of the Thirty Years' War, Heller gained for himself many influential enemies who charged him with favoritism in allotting the taxes to different members of the community. He was accused before the emperor of having written against Christianity and ordered to appear in Vienna before a special tribunal. He was found guilty because he defended the Talmud. His sentence of death was later commuted by the emperor to the payment of a large sum of money to the treasury. After a confinement in prison for forty days, he was released upon the payment of the first installment of the fine. He returned to Prague in broken health, but stayed there for a short time only. In 1632 he became rabbi of Nemirov in Russia and in 1643 was called to the rabbinate of Cracow, where he died in 1654. In the *Megillah* which he wrote, in which he gives the details of all his troubles, he enjoined upon his family to observe the fifth day of Tammuz, the day when his troubles began, as a fast day, and the first day of Adar, the day when he was installed as rabbi of Cracow, as a Purim, a day of rejoicing and merrymaking. He writes that he hesitated to have his Purim following immediately upon the fast day, since at that time he was still in danger of his life.

PURIM OF TIBERIAS[8]

CECIL ROTH

Tiberias had recently been reestablished by Sheikh Dair el Amar, who invited Isaac Abulafia to induce some of his brethren to settle in it with him. This pre-Zionist experiment met with some success, and the little community seemed to be firmly establishing itself. In 1743, however, Suleiman Pasha, Governor of Damascus, determined to assert his overlordship and laid siege to the city. During the eighty-three days of the investment the Jews cooperated manfully in the defense, for they knew that capture would spell disaster for them. At last the Pasha was forced to raise the siege (August 27); and a short time afterwards, while he was preparing a second attack, he suddenly died. The Jews of Tiberias accordingly instituted the anniversaries of these two dates (Elul 7 and Kislev 4) as local Purims, which are still annually observed.

DAY OF THE MIRACLE[9]

HAKAM EZRA REUBEN DANGOOR

In Basra one day in the year is celebrated as *Yom ha-Nes,* and this happens on the second day of the month of Nisan. They read a scroll and call it *Megillat Paras,* or the Scroll of Persia, which was compiled by R. Jacob Elyashar, the messenger of the Jews of Hebron, who was in Basra. He was the grandfather of Rabbi Jacob Saul Elyashar, the present Hakam Bashi of Jerusalem.

This is the story: In the month of Nisan of the year 5534 (1774) came Karim Khan, the Vizir of the Shah of Persia, with the Persian armies and besieged Basra. At that time Suleiman Pasha, a lover of Israel, an upright man, was the Wali of Bara, and the Saraaf Bashi, Jacob ben Aaron, was the *Nasi* (leader of the Jewish community). Suleiman Pasha fought against the Persian Vizir, and there was a great famine, and they could not prevail against the Persians. On the 27th of Nisan the gates of the city opened and the Persian army entered, and they robbed and pillaged and captured women . . . . and on the day of the New Moon of Iyar, Karim Khan established his rule over Basra, and imposed fines on the people and imprisoned many of the leaders of the city in order to take away their money. Suleiman Pasha, his family and household, Jacob ben Aaron, his wife and children were sent prisoners to the Shah in Shiraz.

The Persian soldiers in Basra were capturing women and ravishing them. Many of the Jewish women threw themselves into fire and died, in order not to fall into the hands of these wicked people. The Jews thereupon turned to the above-mentioned rabbi, gathered in the synagogue and uttered supplications, crying and weeping. God Almighty heard their cries and directed the heart of the Vizir to fight with the Arabs that were in the neighborhood of Basra, but he could not conquer them. The Arabs defeated his armies and the Vizir returned to Basra. A second time he gathered a mighty army and fought with them among the waves of the sea and floods of the rivers. This time again he was unsuccessful, and his armies perished and died, many of them in the rivers and a good many in open battle. The Vizir wanted to try a third time, but his armies poisoned him and he died on the 27th of Adar, 5535 (1775). And when the Shah heard that his Vizir died and his armies were lost, he commanded the remnant to return to Persia by secret flight. On the second day of Nisan, 5535, not one of them remained in Basra, and Basra returned to her former greatness. The Jews made a great rejoicing, like the days of Purim, and called it *Yom ha-Nes*. And they pledged themselves to keep this day from year to year for all generations. The above-mentioned rabbi composed for them songs and called them *Megillat Paras*. He instituted that they should read this *Megillah* yearly on this day in the synagogue, as they do with the Scroll of Esther, that they should cease from all work, give gifts to the needy and presents to each other, and make a festive meal as on Purim.

PURIM OF BANDITS[10]

CECIL ROTH

The Jews in Gumeldjina, in European Turkey, near Adrianople, lived together in one bastion of the fortifications. In 1786, a band of five thousand mountain brigands, intent on pillaging the town, made their entrance at this point. The whole city, and the Jews especially, stood in great danger, but the invaders were driven off. The Jews were, however, accused of complicity; they had, it was alleged, intentionally admitted the brigands to pillage the town. They vindicated their innocence, though not without some difficulty. In memory of this double escape, from plundering and from a false accusation, the rabbis instituted a special feast which is still observed year by year, on Heshvan 22, under the name *Purim de los Ladrones* (Purim of Bandits).

PURIMS OF TRIPOLI[11]

A. R. MALACHI

In addition to the holiday of Purim, the Jews of Tripoli celebrate two other Purims, the Purim of Sharif and the Purim of Burgel. The first falls on the 24th of Tebet, and the second on the eve of the New Moon of Shebat. These extra Purims were established in commemoration of two miracles that happened to the Jews of Tripoli, the first in the year 1745, and the second in 1793.

The Purim of Sharif is not especially important and is treated as a secular custom. There is no fasting on the eve of the holiday, nor reading of a Purim Scroll. For that reason, it is popularly called by the name of *False Purim*, to distinguish it from the traditional Purim.

But the Purim of Burgel is celebrated according to the letter of the law. On the eve of the holiday the men fast, and that night they read a scroll in which the story of the miracle is related. One of the sages of Tripoli, Rabbi Abraham Kalfone, wrote this scroll at the time of the event. On the morning of the holiday, the Jews of Tripoli perform no work whatsoever. They prepare feasts and send one another gifts, exactly as though it were the actual Purim.

The Purim of Sharif commemorates the miracle that took place when the ruler of Tunis besieged Tripoli, and threatened to kill all the inhabitants of the city. Before he could conquer the last fortress, however, an epidemic spread among his soldiers and he was forced to flee with the remnants of his army. The city was saved and the Jews with it. In memory of the miracle, the Jews of Tripoli undertook on behalf of themselves and their descendants to celebrate the day with praise and thanksgiving to God who had redeemed their souls from disaster.

The Purim of Burgel has its source in political intrigues and rivalry between rulers. A Jewish woman, called "the Tripolitan Queen Esther," plays an important part in this Purim.

The Tripolitan pasha in those days, Ali Karamenli, ruled under the dispensation of the Turkish sultan. The pasha was an old, weak man, but sensual and rapacious. He oppressed all the inhabitants of Tripoli; he laid an especially heavy hand on the Jews and passed severe decrees against them.

The Jews were rescued from their evil straits by the hand of "Queen Esther." The Tripolitan Esther was the wife of the head of the Jewish community of Tripoli. She was a wise and energetic woman, wealthy and influential. She had many friends and acquaintances in the court of the ruler. They interceded in her behalf and she managed to obtain an interview with Ali Pasha. Through her wisdom and talent at telling lovely and jolly tales, she won favor in the eyes of the old ruler. The pasha asked her to come to his home daily to delight him with comments about political affairs and royal manners, in which she was well versed.

Esther complied with the wish of the pasha and began to visit him every day. She spoke up each time in behalf of her fellow Jews, until she succeeded in awakening the pasha's compassion and he relaxed his severity.

Queen Esther's influence over the pasha grew to such an extent that he introduced her into governmental secrets and did nothing without consulting her, whether it was an important matter or not.

In those days quarrels and divisions broke out among the sons of the pasha, concerning the division of the rule among them after the death of their father.

The civil war lasted a few years. The pasha's sons first fought among themselves, and afterwards rose against their father. One of the sons who rebelled against his father laid siege to Tripoli for two years. Impoverished by the burden of the war, the heads of the city finally handed the city and its fortresses over into his hands.

Ali Burgel, who seized the reins of the government, oppressed all the inhabitants of Tripoli and drew off their blood and their money. In particular, he vented his anger upon the Jews. On the very first day of his rule, he called together the heads of the community and threatened them with death if they would not give him 240,000 francs — a very large sum in those days. Burgel Pasha continued his cruel course, imprisoning many of the most important men in the community.

When Ali Burgel heard of "Queen Esther's" influence in the palace of the pasha and her efforts in behalf of the Jews, he decided to take revenge upon her. At his command, she was locked in prison, where, in order to humiliate her and to torment her further, her arms and legs were chained with irons. She remained in that sorry state until her family redeemed her by paying a considerable sum of money.

While the Jews of Tripoli were in these severe and adverse circumstances, a miracle took place. Burgel Pasha went off to war with the ruler of Tunis and suffered a severe defeat. The inhabitants of Tripoli thereupon removed him from his position. The Jews were saved; Ali Pasha was returned to his office and, with him, "Queen Esther," who resumed her former glory and greatness. She lived seven more years and died in 1800.

The downfall of Burgel took place on the 29th of Tebet,

1793. In commemoration of their redemption, the Jews of Tripoli and Bengazi established that day as a day of festival, when they read a scroll describing the event and send one another gifts; nor do they recite any penitential prayers on that day. To this day that holiday is called the Purim of Burgel.

MIRACLE OF THE BOMB[12]

CECIL ROTH

In the spring of 1796, the French armies were laying siege to Fossano — that little city to the south of the Alps to which some refugees of the Jewish communities of France had escaped in the fourteenth century. Easter had passed, with its reminder of the Passion. The perilous Passover season had arrived; and, in the midst of the siege, the Jews had the audacity to celebrate the festival of freedom in accordance with their ancestral rites, assuredly a manifest token of sympathy with the enemy. On the fourth night (Monday, April 26, 1796), when the enemy opened his usual bombardment, apparently with more deadly results than ordinarily, the rabble of the city could bear it no longer. Snatching up any weapons which they could find, they made their way to the Jewish quarter, confident there at least of a signal victory.

The ghetto at Fossano (now the Via dell' Orfanotrofio) is a long narrow street close to the city wall. The mob rushed thither and gained access without opposition. Once entered, they did as they pleased, hacking down the doors with axes, breaking into the shops and houses, and pillaging them of whatever they contained. The Jews were entirely in their power. They were absolutely cut off from the rest of the town. Here, moreover, the soldiers of the garrison were otherwise engaged, while the more moderate elements in the population, alarmed by the bombardment which had just opened, remained cooped up in their houses. All appeals for assistance thus remained unanswered. Meanwhile, the Jews sought refuge in their diminutive synagogue, trusting in its sanctity to protect them.

The synagogue stood (in accordance with a fairly common architectural convention of the period) on an upper story at the far end of the street, access being gained by a narrow staircase leading into a little vestibule. From the far end of this, there opened out of the synagogue itself a small but picturesque structure, which still preserves its original form, in spite of a restoration in 1812. Here, the members of the little community were huddled together, awaiting the attack. Massacre seemed inevitable, unless a miracle intervened.

According to local legend, that is precisely what happened. Just as the first of the mob arrived at the top of the staircase, an enemy cannon fired almost at a venture. The shell burst through the wall of the vestibule, midway between the surging mob and their cowering victims. As it happens, it did no great material damage. But the assailants, terror-stricken, took to their heels and fled, throwing away a great part of their spoil as they ran. The community was saved. Very shortly afterwards, the French entered the city, and all danger was, for the moment at least, removed.

This marvellous escape seemed a direct act of God. Searching of conscience and repentance appeared insufficient to commemorate so signal a deliverance. Accordingly, the anniversary of that event, the fourth night and day of Passover, was declared by the leaders of the community a special holy day.... The aperture through which the providential cannon-ball burst its way into the synagogue building has never been repaired. It survived the reconstruction of sixteen years later, and it is still to be seen today by the visitor. It now serves as a window, to throw

much-needed light upon the internal obscurity. Around it
is written in Hebrew, in letters of gold, the simple phrase
נס של הבומב״א, "The Miracle of the Bomb."

PURIM OF THE POISONED SWORD[13]

M. Franco

In 1807, Passvanoglu, the feudal lord of the region of
Widdin on the Danube, had in his service as physician
(*Hakim Bashi*) a person named Cohen. Passvanoglu having
become mortally ill through contact with a poisoned sword,
the Mohammedan population accused the Jewish physician
of having made an attempt on the governor's life, and the
Jewish community was threatened with a general massacre.
Fortunately, the dying man himself energetically defended
his physician, and the threatened calamity was averted.
Hence the ninth and tenth of Heshvan, the dates of the
events, were declared days of Purim.

PURIM TAKA[14]

Elkan Nathan Adler

Ludwig A. Frankl gives the origin of the *Purim Taka*,
or "Window Purim," still celebrated by the Sephardic Jews
of Hebron on the anniversary (Tebet 14) of their deliverance
from an intolerable tax. It appears that once there was a
pasha there who was very fond of money. Fired by the
memory of the methods of King Richard the Lion-Hearted,
or perhaps of his own sweet initiative, for great minds think
alike, His Excellency determined to get money out of his
Jewish subjects. He demanded fifty thousand piasters
under threat of killing the leading members of the community and selling the rest into slavery. The rabbis were direly
perplexed, for they could not scrape the sum together. At

last, they could think of no other expedient than to write
to the Patriarchs about their trouble. They did so, and
bribed the watchman of the Mosque to lower the petition
by a string into the cave of Machpelah, for, of course, even
he dared not enter there. That night the pasha woke up
and, at his bedside, found three venerable looking sages, who
demanded fifty thousand piasters of him, and threatened
him with death if he did not pay. The pasha saw that they
were in earnest, went to his money-bags, and paid the fifty
thousand to the three weird old men. Next morning, at break
of day, the pasha's soldiers came to the Jewish quarter to
fetch the fifty thousand subsidy he levied upon them. The
Jews are all in synagogue, praying, for they know their last
hour has come. The soldiers knock at the door, and the
beadle hurries to open it, when he notices a bag of money in
the hall, just where the people wash their hands before
entering the synagogue. He brings it to the *Parnas*, who
hands it to the pasha. The pasha recognizes both purse and
money as his own, and declares that Abraham, Isaac and
Jacob themselves rose from their grave to keep him from
an evil deed, and that the Jews must, indeed, be a people
dear to Allah, if the Patriarchs, after so many thousands of
years, would come to life again merely to protect them from
injury. He makes the community a present of the money,
but requires them to promise to pray for him if ever he
should be in trouble. There are elements of truth in this
story, and obviously it is capable of a very rational explanation.

PURIM OF IBRAHIM PASHA[15]

Joseph Meyuhas

When Ibrahim Pasha made war on Palestine in 1832, he
decided to attack Hebron. On the road, seeing that his
men were very tired, he resolved to halt at Mount Itan near

Solomon's Pools. The inhabitants of Hebron hearing of this, gathered a large army together, and, issuing to where the pasha's men were resting, charged at the enemy and killed three thousand of them. The pasha's anger was kindled and he vowed to attack Hebron and wipe out all its inhabitants. When this reached the ears of the Jews, terror fell upon them; they shut themselves in the courtyard and prayed unto the Almighty to save them. But what was their astonishment when they beheld the pasha, on entering Hebron, post soldiers outside the courtyard of the Jews to protect them. At the same time terrible treatment was meted out to the rest of the population. On enquiring as to the reason for their escape, they learned that the Jewish generals of the house of Farhi of Damascus who had accompanied Ibrahim Pasha, intervened for their brethren in Hebron and the pasha acceded to their pleas.

In memory of this event, the day of the New Moon of Ab has been set aside in Hebron for rejoicing and is known as "Purim of Ibrahim Pasha."

CHAPTER III

PURIM IN MANY LANDS

PURIM CELEBRATION OF SEIXAS' FAMILY, NEW YORK[1]

IN a letter from Gershom Mendes Seixas we have a pic-
utre of the family's Purim celebration in 1813 "with all the
merriment & festivity usually practised in my family, the
Children seated at our large Table, in the Parlour, with two
lighted Candles, & a great display of *fair* Tea (no water and
milk for a mockery) — a sweet loaf, gingerbread, & some
few nic-nacs from our friend L in Broad st. — sent in the
morng for *Shalah Monot* in fact they were so full of the
frolic, that everyone reserved some of their allowances for
the next day — they stayed up until ½ past 8 o'clock, & I
entertained them with quite a romantic biographycal history, & we of larger growth entertained each other, with the
occurrences of last *Purim*, in which you were one of the
chief characters of the Drama . . . ."

PURIM IN ENGLAND[2]

Israel Zangwill

At Purim a gaiety, as of the Roman carnival, enlivened
the swampy Wentworth Street, and brought a smile into
the unwashed face of the pavement. The confectioners'
shops, crammed with "stuffed monkeys" and "bolas" (balls),
were besieged by hilarious crowds of handsome girls and
their young men, fat women and their children, all washing

down the luscious spicy compounds with cups of chocolate; temporarily erected swinging cradles bore a vociferous many-colored burden to the skies; cardboard noses, grotesque in their departure from truth, abounded. The Purim *Spiel*, or Purim play, never took root in England, nor was Haman ever burnt in the streets, but *Shalah Monot*, or gifts of the season, passed between friends, and masquerading parties burst into neighbors' houses.

AN ENGLISH PURIM OF LONG AGO[3]

Gabriel Costa

Where is the Purim of yester-year? Let me carry you back to the London ghetto before the days of telephone, electric tram and automobile; let me draw the curtain from a picture that is fast fading and tell you of happy Purims that have been. Come with me to Goulston Street in the 'seventies. Goulston Street is hard by Petticoat Lane, the mart of Israel, famed the world over for the multiplicity of its wares. Here are swings and roundabouts (merry-go-rounds), clowns and donkeys, peddlers of Purim sweets galore, and young rascals in quaint array who besprinkle flour with aggravating liberality upon unsuspecting passers-by. Remonstrate with the gentleman who shows so little regard for your Sabbath clothes, and lo and behold! a larger share than ever transforms you into a baker's man.

Brothers and sisters are dressed in each others' attire, for no one cares for Mrs. Grundy on this day of days. And the Gentiles from far afield foregather to a piece of waste ground, where the effigy of Haman is consigned to the flames with all due ceremony. Down in the Dutch Tenter Ground, where lived good folks from the land of dykes, they kept Purim after a fashion that lacked nothing in the way of thoroughness. These Hollanders of the sweet tooth, their tables groaning under the weight of good things, welcomed with open arms the *Purimspielers*, with their songs, their jests and jargon ballads. To them, every house was liberty hall, and choice fare their perquisite. That their songs became less melodious and their jests less keen was the fault of the *Shnaps* and the good things aforesaid.

Nowadays, there is no such thing as the Anglo-Jewish ballad; for that was a product of the times. We have grown out of this, likewise. There were ballads for all sorts of occasions. One, I recall, was much in demand at *Bar Mizvah* parties. I only mention this because it is one of the two creations that have survived in an age when the English song, humorous and sentimental, rules the roast. The ballad, to which I would particularly refer, is still remembered by elderly Jewish ladies, though one is enabled to secure just a few incomplete fragments of what must have been a most amusing effusion. Here is one verse, the complete accuracy of which cannot be vouched for:

> Then said Haman to his wife:
> "Angelina, take this knife,
> And cut this sheet of paper into pieces,
> Put on each a day and month,
> Let all this be done at once,
> We'll make the Jews look as green as water-cresses!"

This, of course, refers to the episode of casting lots, but the complete ballad would bring joy to the hearts of many of us today. To travel back still further down the corridor of time, what a contrast with the English Purim of two centuries back! From data in our possession, it is possible to reconstruct the average year of the earliest Anglo-Jewish settlers, the Crypto-Jews (Marranos), and pass with them in imagination from the beginning to the end of the Jewish calendar. Much of the spirit in which they celebrated Purim may be gathered from the old Spanish archives of the Sephardic congregation. They cast aside, on this Feast of Lots, their natural pessimism as a garment. In their eyes, the story of the deliverance of the Jews of ancient Persia from the machination of the wily Haman was as fresh and as real as if it had happened in the previous year. Congregational decorum was thrown to the winds. Children and adults gave themselves up to festivity and frolic. A day of merrymaking and rejoicing, it was nevertheless "sternly prevented from passing the threshold of the synagogue." Even so, the synagogue itself provided a setting for such revels as can be imagined. In the old "snoga" (synagogue) at Bevis Marks on the night of Purim, the congregants would hold a "service" of their own. They appointed their own Haman, *Hazan* and *Parnas* (lay head). They burlesqued the beadle and poked fun at the autocratic *Gabay*. The reader recited the *Hallel* after his own fashion, the musical portion being taken up by the revellers with little regard to its tuneful rendering.

Buffoonery and burlesque were the keynote of the revel, and although for a time the Elders looked on with a blind eye, they came to realize that these things could not be tolerated year after year, having regard to the growing importance of the congregation and to the need for acting circumspectly in a Christian country. So it came about that the *Ma'amad* (Board of Management) framed certain regulations for ensuring decorum in the synagogue on the eve of Purim and on the eventful day itself. These regulations are still to be found, and they read passing quaint in these days. The first had reference to the masquerade and set forth "That in future no person of our nation of either sex shall in Purim, or at any other time of the year, appear in the streets in masquerade, or disguised in the dress of the other sex, though it is only to go from one house to another, this being as well in violation of decency, as of the laws of God and of this kingdom."

No less entertaining was a further law framed with the idea of preserving decorum in the Bevis Marks Synagogue on Purim eve. This very law was destined to make history in later years. It reads as follows: "Also, in future, on the evening and morning of Purim while the *Megillah* is said, or at any other time, no person of whatever condition, age or sex, shall beat or make a noise in synagogue with a hammer, or any other instrument, since, independently of the scandal such a bad custom would give rise to, it may prevent many devout persons of our congregation from going to synagogue on these occasions; and should anyone transgress this order, the *Ma'amad* shall fine him in a sum not exceeding twenty pounds for *Zedakah* (charity)."

Excepting on one occasion, it is hardly likely that this curious *Askamah* (regulation) was ever enforced, for it is an unwritten law that on the eve of Purim the name of Haman should be greeted with a stamping of feet and a volley of raps on the shiny wooden benches. The elder members of the congregation were wont to look up in mild surprise at this breach of decorum, and one would never suspect them of being the greatest offenders!

It was this very *Askamah* that led to the apostasy of the Isaac Mendes Furtado, who built Purim Place in London — demolished many years now — to perpetuate the episode. The story is fairly well known, but it merits a repetition as indicating the unwillingness of conservative Sephardim, then as now, to give up time-honored customs without a struggle. Some of the members of Bevis Marks Synagogue in 1783 resented this attempt to enforce decorum on Purim. They had always made a clatter when Haman's name figured in the *Megillah*. Indeed, it would not be a real Purim without it. Furtado and some of his cronies treated the new law with contempt, and this memorable Purim culminated in a riot in which the interference of the police was found necessary. Furtado, though one of the most prominent offenders, refused to make *Shalom* (peace) with the Elders, and withdrew from the community. They were easily piqued, these Sephardim of other days.

When I lament the passing of the old-fashioned English Purim, I would not say that it is quite extinct in 1913. By no means. What semblances of life it possesses in these bustling times is imparted to it by the younger generation.

There are donkey-rides in the ghetto, ample supplies of "Haman's ears" and flags depicting the Amalekite and his sons suspended from the gallows of their own fashioning. Flour-throwing is still a favorite Purim pastime, and there are many streets in the ghetto that resemble millers' yards when Purim day is over.

But, comparatively speaking, the Purim of to-day is a half-hearted affair. It is nobody's fault. It is just typical of an age in which there is little time to go romancing; although this romance of ancient Persia is worthier of a far better fate.

PURIM IN BENGHAZI, NORTH AFRICA[4]

MOSHE MOSENSON

Excerpts from the diary of a Palestinian Jew in the British Army
March 21, 1943.

In one of my letters I told you briefly that we had set up a Hebrew school in the city next to which we are stationed. Each one of the units offered a member as teacher. Four teachers organized the school. The children, bewildered, depressed and melancholy, were taken in hand by these boys and put into school after three years of absence from their studies. . . .

And now, three weeks after the school was started, they arranged a Purim play and invited us, the soldiers, to attend. The play took place in the hall of a fascist bank, the very bank where long lines of beaten Jews were corralled before they were taken to the concentration camps. The hall was packed full. . . .

A boy of fourteen got up on the pleasantly decorated stage and said: "The children of the school at Benghazi will now present their Purim program to the Jewish soldiers. After three years away from their studies, the school was set up, and it is now three weeks since it was opened. Therefore our program is short and modest. But we want the soldiers to know that it is offered them in love and affection. This is a Purim gift from the Jewish youth of Benghazi to the Jewish soldier." The curtain was raised. At that moment I thought that I was back at Naan, at a play given by our school and our kindergarten. We saw a scene that had been composed by one of our comrades, a teacher. Children are playing at Purim games. Their mother comes in and sends them to sleep. The children lie down on mattresses and fall asleep. The light grows fainter and there is semi-darkness. In the distance you can see the hills of Galilee outlined on the horizon (the decoration was painted by one of our comrades). Behind the scenes a beautiful woman's voice is heard singing,"There are melodies in the mouth of a flute." While she is singing the children are sleeping. Palestinian children enter with palm leaves in their hands and bands across their foreheads bearing the names of the different settlements in Palestine. They stumble over the sleeping children and ask, "Who are they?" Then the biggest girl among them says, "Do you not recognize them, children? They are our brothers, the children of the Diaspora who have been persecuted by the enemy. We have been waiting for them impatiently, waiting for them to come to us so that together we may rebuild our ancient homeland." One of the children says bitterly, "In every generation there are Hamans who rise up to destroy us — why should we not take the children of the *Galut* (Diaspora) and bring them to Palestine so that they may live with us and be happy?" A second child answers, "Patience, children, the gates to our country are closed and the keys are not in our hands, but we have sworn to ourselves that these children shall find a home among us, in their homeland, in the hills of Galilee and in the valleys of Jezreel. We shall not rest or sleep until the remnant of Israel shall return to our motherland." Then the Palestinian children begin singing *Anu Banu Arzah* (We have come to the land to build and to be rebuilt there). Near me stood the father of one of the little girls who was acting; he was weeping quietly.

The play went on. Suddenly one little boy whispers, "Sh-sh — they're waking up. The children of the *Galut* are awaking." They rub their eyes and ask: "Where are the children from Palestine?" Then the mother enters again and they tell her that children from Palestine have been visiting them. The mother is surprised and astonished, but they insist that it was so. One little girl says, "They sang us one of their songs and they swore an oath that they would bring us to Palestine quickly." Then the mother says, "All this was only a dream that you dreamed, children. A beautiful dream, a holy dream about Palestine. It is true that the children of Palestine are waiting for you, and you must learn Hebrew well and be good and strong and perhaps we will all celebrate next year's holiday in Jerusalem." Then she asks, "What was the song, children, do you remember?" And the children burst into song, "We have come to the land to build and to be rebuilt there!"

Then the audience, with hundreds of Jewish soldiers among them, rose to their feet suddenly and sang with them,

"We have come to the land to build and to be rebuilt there!"
When the lights were lit in the hall many of us were ashamed
to lift our heads because of the tears in our eyes . . . .

The program continued. Soldiers and children took part in
it alternately. Finally all the school children went up on the
stage, stood opposite the soldiers and *Hatikvah* burst from
their throats with fervor and enthusiasm. When have I ever
sung it that way?

PURIM IN CAIRO[5]

HERBERT FRIEDENWALD

If the Jews of the Occident wish to see some of our festivals celebrated with much of the old-time spirit, they must
go to the Orient.

Purim in Cairo is very different from Purim in Philadelphia or New York. With the exception of the inhabitants of
New Orleans, few Americans know anything of the carnival
season. At Cairo, however, in spite of its being a Mohammedan principality, the authorities permit of the existence,
with every degree of freedom, of all religious beliefs, and
their festival occasions are allowed to be observed in almost
any manner the individual sees fit. . . .

Beginning with the evening the gaiety is continued
through all of Purim day and much of the night.

Purim eve, guided by one of the prominent merchants of
the place, we were piloted through the narrow, crooked,
dirty lanes of a portion of the Jewish quarter of Cairo until
we reached our destination, the synagogue, a small, unim-
posing-looking structure about two stories in height.

After the regular evening service, a very untidy-looking
individual, whose attire suggested that of the donkey-boy
of the streets, illuminated the building as far as it was possible and then went the rounds of the congregation present-

ing each person in turn with a tallow candle. These preparations finished and all the candles lighted, the reading of the *Megillah* was commenced. The reader, a very young man, seemingly made no attempt to rush through, yet he made very good time and concluded within twenty-five minutes. The mention of the name of Haman was met with shouts and stamping of feet, and one small boy with some of the spirit of young America had the temerity to set off a firecracker, a proceeding which created no unusual interest or concern other than a few hisses of disapproval. . . .

From the beginning of the reading to the end, beggars, in all stages of misery and of all ages, took full advantage of the privileges accorded them and went about asking each in turn for alms. Just before the conclusion they formed a column of about twenty men and once more made the tour. Few, if any, refused to give *Baksheesh* (gratuity), and the miserable mortals were well repaid for their exertions.

During the day, masqueraders took full possession of the town and went about from street to street thoroughly enjoying their lark. All sorts and conditions of fancy costumes are called into requisition, and men of nearly middle age are seen together with boys and girls hardly yet in their teens. Once in a while one comes across some jolly party, more fortunate as to this world's goods, who have procured a carriage or other vehicle in which they ride about, while occasionally a still more ambitious crowd are preceded in their wanderings by a band of music of a very amateurish variety. The vast majority of those who do not go about on foot make use of the ubiquitous donkey, whose striped, dyed and often emaciated body lends additional ridiculousness to the general make-up. There is no doubt that all are having a good time, and, as with all those engaged in celebrating a carnival, the more noise that can be created the better do those indulging enjoy it.

The coming of the night finally puts an end to the revellers' enjoyment, when tired and often footsore they disappear into their homes.

PURIM IN POLAND[6]

MENDELE MOKER SEFARIM

That winter was very hard for Reb Hayyim, very hard and very bad indeed.

On Purim eve, Reb Hayyim sat at the table, at the head of his family, and strained his powers to their utmost in order to keep the Purim feast in the traditional manner, joyously and by sending gifts to the poor, as was his yearly custom. The poor entered and Reb Hayyim gave. He gave with a friendly eye and a good word. The sons of householders were wont to come with kerchiefs to ask charity for others — for the secretly poor who had lost their money and whose families were in want of bread; for a teacher whose strength had failed in the course of time, leaving him naked and penniless; and for So-and-So, a righteous man, the husband of a wife, and father of five children, who had no income all year round and had not a penny to provide for the coming Passover — and Reb Hayyim would hear and give, give with great compassion, and honor them meanwhile with Purim delicacies.

The "holy servants" would come in a band: the caretakers of the synagogues and the caretakers of the bathhouses, the society of the musicians and the professional clowns, the ne'er-do-wells and the nasty fellows. Reb Hayyim would give to all of them with a generous spirit and a friendly face.

And Sarah his wife would be busy at the same time receiving gifts from relatives and neighbors, that boys and girls, *Yeshibah* students and maids brought on covered plates. The gifts consisted of all kinds of sweets and dainties, honey cakes, and cookie figures with many strange decorations,

3. *PURIM IN THE HOME*

Painting

Moritz D. Oppenheim, 19th Century

and with the names Vashti, Zeresh and Queen Esther, written on them in sugar and honey-of-the-comb. Dry plums or some almonds and nuts would cap off these gifts. Sometimes, in place of these delicacies, there would come pickles — spiced and stewed in vinegar and honey — that would be a gift sent by a householder who was one of those rude souls. "Grace, " they say, "is deceitful and beauty is vain," and they can conceive of nothing in this world but the tangible. The children would look over the gifts that were brought in and do business with one another, exchanging and trading gifts — for rolls they'd exchange honeycakes; for Vashti, Queen Esther; and for the plums, a red apple. Their opinions would be divided; one would say one thing, and one another, but the joy would not be spoiled. For it was Purim that night and everybody was easily appeased.

It would seem that Purim this year was no different in the home of Reb Hayyim, and everything was as it had been the year before. Yet, nevertheless, it wasn't quite the same. There were the same poor folk, and the same paupers; there was no lessening of those who came, far be it, but the gifts for the poor had diminished. Of the many visitors, the friends of Reb Hayyim who used to come to his feasts in the past and would eat and drink with him and dance all that night, this year there appeared only a few of his poor relations. Reb Hayyim sang *Shoshanat Ya'akob* (Lily of Jacob) and those sitting at the table lent him vocal assistance, but his voice wasn't the same as it had been in the past. Audible in his singing was something like a sob issuing from a saddened soul, something like the *Lamentations* of the Ninth of Ab. This year's "Lily of Jacob" was like a plucked lily, still beautiful to the eye but hollow within; her perfume fled and her vital source drying within her. She was dying! Reb Hayyim tried hard to subdue his melancholy. He stirred up enthusiasm and, turning to his poor relatives

with words of consolation, said, "Be strong, O Jews! Have
faith, have faith, O children of believers. Do not fear; behold the God of our salvation will care for us!" But the anxiety in his heart was sucking away his blood like a cupping
glass, and sorrow and anguish peered out of his eyes.

PURIM IN A LITHUANIAN TOWN[7]

A. S. SACHS

After the Purim feast, everybody went to the home of
the head of the *Yeshibah*, where the *Yeshibah* students would
produce their "play." On Purim, the *Yeshibah* folk were
the heroes of the day. That day marked the end of the winter term. The *Rosh Yeshibah* ceased the daily recitation
and the supervisor no longer had his grip on the poor
youths, who were preparing to return to their homes, with
their store of learning and indigestion after eating "days."
The *Yeshibah* students were now in a happy mood, and
when they felt happy they sang and improvised witticisms
in rhyme, and the gifted ones were good at singing and ban-
tering. These were indeed gifted all around. Some were endowed with genuine talent. All through the year they could
not show it. Purim was the day for them; then it was that
they gave utterance in word and song to whatever weighed
heavily on their minds. They "roasted" the housewives
who gave them meals; the *Rosh Yeshibah* for his intermin-
able pilpuls; the supervisor for his "snitching"; the *Rosh
Yeshibah's* wife for her "billy-goat," and everybody else.
The *Rosh Yeshibah's* daughters, however, fared better at
their hands. The *Yeshibah* fellows got along well with them
— too well, evil tongues said — and if there was to be a female part in the play, the students would borrow skirts from
the rabbi's daughters.

In the celebrated *Yeshibot* of Telz and Voloshin, the

4. *THE PURIM RABBI*   Painting
Megillah, 18th Century

students would elect a Purim rabbi. This rabbi was king
in the *Yeshibah*. He would don a long silk coat, put a girdle
around his waist, a fur-edged cap on his head, whiskers and
sidelocks, exactly like the actual rabbi or *Rosh Yeshibah* of
the year. At the Purim feast, the Purim rabbi would recite
the lesson of the day and the real *Rosh Yeshibah* would sit
at the table, like an ordinary *Yeshibah Bahur* and listen to
the pilpul of his pupil, who was wearing the *Rosh Yeshibah's*
clothes. . . .

The chant and form of the Purim pilpul were like those of
every day, but the substance and content was a burlesque on
the daily regime of the *Yeshibah*. All the weaknesses of the
Rosh Yeshibah and his aides were mocked in this pilpul, and
the latter could clearly see in what regard his students held
his erudition and what they thought of his management.
Occasionally the *Rosh Yeshibah* had to listen to sharp caus-
tic criticism of himself, but he would grin good-naturedly
and bear it.

"What do you think, Rebbi, of the Talmud lesson that
the rascals read today?" Yossel Reb Zissel's, a youthful
scholar with aspirations for the post of *Yeshibah* supervisor,
asked the *Rosh Yeshibah*. The latter, with a sweet, good-
humored smile all over his face, replied: "I am vanquished,
my son, I am vanquished. . . ."

PURIM IN MINSK, WHITE RUSSIA[8]

Daniel Persky

There is no recounting the manifold delights of Purim, which to some extent relieved our depressed spirits. One important aspect of Purim may not be visible at first glance. It may be a surprise to you, but I dare to make the following generalization: Purim developed our craftmanship and technical skills.

Nowadays, you can buy small noisemakers readymade — and everything is all right. But I remember, in my childhood days, the children of the poor and the rich alike used

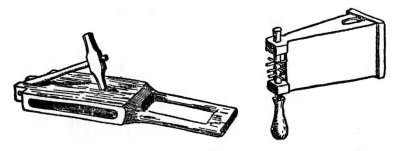

5. HAMAN HAMMER AND NOISEMAKER
End of the Middle Ages

to make those instruments *with their own hands*. A very large amount of creative power was sunk into the production of Purim utensils. I, for example, excelled only in casting teetotums for Hanukkah. My elder brother, on the other hand, was a real "wonder" when it came to manufacturing noisemakers. About a month before Purim he was already busy making this "machine" of his — an "original" machine that gave forth a powerful and earsplitting clamor.

I was amazed on Purim eve, during the course of my visits to various adjacent synagogues, at the sight of all sorts of large and strange noisemakers, which occupied large areas of space. There was one wonderful hammer that was pounded on top of an anvil whenever the name of Haman was heard in the House of Prayer. There was a heavy stone that was released to fall with a loud thud whenever a certain rope was pulled. There were noisemakers as big as a table. When these engines of destruction opened their mouths, you would think there was an earthquake. Every artisan tried his best to excel every other in the magnitude of the din which his contrivance could create.

A few minor "tragedies" are still engraved in my memory. I remember how more than once boys, who had pressed all their comrades to come to their synagogue during the reading of the Scroll to watch the marvellous accomplishments of their wonderful noisemakers, would set out to "beat Haman" to the edification of their own personal claque — but, lo and behold, desolation and ruination: the noisemakers didn't work at all! Apparently, their Frankensteins had turned antisemite at the last moment and hadn't wanted to disgrace the name and memory of Haman the son of Hammedatha.

There was no limit to the variations and technical achievements possible. Our neighbor, the tinsmith, and his two sons were expert workingmen. So they made themselves a sort of tin noisemaker with chambers in which little tin balls used to roll back and forth, jingling and jangling.

There were practical jokers who imitated the voices of animals, by growling like bears, roaring like lions, barking like dogs, bleating like goats — all for the edification of the son of Hammedatha, who had to be confounded by their shouting and screaming.

At times it seems to me that all the violent hubbub which

we make on Purim conceals a secret symbolic meaning. What we are trying to do is *silence* our pains by our yelling. Screams are the fit accompaniment to misery. The cry for help is the fit accompaniment to redemption. Speaking the language of military tactics, we might say: We are flying in airplanes above the heights of the eternity of Israel to drop bombs in the form of noisemakers to shatter the ranks of our foes, spiritually and physically, to wipe their evil from our hearts, to cause the murmur of our sorrow, the flame of our humiliation and the slings and arrows of our outrageous fortune, to be forgotten in a firmament-shattering and earth-shaking racket.

PURIM GIFTS IN VITEBSK, RUSSIA[9]*

BELLA CHAGALL

A white snow, a pale sun. With the early morning Purim has come. A thin frost has carved white horses with heroic riders on the window panes. A little wind brings the tidings: today is a holiday!

My brother Abrashke and I have run to meet it. We received Purim money. The copper coins clinked in our hands. We ran to the meat market on the square. We found it already full of stir like a fair.

The old, dilapidated tables were blanketed with white hole-riddled tablecloths as with snow blown in. The tables were set as for a wedding. Women and children stamped around the tables, as the men do in *Shul* during the ceremony of *Hakkafot* (ceremonial procession around the synagogue). The tables were dazzling, bewitching.

A whole world of little beings of frozen candy was spread on the tables. Little horses, sheep, birds, dolls and cradles

*Reprinted from *Burning Lights*, by Bella Chagall, by permission of Schocken Books, New York. Copyright, 1946, by Schocken Books, New York.

— their red-yellow dots seemed to wink at us, to show that they were still alive, that they were not yet quite dead. Little golden fiddles looked as though they had fallen asleep while playing a last melody. Mordecais and Ahasueruses on horseback seemed to be raising themselves in the saddle.

The cold sun occasionally cast his rays on all these dream-like Purim gifts and hardly warmed their coats of sugar. Abrashke and I elbowed up close to the tables, as if we were trying to rescue the frozen toys with our own breath. We wanted to take them all with us. On the street here, wouldn't they be frozen to death?

"Children, let's get on with it! Choose your presents and go home!" The freezing vendor interrupted our dreams.

As though it were easy to choose! Our hearts pounded. We looked at the Purim toys, hoping that they themselves would tell us which of them wanted to go with us, which to remain.

How could one let them go out of one's hands? And what should we take? A big horse or a small one? My friend Zlatke might think that in giving her the bigger horse I wanted to show off, yet she would be more pleased with it than with the smaller one. So I touched the little horse in front and in back.

"Bashke, what are you doing? It's dangerous to touch it!" my brother teased me.

I let go of the horse, as though I feared that it might bite me. My teeth were chattering, either from cold or from the temptation of the thought whispering to me that all these little horses and little violins were the sweetest of all sweets, and that it would feel good to be crunching them alive in one's mouth.

"If you wish, I'll deliver your Purim presents," said a tall, scrawny boy coming up to us.

"Sure, yes — come with us!"

His round, sad eyes, the eyes of a much-beaten dog, drew us after him. And like a dog he ran in front of us.

"What's your name?" we asked him.

"Pinye."

Pinye? That is a strange name, like a bird's.

"Can you whistle?"

At home we spread our Purim gifts on two plates, one plate for Abrashke and the other for me.

The little sugar animals seemed to come back to life in the warm air. Their little cheeks began to glisten. Frightened, I blew on them, so that they should not melt from the heat. That would be the last straw — that our presents should melt, fall apart in little bits. More than once we changed the plates, picked among the presents, sorted them. I clung particularly to the little candy violin. It nestled in my fingers, stroked them, like a toy bow, as if it were trying to play a melody on them.

"And if I send the little violin to my friend, it will surely never come back to me," I thought, feeling a stab in my heart.

But Pinye, the errand boy, was shuffling his feet, waiting for our presents. Trembling with emotion, we gazed for the last time on our plates, wrapped them each in a kerchief, and gathered together the corners.

"Pinye, see, here are our Purim gifts. But you mustn't run, mind you! Better walk slowly! You must not — God forbid — slip on the wet snow with the plates. And don't turn around! You might be pushed! What is the matter, are you asleep? Why do you look at us in a dream?" And we shook the boy by his shoulder.

Pinye started from his place and at once began to run. The plates shook in his hands.

"Don't rush like that, Pinye! Have you no time? What's

6. THE MESSENGER   Pen and Ink

Marc Chagall

the hurry? Watch out, hold fast to the corners of the kerchiefs!" we shouted after him.

Oh, he'll make trouble, that boy, I said to myself. He
has such long legs! Our presents will tumble over on one another. And suppose an ear of the horse breaks off on the

way, or the top of the curved little violin falls off? What will our friends think? That we sent them broken presents!

"Where are you, Pinye?"

But Pinye has vanished.

Right now, I keep thinking, Pinye has turned into the little street where my friend Zlatke lives. The black latch of the door is lifted from inside, and from behind the door Zlatke appears, as though she had been waiting for the messenger.

"Are the two for me?" And Zlatke stretches out both hands.

"No, this one is yours!" And Pinye probably confuses our plates.

Zlatke snatches the little plate from Pinye's hands and runs to her bedroom. Pinye remains standing there.

In the kitchen, Zlatke's mother is busying herself. With a long iron fork she lifts a big black pot and pushes it into the oven. Pinye's tongue hangs out of his mouth. He wants to eat. The roasted meat and potatoes smell so good.

"Zlatke, why does it take so long? Have you fallen asleep there, or what? *Ai*, what children get excited about! Going wild over nothing!"

Zlatke's mother turns to the boy with a cry. "What are you standing for, you ninny? For the same money you can sit down!"

Zlatke is somewhat fat, with short little legs, and she wears her hair in a long, heavy pigtail on her back. And she always walks so slowly that I get bored looking at her. Even her big eyes stare as if frozen in her face. Before she gets through with the Purim gifts, the Messiah himself might come. She probably examines my plate from all sides, touches the little horse and the golden lamb. She puts them to her nose, to her ears.

Her long pigtail wiggles on her back as though it were helping her to think. She is unable to fix her attention on anything. And suppose Zlatke wants to keep the whole plate?

Oh, why do I think up such false accusations? I shame myself. Probably Zlatke runs to the drawer where she keeps her own presents, spreads out her little horses and lambs, and compares them with mine.

"She is taking the sweet little violin from my plate!" I think with pounding heart.

And what will she put in its place? Oh, why doesn't the boy come back? He has vanished as though forever! I begin to question Abrashke: "Do you think Pinye has already been at my friend's?"

But my brother teases me. He thinks that being older than I, and a boy to boot, he can make fun of me. So he bursts into laughter.

Let him laugh, by all means! I know nevertheless that he too is waiting for Pinye, that he is dying to see what has remained on his plate, and what gifts for him have been added on it. To whom is he boasting? Don't I see that he keeps looking out of the window, watching for the return of our Pinye?

"You know, Bashke," he says, "Pinye probably won't be back for at least an hour. You know that my friend Motke lives on the other side of the river. And by the time that dreamy Pinye crosses the bridge, we shall be falling asleep. How can you expect him not to stop to have a look at what is going on in the river? Perhaps the ice has begun to break!"

And what if Abrashke is right? I am bursting with grief.

"Pinye is capable of anything," I agree with my brother. "That's all he has to do — inspect the whole river! He won't even be back for the meal!"

"You dumb cluck, you believe everything! I've just made that up!"

My brother is now rolling with laughter.

Suddenly he pushes me to one side and, like a cat, scrambles down all the stairs that lead to the kitchen. Pinye is knocking at the door.

"Ah, you brats, why do you make so much noise?" the fat cook yells at us. "You idlers! All day long you roam about here — you don't give me a chance to do anything. Out of the kitchen!"

We drag Pinye into the house. First we look into his eyes, then into the plates. He has probably seen what kind of presents have been sent us in exchange for ours.

Well, the little violin must be gone! I read it in Pinye's sad eyes. I open the kerchief on my plate. Yes, she did take the pretty little violin! And I have no other violin, and I don't

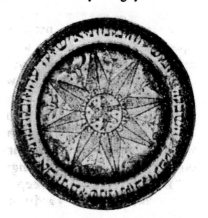

7. *PURIM DISH*   Pewter

1787

need the doll she has given me. I've got two like it. Abrashke has given me his. And that's what made her fuss for a whole hour! In anger I bite my lips.

What? He is laughing again, Abrashke, and even that silly Pinye too! I can't look at them any more.

Abrashke is lucky. He can afford to be in a good mood. Motke has put a big horse on his plate. In his enthusiasm, Abrashke neighs like a real horse.

Weeping, I run to the kitchen.

"Why do you make such a long face?" The cook throws the words at me while chopping onions. "What is the matter, did you get a bad Purim gift?" And she keeps on babbling in her usual fashion, as though she were chopping the onions with her tongue, and she spatters me with wet crumbs. "What a misfortune that is! May you have no greater grief until your hundred-and-twentieth year! Silly girl, you'll surely forget about it before your wedding!"

Whether because of the onions or because of her words, my eyes begin actually to drop tears.

"Here, take your little *Hamantash*." And the cook squeezes into my hands a triangular cake, bursting with heat and with the poppyseed with which it is stuffed.

My hands at once become wet and warm as though somebody had kissed them.

"You see, Bashutke, there is no reason for crying." Sasha cheers me with her smile. "You know what? Just wait a while — when I'm through with my work, I'll run out for a minute and exchange your doll for a violin."

"Darling Sasha!" I creep into her skirts, stuffed underneath like a whole wardrobe, and wipe my eyes on her sleeves.

"That's enough, Bashutke, go now, let me work! It will be meal-time soon! Why do you keep spinning around me, you crazy girl?" And she pushes me away gently.

In the dark rear shop I bump into something hard. Aha, a woven basket! This must be mother's Purim gifts prepared for our uncles and aunts. A basket packed full of good things! How can mother send them away so improvidently? The basket will have bottles of red and white wine, bottles of sweet syrups, big pears, wooden boxes with cigars heaped on one another like blocks; and there will be cans of sprats and sardines, and amidst all this a new red tablecloth with painted flowers.

Mother has been busy in the shop, as always, and probably has forgotten her Purim presents. Doesn't she even think of them? The basket will soon be carried away! And isn't she waiting at all for the presents that she will get?

I imagine my good Aunt Rachel's delight over mother's presents: "Lord of the Universe! So many good things! And all that for me! Ah, Alta, you'll spoil me altogether!"

My aunt's weak heart is choked with joy. She sniffs at the basket; she seems instantly to be made drunk by all the good smells, for she closes her eyes. Then she awakens as if from a dream. She feels the tablecloth, lifts it in the air, strokes it. She might be saying a benediction: "Thank you, Altinke! May God in heaven grant you many healthful and happy years! How could you guess so truly? I really needed a new tablecloth for *Pesah*, to honor my guests."

And suddenly my aunt fancies that a speck of dust has fallen on the new tablecloth. She blows away the speck, and fearing the tablecloth may become soiled before Passover, she carefully lays it in its folds.

How many baskets with presents have been carried through the streets from one house to another! And the things they were filled with! The scrawny woman messengers were hardly able to hold them up.

PURIM IN SWISLOWITZ, RUSSIA[10]*

Shmarya Levin

Soon after the fifteenth day of Shebat the town began to liven up — Purim was coming — the festival which commemorates the triumph of the Jews of Persia over Haman the persecutor in the days of Ahasuerus, Esther and Mordecai. Now Purim itself is certainly not among the major festivals, but it is the merriest and most jovial of them all. And the Jews of Swislowitz looked forward to it less on its own account than for the sake of the Purim players, the only approach to a theater known to us.

*Condensed from *Childhood in Exile*, by Shmarya Levin, copyright, 1939, by Harcourt, Brace and Company, Inc.

The Purim players of Swislowitz were preparing that year to give two grand performances: *The Story of Esther* and *The Selling of Joseph.* The first of these was the authentic play of the festival, a sort of mystery or miracle play, given every year. It already had its trained actors, some of whom conserved their roles for several years in succession. But for *The Selling of Joseph* new forces had to be trained, and a tremendous hubbub arose in the town concerning the distribution of the roles. There were three candidates for every role, and it was impossible to satisfy even the successful candidates. And the quarrels spread from the candidates to their families, and from the families to their friends, and the whole town seethed with claims and counter-claims, ambitions and artists' passions.

The general organizer of the plays was Bencheh, son of Cherneh the widow. He was *regisseur*, stage-manager and promoter rolled into one. He had a heart-breaking task in front of him, for no matter whom he chose, he alienated more than he won over. But to the honor of his memory be it said, he was an honest man. He chose his actors without fear or favor, solely on their merits and without regard to their influence and family connections. He was an artist in search of artists. He put all the candidates through their paces, tested their elocution and their memory. Perhaps he would not have been so stern and masterly if he had not had behind him his mother — Cherneh the widow. And Cherneh the widow was an important factor in the life of Swislowitz.

Bencheh was an old bachelor in the neighborhood of thirty — old bachelor being the designation for any Jew who had not taken a wife unto himself before he had passed the early twenties ....

Bencheh was by instinct a vagabond, a hobo. Swislowitz was too narrow for him, and from childhood on he was tormented by the *Wanderlust* of the gypsies ....

For the Purim I am now speaking of, he had returned from Kiev, after an absence of some months. In that metropolis he had picked up another, more modish pronunciation of Yiddish, and he made fun of our peasant thickness of speech. He expressed his superior culture in other ways, too: he was the only one in the town to wear a short coat instead of the usual long *Capote*: he wore a derby instead of a cap, and his trousers had cuffs at the bottom — the only trouser-cuffs in Swislowitz. He walked apart, like an aristocrat whom evil fate had cast among boors and savages. But in spite of his contempt for us, he loved to gather crowds around him and recount the marvels of the vast world he had sojourned in. . . .

Whenever I think back on Bencheh, with his lean figure, his gestures, his wild tricks, I am reminded of Charlie Chaplin. I am convinced till this day that Bencheh was a man of real gifts, a born artist. His *Wanderlust* was only the expression of his thwarted hunger to live himself out. And he had to satisfy his artistic longings by organizing the Purim plays of the town.

No easy task, this. Where were the men, the means, the interest, to come from? But Bencheh was not only an artist, but a man of restless, enterprising spirit. The first thing he did was to create a fund. He asked nothing for himself; his gifts and his labors he gave away, like a true artist. But there were many things to be bought, and neither he nor his mother — who supported him in this enterprise with all her moral force — could spend money of their own. The first thing that Bencheh did, then, was to tax each one of the actors. After all, they were not real artists, and they were actually getting instructions in the art from the incomparable Bencheh. The levy was graduated according to the importance of the role and the number of lines assigned to it.

The heaviest taxes were laid on Pharaoh and Ahasuerus; next came Haman and Joseph, and after them Jacob and Mordecai. Vaizatha, the clown of the Esther stories, got off scot-free. A second factor in the levying of taxes was the expense tied up with every role. The kings were ruinously costly, and their ministers were only slightly less so. Jacob and Mordecai were only two old Jews, and clothes for the former might be borrowed from the *Rab*, while clothes for the latter — who had to appear in the tattered raiment of a beggar — could be obtained from the water-carrier. Toward the end of the play, of course, Mordecai did become an important figure; he was elevated to Haman's place. But Haman having been hanged, his clothes could be used for Mordecai — an economic stroke and a fine symbolic act in one. The levies raised from the actors could not cover the costs; and here Cherneh the widow threw herself into the struggle. She advanced her own money on the basis of the income of the two performances; it was at least as good an investment as selling pancakes on credit to hungry *Heder* boys. . . .

Bencheh next set about the training of the actors. For himself he reserved the role of Haman the wicked. True, the role of the tyrant and Jew-hater — the greatest Jew-hater the world has ever known — is not a grateful one. But Bencheh was an artist, and he chose a role that had plenty of action. Besides, the more hateful the role, the more room there was for skill and subtlety.

The severest test of his managerial ability came in the choosing of Vashti and Esther. If it had been up to Bencheh, he would have stopped at nothing, and actually invited girls into the drama. But modern realism was beyond the taste — and the morals — of the Jews of Swislowitz, and neither the *Rab* nor the elders of the community would have tolerated it. Bencheh, brought up short by this iron wall, gave in and found boys for the roles. Of the two, Esther was the easier to satisfy. He needed a good-looking boy and some women's clothes. But in the case of Vashti a fearful historical complication arose.

The role of the rejected and humiliated queen was a short one. She appeared on the stage just once. But when she did appear, she had to satisfy the traditional history of Vashti. And tradition says that the incident which set in motion the drama of Purim, and the saving of the Jews of Persia from the enmity of Haman the wicked, namely, the refusal of Vashti to appear in all her beauty before the assembled guests of the tipsy monarch, had a most ludicrous and pitiful explanation. Far from being a woman of innate modesty and good taste, Vashti the queen was as wicked as her husband was foolish; *but* on the day when she was summoned to display herself to the banqueters, something exceedingly ugly and exceedingly immodest grew out on her forehead. And the modesty which prevents me from saying exactly what it was that grew out on her forehead, also prevented the historic presentation of the role of Vashti the queen. And yet how could all allusion to this providential, if shocking, accident be entirely omitted? . . . .

As is to be expected, every boy in Swislowitz knew what had happened to Vashti the queen, and what the biblical account does not mention. Who told me, I cannot remember, but it was certainly neither the rabbi nor my mother. We just knew. And we asked each other, "Do you know what grew on the forehead of Vashti the queen?" Therefore, neither historical accuracy nor public curiosity would have been satisfied unless Vashti was in one way or another properly represented. Of course, Bencheh could have wriggled out of it — as most Purim players did — by putting a few allusive words into the mouth of another character. But Bencheh was made of sterner stuff. He could not bring himself to such intellectual dishonesty. After fearful inner tortures, he found a way out. Vashti would appear on the stage. But besides her crown she would wear a veil covering half her face. What was under the veil could be left to the imagination. The town applauded Bencheh's ingenuity — and the arrangements continued.

Other inspirations came to Bencheh in the course of the preparations. He felt that his talents and his dignity entitled him to a special mark of distinction on the stage. He who had looked upon the actors of Kiev in all their glory would not appear on the stage in the same pitiful village make-up as the amateurs of Swislowitz, with their paper crowns, their imitation robes and their wooden swords covered with gilt.

He felt, moreover, that the king's first minister, the actual overlord of one hundred and twenty-seven provinces stretching from Ethiopia to India, could not appear in the makeshift rags of a silly *Heder* boy. And Bencheh found a way out. By devious ways, through backstairs influence and perhaps with the use of a bribe, he obtained a cast-off uniform of the district commissioner himself. The coat lacked epaulettes, but these he supplied. By the same obscure and circuitous routes he obtained an ancient sword discarded by the town sergeant, unbent it and polished it up. And he had a regular crown made for himself by the cooper, so that he towered above his fellow actors not only by virtue of his superior talents, but by virtue of accoutrements never before seen among Purim players of Swislowitz.

In the second play, *The Selling of Joseph*, he took the role of the hero and had his brother-in-law, Mottye, the best ladies' tailor in Swislowitz, make him the famous coat of many colors. But *The Selling of Joseph* was only dessert to the banquet. It was in the real Purim play that Bencheh took the town by storm.

8. PURIM JESTERS

Engraving

Johan van den Avele, 17th Century

The preparations for the Great Show lasted about a month. The actors — most of them apprentices to various trades — were occupied during the day, and Bencheh himself had been driven by the need to take up again the despised needle. So only the evenings were free. The training therefore had to be intensive. Cherneh's home — a two-room cottage — became for that one month a dramatic school with Bencheh as the director. . . .

No spectators were permitted at the rehearsals. To begin with, Bencheh's home was hardly large enough for the actors. But more than this, his instincts revolted against a display of talent in the making. Close relatives of Cherneh, and one or two chosen friends, were excepted. But it was impossible to keep away the crowds which gathered at the windows and looked on from outside. The winter having relaxed its grip, the boys and girls used to gather eagerly outside Bencheh's home on the evenings before Purim, and get their first glimpses of the preparations for a play. I, because of the close friendship between Cherneh and my mother, was once admitted to the sanctum, and great was my pride and the envy of my playmates.

Parallel with these formidable preparations, the Jewish community went about the minor tasks which preceded the unimportant festival. And among these the most important was the preparation of the rattler for the young people. The rattler is a simple instrument for the production of noises whereby, during the synagogue services of the Purim festival, the children express their contempt whenever the name of Haman is mentioned. It consists of a toothed wooden disk, circular in shape, attached to a handle. A rotating frame-work brings against the teeth of the disk an elastic wooden prong, with ear-splitting results. This was the sole weapon allowed us in our war against the memory of "Haman, son of Hammedatha, the persecutor of the Jew."

After a brief family reunion at the house of my grandfather, we came home to the grand Purim banquet. The table was more richly prepared than for any other meal in the year — foods and drinks of all kinds: twisted loaves that shone yellow, a huge baked fish touched up with saffron, golden colors that harmonized with the light of the candles stuck in the big Menorahs, or seven-branched candlesticks, that burned brilliantly, one at each end of the table. But in the center of the table, and near each Menorah, had been placed three piles of plain boiled chick-peas. I asked my mother why these plebeian dishes had been permitted in the midst of this glorious company. And she explained that they were commemorative of the extreme piety of Esther the queen. For Esther was a good Jewish daughter and, though she lived in the luxurious and profligate palace of the great king, she would touch none of their food. Haman the wicked, knowing of the laws of the Jews, had forbidden the presence of a *Shohet*, or ritual slaughterer, in the palace. And Esther therefore contented herself, at all the feasts, with plain peas and beans; yet on this diet she was as well fed, and as beautiful, as those that gorged themselves on the most tempting dishes.

And then, after the banquet, came the sublime moment for the youngsters. The door was flung wide open and the Purim players, accompanied by a host of children and grown-ups, poured into the house. Our dining room was probably the largest in Swislowitz, but on this occasion it was too small, and protesting voices began to rise: "Let me in, I'm Haman's brother." "Let me in, I'm the queen's first cousin. . ." And when order of a kind had been established in the pent room, the players began. Of course, I knew every one of the players personally, and could have told you to a man who was hidden behind that flaxen beard or within those girlish clothes. But the hunger for illusion was strong, and I felt that these boys were the same, and yet not the same.

And when Vashti, a young *Yeshibah* student, dressed in women's clothes, with a little crown on his head and a veil half covering his face, piped the first lines: "Would that I were a little bird; would that I were a little flower, nay even a little worm," my heart melted toward the unhappy queen. Ahasuerus sat in glory, sullen, gross, almost wordless, as befitted the stupid monarch. And then the word of the chamberlain Mehuman was heard: "Come forth, come forth, O Haman the prince," and Bencheh himself strode into the center of the room, magnificently caparisoned, and taking up a haughty pose, glared upon the players and spectators with the look of an outraged general — nay, a field marshal. The Jews of Swislowitz had never seen the inside of a theater, but instinct told them that here was no ordinary village Purim player; here was a man who understood both make-up and histrionics. Before Bencheh had spoken a word, a shudder ran through the audience: here was Haman himself, an enemy implacable and resourceful. His furious gestures, his bitter glances, his intolerant bearing, said, "There stands before you the Persecutor, the Eternal Persecutor, who will pursue you to the gates of Destruction."

The play took up half an hour and was followed at once by the presentation of the second play, *The Selling of Joseph*. But the addition of the program was not a success. For Vashti the queen suddenly became Joseph the victim, and Haman became Reuben, and Mordecai became Joseph. And in the center of the room a barrel was placed, end up, to represent the pit into which the older brothers threw the spoiled darling of their father.

A second banquet followed the close of the performance, and for the remainder of the evening Bencheh was the hero of Swislowitz. He told again the stories of his wanderings, the marvels of Kiev, and the glories of the theater. We sat up very late that night. The older people were sleepy, and I could hardly keep my eyes open. My thoughts became confused; Haman ears, the Scroll of Esther, rattlers, drama, banquet, beards, everything flowed into everything else, and the entire tumult moved slowly, dimly, into the darker spaces of my mind. At last everything sank into a dream, the misty and eternal dream of a people forever at war with an invisible enemy.

TEL AVIV—THE CITY OF PURIM
Mortimer J. Cohen

When the month of Adar approaches, the new all-Jewish city of Tel Aviv undergoes a magical change. Purim is coming and the voice of the merrymakers is heard in the land.

Purim was born in the *Galut* but has been adopted by Tel Aviv as its very own. Let Jerusalem have its pilgrim festivals! Let little Meron rejoice over Lag ba'Omer and proud Modin over Hanukkah! Tel Aviv, Palestinian child of the *Galut*, embraces tenderly, joyously and passionately happy Purim, festival of the *Galut*. In Tel Aviv, Purim is no minor event. Outside Palestine, Jews set aside two days for most holidays and give only one to Purim; but in Tel Aviv it is different — one day for most holidays, but for Purim two, and even more! Thus, Tel Aviv has become the City of Purim, and he who has not celebrated Purim in Tel Aviv has not known true Purim joy.

Old and New in Celebrations

All that previous generations have devised in honor of Purim can still be found in Tel Aviv — the reading of the *Megillah* evening and morning, accompanied by the *Groggers'* raspy protests at the mention of Haman's name; the friendly interchange of *Shalah Monot*; the masquerade balls; the *Hamantashen* made of prune-jelly or black poppy-seed, *Mohn*; and home parties that last into the wee hours of the morning.

But new ceremonies and celebrations have been created to express in modern idiom the spirit of this ancient festival of Queen Esther. This has ever been the Jewish way — to hold fast to the old that has grown precious with time, but to garb it in new apparel of beauty and splendor. It is these new ways of celebrating Purim that intrigue the visitor in Tel Aviv.

The municipality of Tel Aviv does not leave the celebration of Purim to vagrant chance. It takes the lead in the festivities. It instructs the populace about the decorations of the buildings and streets, the types of costumes to be worn and the general behavior of the celebrants. Months in advance of the holiday it initiates the Purim activities, and for many weeks makes them in all circles the topic of vigorous discussion and planning.

Since 1933, Tel Aviv has issued an official guide — suspended during the war years — named *Kerobez*. Its name is made up of the first letters of the Hebrew words: *Kol rinah vi'yeshuah be-ohale zadikim* (Psalm 118.15), making K'ro'be'z. *Kerobez*, explains the editor, "is an original Hebrew name. . . and expresses the true spirit of Jewish joy," for the words of the Psalmist declare that the righteous rejoice when God makes justice triumph in the world. Thus, in *Kerobez* the ethical note of triumphant righteousness is sounded in a new way.

TEL AVIV EXPANDS WITH JOY

Tel Aviv does not regard Purim as a local, but as a national, even an international, Jewish event, for Jews assemble there to celebrate it from all parts of Palestine, and even from the four corners of the earth. Colonists from the Emek, industrialists from Haifa, students from Jerusalem, orange growers from Petah Tikvah, Yemenites, Bukarim, Morrocans, Ashkenazim, Sefardim, Hasidim, American and English tourists — a multitude of Jews, a motley assembly, who crowd every nook and corner of the city. Here and there in the crowded streets Arabs can be seen, clad in their flowing robes, lured from Jaffa and neighboring towns and villages. By train, bus, auto, wagon, bicycle, donkey, in every conceivable kind of conveyance, and some even on foot, the revelers pour into Tel Aviv. The little city expands, bulges and spreads until, as Judah Karni, a Palestinian poet, declares:

> Each pilgrim makes her boundaries wider,
> Expanding them yet more and more,
> Until they spread and, in our own day,
> She'll stretch beside the sea's long shore.

The streets are aflutter with flags, multi-colored bunting and decorations. Private homes and public buildings present a mass of riotous colors. The shop windows with their lavish displays reflect the gay spirit of the festival. Tall arches, painted white, are erected over the city's main intersections, where processions pass to the shouts and applause of the spectators. By day these arches gleam in the sun like monuments of burnished gold, and by night they sparkle with the silver light of moon and stars.

The names of the streets have undergone a strange transformation; they have been temporarily changed to others more appropriate to Purim, being derived from the Book of Esther. Thus, Herbert Samuel Street is called "Next-to-the-King"; Eliezer ben Yehudah Street becomes "He-spoke-in-the-language-of-his-people"; Rothschild Boulevard is renamed "He-who-seeks-the-good-of-his-people"; Herzl Street is "Great-among-the-Jews"; and Allenby Road, "Shushan-the-Capital."

The streets, the avenues and the boulevards of the city provide the locale for the main celebration of Purim. These are inadequate to accommodate all the spectators and participants; even those who merely watch share in the celebration. Only a part of the crowd finds observation posts on the balconies and rooftops of the houses that line the main thoroughfares where the milling throngs eddy about, jostling each other.

The young people do not seek dance halls; the streets afford them more spacious pavilions. Morning, noon and night they can be seen dancing, prancing, swirling, chains of them, linked arm in arm, taking possession of broad "Shushan-the-Capital," singing, swaying, hopping, skipping. Occasionally, a group of them will suddenly stop, form a circle and, with abandon, untiringly dance the *Horah*.

The Megillah under the Stars

On Purim evening, that is, the 14th of Adar, at six o'-clock precisely, heralds scurry out of the City Hall in automobiles to announce by their trumpet-peals the beginning of the festival and its ceremonies. They rush from street to street, playing on their trumpets the traditional musical notes used when reading the *Megillah*, adapted by one of Palestine's musicians.

A short time later, the reading of the *Megillah* takes place in the Great Synagogue at "Shushan-the-Capital" and "A-certain-Jew" Streets. All the synagogues are crowded, but tremendous throngs mass in front of the Great Synagogue under the open and friendly sky. There, by the light of the full moon and the winking stars, many follow the reading of the *Megillah* broadcast from inside over loudspeakers. When Haman's name is read, the din of the *Groggers* is enough to frighten every living antisemite in the world, if he could but hear their half-angry, half-mocking roar. All traffic in the vicinity of the Great Synagogue has been stopped, and the only sounds heard are the reader's voice and the growling of the *Groggers*.

An hour later sees the crowds surge towards the eastern section of Tel Aviv, at the end of "A-certain-Jew" and "He-who-seeks-the-good-of-his-people" Streets, where the authorities have erected a spacious stage and a stately, oriental edifice appropriately named the "Palace of Esther" on grounds called the "King's Courtyard." Here the Mayor of Tel Aviv formally opens the celebration with a short speech of welcome.

The spirit of this address can be caught from some of the words of the late Mayor of Tel Aviv, Meier Dizengoff, spoken in 1934, one year after the Hitler earthquake in Germany.

> The City of Tel Aviv opens again its traditional celebration of the festival of Purim, and heartily welcomes the thousands of visitors who have come from near and far-off places with the greeting: "May your coming be in peace! Blessed are you who have come!"

Then he spoke of the misfortunes that had befallen the Jews of Europe and expressed the sympathy felt by the Jews of Palestine for their stricken brothers. He concluded:

> Do not despair!... Come and build this land together with us! This old-new homeland, in which we are pioneers, is ready to receive you with open arms and with brotherly love.... Tel Aviv stands at the gates of Zion and is happy to gather within her more and more of the communities of the *Galut*, the scattered tribes of Israel, and to unite them into one people...

And now the festival of Purim is declared open! *The Jews had light and gladness, and joy and honour.* And the City of Tel Aviv rejoiced and was glad.

The festivities now begin with plays and spectacles telling the story of Purim in different versions for adults and children. Choral singing and orchestral music fill the air with Purim melodies. For the children a special pageant is prepared dramatizing the Book of Esther. Like a living *Megillah*, the characters of the story step out of the pages of a gigantic scroll, or book. Guest artists and singers, dancers, musicians and actors participate in these performances.

QUEEN FOR A DAY

One of the most important events of the Purim celebration is the election of Queen Esther, who reigns over Tel Aviv. Paralleling the words chanted on *Kol Nidre* night, the elected Queen is declared ruling monarch *Mi-yom Purim zeh ad yom Purim ha-ba*, that is, "From this Purim unto the Purim to come!" Not always is the most beautiful young girl crowned Queen Esther. Sometimes she is chosen for beauty, but sometimes from patriotic motives, and at other times even to strengthen local pride. One year an Ashkenazic girl is chosen, then perhaps a Sefardic beauty. Once a Yemenite maiden of Neve Zedek, a quarter bordering on Tel Aviv, was crowned queen. It was, indeed, a Cinderella story of a poor orphan girl who was queen for a day. The joy of the Yemenites was unbounded. At last they had come into their own. They were now considered the full equals of other Jews. Thus, the selection of the queen is used to foster the sense of Jewish unity. Parodying a well-known statement of the rabbis, a wit in *Kerobez* declares: *Kol Yisrael yesh lahem helek be-Esther ha-Malkah*, which means that all

Israel is united in the pride they share in glorious Queen Esther.

For the more serious-minded, special dramatic performances are given by the brilliant theatrical troupes of the *Ohel* and the *Habimah*, famous theaters of Palestine. The *Matate*, equally well-known for its humorous and satirical dramas, arranges entertainment suited to the occasion. Long in advance of Purim, tickets of admission to all these performances are at a premium.

The famous Agadatti is largely responsible for the main masquerade balls. A group of buildings is taken over for the holiday. The walls are freshly decorated with modernistic interpretations of the Purim story by such Palestinian artists as Lubin, Rubin and Zaretsky. Orchestras play in several halls. In the courtyard the slow-moving, stately camel may be seen bearing aloft on his mountainous back cheering, exuberant young people. All the public halls and masquerade parties are jammed beyond normal capacity. People rush from one place to the other, eagerly expectant and excited, unwilling to miss anything.

The evening celebration comes to its climax in a brilliant display of bursting fireworks set off in the "King's Courtyard." And the young people dance on and on through the starlighted, moon-drenched night.

First Day of Purim Dawns

The first day of Purim is given over to the children and to sports. In the morning, about ten o'clock, the children gather at the "Palace of Esther," where they join in community singing of Purim songs, hear a special reading of the *Meggillah* for children, and participate in group dances and plays.

9. PURIM FESTIVAL IN TEL AVIV   **Photograph**

Masquerade parties, marionette shows and camel rides are among the special amusements for the children. Every child has at least a mask and almost everyone a costume. There are Queen Esthers, Mordecais, Arabs, Hasidim, Haluzim, clowns, pirates, sailors and every conceivable character of kings and queens. Mordecais and Esthers are numerous, but a Haman is rarely seen, for no child wants to impersonate the prototype of the oppressors of the Jews throughout the ages. Some costumes portray the products of Palestine; some are modelled on the Jewish National Fund box. Not only the children but their elders, too, are masked and costumed.

In the afternoon, the many sports clubs of Palestine — Betar, Hakoah, Makkabi, Atid and others — stage a great Sports Carnival. Displaying their insignia and carrying aloft their distinctive banners, the clubs march in groups, led by bands, to the "Palace of Esther." On the level fields of the "King's Courtyard" they engage in games, contests, athletic dances and gymnastics. Prizes are awarded for special excellence.

THE SECOND DAY — CLIMAX! ADLOYADA! ADLOYADA!

This word is heard on every side.

The second day of Purim is the day of the great Carnival, the climax of the Purim festivities. Originally, the Purim celebration was called Carnival, but this name was felt to be unfitting for this unique, Jewish observance. The Jews of Tel Aviv wanted a Hebrew name for this national, Jewish and Palestinian celebration. A committee of prominent literary men was appointed to search for an appropriate name. An announcement was made asking that suggestions be sent to the committee, and over two hundred names were submitted. The committee finally chose the one that

has become fixed in the heart and mind of every citizen of
Tel Aviv and has spread throughout the world — *Adloyada*
— which means "Until one knows not!" It is part of the
talmudic dictum that on Purim "one is obligated to drink
until one knows not the difference between 'Blessed be
Mordecai' and 'Cursed be Haman.'"

About two-thirty o'clock in the afternoon the parade of
the floats begins, wending its way through the crowded
streets. Beautifully executed tableaux portray diverse
themes taken from the Bible, Jewish history, current events
and the achievements of the *Yishub* in Palestine, its agriculture, industry and science. Schools, youth organizations,
the colonies and other groups depict their particular interests by cleverly and attractively designed floats.

A corps of motorcycles and cyclists with decorated bicy-
cles, performing daring stunts, and bands playing lively
tunes are all part of the long procession. Huge balloons,
floating in the air and bobbing about, add to the color and
excitement. Mighty, grotesque figures, caricaturing the
living and the dead, receive the stormy applause of the
massed spectators.

Hail and Farewell, Purim in Tel Aviv!

With the falling of night, the second day of Purim has
ended. The people of Tel Aviv and the visitors among them
retire, wearied physically but renewed in spirit. Symboli-
cally, they have once more celebrated the triumph of good
over evil. Once again they have tasted the sweet wine of
hope for the future. In song, dance, pageant, sport, drama,
prayer and *Adloyada*, they have offered thanks to God for
their survival and their redemption. With uplifted hearts
they face the coming months of labor and creation for themselves and for all Israel.

And so, we say farewell to Purim in Tel Aviv.

PURIM AMONG THE YEMENITES[11]

Samuel ben Joseph

It is our custom that the privilege of reading the *Megillah* shall be bought by donating oil and wax for the synagogue light when the reader holds a feast for all the people. As a general rule, bridegrooms are the purchasers. On one occasion several bridegrooms quarreled among themselves, one saying: "I shall bring oil and wax," and the other saying: "I shall bring oil and wax." The *Bet Din* (Court of Justice) in our town proclaimed that it should be put up for public auction, and go to the highest bidder, who should then bring the oil and wax he had bid.

It was the custom, before the *Megillah* was read, to recite certain verses fixed by the ancients for extolling the miracles and mercies of the Almighty, such as " I shall make mention of the loving kindness of God." When the time came for reading the *Megillah*, the reader would call out to him in a loud voice: "Blessed be so-and-so, the Bridegroom." The latter would then stand up and take the Scroll, open it and say: "With your permission, Sirs," and they would answer: "With the permission of Heaven!" Then he would pronounce the benediction and proceed to read.

It is our custom for the reader of the *Megillah* to recite one half of the verse. The congregation whispers it after him, but finishes the second half of the verse in a loud voice. The reading of the *Megillah* with us is divided between two bridegrooms; one reads the first half and then the reader calls the second and the same formula as above is repeated. The second reader then continues: "Go, gather together all the Jews, etc." In the morning the order is reversed: the one who commenced the night before, now reads the second half, and vice versa. This has been our custom of old. It is also our custom, during the reading of the *Megillah*, at both the evening and morning services, to light ten wax candles in a circle, representing the ten sons of Haman, and the custom of our forefathers is law.

PURIM IN CHINA[12]

GABRIEL BROTIER

You would perhaps believe that the Jews of China have no other books of the Holy Scriptures than the Pentateuch; and you would be mistaken. They have others not a few; but they regard not as canonical any but the Pentateuch.

10. *PURIM GREETING CARD*

Fritz Melchior

*Used by Jewish Soldiers of the U. S. Armed
Forces in Shanghai*

The other books they call the *San-tsao*, which is the Supplementary, or separate books.

The books of Nehemiah and Esther are . . . imperfect. The Jews of China have for this Princess the most profound veneration; they call her always *Issetha Mama*, the Great Mother. Their reverence extends also to Mordecai, whom they call *Mo-to-kai*; they regard them as the saviors of Israel.

WITH MORDECAI AND ESTHER IN SHUSHAN[13]

WALTER J. FISCHEL

One of the most remarkable things observed in the religious life of the Oriental Jews is their desire to make pilgrimages. To make a pilgrimage, at certain seasons or on certain occasions, to the grave of some great ancestor has long been an integral part of the religious forms of the Oriental Jew.

Doubtless this custom, so alien to the spirit of Judaism, must be traced back to the influence of the Islamic environment in which these Jews live.

The most important holy place of the Persian Jews is the tomb of Esther and Mordecai, located at Hamadan, which supposedly is on the site of the biblical *Shushan ha-Birah* (Shushan the Capital).

I must confess that a curious sense of solemnity filled me when, on my way from Jerusalem via Bagdad into the interior of Persia, I found myself in *Shushan ha-Birah*, at the graves of Mordecai and Esther. First came the impressive road from the Tigris plain to the high Persian plateau, a stair-like, rising pass, on which for thousands of years the armies of all kings, merchants and pilgrims of all nations have traveled — that ancient caravan road to China which is a natural passage connecting East and West. Here the most ancient history of humankind has left its traces. High up in the mountains stands the historically important Behistan Inscription of Darius, hewn into the rock, its reliefs and old, time-worn incisions still clear today.

Then there is Hamadan itself, one of the most ancient of cities, standing on the ruins of old Achmetha, the summer residence of the kings of the Medes.

11. *PRESUMED TOMB OF MORDECAI AND ESTHER IN SHUSHAN*

But there was another reason why I felt that in this city I stood on holy ground; I recalled the *Megillat Esther*, the characters of which come to life as one stands beside the tomb of its heroes. One can fairly see the procession of mourning, fasting Jews, Mordecai in sackcloth and ashes, beautiful, graceful Esther, hate-filled Haman, the vacillating king and then the messengers who bear the tidings of salvation to all the Jewish communities of the great Persian empire, the festive rejoicing of the Jews.

No wonder that at Purim everybody wants to make a pilgrimage to the graves of these heroes of the *Megillah*. Dark and narrow though the tomb is, everybody wants to perform the special *Mizvah* of hearing the reading of the *Megillah* at the historic site of the actual events.

PURIM IN PERSIA, 1945[14]

Ralph M. Weisberger

The American flag has been carried to the far-flung corners of the earth. Our young servicemen and women unfurled it over scattered and isolated outposts whose common responsibility it was to defend democracy against the tyranny of the "master-race." The uniform of our country was a welcome sight that cheered the hearts of many suffering peoples. In return, some of our servicemen were presented with an opportunity to visit world-famous cities and sites and much-talked about buildings and cathedrals, such as those in France and Germany. There were still others, however, who were sent by the chances of war to a part of the world where history stood still and present conditions mirror the state of civilization of one and even two thousand years ago. They saw "the dead walking," the scenes of history being enacted with living characters — they went to the Persian Gulf Command.

The Persian Gulf Command covered Iran, Iraq and the Persian Gulf. It was our mission to serve as the lend-lease supply line to our ally, Russia. . . .

When our people was yet young (as the Almighty counts time, although not too young to have already experienced the major tragedy of the destruction of the first Temple), those who were in this part of the world were aroused to self-defense before the original Haman who schemed to exterminate the Jewish people. In those days, Iraq was known as Babylonia; and Iran was known as Persia and Media. The ruler of Babylonia, Nebuchadnezzar, had driven our fathers from their home; and the ruler of Persia, Cyrus, had granted them royal permission to return to re-build Palestine. When I inquired of the native Iranian Jews, "How long have Jews been in Iran?" they looked at me in wonder at my question. "From the time of Mordecai and Esther," they would reply, "we have been in Persia." Even if one receives this boast in skepticism, there is no question, if one accepts archaeological evidence, that the locale of the biblical Book of Esther was in this country, and even the exact location has been clearly identified. One hundred and fifty miles north of Khorramashar, one of the larger ports at which the Liberty ships unloaded their lend-lease supplies, lies the decrepit Mohammedan village of Shush. Close by are the excavations from which the archaeologists derived their evidence that this was ancient Shushan. Rising from amidst the pits is "Esther's castle," a replica of the original castle of biblical days, according to the imagination and estimation of those who investigated the ruins. Mixed among the material are cuneiform-inscribed bricks which were dug up at the site. Perhaps Esther and Mordecai walked upon them. Perhaps they were in the wall of the room where Queen Esther prepared herself for the ordeal of pleading for her people before the mighty ruler, Ahasuerus. Practically all of south Iran is a vast salt desert; it is only along the few streams that trees grow. A small stream flows close to the base of Queen Esther's castle.

Perhaps at this very spot stood the tree which served as the instrument by which Haman reaped his just retribution. The castle is the highest spot on the surrounding desert plain. . . .

In ancient times, the vicinity of Hamadan was known as Ecbatna, when it was the capital of the Persian empire. In this village there is a sacred shrine of Iranian Jewry, namely, the tomb of Mordecai and Esther. Ancient folk-traditions are associated with the comparatively modern structure, and I listened, fascinated even though skeptical, to a Persian Jew telling of his grandfather's visit there when the original crown of Queen Esther was still to be seen.

It is little wonder that Purim has been appropriated by the Jews of the Middle East as their special holiday. As a matter of fact, they find it hard to understand that Jews in other parts of the world also celebrate it. One Iraqi Jew, who was living in Iran, was puzzled at my interest in their celebration of the holiday. "Do they observe Purim in America, too?" he inquired . . . . I could not help but feel, however, that, unfortunately, the Iranian environment made it hard for the Jews of Iran to celebrate the ancient liberation, while they still lived in the shadow of modern tyranny . . . . The fear of the Arab majority, from whom they are "different," is still real; Amalek, Haman and Hitler are one and the same. One of the Hebrew teachers there explained this to me, with the aid of a bit of generous arithmetical calculation. The sum of the numerical values of the Hebrew letters in the name Amalek totals 15 (7, 4, 3, 1); Haman totals 14, but is generously amended to 15 (5, 4, 5, plus 1); and Hitler (with a *Toph*) totals 14, but is amended to 15. (This result is obtained by considering only the digit and not the cipher, that is, 70 becomes 7; then a unit is added where necessary.)

The Purim season, of course, begins with *Shabbat Zakor*. Besides the special Pentateuchal reading, the service is marked by the rendition of special songs dealing with Purim and Haman. When I entered the synagogue, I saw the children waiting about expectantly, and dressed somewhat *Yomtobdig*, in holiday mood. When the reading of the Torah was reached, they stood around the Torah and led in the singing; they did the same after the conclusion of the *Haftarah*. Then most of them returned to their routine of play outside the *Shul*, even as in America.

With the approach of *Taanit Esther* (Fast of Esther), however, the color and drama of Purim in Persia made themselves evident, and remote antiquity came to new life in our own day. As in days gone by, even a thousand years ago in gaonic times, the children constructed an effigy of Haman, which they proceeded to burn. A cardboard figure clothed in rags was fixed to a wooden stake, which was inserted in a hole in the brick floor of the courtyard of the synagogue. Perhaps this was just a chance crack, but it seemed to me the hole had been left in the floor expressly for this purpose. Children of all sizes, boys and girls, jumped impatiently, each armed with a long stick. When all was in readiness, the teacher gave the order and kerosene was poured about the kindling wood at the base of the figure. The flames curled about its feet. The children circled the flaming figure, chanting as they moved. Their chant was in Arabic and, as translated for me into Hebrew, meant: "This is Haman and Purim; and the basket is on his head." Why the "basket"? Could it be a reference to the story of Joseph and his interpretation of the steward's dream (Genesis 40.16), where the basket on the steward's head was an omen that he would be hanged? As the flames mounted, the children beat the figure with their sticks. Sometimes they changed the "Haman" of their chant to "Hitler." The older people, who stood about, clapped their hands in Oriental fashion, in time with the chant. When the figure was completely consumed in the still crackling flames, some daring youngsters jumped across the flames. I pointed them out to the teacher, and was afraid they would fall into the fire and be injured. It was only when I repeated the story at the Jewish Theological Seminary that I learned that this custom was the same as that described in the gaonic accounts of the celebration a thousand years ago.

In the evening, the usual *Megillah* reading took place. In Iraq, the Jews pronounced this as *Mejilla*; in Iran as *Me'khilla* (the *Gimmel* becoming a guttural-voiced *Het*). Practically no one but the *Baal Kore* had a *Megillah*, or even a *Humash*, due to the general poverty. Some youngsters observed the spirit of the occasion and gave some American soldiers, who were in Iraq for the first time, a good scare, since they thought they were in a non-combatant theater, by throwing fire crackers around at people's heels. This, however, was indiscriminate, and was not timed to bring sympathetic magical harm upon the name and memory of Mister Haman. Besides the usual two readings of the *Megillah*, on the evening and morning of Purim, the *Megillah* was repeated a third time the next evening in observance of Shushan Purim.

Our men left the environs of the Persian synagogue and the Persian Purim, and returned to our artificially-created tiny section of the United States, the military post over which Old Glory waved. Here we held our American Purim. No, not American alone, as we had guests from among the Palestinian civilians. Let us rather call it a "Free Man's Purim." The Palestinians entertained us with their orchestra and presented Palestinian and Yiddish folk music. To say that our perennially homesick GI's ate it up, is putting it mildly. And why not? Deep in the heart of Iran, we enjoyed *Hamantashen*.

We had brought the spirit of America to the deserts of Iran. We had caught a glimpse of the Purim of the centuries in ancient Persia. In their day, Mordecai and Esther rose to the aid of their people. In our day, our country sent its young manhood and womanhood to strange countries and climes, in order to stamp out the Amaleks of our time. We have returned home; our hearts still feel for our brethren to whom Purim is not merely an annual holiday-time but an every-day shadow. We, who knew them as living men, women and children, as fellow-Jews, must not know rest, until we have striven to make this a better world, not merely for our own blessed children of America, but for the scattered and suffering remnants of our people. May the dispersed of Israel find peace!

BOOK TWO

Purim in Literature, Art and Music

> And all the acts of his power and
> of his might, and the full account
> of the greatness of Mordecai, how
> the King advanced him, are they
> not written in the book of chron-
> icles of the Kings of Media and
> Persia?
>
> ESTHER 10. 2.

CHAPTER IV

PURIM IN THE BIBLE

T HE Book of Esther, the last of the five *Megillot*, or
scrolls, is found in the third part of *The Holy Scriptures*
known as "The Writings" (in Hebrew, *Ketubim*).

It is the only biblical book which does not contain
the name of God, and, yet, His Divine Providence is felt to
be present throughout. The Book of Esther stands as a
warning to the world of the eternal truth that suffering and
tribulation, both for persecutor and persecuted, inevitably
accompany the rise of prejudice.

Megillat Esther, popularly known as *the Megillah*, has
become endeared to the hearts of the Jewish people.

THE BOOK OF ESTHER[1]

AHASUERUS DETHRONES QUEEN VASHTI

Now it came to pass in the days of Ahasuerus — this is
Ahasuerus who reigned, from India even unto Ethiopia,
over a hundred and seven and twenty provinces — that in
those days, when the king Ahasuerus sat on the throne of
his kingdom, which was in Shushan the castle, in the third
year of his reign, he made a feast unto all his princes and
his servants; the army of Persia and Media, the nobles and
princes of the provinces, being before him; when he showed
the riches of his glorious kingdom and the honour of his
excellent majesty, many days, even a hundred and fourscore
days. And when these days were fulfilled, the king made a

12. *AHASUERUS' BANQUET*

Megillah, 17th Century

feast unto all the people that were present in Shushan the
castle, both great and small, seven days, in the court of the
garden of the king's palace; there were hangings of white,
fine cotton and blue, bordered with cords of fine linen and
purple, upon silver rods and pillars of marble; the couches
were of gold and silver, upon a pavement of green, and white,
and shell, and onyx marble. And they gave them drink in
vessels of gold — the vessels being diverse one from another — and royal wine in abundance, according to the
bounty of the king. And the drinking was according to the
law; none did compel; for so the king had appointed to all
the officers of his house, that they should do according to
every man's pleasure.

Also Vashti the queen made a feast for the women in the
royal house which belonged to King Ahasuerus. On the
seventh day, when the heart of the king was merry with
wine, he commanded Mehuman, Bizzetha, Harbona, Bigtha,
and Abagtha, Zethar, and Carcas, the seven chamberlains
that ministered in the presence of Ahasuerus the king, to
bring Vashti the queen before the king with the crown

royal, to show the people and the princes her beauty; for she was fair to look on. But the queen Vashti refused to come at the king's commandment by the chamberlains; therefore was the king very wroth, and his anger burned in him.

Then the king said to the wise men, who knew the times — for so was the king's manner toward all that knew law and judgment; and the next unto him was Carshena, Shethar, Admatha, Tarshish, Meres, Marsena, and Memucan, the seven princes of Persia and Media, who saw the king's face, and sat first in the kingdom: 'What shall we do unto the queen Vashti according to law, for as much as she hath not done the bidding of the king Ahasuerus by the chamberlains?'

And Memucan answered before the king and the princes: 'Vashti the queen hath not done wrong to the king only, but also to all the princes, and to all the peoples, that are in all the provinces of the king Ahasuerus. For this deed of the queen will come abroad unto all women, to make their husbands contemptible in their eyes, when it will be said: The king Ahasuerus commanded Vashti the queen to be brought in before him, but she came not. And this day will the princesses of Persia and Media who have heard of the deed of the queen say the like unto all the king's princes. So will there arise enough contempt and wrath. If it please the king, let there go forth a royal commandment from him, and let it be written among the laws of the Persians and the Medes, that it be not altered, that Vashti come no more before king Ahasuerus, and that the king give her royal estate unto another that is better than she. And when the king's decree which he shall make shall be published throughout all his kingdom, great though it be, all the wives will give to their husbands honour, both to great and small.' And the word pleased the king and the princes; and the king did according to the word of Memucan; for he sent letters into all the king's provinces, into every province according to the writing thereof, and to every people after their language, that every man should bear rule in his own house, and speak according to the language of his people (1.1–22).

ESTHER CHOSEN QUEEN

After these things, when the wrath of king Ahasuerus was assuaged, he remembered Vashti, and what she had done, and what was decreed against her. Then said the king's servants that ministered unto him: 'Let there be sought for the king young virgins fair to look on; and let the king appoint officers in all the provinces of his kingdom, that they may gather together all the fair young virgins unto Shushan the castle, to the house of the women, unto the custody of Hegai the king's chamberlain, keeper of the women; and let their ointments be given them; and let the maiden that pleaseth the king be queen instead of Vashti.' And the thing pleased the king; and he did so.

There was a certain Jew in Shushan the castle, whose name was Mordecai the son of Jair the son of Shimei the son of Kish, a Benjamite, who had been carried away from Jerusalem with the captives that had been carried away with Jeconiah king of Judah, whom Nebuchadnezzar the king of Babylon had carried away. And he brought up Hadassah, that is, Esther, his uncle's daughter; for she had neither father nor mother, and the maiden was of beautiful form and fair to look on; and when her father and mother were dead, Mordecai took her for his own daughter.

So it came to pass, when the king's commandment and his decree was published, and when many maidens were gathered together unto Shushan the castle, to the custody of Hegai, that Esther was taken into the king's house, to the custody of Hegai, keeper of the women. And the maiden pleased him, and she obtained kindness of him; and he speedily gave her her ointments, with her portions, and the seven maidens, who were meet to be given her out of the king's house; and he advanced her and her maidens to the best place in the house of the women. Esther had not made known her people nor her kindred; for Mordecai had charged her that she should not tell it. And Mordecai walked every day before the court of the women's house, to know how Esther did, and what would become of her.

Now when the turn of every maiden was come to go in to king Ahasuerus, after that it had been done to her according to the law for the women, twelve months — for so were the days of their anointing accomplished, to wit, six months with oil of myrrh, and six months with sweet odours, and with other ointments of the women — when then the maiden came unto the king, whatsoever she desired was given her to go with her out of the house of the women unto the king's house. In the evening she went, and on the morrow she returned into the second house of the women, to the custody of Shaashagaz, the king's chamberlain, who kept the concubines; she came in unto the king no more, except the king delighted in her, and she were called by name.

Now when the turn of Esther the daughter of Abihail the uncle of Mordecai, who had taken her for his daughter, was come to go in unto the king, she required nothing but what Hegai the king's chamberlain, the keeper of the women, appointed. And Esther obtained favour in the sight of all them that looked upon her. So Esther was taken unto king Ahasuerus into his house royal in the tenth month, which is the month Tebeth, in the seventh year of his reign. And the king loved Esther above all the women, and she obtained grace and favour in his sight more than all the virgins; so that he set the royal crown upon her head, and made her queen instead of Vashti. Then the king made a great feast unto all his princes and his servants, even Esther's feast;

13. *THE CROWNING OF ESTHER*

Megillah, 17th Century

and he made a release to the provinces, and gave gifts, according to the bounty of the king.

And when the virgins were gathered together the second time, and Mordecai sat in the king's gate — Esther had not yet made known her kindred nor her people; as Mordecai had charged her; for Esther did the commandment of Mordecai, like as when she was brought up with him — in those days, while Mordecai sat in the king's gate, two of the king's chamberlains, Bigthan and Teresh, of those that kept the door, were wroth, and sought to lay hands on the king Ahasuerus. And the thing became known to Mordecai, who told it unto Esther the queen; and Esther told the king thereof in Mordecai's name. And when inquisition was made of the matter, and it was found to be so, they were both hanged on a tree; and it was written in the book of the chronicles before the king (2.1–23).

HAMAN SEEKS TO DESTROY THE JEWS

After these things did king Ahasuerus promote Haman the son of Hammedatha the Agagite, and advanced him, and set his seat above all the princes that were with him.

And all the king's servants, that were in the king's gate, bowed down, and prostrated themselves before Haman; for the king had so commanded concerning him. But Mordecai bowed not down, nor prostrated himself before him. Then the king's servants, that were in the king's gate, said unto Mordecai: 'Why transgressest thou the king's commandment?' Now it came to pass, when they spoke daily unto him, and he hearkened not unto them, that they told Haman, to see whether Mordecai's words would stand; for he had told them that he was a Jew. And when Haman saw that Mordecai bowed not down, nor prostrated himself before him, then was Haman full of wrath. But it seemed contemptible in his eyes to lay hands on Mordecai alone; for they had made known to him the people of Mordecai; wherefore Haman sought to destroy all the Jews that were throughout the whole kingdom of Ahasuerus, even the people of Mordecai. In the first month, which is the month Nisan, in the twelfth year of king Ahasuerus, they cast *pur*, that is, the lot, before Haman from day to day, and from month to month, to the twelfth month, which is the month Adar.

And Haman said unto king Ahasuerus: 'There is a certain people scattered abroad and dispersed among the peoples in all the provinces of thy kingdom; and their laws are diverse from those of every people; neither keep they the king's laws; therefore it profiteth not the king to suffer them. If it please the king, let it be written that they be destroyed; and I will pay ten thousand talents of silver into the hands of those that have the charge of the king's business, to bring it into the king's treasuries.' And the king took his ring from his hand, and gave it unto Haman the son of Hammedatha the Agagite, the Jews' enemy. And the king said unto Haman: 'The silver is given to thee, the people also, to do with them as it seemeth good to thee.'

Then were the king's scribes called in the first month, on the thirteenth day thereof, and there was written, according to all that Haman commanded, unto the king's satraps, and to the governors that were over every province, and to the princes of every people; to every province according to the writing thereof, and to every people after their language; in the name of king Ahasuerus was it written, and it was sealed with the king's ring. And letters were sent by posts into all the king's provinces, to destroy, to slay, and to cause to perish, all Jews, both young and old, little children and women, in one day, even upon the thirteenth day of the twelfth month, which is the month Adar, and to take the spoil of them for a prey. The copy of the writing, to be given out for a decree in every province, was to be published unto all the peoples, that they should be ready against that day. The posts went forth in haste by the king's commandment, and the decree was given out in Shushan the castle; and the king and Haman sat down to drink; but the city of Shushan was perplexed (3.1–15).

Mordecai Appeals To Esther

Now when Mordecai knew all that was done, Mordecai rent his clothes, and put on sackcloth with ashes, and went into the midst of the city, and cried with a loud and a bitter cry; and he came even before the king's gate; for none might enter within the king's gate clothed with sackcloth. And in every province, whithersoever the king's commandment and his decree came, there was great mourning among the Jews, and fasting, and weeping, and wailing; and many lay in sackcloth and ashes.

And Esther's maidens and her chamberlains came and told it her; and the queen was exceedingly pained; and she sent raiment to clothe Mordecai, and to take his sackcloth from off him; but he accepted it not. Then called Esther for Hathach, one of the king's chamberlains, whom he had appointed to attend upon her, and charged him to go to Mordecai, to know what this was, and why it was. So Hathach went forth to Mordecai unto the broad place of the city, which was before the king's gate. And Mordecai told him of all that had happened unto him, and the exact sum of the money that Haman had promised to pay to the king's treasuries for the Jews, to destroy them. Also he gave him the copy of the writing of the decree that was given out in Shushan to destroy them, to show it unto Esther, and to declare it unto her; and to charge her that she should go in unto the king, to make supplication unto him, and to make request before him, for her people.

And Hathach came and told Esther the words of Mordecai. Then Esther spoke unto Hathach, and gave him a message unto Mordecai: 'All the king's servants, and the people of the king's provinces, do know, that whosoever, whether man or woman, shall come unto the king into the inner court, who is not called, there is one law for him, that he be put to death, except such to whom the king shall hold out the golden sceptre, that he may live; but I have not been called to come in unto the king these thirty days.' And they told to Mordecai Esther's words.

Then Mordecai bade them return answer unto Esther: 'Think not with thyself that thou shalt escape in the king's house, more than all the Jews. For if thou altogether holdest thy peace at this time, then will relief and deliverance arise to the Jews from another place, but thou and thy father's house will perish; and who knoweth whether thou art not come to royal estate for such a time as this?' Then Esther bade them return answer unto Mordecai: 'Go, gather together all the Jews that are present in Shushan, and fast ye for me, and neither eat nor drink three days, night or day; I also and my maidens will fast in like manner; and so will I go in unto the king, which is not according to the law, and if I perish, I perish.' So Mordecai went his way, and did according to all that Esther had commanded him (4.1–17).

ESTHER APPROACHES THE KING

Now it came to pass on the third day, that Esther put on her royal apparel, and stood in the inner court of the king's house, over against the king's house; and the king sat upon his royal throne in the royal house, over against the entrance of the house. And it was so, when the king saw Esther the queen standing in the court, that she obtained favour in his sight; and the king held out to Esther the golden sceptre that was in his hand. So Esther drew near, and touched the top of the sceptre. Then said the king unto her: 'What wilt thou, queen Esther? for whatever thy request, even to the half of the kingdom, it shall be given thee.' And Esther said: 'If it seem good unto the king, let the king and Haman come this day unto the banquet that I have prepared for him.' Then the king said: 'Cause Haman to make haste, that it may be done as Esther hath said.' So the king and Haman came to the banquet that Esther had prepared. And the king said unto Esther at the banquet of wine: 'Whatever thy petition, it shall be granted thee; and whatever thy request, even to the half of the kingdom, it shall be performed.' Then answered Esther, and said: 'My petition and my request is — if I have found favour in the sight of the king, and if it please the king to grant my petition, and to perform my request — let the king and Haman come to the banquet that I shall prepare for them, and I will do to-morrow as the king hath said.'

Then went Haman forth that day joyful and glad of heart;

14. *ESTHER BEFORE AHASUERUS* Engraving

M. Merian, the Elder, 17th Century

but when Haman saw Mordecai in the king's gate, that he
stood not up nor moved for him, Haman was filled with
wrath against Mordecai. Nevertheless Haman refrained
himself, and went home; and he sent and fetched his friends
and Zeresh his wife. And Haman recounted unto them the
glory of his riches, and the multitude of his children, and
everything as to how the king had promoted him, and how
he had advanced him above the princes and servants of the
king. Haman said moreover: 'Yea, Esther the queen did
let no man come in with the king unto the banquet that she
had prepared but myself; and to-morrow also am I invited
by her together with the king. Yet all this availeth me
nothing, so long as I see Mordecai the Jew sitting at the

king's gate.' Then said Zeresh his wife and all his friends
unto him: 'Let a gallows be made of fifty cubits high, and
in the morning speak thou unto the king that Mordecai may
be hanged thereon; then go thou in merrily with the king
unto the banquet.' And the thing pleased Haman; and he
caused the gallows to be made (5.1–14).

Mordecai Honored By The King

On that night could not the king sleep; and he commanded
to bring the book of records of the chronicles, and they were
read before the king. And it was found written, that
Mordecai had told of Bigthana and Teresh, two of the king's
chamberlains, of those that kept the door, who had sought to
lay hands on the king Ahasuerus. And the king said: 'What
honour and dignity hath been done to Mordecai for this?'
Then said the king's servants that ministered unto him:
'There is nothing done for him.' And the king said: 'Who
is in the court?' — Now Haman was come into the outer
court of the king's house, to speak unto the king to hang
Mordecai on the gallows that he had prepared for him. —
And the king's servants said unto him: 'Behold, Haman
standeth in the court.' And the king said: 'Let him come
in.' So Haman came in. And the king said unto him: 'What
shall be done unto the man whom the king delighteth to
honour?' — Now Haman said in his heart: 'Whom would
the king delight to honour besides myself?' — And Haman
said unto the king: 'For the man whom the king delighteth
to honour, let royal apparel be brought which the king
useth to wear, and the horse that the king rideth upon, and
on whose head a crown royal is set; and let the apparel and
the horse be delivered to the hand of one of the king's
most noble princes, that they may array the man therewith
whom the king delighteth to honour, and cause him to ride

15. *MORDECAI'S TRIUMPH*   Painting

Cassone panel, 15th Century

on horseback through the street of the city, and proclaim
before him: 'Thus shall it be done to the man whom the
king delighteth to honour.' Then the king said to Haman:
'Make haste, and take the apparel and the horse, as thou
hast said, and do even so to Mordecai the Jew, that sitteth

at the king's gate; let nothing fail of all that thou hast spoken.' Then took Haman the apparel and the horse, and arrayed Mordecai, and caused him to ride through the street of the city, and proclaimed before him: 'Thus shall it be done unto the man whom the king delighteth to honour.'

And Mordecai returned to the king's gate. But Haman hastened to his house, mourning and having his head covered. And Haman recounted unto Zeresh his wife and all his friends every thing that had befallen him. Then said his wise men and Zeresh his wife unto him: 'If Mordecai, before whom thou hast begun to fall, be of the seed of the Jews, thou shalt not prevail against him, but shalt surely fall before him.' While they were yet talking with him, came the king's chamberlains, and hastened to bring Haman unto the banquet that Esther had prepared (6. 1-14).

ESTHER PLEADS FOR HER PEOPLE

So the king and Haman came to banquet with Esther the queen. And the king said again unto Esther on the second day at the banquet of wine: 'Whatever thy petition, queen Esther, it shall be granted thee; and whatever thy request, even to the half of the kingdom, it shall be performed.' Then Esther the queen answered and said: 'If I have found favour in thy sight, O king, and if it please the king, let my life be given me at my petition, and my people at my request; for we are sold, I and my people, to be destroyed, to be slain, and to perish. But if we had been sold for bondmen and bondwomen, I had held my peace, for the adversary is not worthy that the king be endamaged.'

Then spoke the king Ahasuerus and said unto Esther the queen: 'Who is he, and where is he, that durst presume in his heart to do so?' And Esther said: 'An adversary and an enemy, even this wicked Haman.' Then Haman was terrified before the king and the queen. And the king arose in his wrath from the banquet of wine and went into the palace garden; but Haman remained to make request for his life to Esther the queen; for he saw that there was evil determined against him by the king. Then the king returned out of the palace garden into the place of the banquet of wine; and Haman was fallen upon the couch whereon Esther was. Then said the king: 'Will he even force the queen before me in the house?' As the word went out of the king's mouth, they covered Haman's face. Then said Harbonah, one of the chamberlains that were before the king: 'Behold also, the gallows fifty cubits high, which Haman hath made for Mordecai, who spoke good for the king, standeth in the house of Haman.' And the king said: 'Hang him thereon.' So they hanged Haman on the gallows that he had prepared for Mordecai. Then was the king's wrath assuaged (7.1–10).

The King Grants Esther's Request

On that day did the king Ahasuerus give the house of Haman the Jews' enemy unto Esther the queen. And Mordecai came before the king; for Esther had told what he was unto her. And the king took off his ring, which he had taken from Haman, and gave it unto Mordecai. And Esther set Mordecai over the house of Haman.

And Esther spoke yet again before the king, and fell down at his feet, and besought him with tears to put away the mischief of Haman the Agagite, and his device that he had devised against the Jews. Then the king held out to Esther the golden sceptre. So Esther arose, and stood before the king. And she said: 'If it please the king, and if I have found favour in his sight, and the thing seem right before the king, and I be pleasing in his eyes, let it be written to

16. PURIM GREETING CARD

reverse the letters devised by Haman the son of Hammedatha the Agagite, which he wrote to destroy the Jews
that are in all the king's provinces; for how can I endure to
see the evil that shall come unto my people? or how can I
endure to see the destruction of my kindred?'

Then the king Ahasuerus said unto Esther the queen and
to Mordecai the Jew: 'Behold, I have given Esther the
house of Haman, and him they have hanged upon the gallows, because he laid his hand upon the Jews. Write ye also
concerning the Jews, as it liketh you, in the king's name, and
seal it with the king's ring; for the writing which is written
in the king's name, and sealed with the king's ring, may no
man reverse.' Then were the king's scribes called at that
time, in the third month, which is the month Sivan, on the
three and twentieth day thereof; and it was written according to all that Mordecai commanded concerning the

Jews, even to the satraps, and the governors and princes of the provinces which are from India unto Ethiopia, a hundred twenty and seven provinces, unto every province according to the writing thereof, and unto every people after their language, and to the Jews according to their writing, and according to their language. And they wrote in the name of king Ahasuerus, and sealed it with the king's ring, and sent letters by posts on horseback, riding on swift steeds that were used in the king's service, bred of the stud; that the king had granted the Jews that were in every city to gather themselves together, and to stand for their life, to destroy, and to slay, and to cause to perish, all the forces of the people and province that would assault them, their little ones and women, and to take the spoil of them for a prey, upon one day in all the provinces of king Ahasuerus, namely, upon the thirteenth day of the twelfth month, which is the month Adar. The copy of the writing, to be given out for a decree in every province, was to be published unto all the peoples, and that the Jews should be ready against that day to avenge themselves on their enemies. So the posts that rode upon swift steeds that were used in the king's service went out, being hastened and pressed on by the king's commandment; and the decree was given out in Shushan the castle.

And Mordecai went forth from the presence of the king in royal apparel of blue and white, and with a great crown of gold, and with a robe of fine linen and purple; and the city of Shushan shouted and was glad. The Jews had light and gladness, and joy and honour. And in every province, and in every city, whithersoever the king's commandment and his decree came, the Jews had gladness and joy, a feast and a good day. And many from among the peoples of the land became Jews; for the fear of the Jews was fallen upon them (8.1–17).

The Jews Defend Themselves

Now in the twelfth month, which is the month Adar, on the thirteenth day of the same, when the king's commandment and his decree drew near to be put in execution, in the day that the enemies of the Jews hoped to have rule over them; whereas it was turned to the contrary, that the Jews had rule over them that hated them; the Jews gathered themselves together in their cities throughout all the provinces of the king Ahasuerus, to lay hand on such as sought their hurt; and no man could withstand them; for the fear of them was fallen upon all the peoples. And all the princes of the provinces, and the satraps, and the governors, and they that did the king's business, helped the Jews; because the fear of Mordecai was fallen upon them. For Mordecai was great in the king's house, and his fame went forth throughout all the provinces; for the man Mordecai waxed greater and greater. And the Jews smote all their enemies with the stroke of the sword, and with slaughter and destruction, and did what they would unto them that hated them. And in Shushan the castle the Jews slew and destroyed five hundred men. And Parshandatha, and Dalphon, and Aspatha, and Poratha, and Adalia, and Aridatha, and Parmashta, and Arisai, and Aridai, and Vaizatha, the ten sons of Haman the son of Hammedatha, the Jews' enemy, slew they; but on the spoil they laid not their hand.

On that day the number of those that were slain in Shushan the castle was brought before the king. And the king said unto Esther the queen: 'The Jews have slain and destroyed five hundred men in Shushan the castle, and the ten sons of Haman; what then have they done in the rest of the king's provinces! Now whatever thy petition, it shall be granted thee; and whatever thy request further, it shall be done.' Then said Esther: 'If it please the king, let it be granted to the Jews that are in Shushan to do to-morrow also according unto this day's decree, and let Haman's ten sons be hanged upon the gallows.' And the king commanded it so to be done; and a decree was given out in Shushan; and they hanged Haman's ten sons. And the Jews that were in Shushan gathered themselves together on the fourteenth day also of the month Adar, and slew three hundred men in Shushan; but on the spoil they laid not their hands.

And the other Jews that were in the king's provinces gathered themselves together, and stood for their lives, and had rest from their enemies, and slew of them that hated them seventy and five thousand — but on the spoil they laid not their hand (9.1–16).

The Establishment Of Purim

On the thirteenth day of the month Adar, and on the fourteenth day of the same they rested, and made it a day of feasting and gladness. But the Jews that were in Shushan assembled together on the thirteenth day thereof, and on the fourteenth thereof; and on the fifteenth day of the same they rested, and made it a day of feasting and gladness. Therefore do the Jews of the villages, that dwell in the unwalled towns, make the fourteenth day of the month Adar a day of gladness and feasting, and a good day, and of sending portions one to another.

And Mordecai wrote these things, and sent letters unto all the Jews that were in all the provinces of the king Ahasuerus, both nigh and far, to enjoin them that they should keep the fourteenth day of the month Adar, and the fifteenth day of the same, yearly, the days wherein the Jews had rest from their enemies, and the month which was turned unto them from sorrow to gladness, and from mourning into a good day; that they should make them days of feasting and gladness, and of sending portions one to another, and gifts to the poor. And the Jews took upon them to do as they had begun, and as Mordecai had written unto them; because Haman the son of Hammedatha, the Agagite, the enemy of all the Jews, had devised against the Jews to destroy them, and had cast *pur*, that is, the lot, to discomfit them, and to destroy them; but when she came before the king, he commanded by letters that his wicked device, which he had devised against the Jews, should return upon his own head; and that he and his sons should be hanged on the gallows. Wherefore they called these days Purim, after the name of *pur*. Therefore because of all the words of this letter, and of that which they had seen concerning this matter, and that which had come unto them, the Jews ordained, and took upon them, and upon their seed, and upon all such as joined themselves unto them, so as it should not fail, that they would keep these two days according to the writing thereof, and according to the appointed time thereof, every year; and that these days should be remembered and kept throughout every generation, every family, every province, and every city; and that these days of Purim should not fail from among the Jews, nor the memorial of them perish from their seed.

Then Esther the queen, the daughter of Abihail, and Mordecai the Jew, wrote down all the acts of power, to confirm this second letter of Purim. And he sent letters unto all the Jews, to the hundred twenty and seven provinces of the kingdom of Ahasuerus, with words of peace and truth, to confirm these days of Purim in their appointed times, according as Mordecai the Jew and Esther the queen had enjoined them, and as they had ordained for themselves and for their seed, the matters of the fastings and their cry. And the commandment of Esther confirmed these matters of Purim; and it was written in the book (9.17–32).

17. *ESTHER AND MORDECAI WRITING LETTERS
TO THE JEWS*

Illuminated Manuscript

Alba Bible, 15th Century

Mordecai Advanced To Greatness

And the king Ahasuerus laid a tribute upon the land, and upon the isles of the sea. And all the acts of his power and of his might, and the full account of the greatness of Mordecai, how the king advanced him, are they not written in the book of the chronicles of the kings of Media and Persia? For Mordecai the Jew was next unto the king Ahasuerus, and great among the Jews, and accepted of the multitude of his brethren; seeking the good of his people and speaking peace to all his seed (10.1–3).

CHAPTER V

PURIM IN POST-BIBLICAL WRITINGS

THE ADDITIONS TO THE BOOK OF ESTHER

BESIDES the Book of Esther, there are less well known "Additions." They are found in the Apocrypha and were incorporated at an early date in the Septuagint, the Greek version of the Bible.

The name Apocrypha, meaning hidden or secret books, implies that these books were excluded from the biblical canon, although in a sense they are a continuation of it. Hence, the apocryphal *Additions to the Book of Esther* supplement and expand the canonized book. They furnish that religious element which on the surface is lacking in the canonical Book of Esther.

THE DREAM OF MORDECAI[1]

In the second year of the reign of Artaxerxes the Great, on the first day of Nisan, Mordecai the son of Jair, the son of Shimei, the son of Kish, of the tribe of Benjamin, had a dream. He was a Jew, and lived in the city of Susa, an important man, in attendance at the royal court; he was one of the captives that Nebuchadnezzar, king of Babylon, had brought from Jerusalem, with Jeconiah, king of Judah. And this was his dream: behold, noise and tumult, thunders and earthquake, uproar on the earth. And here came two great dragons, both ready to wrestle, and they uttered a great roar. And at their roar every nation made ready for war, to fight against the nation of the upright. And behold, a day of darkness and gloom, affliction and anguish, distress and great tumult, upon the earth. And the whole upright nation was troubled, fearing their own hurt, and they prepared to perish; and they cried out to God. And at their cry there arose as though from a tiny spring, a great river, with abundant water; light came, and the sun rose, and the humble were exalted and consumed the glorious.

When Mordecai, who had had this dream, and had seen what God had resolved to do, awoke, he kept it in his mind, and all day sought by all means to understand it (11.2–12).[1]

The Prayer Of Mordecai

And he besought the Lord, calling to mind all the doings of the Lord, and said,

"Lord, King, who rules over all, for all is in your power, and there is no one who can oppose you when you choose to save Israel, for you made heaven and earth, and every wonderful thing under heaven, and you are Lord of all, and there is no one who can resist you, who are the Lord; you know all things; you know, Lord, that it was not in insolence or arrogance or vainglory that I did this, and refused to bow down to this proud Haman, for I would have been willing to kiss the soles of his feet, to save Israel. But I did it so as not to set the glory of man above the glory of God, and I will bow down to no one but you, my Lord, and I will not do it in pride. Now, Lord God and King, God of Abraham, spare your people, for they are looking at us to consume us, and they desire to destroy the inheritance that has been yours from the beginning. Do not be indifferent to our portion, which you ransomed for yourself from the land of Egypt. Hear my prayer, and have mercy on your heritage; turn our mourning into feasting, so that we may live, and sing praise to your name, Lord; do not destroy the mouth of those who praise you."

And all Israel cried out with all their might, for death was before their eyes (13.8–18).

The Prayer Of Esther

Then Esther, the queen, overwhelmed with deadly anxiety, fled to the Lord; she took off her splendid clothing and put on garments of distress and mourning, and instead of the rarest perfumes, she covered her head with ashes and dung, and she abased her body utterly, and every part that she delighted to adorn she covered with her tangled hair. And she prayed to the Lord and said,

"My lord, our King, you stand alone; help me who am alone, and have no helper but you; for my danger is in my hand. Ever since I was born, I have heard in the tribe of my family that you, Lord, took Israel from among all the nations, and our forefathers from among all their ancestors for an everlasting possession, and that you did for them all that you promised. But now we have sinned before you, and you have handed us over to our enemies, because we glorified their gods; you are upright, Lord. And now they are not satisfied that we are in bitter captivity but they have made an agreement with their idols to abolish what your mouth has ordained, and destroy your possession, and stop the mouths of those who praise you and quench the glory of your house, and your altar, and open the mouths of the heathen to praise unreal gods, so that a mortal king may be magnified forever. Lord, do not give up your scepter to those who have no being, and do not let them mock at our fall, but turn their plan against themselves, and make an example of the man who has begun this against us. Remember, Lord; make yourself known in this time of our affliction and give me courage, king of the gods and holder of all dominion. Put eloquent speech in my mouth, before this lion, and change his heart to hate the man who is fighting against us, so that there may be an end of him, and of those who support him. But save us by your hand, and help me, who stand alone, and have no one but you, Lord. You know everything, and you know that I hate the splendor of the wicked, and abhor the bed of the uncircumcised and of any alien. You know what I am forced to do — that I abhor the symbol of my proud position, which is placed upon my head on the days when I appear in public; I abhor it like a filthy rag, and never wear it in private. Your slave has not eaten at Haman's table, and I have not honored the king's feast, or drunk the wine of the libations. Your slave has had no joy from the day I was brought here until now, except in You, Lord God of Abraham. O God, whose might is over all, hear the voice of the despairing, and save us from the hands of evil-doers, and save me from what I fear" (14.1–19).

The Decree Of Artaxerxes
Concerning The Jews

Of this letter the following is a copy:

"The Great King, Artaxerxes, sends greeting to the rulers of countries in a hundred and twenty-seven provinces, from India to Ethiopia, and to those who are loyal to our rule. The more frequently they are honored by the excessive favor of their benefactors, the prouder many men become, and not only seek to injure our subjects, but, in their inability to bear prosperity, they undertake designs against their own benefactors, and not only uproot gratitude from among men, but intoxicated by the boasts of foolish men they suppose they will escape the evil-hating justice of the ever all-seeing God. And often many of those who occupy places of authority have by the persuasiveness of the friends who have been intrusted with the conduct of affairs, been made accomplices in the shedding of innocent blood, and been involved in irremediable disasters, when such men by the specious fallacies of their vicious natures beguile the sincere good will of their sovereigns. And what had been impiously accomplished by the baneful conduct of those who exercise authority unworthily, you can see not so much from the venerable histories which have come down to us, as from the scrutiny of matters close at hand. And in order to make our kingdom in the future tranquil and peaceful for all men, we will change our attitude, and always decide the matters that fall under our notice with more considerate attention. For Haman, the son of Hammedathi, a Macedonian, an alien indeed from the Persian blood, and widely removed from our kindliness, being entertained as a guest by us, enjoyed the humanity that we extend to every nation to such a degree that he was called our father, and was continually bowed down to by all, as a person second only to the royal throne. But he in his unbearable arrogance designed to deprive us of our kingdom, and to compass the death of our preserver and perpetual benefactor Mordecai, and of Esther, our blameless partner in the kingdom, together with their whole nation, demanding with intricate deceptions and intrigues that they be destroyed. For he thought by these means that he would find us deserted and would transfer the domination of the Persian to the Macedonians. But we find that the Jews, who were consigned to annihilation by this thrice sinful man, are no evil-doers but are governed by most just laws, and are sons of the Most High, Most Mighty Living God, who has directed the kingdom for us and for our forefathers with most excellent guidance. Therefore please pay no further attention to the letters sent you by Haman, the son of Hammedathi, because the very man who was active in this has been hung with all his house at the gates of Susa, for God, who governs all things, has speedily inflicted on him the punishment he deserved. Therefore put up the copy of this letter publicly everywhere, and let the Jews live under their own laws, and reinforce them, so that on the thirteenth day of the twelfth month, Adar, on that very day they may defend themselves against those who assail them at the time of their affliction. For God, who governs all things, has made this day a joy to them instead of proving the destruction of the chosen race. So you must observe it as a notable day among your commemorative festivals, with all good cheer, so that both now and hereafter it may mean preservation to us and to the loyal Persians, but to those who plot against us it may serve as a reminder of destruction. But any city or country without exception, which shall fail to act in accordance with this, shall be utterly destroyed in wrath with fire and sword; it will be made not only impassable for men, but also hateful to wild animals and birds for all time" (16.1–24).

The Interpretation Of the Dream
Of Mordecai

And Mordecai said,
"This came from God. For I remember the dream that I had about these things; for none of them has failed to be fulfilled. As for the tiny spring that became a river, when light came, and the sun shone and there was an abundance of water, the river is Esther, whom the king married and made queen. And I and Haman are the two dragons. And those who gathered to destroy the name of the Jews are the heathen. And my nation, which cried out to God and was saved, is Israel; for the Lord has saved his people, the Lord has delivered us from all these evils, and God has wrought great

signs and wonders, such as never happened among the heathen. That is why he made two lots, one for the people of God and one for all the heathen, and these two lots came to the hour and time and day when God should judge among all the nations. And God remembered his people, and he acquitted his inheritance. So these days in the month of Adar, on the fourteenth and fifteenth of that month, will be observed by them with assembling together and joy and gladness before God from generation to generation, forever, among his people Israel" (10.4–13).

FLAVIUS JOSEPHUS' *JEWISH ANTIQUITIES*

Flavius Josephus, in his *Jewish Antiquities*, recounted the story of Purim in free paraphrase and included much of the apocryphal *Additions to the Book of Esther*. He added original and novel embellishments of his own to the ancient story. Though the new elements that he introduced may have been derived from an early Midrash, they nevertheless reveal Josephus as something of an historical novelist, possessor of creative imagination and always literary master of the dramatic situation. The selections given below reveal some of these variations and adaptations.

THE LAW AGAINST APPROACHING THE THRONE[3]

Now the king had made a law that none of his people should approach him whenever he sat on the throne, unless he were summoned. And round his throne stood men with axes to punish any who approached the throne without being summoned. The king himself, however, as he sat held a golden scepter which he extended to anyone whom he wished to save of those who approached without being summoned; and whoever touched this was out of danger (XI, 6.3).

Mordecai Discovers A Plot

Some time afterwards Bagathoos (Bigthan) and Theo-destes (Teresh) plotted against the king, but Barnabazos, the servant of one of these eunuchs, who was a Jew by race, discovered their plot and revealed it to Mordecai, the uncle of the king's wife, and he in turn through Esther exposed the plotters to the king. The king, being alarmed, investigated and found out the truth and crucified the eunuchs; as for Mordecai, at the time he gave him no reward for saving his life but only ordered the keepers of the archives to note his name and let him remain in the palace as a very close friend of the king (XI, 6.4).

The King's Sleepless Night

God mocked Haman's wicked hopes, and knowing what was to happen, rejoiced at the event. For that night He deprived the king of sleep, and, as he did not wish to waste his wakeful hours in idleness but to use them for something of importance to his kingdom, he commanded his scribe to bring him both the records of the kings who were before him and those of his own deeds, and read them to him. And so, when he had brought them and was reading them, it was found that a certain man as a reward for his bravery on one occasion had received some land, the name of which was also written. Then, in mentioning another who had received a gift for his loyalty, he also came to Bagathoos and Theodestes, the eunuchs who had plotted against the king and against whom Mordecai had informed (XI, 6.10).

CHAPTER VI

PURIM IN TALMUD AND MIDRASH

THE Purim story in the Book of Esther has been richly embellished with commentary and interpretation by the rabbis of the Talmud and the Midrash beyond proportion to its size. Undoubtedly the characters and incidents of the Purim story appealed strongly to the rabbis' imagination, their poetical instincts and their ethical and moral conscience. Hence, they used the verses of the Book of Esther as a basic text and wove their imaginings in and through its strands, amplifying its meager sentences, supplying the motives that impelled the main characters and humanizing the figures of Esther and Mordecai.

In this way, the Purim of the Bible did not remain a dramatic episode of past history, but became a living and vital experience of their own and later times — an experience from which they and later generations could learn about the Jewish people's patience, courage, sacrifice and heroism. Above all, they piously sought to emphasize, wherever the opportunity presented itself, how God's Presence wrought the Divine Will on the side of Israel in their eternal struggle against hostile environments and evil-designing foes. The result of the sages' creative weaving might well be compared to a large tapestry crowded with gorgeously colored designs spun out of the Jewish heart and worked into the ethical patterns of the Jewish spirit.

The Tractate Megillah of the Talmud devotes numerous pages to an elaboration of the Book of Esther. The *First* and *Second Targum* (Aramaic translations) are more properly running commentaries, reproducing not only every word of the Bible text, but adding here and there new material and interpretations. The profound love of the sages for the *Megillah* can be seen in the fact that of all the biblical books it alone has a second Aramaic translation, much larger than the first and borrowing heavily from many other sources. This is called in Hebrew *Targum Sheni*.

There are numerous *Midrashim* on the Book of Esther, exceeding greatly in number those written on the other books of the Bible, such as: *Pirke de Rabbi Eliezer, Esther Rabbah, Lekah Tob, Abba Gorion, Megillat Esther, Panim Aherim, Aggadat Esther* and *Yalkut Shim'oni*. The same material is often found in more than one *midrash*, with more or less variation. Frequently, similar legends are told in several works although in different words.

The selections given here have been taken from this talmudic and midrashic literature.

ESTHER AND MORDECAI

As myrrh (*Mor*) is the foremost of spices, so *Mor*–decai was the foremost of the righteous of his generation. (*Esther Rabbah* 2.5)

Mordecai raised Esther. She had been named Hadassah (Myrtle), because as the myrtle spreads fragrance, so she spread good works throughout the entire land. She was also named Hadassah because the righteous are compared to myrtle, like Hananiah, Mishael and Azariah, of whom it is said: *And he stood among the myrtle trees* (Zechariah 1.8). She was also called Hadassah because, as the myrtle does not wither in summer or winter, so the righteous do not perish but have a share in this world and in the world to come. Esther remained the same in her youth and in her old age, and never ceased from doing good. She was called Esther, because she was like the planet Venus, which in Greek is *Astara*. (*II Targum* 2.6, 7)

ESTHER CHOSEN AS QUEEN

Esther was led before Ahasuerus in the royal palace, in the tenth month, the month of Tebet, in the seventh year of his reign. And the king loved Esther more than all the women. He said to her: "Pray tell me, who are your people, and where is your birthplace?" She replied: "I am ignorant concerning both my people and my birthplace, because when I was quite a child my father and mother died and I was brought up by strangers." When the king heard these words, he ordered that presents be given to the people in all the provinces, because he thought to himself, "I will do good to all the inhabitants of my land, among whom must certainly be the people of Esther." (*II Targum* 2.16–18)

The change in her worldly position wrought no change in Esther's ways and manners. She retained her beauty until old age and remained as pure in mind and soul as she had been in her simple maidenhood. All the other women who entered the gates of the royal palace made excessive demands, but Esther's demeanor continued modest and unassuming. The others insisted that the seven female servants assigned to them should have certain peculiar characteristics, as for example, that they should not differ in complexion and height from their mistress. Esther, however, uttered no wish whatsoever.

But her unpretending ways were far from pleasing to Hegai, chief of the keepers of the harem. He feared lest the king should discover that Esther made no effort to preserve her beauty, and would put the blame for it upon him, an accusation that might bring him to the gallows. To avoid

18. *ELEVATION OF ESTHER*

Cassone panel, 15th Century

Painting

such a dire fate, he clothed Esther with resplendent jewels, distinguishing her beyond all the other women gathered in the palace, even as Joseph had singled out her ancestor Benjamin by means of costly gifts lavished upon him. (*II Panim Aherim* 63, 64)

Esther was cut off from intercourse with Jews in all other matters, and she was in danger of forgetting when the Sabbath came. She therefore adopted the device of giving her seven attendants peculiar names, to keep in mind the passage of time. The first one she called *Hulta*, "Workaday," and she was in attendance upon Esther on Sundays. On Mondays, she was served by *Rok'ita*, to remind her of *Rek'ia*, "Firmament," which was created on the second day of the world. Tuesday's maid she called *Genunita*, "Garden," the third day of creation having seen plants produced in the world. On Wednesday, she reminded herself by *Nehorita's* name, "the Luminous," that it was the day on which God had made the luminaries, to shed their light in the sky; on Thursday by *Ruhshita*, "Movement," for on the fifth day the first animated beings were created; on Friday, the day on which the beasts came into being, by *Hurfita*, "Little Ewelamb"; and on the Sabbath her bidding was done by *Rego'ita*, "Rest." Thus she was sure to remember the Sabbath day week after week. (*I Targum* 2.9)

On the advice of her uncle, Esther kept her descent and her religion a secret. Mordecai's command was dictated by several motives. First of all, it was his modesty that suggested secrecy. He thought that the king, if he heard from Esther that she had been raised by Mordecai, might offer to place him in some high office. In point of fact, Mordecai was right in his conjecture, for Ahasuerus had pledged himself to make lords, princes and kings of Esther's friends and kinsfolk, if she would but name them.

Another reason for keeping Esther's Jewish affiliations

a secret was Mordecai's fear lest the fate of Vashti also over-take Esther. If such were in store for her, he desired at least to guard against the Jews becoming her fellow-sufferers. Besides, Mordecai knew only too well the hostile feelings of the heathen towards the Jews, ever since their exile from the Holy Land, and he feared that the Jew-haters, to gratify their hostility against the Jews, might bring about the ruin of Esther and her house. (*II Panim Aherim* 64)

THE ELEVATION OF HAMAN

The conspiracy of Bigthan and Teresh caused the king to determine never again to have two chamberlains guard his person. Henceforth, he would entrust his safety to a single individual, and he appointed Haman to the place. This was an act of ingratitude towards Mordecai, who, as the king's savior, had the most cogent claims upon the post. (*Aggadat Esther* 26)

After these things did king Ahasuerus promote Haman the son of Hammedatha (Esther 3.1). The king commanded that all the people should bow down and show reverence to him. What did Haman do? He made for himself an image of an old idol, and had it embroidered upon his dress, above his heart, so that everyone who bowed to Haman also bowed down to the idol which he made. Mordecai saw this, and did not consent to bow down to the idol, as it is said, *But Mordecai bowed not down* (Esther 3.2). (*Pirke de Rabbi Elie-zer* 50)

THE DIVINE DECREE IS SEALED

When this letter was signed and delivered to Haman, he and all his associates went out rejoicing. As it happened, Mordecai was just then walking in front of Haman. He saw three children coming from school and ran after them. Haman and his companions followed Mordecai to see what he would ask the children. When Mordecai came up with the children, he asked one of them to repeat the verse he had just learned. He said: *"Be not afraid of sudden terror, neither of the destruction of the wicked, when it cometh"* (Proverbs 3.25). The second then followed, saying, "I read the Scripture to-day and I stopped at this verse when I left school:

19. *MORDECAI COMFORTED BY SCHOOLBOYS*   Illuminated Manuscript

Ashkenazic Mahzor, 14th Century

Take counsel together, and it shall be brought to nought; speak the word, and it shall not stand; for God is with us" (Isaiah 8.10). Then the third chimed in with the verse: *"Even to old age I am the same, and even to hoar hairs will I carry you; I have made, and I will bear; yea, I will carry, and will deliver"* (Isaiah 46.4). When Mordecai heard this he smiled and was exceedingly glad. Said Haman to him: "Why are you so glad over the words of these children?" He replied: "Because of the glad tidings which they have brought me, that I should not fear the evil designs which you formed against us." Forthwith the wicked Haman grew wroth and said: "I will lay hand on these children first of all." (*Esther Rabbah* 7.17, 18)

When Mordecai, the righteous, heard of the decree which
was issued, and of the letter which was sealed, he rent his
garments in front and in back, and put on sackcloth and
ashes, and lifted up his voice and cried.

Immediately the Holy Ark was brought out to the gates
of Shushan, and the scroll of the Law was taken out, and
they covered it with sackcloth, and they spread ashes upon
it, and then they read therein: *In thy distress when all these
things are come upon thee, in the end of the days, thou wilt return to the Lord thy God; and hearken unto His voice; for the
Lord thy God is a merciful God* (Deuteronomy 4.30, 31).
(*II Targum* 4.1)

MORDECAI CHARGES ESTHER

Then Mordecai addressed a message to Esther as follows:
"Perhaps you imagine that you at any rate are safe, and say
to yourself that you need not pray for Israel; know that if
only a foot of one Jew is injured, do not think that you, of
all Jews, shall escape. Arise, therefore, and pray to your
heavenly Father for your people Israel. He who did justice
to the first generation will also do justice to those who come
after them. Is, then, Haman the tyrant stronger that we
should fear him? Or is his decree of greater duration? Is he
stronger than his ancestor Amalek, who came against Israel,
but whom the Lord removed from the world? Therefore,
withhold not your mouth from prayer, nor your lips from
interceding for mercy from your Creator. For the sake of
the righteousness of our fathers, Israel was delivered from
slaughter more than once; and He who has at all times done
wonders for them will also deliver our enemies into our
hands, and we shall do with them as we please. But, O
Esther, do not fancy that you, of all the Jews, shall be saved

in the house of the king. For if you shall be silent at this time, He who is the Holy One, and the Redeemer of the Jews at all times, will cause redemption to spring up for them from another place, but you and your father's house shall perish. And who knows whether you have not come to the kingdom because of the sins of your father's house." (*II Targum* 4.13-14)

Yielding at last to the argument of Mordecai, Esther was prepared to risk her life in this world, in order to secure her life in the world to come. She made only one request of her uncle. He was to have the Jews spend three days in prayer and fasting in her behalf, that she might find favor in the eyes of the king. At first Mordecai was opposed to the proclamation of a fast, because it was Passover time, and the law prohibits fasting on the holidays. But he finally assented to Esther's reasoning: "Of what avail are the holidays, if there is no Israel to celebrate them, and without Israel, there would not even be a Torah. Therefore it is advisable to transgress one law, that God may have mercy upon us." (*II Panim Aherim* 70-71)

SELECTING THE TREE FOR THE GALLOWS

Let a gallows be made of fifty cubits high and in the morning speak thou unto the king that Mordecai may be hanged thereon. The thing pleased Haman; and he caused the gallows to be made (Esther 5.14). Of what kind of tree was that gallows made? Our sages said: "When he came to make it ready, God called all the trees of creation and said: 'Which will offer itself for this evil man to be hanged on?' The fig-tree said: 'I will offer myself, for from me Israel bring first-fruits, and what is more, Israel is also compared to a first-ripe fruit, as it says, *I saw your fathers as the first-ripe in the fig-tree at her first season*' (Hosea 9.10). The vine said 'I offer myself, since Israel are compared to me, as it says, *Thou didst pluck up a vine out of Egypt*' (Psalms 80.9). The pomegranate said: 'I offer myself, since Israel are compared to me, as it says, *Thy temples are like a pomegranate split open*' (Song of Songs 4.3). The nut tree said: 'I offer myself, because Israel are likened to me, as it says, *I went down into the garden of nuts*' (Song of Songs 6.11). The citron said: 'I offer myself, because Israel take my fruit for a religious ceremony, as it says, *And ye shall take you on the first day the fruit of goodly trees*' (Leviticus 23.40). The myrtle said: 'I offer myself, because Israel are compared to me, as it says, *And he stood among the myrtles that were in the bottom*' (Zechariah 1.8). The olive said: 'I offer myself, since Israel are compared to me, as it says, *The Lord called thy name a leafy olive tree, fair with goodly fruit*' (Jeremiah 11.16). The apple tree said: 'I offer myself, because Israel are compared to me, as it says, *As an apple tree among the trees of the wood, so is my beloved among the sons* (Song of Songs 2.3) and it also says, *And the smell of thy countenance like apples*' (Song of Songs 7.9). The palm-tree said: 'I offer myself, because Israel are likened to me, as it says, *This thy stature is like to a palm-tree*' (Song of Songs 7.8). The acacia trees and fir trees said: 'We offer ourselves, because from us the Tabernacle was made and the Temple was built.' The cedar and the palm-tree said: 'We offer ourselves, because we are likened to the righteous, as it says, *The righteous shall flourish like the palm-tree; he shall grow like a cedar in Lebanon*' (Psalms 92.13). The willow said: 'I offer myself, because Israel are compared to me, as it says, *They shall spring up. . . as willows by the watercourses* (Isaiah 44.4), and they also use me for the ceremony of the four species of the *Lulab*.' Thereupon the thorn said to the Holy One, Blessed be He, 'Sovereign of the

Universe! I who have no claim to make offer myself, that
this unclean one may be hanged on me, because my name is
thorn and he is a pricking thorn; and it is fitting that a thorn
should be hanged on a thorn.' So Haman's servants found
one of these thorn-bushes and they made the gallows. When
they brought the thorn-bush to him, he set it up at the entrance of his house and he measured himself on it to show
his servants how Mordecai should be hanged on it. A *Bat
Kol* answered him: 'For thee is the tree fitting: the tree has
been made ready for thee from the beginning of the world!' "
(*Esther Rabbah* 5.14)

THE TRIUMPH OF MORDECAI

When Haman had satisfied himself that the tree intended
for his enemy was properly constructed, he repaired to the
Bet ha-Midrash, where he found Mordecai and all the Jewish school children, twenty-two thousand in number, in
tears and sorrow. He ordered them to be put in chains, saying: "First I shall kill off these, and then I shall hang Mordecai." The mothers hastened thither with bread and water,
and coaxed their children to take something before they
encountered death. The children, however, laid their hands
upon their books, and said: "As our teacher Mordecai
liveth, we will neither eat nor drink, but we will perish exhausted with fasting." They rolled up their sacred scrolls,
and handed them to their teachers with the words: "For
our devotion to the study of the Torah, we were to be rewarded with long life, according to the promise held out in
the Holy Scriptures. As we are not worthy of this, remove
the books!" The outcries of the children and of the teachers
in the *Bet ha-Midrash*, and the weeping of the mothers outside, united with the supplications of the fathers, reached to

heaven in the third hour of the night, and God said: "I
hear the voice of tender lambs and sheep!" Moses arose and
addressed God thus: "Thou knowest well that the voices
are not of lambs and sheep, but of the young of Israel, who
for three days have been fasting and languishing in fetters,
only to be slaughtered on the morrow to the delight of the
arch-enemy."

Then God felt compassion with Israel, for the sake of His
innocent little ones. He broke the seal with which the heavenly decree of annihilation had been fastened, and the decree
itself He tore in pieces. (*Abba Gorion* 37–38)

On that night, Ahasuerus became restless, and sleep was
made to flee his eyes, for the purpose that the redemption of
Israel might be brought to pass. The archangel Gabriel
descended, and threw the king out of his bed on the floor no
less than three hundred and sixty-five times, continually
whispering in his ear: "O you ingrate, reward him who deserves to be rewarded."

To account for his sleeplessness, Ahasuerus thought he
might have been poisoned, and he was about to order the
execution of those charged with the preparation of his food.
But they succeeded in convincing him of their innocence by
calling to his attention that Esther and Haman had shared
his evening meal with him, yet they felt no unpleasant effects. (*Abba Gorion* 38–39)

That night the throne of the King who is King of kings,
the Holy one, Blessed be He, became unsteady, because He
saw that Israel was in great distress. The sleep of the king
on earth fled, for he had seen in his dream Haman taking the
sword to slay him. He became agitated and arose from his
sleep, and he told the sons of Haman, the scribes, to read in
the book so as to see what had happened to him. They
opened the books and found the incident which Mordecai

had told, but they did not wish to read this, and they rolled up the scroll. The king said to them, "Read what is written before you." But they were unwilling to read, and the writing was read (of its own account) by itself, as it is said, *And they were read before the king* (Esther 6.1). It is not written here, "they read," but "they were read." The king spoke to his servants: "Call Haman to me." They said to him: "Behold, he is standing outside." The king said: "The thing is true which I saw in my dream; he has come only in this hour to slay me." He continued: "Let him come in." Haman entered before the king. The king said to him: "I wish to exalt and aggrandize a certain man; what shall be done to him?" Haman said in his heart, for the seed of Esau speak in their hearts but never reveal their secret with their mouths, as it is said: *And Haman said in his heart* (Esther 6.6): "He does not desire to exalt any other man except me. I will speak words so that I shall be a king just as he is." Haman said to the king: "Let them bring the apparel which the king wore on the day of the coronation, and the horse upon which the king rode, and the crown which was put upon the head of the king."

The king was exceedingly angry because of the crown. The king said: "It does not suffice this villain, but he must even desire the crown which is upon my head." Haman saw that the king was angry because of the crown; he said: *And let the apparel and the horse be delivered to the hand of one of the king's most noble princes* (Esther 6.9).

The king then said to Haman: "Make ready, and go into the royal treasure chambers and take from the wardrobe a purple covering, a raiment of fine silk, adorned with fringes and costly stones and pearls, having bells of gold on its four corners, and golden pomegranates on every side. Bring also from there the large golden crown which was brought to

me from the Macedonian province on the first day that I
ascended the throne. Further, bring from there the sword
and the coat of mail which were sent to me from Ethiopia,
and the two royal veils embroidered with pearls which were
brought to me from Africa; then fetch from the royal stables
the horse whose name is Hippus Regius (Royal Steed) which
I rode on my coronation day, and go invest Mordecai the Jew
with all these marks of distinction." Haman answered and
said: "There are many Jews in Shushan the capital by the
name of Mordecai; to which of them shall I go?" The king
said: "Go to Mordecai, the Jew, who spoke well about the
king, and who sits at my gate."

When Haman heard these words he was in great trouble,
his countenance was changed, his sight grew dim, his mouth
became distorted, his thoughts confused, his loins languid,
and his knees knocked one against the other. He addressed
the king: "My Lord King! There are many Mordecais in
the world, and I do not know about which of them you have
spoken to me." The king in reply said: "Have I not told
you that I mean Mordecai who sits at my gate?" "But," re-
joined Haman, "there are many royal gates, and I do not
know of which gate you have spoken to me." "Have I not
told you," said the king, "that I mean the gate which leads
from the harem to the palace?" Haman said: "This man is
my enemy, and the enemy of my fathers; I would rather
give him ten thousand talents of silver; only let not this
honor be done to him." The king replied: "Go and give him
ten thousand talents, and he shall rule over thy house, and
this honor shall also not be withheld from him." Haman
said to the king: "I have ten sons, let them all be servants
in the royal palace and let them run before the horses, but
let not this honor be done to him." The king replied: "You,
your sons and your wife shall be slaves to Mordecai, and
this honor shall not be withheld from him." Haman said

again: "Messengers with letters and decrees have already been sent out to all the provinces of the king to destroy the people of Mordecai; let these letters be revoked and let not this honor be done to him." The king answered: "The letters which I sent out I invalidate, and this honor shall not be withheld from him." Then the king for the second time rebuked him, and said: "Haman, make haste! Do not fail to do all that I command you!" Now when the wicked Haman saw how his words were received by the king, and that he did not pay any attention to his speech, he went to the royal treasure chambers, bowed down and sad, his head covered like that of a mourner. (*II Targum* 6.10-11)

Then Haman took the apparel and the horse and went and found Mordecai with the rabbis sitting before him.

Haman said to him: "Arise and put on this apparel and ride on this horse, for so the king desires you to do." He replied: "I cannot do so until I have gone into the bath and trimmed my hair, for it would not be good manners to use the king's apparel in this condition." Now Esther had sent and closed all the baths and all the barbers' shops. So Haman himself took him into the bath and washed him, and then went and brought scissors from his house and trimmed his hair. While he was doing so, he sighed and groaned. Said Mordecai to him: "Why do you sigh?" He replied: "The man who was esteemed by the king above all his nobles is now made a bath attendant and a barber." Said Mordecai to him: "Wretch, and were you not once a barber in Kefar Karzum?" (So a sage recorded: Haman was a barber in Kefar Karzum twenty-two years.) After he had trimmed his hair he put the garments on him, and said to him, "Mount and ride." He replied: "I am not able, as I am weak from the days of fasting." So Haman stooped down and he mounted by standing on his back.

As he was leading him through the street where Haman

lived, his daughter who was standing on the roof saw him.
She thought that the man on the horse was her father and
the man walking before him was Mordecai. So she took a
pot and emptied it on the
head of her father. He
looked up at her and when
she saw that it was her
father, she threw herself
from the roof to the ground
and killed herself. (Megillah 16a)

20. *MEGILLAH*

1748

Then Mordecai returned
to the gate of the palace
with great honor and dig-
nity; but Haman went to
his house covered with
shame, sad and his head
covered over. (*II Targum*
6.11–13)

The vast fortune which Haman possessed was divided
into three parts. The first part was given to Mordecai and
Esther, the second to the students of the Torah, and the
third was applied to the restoration of the Temple. (*Tehillim*
22.197)

THE FEAST OF PURIM

With the arrival of the month of Adar, one should be exceedingly joyful. (Ta'anit 29a)

The rabbis said: "Have we not had enough of impending
oppressions? Do you want to increase them by recalling
the oppression of Haman?" Rabbi Samuel b. Nahman said
in the name of Rabbi Jonathan, "Eighty-five elders, including more than thirty prophets, have been unwilling to grant
recognition to the Feast of Purim. They said: 'Moses has

told us that no prophet should add anything to the Law from now and henceforth; and yet Mordecai and Esther desired to create and establish a new institution!' They did not cease to ponder over it, until God opened their eyes and they found justification for it written in the Law, the Prophets and the Writings." (Jerusalem Megillah ch. 1.5)

Should all other festivals cease to be observed, the days of Purim will never be annulled. (*Midrash on Proverbs*, 9.2)

Though all other festivals be abolished, Hanukkah and Purim will never be annulled. (Jerusalem Ta'anit, ch. 2.12)

Rabba said: It is the duty of a man to mellow himself with wine on Purim until he cannot tell the difference between "Cursed be Haman" and Blessed be Mordecai." (Megillah 7b)

All festivals will in the future be abolished except Purim and the Day of Atonement. (*Yalkut Shim'oni* on Proverbs 9.944)

The collection for Purim must be given to the poor for the Purim festival. (Baba Mezia 78b)

THE BOOK OF ESTHER

The Book of Esther was composed under the inspiration of the holy spirit. (Megillah 7a)

Rabbi Joshua ben Levi declared that one of the three things the earthly Court instituted and the Court on High approved is the reading of the *Megillah*. (Makkot 23b)

Our Rabbis taught: Forty-eight prophets and seven prophetesses prophesied to Israel, and they neither took away from nor added aught to what is written in the Torah save only the reading of the *Megillah*. (Megillah 14a)

In the time to come all the other parts of the Prophets and the Writings will lose their worth and only the Torah of Moses and the Book of Esther will retain their value. (Jerusalem Megillah ch. 1.5)

CHAPTER VII

PURIM IN JEWISH LAW

ONE of the characteristics of Judaism as a religion is its unwillingness to permit ideal, sentiment and emotion to go unused and wasted. Hence, Judaism seeks to embody such matters of the heart as study, prayer and even joyful celebration, in laws the intent of which is to make habitual what might otherwise be evanescent, to deepen into practice what might be mere fleeting thought and passing emotion. Thus, so joyous an occasion as Purim gave rise to a distinct body of law.

While the Book of Esther itself instituted the festival of Purim, the oral traditions pertaining to it were set down in Tractate Megillah of the Mishnah, compiled by Judah the Prince (about 135–220 C.E.). This tractate deals with the time, place and manner of reading the Scroll of Esther. Centuries later Moses ben Maimon, better known as Maimonides (1135–1204), systematized the body of Jewish law found in the Talmud in his great work, *Mishneh Torah*, in which are found further laws about Purim. The last outstanding codifier of rabbinical Judaism, Joseph Karo (1488–1575), established the accepted basis for traditional practices in the *Shulhan Aruk*. A notable commentator on the *Shulhan Aruk* was Moses Isserles (about 1520–1572), whose decisions came to be widely accepted. An abridged and popular version of Karo's monumental work was prepared by Solomon Ganzfried (about 1800–1886).

The laws of Purim embodied in these works reflect the invisible but real spirit of the Jews rejoicing not so much in the downfall of their enemies as in the glorious victory of right and justice, and the triumph of the God of Israel.

142

MISHNAH MEGILLAH[1]

The Time of Reading

The Scroll (of Esther) is read on the 11th, 12th, 13th, 14th, or 15th (of Adar), never earlier and never later. Cities encompassed by a wall since the days of Joshua the son of Nun read it on the 15th. Villages and large towns read it on the 14th, save that villages (sometimes) read it earlier on a day of assembly (1.1).

Thus, if the 14th fell on a Monday, villages and large towns read the Scroll on that day, and walled cities on the day after. If it fell on a Tuesday or a Wednesday, villages read it earlier on the day of assembly (Monday, the 12th or 13th), and large towns on the day itself, and walled cities on the next day. If it fell on a Thursday, villages and large towns read it on that day, and walled cities on the next day. If it fell on a Friday, villages read it earlier on the day of assembly (Thursday the 13th), large towns and walled cities on the day itself. If it fell on the Sabbath, villages and large towns read it earlier on the day of assembly (Thursday the 12th), and walled cities on the next day. If it fell on the day after the Sabbath, villages read it earlier on the day of assembly (Thursday the 11th), large towns on the day itself, and walled cities the next day (1.2).

Towns and Villages

What is deemed a large town? Any in which are ten unoccupied men (who can be counted upon to form a quorum of ten necessary for the saying of the prescribed congregational prayers). If there are fewer than this, it is a village. Of these times (when the 14th or 15th of Adar falls on the Sabbath) they have said: They may read it earlier and not later. R. Judah said: This applies (that the reading may be advanced) only to a place where they hold assembly on Mondays and Thursdays; but if they do not hold assembly on Mondays and Thursdays they may read it only at its appointed time (1.3).

MANNER OF READING

He that reads the Scroll may stand or sit. If one reads it, or if two read it, they (that read and that listen) have fulfilled their obligation. Where the custom is to say a Benediction (after it) they say it; where it is not the custom, they do not say it (3.1).

MISHNEH TORAH[2]

MOSES BEN MAIMON

READING OF THE SCROLL

The reading of the Scroll at its prescribed time is a positive commandment of the scribes and it is also well known that it was a decree of the prophets. All are obligated to read it: men, women, proselytes and emancipated slaves; and children are taught its reading. Even priests who are occupied in divine service should put aside their work and come to listen to the reading of the Scroll. The study of the Torah also is interrupted to listen to the reading of the Scroll. It is all the more mandatory that all the other commandments of the Torah be set aside for the reading of the Scroll. There is nothing for which the reading of the Scroll should be postponed except the duty of burying the dead, if there is no one to bury him. For he who chances upon a dead person should bury him first and then read (1.1).

21, 22. *MEGILLAH CASES*   Embossed Silver

It is commanded to read it entirely and also to read it at night and in the daytime. The entire night is proper for the reading at night, and the entire day is proper for the reading in the daytime.

SEWING OF THE SCROLL

The Scroll must be sewn so that all the skins of parchment become one scroll. It is sewn only with threads like a *Sefer Torah*, and if it was sewn without threads it is defective. Nevertheless, it is not necessary to sew all the writing sheets with threads like a *Sefer Torah*; even if it was sewn with three stitches of thread at the end of the writing sheet, three in the middle, and three at the second end, it is suitable, as it is called a letter (2.11).

MANNER OF READING

It is a custom throughout Israel that the reader of the Scroll spreads it out and reads it as a letter to demonstrate the miracle. When he is finished, he rolls it all up again and pronounces the blessing (2.12).

EULOGIZING AND FASTING PROHIBITED

On these two days, i.e., the 14th and 15th (of Adar), it is forbidden to everyone in every place to deliver a funeral address and to fast. The same applies to those who dwell in cities that observe only the 15th (of Adar) and to those who dwell in towns that observe only the 14th (of Adar). On these two days, it is forbidden to deliver a funeral address and to fast both in the First and Second Adar (2.13).

Feasting, Portions to Friends and Gifts to the Poor

On the 14th (of Adar) it is a duty for those who dwell in villages and towns, and on the fifteenth for those who dwell in cities, to make them days of gladness, feasting and of sending portions to friends and gifts to the poor.

Although it is permissible to work (on Purim), nevertheless it is not proper to do so. The sages have said that everyone who does work on the day of Purim will never see the sign of a blessing.

Everyone must send two portions of meat or two kinds of cooked dishes or other kinds of food to his friend, as it is said, *sending portions one to another*, (implying) two portions to one person. And whoever increases the portions to friends is praiseworthy. And if one does not have (enough to send), he should exchange with his friend, each one sending his dinner to the other, to fulfil (the words): *sending portions one to another* (2.15).

One is duty bound on the day of Purim to distribute (gifts) to the poor. One must not give to less than two poor people, giving to each one a present or money or a cooked dish or some other kind of food, as it is said *gifts to the poor*, i.e., (at least) two gifts to two poor persons.

Purim money may not be diverted for any other charity (2.16).

It is better to increase the gifts to the poor than to make for oneself a big meal or to send more portions to friends, for there is no greater or nobler joy than to gladden the hearts of the poor, the orphans, the widows and the strangers. He who makes the heart of the unfortunate to rejoice resembles the Divine Presence, as it is said, *To revive the spirit of the humble, and to revive the heart of the contrite ones* (Isaiah 57.15). (2.17).

COMMENTARY ON SHULHAN ARUK[3]

MOSES ISSERLES

"On Purim a person should drink until he knows not the difference between 'Cursed be Haman' and 'Blessed be Mordecai'." Some authorities say that it is not necessary to get as drunk as all that, but merely to drink more than one's normal allowance, so that he may fall asleep and, because he is asleep, not know the difference between 'Cursed be Haman' and 'Blessed be Mordecai.' It is immaterial whether one drinks a lot or a little, as long as his thoughts are directed to God. No one should fast on Purim except to prevent a bad dream from coming true. There are some people who are accustomed to wear their Sabbath and holiday clothes on Purim, and that is a good custom. . . . Some authorities say that if a man injures his neighbor as a result of too much Purim "joy" he is free from paying damages.

CODE OF JEWISH LAW[4]

SOLOMON GANZFRIED

As soon as Adar arrives all should be exceedingly joyful. If an Israelite has a controversy with a non-Jew, he should go with him to court during this month.

FAST OF ESTHER

All Israel have taken upon themselves the 13th day of the month of Adar as a public fast-day. This is called the Fast of Esther, in order to remember that the Holy One, blessed be He, sees and hears the prayers of every man in time of distress when he fasts and when he returns to God with all his heart, as He had done to our fathers in those days.

Nevertheless this fast-day is not as obligatory as the four

days which are ordained in the Scriptures. Hence, it may be relaxed in an emergency; thus pregnant and nursing women, or even one suffering slightly from his eyes, if the fast would cause them distress, should not fast. A woman within thirty days of giving birth, also a bridegroom in his seven days of rejoicing, need not fast.

Purim is on the 14th of Adar. If Purim occurs on Sunday the fast is observed on Thursday.

HALF SHEKEL

Before Purim has set in, it is customary to give half a standard coin, current in that place and at that time, to commemorate the half shekel they were accustomed to give for the buying of the public offerings.

HONORING THE MEGILLAH

In honor of the *Megillah* one should attire himself in Sabbath garments in the evening, and on his return from the synagogue he should find the lights burning in his house and the table set.

The best way of observing the precept is to hear the *Megillah* read in the synagogue where there is a multitude of people, for in the multitude of people is the king's glory (Proverbs 19.28). One should at least endeavor to hear it in a quorum of ten; but if it is impossible to read it in a quorum of ten, each individual should read it out of a valid *Megillah* with the benedictions that precede it. If one knows how to read it and the others do not, the one who knows should read it and they should listen and thus fulfil their obligations, even if they are not ten.

Reader and Listener

He who reads the *Megillah* is required to have his mind centered upon causing all the listeners to fulfil their obligation. The listener also should bear in mind that he is thus fulfilling his obligation; hence, he should hear every word, for if he did not hear even one word, his obligation is not fulfilled. The reader, therefore, is required to be very careful to cease reading altogether while there is a tumult at the mention of Haman, and wait until the commotion is entirely over. Nevertheless it is mete and proper for each to have a *Megillah* in order that he himself should say word for word in an undertone, as perchance he may not hear one word from the reader.

Mourners on Purim

A mourner in the first seven days of mourning should observe all the laws of mourning, and he is forbidden to witness any manner of festivity, but he is permitted to put on his boots and to sit on a chair, for this is something that everybody can see. At night if he can gather a quorum at his house to read the *Megillah*, it is well; if not, he should pray at his house and go to the synagogue to hear the *Megillah*. If it occurs on the conclusion of the Sabbath, he should go to the synagogue after the third meal while it is yet day, and on the morrow he should go to the synagogue to pray and to hear the *Megillah*.

Sending of Portions and Gifts to the Needy

Everybody, even the poorest Israelite who accepts charity, is obliged to give at least two gifts to two poor persons. If one is in a place where there are no poor, he should keep that money until he will come across some poor people, or he should send it to them.

23. *EXCHANGING OF GIFTS* Painting

Megillah, 18th Century

A mourner, even in the first seven days of mourning, is obliged to send gifts to the needy and portions to his friends; he should not, however, send anything of a joyful nature. But to a mourner, portions are not sent the entire twelve months, even a thing that is not of a joyful nature. If he is a poor man, it is permissible to send him money or some other article that is not of a joyful nature. If only the mourner and one other person are at that place, it is obligatory to send him a gift, in order to perform the precept of sending portions.

Purim Feast

It is obligatory to eat, drink and be merry on Purim. On the night of the 14th one should also rejoice and make somewhat of a feast. . . . Nevertheless one does not fulfil his obligation by the feast that he makes at night, as it is a religious duty to make the feast principally in the daytime, for it is written: *Days of rejoicing.* It is proper to light candles as becomes rejoicing and festivals, even when the meal is had in the daytime. On the night of the 15th also one should rejoice to some extent.

Portions to one's friends and gifts to the needy should be sent in the daytime. And because people are busy sending out portions, a part of the repast is had in the night time. The afternoon prayers are said while it is yet broad day, and the feast is held after the Afternoon Service, at least the greater part of it should be held while it is yet day.

It is well to engage in the study of the Torah for a short time before beginning the feast. A support for this view is found in the verse *For the Jews there was light* (Esther 8.16), and we explain that light refers to the Torah.

Shushan Purim

The 15th of Adar is termed Shushan Purim. It is forbidden to hold a funeral address and to fast thereon. It is customary to make somewhat of a feast and to rejoice thereon, but "We thank thee for the miracles . . ." is not said, and it is permitted to marry on that day, but on the 14th of Adar no marriage should take place, because no joy should be intermixed with another.

On the 14th of the First Adar (in a leap year) neither the Propitiatory Prayers, nor *O God, Who art long suffering*, nor *For the Chief Musician* is said, and it is forbidden to hold a funeral address or to fast thereon. On the 14th somewhat of a feast is made.

CHAPTER VIII

PURIM IN MODERN PROSE

THE HAND OF PROVIDENCE[1]

Isaac Leeser

DOES not the fate of Haman teach us how watchful is the superintendence of God over the affairs of man — and how inefficient are all the cunningly devised plans of the proud and wicked to injure those who are too weak to protect themselves from the impending danger? Little did Haman think that, when he alone was invited to the queen's table, he went to his death; little did he imagine that the sons, of whom he boasted, would perish so soon after him; little did he believe, that Mordecai, for whom he had erected a scaffold, would become the first officer of the king; and yet all this did come to pass, and all Haman's art for evil was rendered as nought, at the moment of his greatest seeming security. Truly may we say, that "the lot is thrown by man, but that to God alone belongs the decision." If then, oppressed one, thou art suffering under severe affliction, if thou seest thy best plans fail of their intended effect: let thy confidence nevertheless remain unshaken in the God by whose favor and will thou wert sent hither, to earn for thyself on earth an immortal happiness. If thou seest the wicked flourish for a while, if thou beholdest their power extending wider and wider; fear thou not, for they, as well as thou, have a limit set to their ambition, and like the waves of the ocean which are broken by the sand against which they dash so furiously, the strength of the unrighteous is exhausted by

the humble resistance which the moral force of the mind of
the lowly good opposes to the fierce onset; for this is the im-
movable and wise decree of God. Cease therefore thy com-
plaining, son of the earth, and be assured, that if thy power
be broken, if thy strength be gone, the powerful Arm held
out over thee for thy protection is one that is never wearied,
that the Providence that watches over thee is never tired. . . .

THE NAME OF GOD[2]

Arthur P. Stanley

Alone of all the sacred books, the Book of Esther never
names the name of God from first to last. Whether this absence arose from that increasing scruple against using the
Divine Name or from the instinctive adoption of the fashion
of the Persian Court, this abstinence from any religious expressions was so startling that the Greek translators thrust
into the narrative long additions containing the sacred
phrases which, in the original narrative, were wanting.

But there is a sense in which this peculiarity of the Book
of Esther is most instructive. Within that Judaic "hard-
ness of heart," behind that "heathenish naughtiness," burn
a lofty independence, a genuine patriotism, which are not
the less to be admired because Mordecai and Esther spoke
and acted without a single appeal by name or profession to
the Supreme Source of that moral strength in which they
dared the wrath of the Great King and labored for the preservation of their countrymen. It is necessary for us that in
the rest of the sacred volume the name of God should constantly be brought before us, to show that He is all in all to
our moral perfection. But it is expedient for us no less that
there should be one book which omits it altogether, to prevent us from attaching to the mere name a reverence which
belongs only to the reality. In the mind of the sacred writer

the mere accidents, as they might seem, of the quarrel of Ahasuerus, the sleepless night, the delay of the lot, worked out the Divine Will as completely as the parting of the Red Sea or the thunders of Sinai. The story of Esther, glorified by the genius of Handel and sanctified by the piety of Racine, is not only a material for the noblest and the gentlest of meditations, but a token that in the daily events — the unforeseen chances — of life, in little unremembered acts, in the fall of a sparrow, in the earth bringing forth fruit of herself, God is surely present. The name of God is *not* there, but the work of God *is*. Those who most eagerly cling to the recognition of the biblical authority of the book ought the most readily to be warned by it not to make an offender for a word or for the omission of a word. When Esther nerved herself to enter, at the risk of her life, the presence of Ahasuerus — *I will go unto the King ... and if I perish, I perish* (Esther 4.16) — when her patriotic feeling vented itself in that noble cry, *for how can I endure to see the evil that shall come unto my people? or how can I endure to see the destruction of my kindred?* (8.6) — she expressed, although she never named the name of God, a religious devotion as acceptable to Him as that of Moses and David, who, no less sincerely, had the sacred name always on their lips.

Esther is, in this sense, the Cordelia of the Bible.

> Thy youngest daughter does not love thee least,
> Nor are those empty-hearted whose low sounds
> Reverberate no hollowness...

THE CHARACTER OF ESTHER[*]

Grace Aguilar

The character of Esther, as an individual and a female, possesses many traits to call for admiration and love. She was not, indeed, a heroine; nor do we perceive in her, that peculiar energy and promptness under danger and trial which we have noticed in the character of Abigail and the Shunamite; but the very want of this quality is consoling, proving, as it does, that the most timid, the most essentially feminine, may be permitted to accomplish great ends, and become instruments in the Eternal's hand for the welfare of His people. Energy of purpose and of action, though essentially woman's attribute, is yet a portion only for the few. There are more to resemble Esther than Abigail; and to those that are timid and fearful, and shrinking from an imperative duty or some imposed task, who would rather remain in sad quiescence than make one effort to conquer an imagined destiny, to them we would point the consoling moral of Esther's history and beseech them, like her, to arm themselves with the arrows of fervent prayers, in the very face of inward trembling and a failing frame, and go forth and do, and leave in kinder hands the rest.

Esther's quiescence and obedience to her destiny was necessity. Chosen as the bride of a heathen monarch, desired by Mordecai not to show her people or her kindred, debarred from all her friends and pleasures of her earlier and happier years, it was her duty to submit patiently and calmly; and her gentle and enduring character enabled her to do so less sufferingly than more energetic minds. But we see that to endure was less painful to her than to act, by her repugnance to go forward when the call of duty came. Her spirit, instead of being roused, by the extreme emergency of the case, shrunk back appalled: and to brave the king's anger, by venturing uncalled into his presence, seemed far more terrible than the danger threatening thousands. To *share* their fate appeared easier far than to court it; and even when, in obedience to Mordecai, she promised to seek the king, it is very evident that her anticipation was failure — and death. Had Abigail or Deborah been in her place, their

24. *ESTHER ON HER WAY TO THE PALACE* Painting

Cassone panel, 15th Century

different character would scarcely have required even the direction of Mordecai; their own energy would have urged them forward and supported them by the inward promise of success.

But that Esther did not naturally possess this strength and firmness, renders her conduct yet more worthy of our grateful admiration. We see her displayed before us, in her woman's weakness, as, indeed, one of ourselves. We behold her in not one point, except in her surpassing loveliness, our superior; nay, to bring her closer to us still, she is a captive in a strange land, even as we are now; and yet was she, this weak trembling girl, the savior, the benefactor of thousands; and her name has come down, through a thousand ages, wreathed with the admiring love of that very people whose ancestors she saved.

That the Bible does give both sympathy and encouragement, even to the most constitutionally weak, is proved by the sweet, gentle, feminine character of Esther. Strength of herself indeed, she had none; but it was asked, and granted, and so it will be unto all.

MORDECAI—MAN OF PEACE[4]

Jacob Hoschander

The eulogy of Mordecai is fully in agreement with our conception of his character. He was pre-eminently a man of peace. This principle governed his whole life. Peace with all the world he considered the acme of human felicity. This thought he expressed in his Letter of Purim: "Words of Peace and Truth." Peace was his life consideration when the letter was not contrary to the principle of Truth. But as soon as these two principles came into collision, he did not hesitate to sacrifice his own happiness for the sake of truth, as he did in his conflict with Haman. Though not having been in sympathy with the zeal of the strict adherents of the Jewish religion, nevertheless he was willing to expose his own life for their sake, and fully identified himself with his brethren who sacrificed themselves for the truth of their religion. The establishment of the festival of Purim commemorating the deliverance of the Jews from

Haman's decree, though ostensibly identical with the Persian New Year festival, was principally due to his desire of avoiding friction with the Gentiles, and to maintain both Peace and Truth. He certainly was solicitous for the welfare of his people, and aimed to safeguard their existence, and to insure for them the blessing of peace. This is, indeed, the ideal of Israel, as the Psalmist expressed himself: *The Lord will give strength unto His people; the Lord will bless His people with peace* (Psalms 29.2). Peace was the theme on which Mordecai dwelt, and which he recommended to his descendants as the highest good: *He was seeking the good of his people and speaking peace to all his seed* (Esther 10.3).

PURIM 5706[5]

LEOPOLD NEUHAUS*

Who does not know the story of Purim, the most popular tale in the twenty-four books of *The Holy Scriptures*, the Scroll of Esther that tells us how the Jewish people was saved from the danger of annihilation at the hands of Haman, the Jew-hater? His plan was crossed by Mordecai and his cousin Esther who later became queen of the land of King Ahasuerus, ruler of its one hundred and twenty-seven provinces. This tale, which kept our forefathers from despair during the dark days of antiquity and the Middle Ages, has always lived in the heart of the Jewish people.

If the entire story and festival of Purim have a quite different tone from Hanukkah, it is because, unfortunately, all too often the religious-moral value of Purim has been too little regarded. True, Hanukkah is a national Jewish festival, possessing as it does heroes like the Maccabees, and

* Rabbi Leopold Neuhaus of Frankfort is the only rabbi who returned from a three year detention in the concentration camp at Theresienstadt to resume his post.

takes place in Palestine, while Purim is more a drama of the
Galut. Nevertheless, this drama of Purim is the *Galut* drama
which, with all its thousand-year-old tendencies and diplo-
macies has ever taught the Jew *Bitahon* (confidence in God)
and showed him that he is not deserted, *Ki lo alman Yisrael*,
that Israel is not forever orphaned. Purim has confirmed
the Jew time and again in the affirmation of his Judaism,
even though the foes of Jews labored to bring about their
downfall. That is why the Jewish people have connected
Purim with the idea of rescue so that, for example, there
have been many Purims.

This festival has been so popular — one might say, unfortunately — because we have suffered so many persecutions, which God has turned to our benefit. Yet Purim has
been no festival of national exultation, but rather the celebration of the *Sherit ha-Pletah* (remnant of the escaped
ones) of a scattered people given into the hands of Haman
and his comrades, of a people that can hope for help through
the intervention of God. This characteristic element of
Purim becomes even interesting by virtue of the fact that
God Himself, who every Purim rescues His people, Israel,
does *not* appear by His name, "The Eternal," in the entire
Scroll of Esther, but is concealed between the lines reading,
relief and deliverance will arise to the Jews from another place
(Esther 4.14). What "another place" could there be, but
the place of God? This profound Jewish psychology, revealing the secret that the Eternal stands behind every
event, is the anchorage of the soul of the Jewish people in the
thought of God, a concept of eternity held by the Jewish
people in which its most insignificant adherent recognizes
the Eternal's bond. It is for this reason that the *Zohar*
says: *Ha-Kadosh Baruk Hu ve-Yisrael ve-Erez Yisrael —
Ehad Hu* (The Holy One, blessed be He, the people of Israel
and the land of Israel are one).

That is the reason why the festival of Purim has been rooted firmly in our hearts for these thousands of years. And one would not wish to miss it as a comforter in hard times. That is the reason why it has become a popular festival for old and young in modern times in Palestine and, from being the drama of the *Galut* Jews, has become a popular festival for all who, as righteous Jews like Mordecai, do not wish to bow before hostile forces; we do not wish to be two-faced souls who bow to those above but trample upon those below. It is this same Purim that teaches us to be righteous people and to overcome the *Galut*. With such an idea in mind, Purim becomes a festival of the Jewish people that is tied to innumerable folk customs.

One may affirm with justice and right that Purim has become a considerable factor in the Jewish life of the masses and that, when we celebrate Purim in the year 5706, we ought to say the *Sheheheyanu* ("Thou hast kept us alive") before reading the Book of Esther, giving particular thanks to God, because the Almighty has left the world a *Sherit ha-Pletah*, from which a new Jewish life may again arise.

THE CARNIVAL SPIRIT[6]

DAVID FRISCHMAN

All of us are reclining. We are all seated at the table, celebrating our festival, and I , too, am among those who are seated. The mistress of the house set the table, poured the wine, baked delightful doughnuts and enchanted me with her eye. And she made cakes too, "king's messengers," filled with cheese. It's Purim today, all over the land! A spirit of peace and pleasure, a spirit of freedom and ease pervades this festival which has become the delight of every soul. For this is a festival that was not bound to us by heavy ropes, nor were we bound with heavy ropes to it, and it is not called "a holy convocation," that it may not seem to be a creditor, but rather a brother and friend. If the other festivals are called "festivals by act of heaven," then we may be justified in calling this holiday a "festival by act of man."

And the facial cast of this holiday resembles the features of the holiday of masks which the Gentiles have and which they call carnival. The voice of rejoicing and the voice of joy are heard in the streets, the voice of male singers and of female singers, and shoutings for happiness ring out on every side; the face of every celebrant glows as did the face of the drunken Lot, concealed by the mask poured over it and by the drink poured into them. And it shall come to pass that that man who would turn his face away in anger might approach us and bring us to reproof because of our iniquities and sate us with the bitter truth, and we must perforce hear our shame and our reproof nor be able to return them whence they came. . . for that is the reason why he has assumed a secret face, that he might be spirit-free, and without constraint.

It is the law unto Israel, and a law unto the nations of the earth, to celebrate the festival of the mask, and we know not who adopted the custom from whom: whether Israel from the nations, or they from us. But sufficient unto us is what our eves see, that the custom of the carnival is the same everywhere. Why, therefore, ought we at once to investigate and rudely to research into such matters, at a moment when we have come only to investigate masks, and to delve into doughnuts and cakes. Let the poor man eat; perhaps he will forget his poverty! Let the rich man drink; perhaps he will forget his wealth! And let the investigators, and their investigations, the delvers and their delving pass utterly from our memory, nor let them come to mind again!

THE LAST PURIM PAGEANT[7]

JOEL BLAU

... cause him to ride on horseback through the street of the city, and proclaim before him: *Thus shall it be done to the man whom the king delighteth to honour* (Esther 6.9).

A wakeful restless night. *On that night the king could not sleep* (6.1). Uneasy lies the head even of him who has a hundred and seven and twenty provinces at his beck and call. A spirit of uneasiness sweeps through the palace; something uncanny and weird and fateful broods over its vast halls, its dark corridors; over the king's chamber even. Ahasuerus, tossing on his couch, knows not what this Namelessness is that lies upon him, depriving him of sleep, of the pleasant visions of the night. Ah, if he knew what mighty forces, mightier than himself, were tossing him about! But he did not know. Do kings ever know? And is there any one mightier than he? And yet — and yet — he who could command thousands of slaves to do his bidding could not command sleep to descend upon his tired eyelids. And the king could not sleep. . . .

Suddenly — was it to beguile the wakeful hours, or did he act unwittingly under the impulsion of the strange forces that were about him? — suddenly he calls for *the book of records of the chronicles* (6.1). If he cannot dream he can at least remember. If the dark-pinioned night took from him the visions of future glory, he himself can bring back on the wings of memory the recollection of all his past exploits, all the deeds for which he is famous throughout Persia and Media. Suddenly (why do things happen in such unaccountable ways?) his reader comes upon an entry that causes the king to start. His life had been in danger at the hand of plotters and someone had saved it. Someone — it was Mordecai; son of a race despised and hated, against which he had already signed a decree of total extermination! And has anything, any honor or dignity, been done to this Mordecai for his service to the magnanimous king? No — nothing. *There is nothing done for him* (6.3).

In the meantime, the first gleam of the rising morn has begun to dissipate the darkness. It lifted the uncanny Namelessness from the royal breast, leaving only one troubling thought — his failure to reward the man who had saved him. The palace is already astir with the life of the new day. *Who is in the court?* (6.4). Haman! The great, strutting favorite of the monarch! *Let him come in* (6.5). And Haman came in. And from his arrogant expectation of fresh favors resulted that procession in which Mordecai the Jew was led about with great pomp and circumstance through the streets of Shushan, while heralds cried before him: *Thus shall it be done unto the man whom the king delighteth to honour* (6.11).

It was the first Purim Pageant.

Eternal Vigilance. Stupendous, everlasting, divine watchfulness. Do earthly kings alone keep vigil? God, the King of kings, watches above the stars. *Behold He that keepeth Israel doth neither slumber nor sleep* (Psalms 121.4). And before the Ancient of Days there lies unrolled the Book of Chronicles which is the Book of Destiny. The record of kings and peoples, of high and humble; the fate of kingdoms and powers, of men and matters, is inscribed in this book: past, present and future are as one here, in this mysterious scroll. But few mortals, of the most clear-visioned, have glimpsed the secrets of this timeless, ageless book: Moses with his tablets; Zechariah with his "flying roll. . . ."

And I wonder, as the King of kings reads, and He comes upon the case of the Jew, does He ask the question, What has been done unto him, what honor, dignity or reward to

25. *READING OF THE CHRONICLE TO AHASUERUS; MORDECAI'S TRIUMPH*   Illuminated Manuscript

Alba Bible, 15th Century

this despised of all peoples, to this Mordecai among the nations?

Mordecai, sitting in the King's gate! He has been sitting there for centuries untold. He has acted as the wise lookout, constantly on guard against possible dangers to the King's cause on earth. His has been an eternal vigilance, matched only by the mysterious divine watchfulness above. He has performed a service whose like history does not record. He has spread the knowledge about the King — the King's goodness, the King's greatness, and all that the King cherishes and holds dear — throughout the world. Occupying as he did the place in the gate, at the world's threshold, he has given information to all passers-by of the splendor of the palace and the graciousness of the King enthroned therein. And for this, what has been done unto him? Nothing!

Nothing? He has been despised and driven. He has been hated, hooted and hunted. Homeless and without honor, the pariah of peoples, every human dignity has been denied him. Victim of the Hamans of all time, never certain of his fate, never having assurance of his life, vainly clamoring for a fair deal and being laughed to scorn even in so-called civilized lands that boast of their liberty: the butt of the hoodlum in low and high places — he, the Jew! Of all the Jews that ever lived and labored for the King's sake — curiously enough — only one Jew has been singled out for the world's honor: a Jew who rose so high in the world's esteem that in his rise he dragged down all his brethren for all time into a pool of common degradation. And in the name of this one Jew all Jews have been made to suffer all the more. Nothing, if it were only nothing! If the world withholds from the Jew its merited rewards, why does it not spare him its unmerited revenges?

Yet on Purim the Jew laughs and makes merry — the strange ritual laughter of his religion!

The Jew laughs, because he is inspired by something deeper than a mere ceremonial motive. His is the confidence that springs from unconquerable faith. He has glimpsed the writing on the page lying before God. He knows its meaning. He understands the long swing of God's thought. He shares, with the patience of the terribly meek, the divine watchfulness. God watches above, Israel — below. Both watch for the victory of the Good. And when the day of victory comes, and all hate is banished from this blood-bathed earth, it will be the day of Israel's rehabilitation. On that day will the nations gather in a mighty throng and bring homage to the long despised: "Thus shall it be done unto the people that the King delighteth to honor!"

And that will be the last Purim Pageant!

CHAPTER IX

PURIM IN THE SHORT STORY

TWO DEAD MEN[1]

Sholom Aleichem

YOU may think this is a strange title for a Purim tale; Purim — when it is fitting and proper for a Jew to act the drunkard and a storyteller to play the fool! Reader, I know that today is Purim and you are supposed to act the drunkard and I the fool; and nevertheless I'll give you a story about two dead men. That's final. All I can do for you is give you this advice: if your nerves are weak, don't read this tale before going to sleep.

I

Chlavne, a short, dark, heavy-set man, had always loved a drink. Fortunately he was brought up in a decent and temperate home, or he would surely have grown up a drunkard. I do not guarantee that it was only his upbringing that saved him from a drunkard's fate. It is possible that in spite of that he might have been able to outdrink a squad of cannoneers, if only he had the means. But his wife Gittel managed all his finances and did not let him have a *Groshen* to spend. Wherever money was involved Gittel took care of it. The work itself, the labor that earned their bread, was done by Chlavne (he was, alas, a shoemaker), but when the work was finished it was Gittel who delivered it and collected the money. And naturally Chlavne was not pleased with this state of affairs.

"What do you think I am? A thief — or what?"

That is what Chlavne said to his wife Gittel, and he received a clear, unequivocal answer on the spot.

"Heaven forbid! Who said you were a thief? All you are is a soak. Do you dare tell me you aren't?"

To deny it outright was not easy. And yet to go ahead and confess that he loved to take the bitter drop was not so agreeable either. So he took refuge in a pun, as he frequently did, because Chlavne the shoemaker was fond not only of a glass of brandy, but also of a quip, a pun, a pithy saying, for he was a true Kasrielevkite. So he scratched his beard, looked up at the ceiling, and said:

"Listen to the woman! All she can say is soak. Soak! If I have a bottle in my hand, do I ever soak anybody with it? All I do is drink it."

"Oh, go to the devil!" his wife sputtered.

"Together with you, beloved, I'd go through the fires of hell."

"Here, go with this!" cried Gittel, and from the other side of the room she heaved a boot at him. This, too, Chlavne caught with a laugh, and he replied with a quip, as always.

And what did he do when Gittel came home with some money and handed him a few *Groshen* to go buy thread and wax and brushes? He became soft as butter and sweet as honey. And his respect for women in general and Gittel in particular rose immediately. He stroked his high, white forehead (all shoemakers have high, white foreheads) and mused thoughtfully, philosophically:

"I can't understand what a wise man like King Solomon had against you women. Do you know what King Solomon said about women? Or don't you?"

"Who cares what King Solomon said? You go to the

market for thread and wax and brushes. And see that you don't lose your way in some tavern."

At this far-fetched idea, Chlavne burst out laughing.

"Next you'll be telling me not to wear my heavy mittens in July, or eat *Matzah* on *Yom Kippur!* Which way is the market place and which way are the taverns? And besides, who would think, in the middle of the week, on a working day, of going off for a drink?"

But even while he was talking he was counting the money Gittel had given him by transferring it, coin by coin, from one hand to the other and, looking philosophically up at the ceiling with one eye closed, was figuring out exactly how much he would need for thread, how much for wax and how much for brushes. And with a deep, deep sigh he quietly went out of the house, and straight to the tavern.

II

Who was that wise man, that sage, who after deep thought announced that on Purim all drunkards are sober? I doubt if he knew what he was talking about. Why should a drunkard miss his chance on a day when it is fitting and proper for everybody to get drunk as a lord? The first to protest against a notion like that would have been Chlavne the shoemaker. How eagerly he awaited that one day! What agony he suffered before it came! And when it finally arrived he went to the synagogue with everybody else, to settle his account with Haman and hang him up on a gallows fifty ells high together with his ten sons. And afterwards, instead of going home to taste the festive *Hamantash*, he stopped off for a while at the homes of one or two of his shoemaker friends, old comrades of the bottle, for a holiday toast. "May the good Lord spare Haman and his ten sons for another year so we can get together next Purim and hang them again on a fifty-ell gallows and take another drink in their honor. Amen."

And after this series of toasts our hero became so foggy that no matter how far he went, no matter how many corners he turned, he was unable to find his way home. It began to look as if the street in which he lived had decided to play hide-and-go-seek with him. There it was in front of him, winking to him with all the flickering candles in all the small windows, and when he took another step he found himself bumping his forehead into a wall. Where did the wall come from? As long as he could remember, there had never been a wall here in the middle of the street. Someone must have put up a woodshed here. Imagine the impudence — building woodsheds right in the middle of the street! Who would dare do a thing like that? It must have been Yossi the *Nogid's* doings. But he'd never get away with it!

"As sure as my name is Ahasuerus, King of Persia!" cried Chlavne, and he reached up both hands to tear down the wall that Yossi the *Nogid* had dared to build right in the middle of the street. But just then the wall moved away, Chlavne lost his balance, and stretched himself out like a baron, full length in the famous Kasrielevky mud.

And there let us leave him for a while, till we have introduced you to the second hero of our tale, a man who was known in our town by the glorious and opulent name of — Rothschild.

III

He was given the name of Rothschild in Kasrielevky obviously because he was the poorest man in town. Though poor people were as numerous in Kasrielevky as the stars in heaven, a pauper as completely wretched and miserable as he could not be duplicated even there. There is a proverb (it must have originated in Kasrielevky) that it takes a special kind of luck to be that unlucky. And as you know, every proverb is founded on truth.

As long as this poor man had been known as Rothschild no one in Kasrielevky had ever seen him approach anyone with a plea for food, a request for drink or lodging, although every one knew very well that he was always hungry and had no place to lay his head. In Kasrielevky there are experienced authorities on the subject of hunger, one might even say specialists. On the darkest night, simply by hearing your voice, they can tell if you are simply hungry and would like a bite to eat, or if you are really starving. No doubt they have their symptoms to judge by, like doctors who prod you here and there and can tell if you are slightly indisposed or are on the verge of giving up your ghost.

If we are to distinguish between the various degrees of hunger, between those who are simply hungry and those who are dead-hungry, we must say without hesitation that our hero Rothschild was in the rank of the dead-hungry. He was a man who frequently went along for days on end with nothing at all in his mouth. And more than once he would surely have passed out right on the broad highway if some kind soul had not of his own accord noticed that here was that unfortunate wretch, Rothschild. If you gave him something he did not refuse it, but if you asked him if he was hungry he never answered. And if you asked if he was very hungry he still did not answer, but his yellow, emaciated face wrinkled up into something like a smile and his frightened eyes looked down, apparently ashamed that a person could ever be as hungry as he was, and a weak little sigh stole out unwillingly. And who knows what that sigh meant?

It is possible that there would have been plenty of people in Kasrielevky to look after him and he would not have had to hunger at all. But who is to blame if this penniless wretch would rather die than hold out his hand for help? And besides, is Kasrielevky expected to support every pauper who comes her way? Do not the people have troubles and heartaches and anxieties enough of their own in their struggle for a livelihood? They thank the Lord that they are able to survive the day and live through the week with their wives and children.

And yet — let the truth be known — when the Holy Sabbath came around, Rothschild was provided for. All Kasrielevky was in the synagogue that day, and Rothschild was in front of their eyes. And seeing him there, would the people let him go hungry — on the Sabbath? After all, an extra person at the table means only that you lay another spoon. So one family or another would take him home.

Great is the power of the Holy Sabbath! On that day you would scarcely recognize the householder of Kasrielevky, or his guest, the derelict Rothschild.

IV

Having fasted the whole day according to custom, the good householders of Kasrielevky finally saw the sun sinking and hastened to the synagogue to celebrate the Purim services, to chant the Book of Esther and take revenge on Haman. And having hurried through the final prayers standing on one foot, the hungry Kasrielevkites rushed out in a body the quicker to come home and the quicker to break the fast, each one under his own grapevine and his own fig tree, with a fresh, warm *Hamantash* full of poppyseed. And in their great haste and desire to partake of food they completely forgot about Rothschild, as if there had never been a Rothschild in the whole world. And Rothschild, seeing that everyone was hurrying, hurried off too, with his short strides, over the muddy roads and alleys of the blessed Kasrielevky, without knowing where he was going.

Running past the half-fallen and dimly lighted shacks and cottages, from time to time our hungry hero stole a glance through a window and saw cheeks and jaws and necks, chewing and grinding and swallowing. What the bulging cheeks enclosed, what the jaws were grinding and the necks were swallowing, he could not see, but he felt fairly certain that it must be those sweet and fresh and wonderful triangular *Hamantashen*, stuffed with honeyed poppyseed that melted in your mouth and tasted like something in Eden. And something woke inside of Rothschild and pulled at his heart and said to him, "Fool, why do you wander around in the darkness? Open one of those doors, go into the house and say, 'Good evening and a happy Purim. Do you have something that a person can break his fast with? It is the third day now since I have eaten anything.' " And Rothschild became frightened by his boldness. Such a thought had never come to him before — to force his way into a stranger's house like a thief! And lest his Evil Spirit take hold of him again, he turned from the houses directly into the middle of the road where the mud was deepest, and in the darkness collided with something soft and broad and alive, and before he could regain his balance fell headlong over our hero number one — Chlavne the shoemaker.

Let us leave our Rothschild alone for a while and find out how Chlavne the shoemaker was doing.

V

Chlavne the shoemaker (we beg his pardon a hundred times for letting him lie in the mud so long) did not feel nearly as wretched in his new surroundings as the reader would imagine. It is an old-established trait of man to adapt himself to his surroundings, no matter how unfavorable they might be. As soon as he found that before resuming his journey he was destined to pause a while in this bed of mud, the famous Kasrielevky mud, he saw to it that he did it like a man, productively, and not idly and wastefully. Without rest and without pause he proceeded to pour his wrath out on the wealthy of the earth, and especially on Yossi the *Nogid*. Did Yossi think that he, Chlavne, was drunk? He swore on his honor that he was not. Who could have started that rumor that he, Chlavne, was a drunkard? It must have been that wife of his, Vashti.

And having uttered the name Vashti, Chlavne the shoe-maker became silent and thoughtful. This name — Vashti — came back to his mind again and again like nails being hammered into a shoe. He remembered quite clearly that his wife's name used to be Gittel — and now suddenly it was Vashti! How did that happen? Gittel-Vashti? And it was not only her name. Everything else about her was changed, too. She was dressed like a queen with a golden crown, and everything she wore from head to foot was gold. He decided that this was not the time to start a fight with her. With a beauty like that you made your peace. And he pulled himself through the mud, closer and closer to her; but she drew away. She spurned him. Apparently because of his other passion, drink. The devil take her! She was too proud to have people think that her husband was a drunkard!

"May I never live to get up from this spot if I ever let another drop of brandy touch my lips!" he swore.] "Do you hear, Vashti? If you don't believe me, here is my hand. I promise. . ."

And Chlavne stretched out the thick, blackened hand with its stubby black fingers in the mud — and he was surprised to find that Vashti's hand was wet and cold and Vashti's fingers were damp and slippery. It was impossible to put one's arms around a woman like that. And once more he held out his arms, and embraced — the bony, shivering body of the unhappy Rothschild.

VI

Philosophers tell you that many things can happen as a result of a shock. A woman can have a miscarriage because of a sudden fright. If the shock is great enough a person can go out of his mind, and in some cases — Heaven forbid! — it has even been suggested that it was possible for a drunkard to become suddenly sober. So say the philosophers. And, therefore, we should not be too much surprised to learn that as soon as our hero, Chlavne the shoemaker, had embraced the unfortunate Rothschild, he too became sober. That is, not entirely sober, not sober enough to pick himself out of the mud and stand like a man, but enough to make him regain his senses one by one. First of all, through his sense of touch, he became aware that Vashti was a man with a beard. Then, with the return of his sense of hearing, he made out these words distinctly: *"Shema Yisroel!* Help! Help! Save me!"* Through his sense of sight he became aware that the two of them were lying in the mud, in the thick, suffocating Kasrielevky mud. But try as he might, he could not distinguish the person who was in his arms, for just then the moon had hidden behind a thick cloud and the dark night had spread its sable wings over all of Kasrielevky.

Rothschild too began slowly to collect his thoughts. His deathly fear gradually disappeared, and together our heroes recovered their speech. And what they said shall now be repeated, word for word:

CHLAVNE: Who are you?

ROTHSCHILD: It's me.

CHLAVNE: What are you doing here?

ROTHSCHILD: Not a thing.

CHLAVNE: How the devil did you get here?

ROTHSCHILD: I don't know.

CHLAVNE: Don't you know anything at all? What are you? One of us? A shoemaker?

ROTHSCHILD: No.

CHLAVNE: What then? A businessman?

ROTHSCHILD: Oh, no! No!

CHLAVNE: Then what on earth are you? Do you know? What are you?

ROTHSCHILD: I'm. . . . I'm. . . . dead. . . . hungry. . .

CHLAVNE: So that's the story? You're dead-hungry, and I'm dead-drunk. But wait! If I'm not mistaken, aren't you Mr. Rothschild? Of course. I knew you at once. If that's the case, Brother Rothschild, maybe it would be a good idea if you helped me crawl out of this mud, and then if you are strong enough the two of us can go to my house and have a bite to eat. Something tells me that there is some sort of holiday being celebrated today. *Simhat Torah?* Purim? I'm not sure which, but I know it's a holiday. If all the kings of the east and west insisted that it wasn't, I'd. . .I'd spit in their faces! . . . .

It took a little while before the two of them managed to drag themselves out of the mud, and with great effort they started on their way, each one holding on to the other. That is, Rothschild was doing his best to keep Chlavne upright, because so far only the shoemaker's head had sobered up. His feet still went this way and that. And when they came to. . . .

But at this point let us leave both our heroes, and let us glance for a moment into the home of Chlavne the shoemaker, to see how his wife Gittel was getting along.

VII

No matter how much she may be criticized by cynics, no matter how much the humorists may joke about her, a wife is still a wife. As soon as it was dark, Gittel began to get things ready for her husband who ought to be coming home soon from the synagogue after his long day of fasting. In his behalf she spread a festive tablecloth and brought out those things that Chlavne loved so well — a bottle and a glass. It is possible that the bottle held no more than a single glassful or perhaps, in recognition of the holiday, enough for two glasses. On the other hand, the *Hamantash* which she placed on the table was a huge one. It was a giant of a *Hamantash*, rich and golden, with honeyed poppy-seed oozing out of its three corners. It cried aloud to be eaten. You could almost hear it plead: "Chlavne, where are you? Chlavne, come eat me!" But Chlavne did not hear. At that moment he was sitting with the other shoemakers pouring long drinks in honor of the Holy Purim.

In vain did the shoemaker's wife look out of the window, in vain did she listen for a sound at the door. Every step she heard outside sounded like Chlavne's. But Chlavne was not walking just then. Chlavne was stretched out in the deep mud, whispering to Vashti. Gittel thought all the thoughts that a wife could ever think about her husband, but when it became really late she tore her jacket off its hook, threw it over her shoulders, and went out to search for Chlavne. She did not find him. The shoemakers with whom he had stopped to take a few drinks in honor of the holiday swore that they hoped they would not live till next Purim if Chlavne had not hurried straight home from the synagogue. And they swore that not one of them has so much as touched a single drop that evening.

VIII

Sad and dejected, Gittel came home again, glanced at the *Hamantash* on the table, and it seemed to her that the *Hamantash* looked back at her and said: "What's the matter with Chlavne?" In her grief she threw herself on the bed and lay there so long that she fell asleep. She dreamt that someone knocked on the window and called her by name. Without moving she asked, "Who is that?" And she received the answer that it was Hanna-Zissel and the *Shammes* of the burial society who had come to her for a shroud. Gittel felt so faint that she could not understand where she got the strength to ask as coldly as she might ask the butcher for a chicken-wing: "Were they burned to death?" "Yes, they were burned to death." "Both together?" "Together."

In terror she sat up and heard something stirring on the other side of the door, as if several hands were passing over it. She was barely able to ask:

"Who is that?"

"Us."

"Who is us?"

"Unlock the door and you'll see."

"The door is unlocked."

"But we can't find the handle."

Gittel recognized her husband's voice. She sprang to the door, opened it, and saw two creatures covered with mud like some fiends from the depths of the earth. At this sight she leaped back.

"Happy Purim, my Gittel," said one of them, staggering into the room without letting go of his companion. "I'll swear that my name isn't Chlavne," he went on, "that you'll never guess who has come to see you. You have two guests for Purim, Gittel. Two dead men. . . . God in heaven, Gittel, why do you look so scared? . . . . .Yes, we are dead,

but we do not come from the Other World. One of us is
dead drunk, the other dead hungry. And which is drunk
and which is hungry you'll have to guess for yourself. . . .

"What are you staring for, Gittel? Don't you know who
this is? It's Rothschild. May Reb Yossi sink into the earth
together with the Kasrielevky mud! Rothschild is so covered
with mud that you can't recognize him. You'd think he'd
been rolling around in a pigsty."

Chlavne looked around the room, looked long at the
table.

"Do you know, Gittel? You're a wise and thoughtful
woman. Compared to you, Vashti is a silly little hen.
You've put a bottle on the table, I see. Something told you
what a holiday the whole world is celebrating today, and
how we ought to celebrate it — with a prayer and a drink
and a *Hamantash*. To your health, Rothschild! May the
Lord save Haman for another year, so we can hang him
again with his ten sons on one gallows, fifty ells high!

"Gittel — why don't you say amen?"

THE JUDGMENTS OF REB YOZIFEL[2]*

MAURICE SAMUEL

Based on the story by Sholom Aleichem

"Lilies that fester smell far worse than weeds," sang a
poet unknown to old Kasrielevky — a poet old Kasrielevky
might have loved because as many commentaries have been
written on him as on the Talmud, and as many interpretations grown up round his text as round that of the Torah.
The Kasrielevkites were so organically interpenetrated
with religion that they had nothing to be good with except

*Pp. 90–101 from *The World of Sholom Aleichem* by Maurice Samuel by permission of Alfred A. Knopf, Inc. Copyright 1943 by Maurice Samuel.

religion, and nothing to be bad with except religion. (Some-where among the old prayers there is one which runs approx-imately thus: "O Lord, let me worship Thee not only with my good inclination, but also with my evil inclination.")

Shalah Monot, the sending round of sweetmeats on the festival of Purim, was not a religious rite, properly speaking. But it had a semi-religious character, and in any case it was a charming tradition; certainly it added, or was supposed to add, to the jol-lity of the celebration and the sweetness of life.

The Kasrielevkites sent one another plates of *Ha-mantashen*, of *Teiglah*, tiny squares of dough boiled in honey, chopped nuts and spices, of cakes, tarts, bis-cuits, cookies, scones with raisins and scones with cur-rants; they sent one another everything that the inge-nuity of the housewife could devise with flour, eggs, milk, sugar, fruits, and an oven. All day long, as we have seen, boys and girls, messengers and maid-servants, scurried through the streets of Kasrielevky, carrying gifts and return gifts from neighbor to neighbor, acquaintance to acquaintance, relative to relative and re-ceiving a little cash reward — Purim money. A lovely and gracious tradition it was, which gave a special tone and color to Purim, the most secular of the festivals.

26. *PURIM DISH*   Pottery

18th Century

Lovely and gracious, that is to say, in the spirit, and for that matter in the execution too, most of the time. But how can one ensure a lovely and gracious tradition against petrifaction into the formal and snobbish? How can we prevent the gifts of Father's Day and Mother's Day and Wedding Day and Birthday and Christmas from degenerating into — well, into missiles instead of missives? Consider a housewife of Kasrielevky, with her Purim list of relatives, in-laws, friends and acquaintances, each one of whom had to be considered individually. There were gradations and standards and precedents, featherweight distinctions in the sending and return of *Shalah Monot*; particularly in the return, if you happened to be the first recipient. For instance, two *Hamantashen*, five cookies, a currant scone, and a slice of honey cake called exactly for one *Hamantash*, two tarts, eight biscuits, and a raisin scone or its equivalent, three slices of honey cake, a slab of *Teiglah*, two currant scones, and three cookies. Of course, the size of the slices and the density of the baking also entered into the reckoning.

You had to know your way about these usages; it was a question of feeling rather than of weights and measures. You had to be the possessor of a massive memory, as well as of a delicate sense of social values. For a disparity in gifts was permissible, or, rather, expected, as between the poor and the well-to-do; the former were not abashed to receive a plateful of good things out of all proportion to their own sending; the latter did not expect in return more than a token greeting. But God help you if you sent more than you received to one whose inferior status was not established and acknowledged; or less than you received if your own inferiority was not similarly established and acknowledged. The *Nogid*, or rich man, ranked everybody except the other *Negidim*; the trustees of the synagogue were in the upper brackets; the rabbi, the cantor, and the ritual slaughterer were in the middle class for substance, but high up for honors. There were class and personal distinctions, individual and group subtleties — all in all an etiquette as complicated as the hierarchies of the Byzantine court and the rigid ceremonial compulsions of the hidalgos. And people knew their rights and stood on them.

A particular sense of delicacy was needed by the first sender of *Shalah Monot*, especially as the gifts might be crossing and still had to correspond to the weights and measures of the code. Here was where memory came in, the *Shalah Monot* of previous years, the relative standing of the parties, and the interpretation thereof in *Shalah Monot* rating.

How deep the code went, and what calamities might follow from the contravention of it, we learn from the incident of the two Nehamahs, or rather of their employers. Nehamah the black and Nehamah the red were two servant girls. Nehamah the black worked for Zlota, the wife of Reb Isaac the storekeeper, and her pay was four and a half roubles the season — six months — with clothes and shoes. Nehamah the red worked for Zelda, the wife of Reb Yossie the storekeeper, and her pay was six roubles the season, no clothes and shoes. On a certain muddy Purim — that is to say, on a certain Purim, for the festival occurs in the early spring, when the unpaved streets and alleys of Kasrielevky were covered by six inches of ooze — Nehamah the red and Nehamah the black came face to face as they were carrying their covered trays of *Shalah Monot*, Nehamah the red on her way to the employers of Nehamah the black, and vice versa. A happy meeting! The girls were tired with delivering gifts in all quarters of the town. So they sat down on a doorstep to swap experiences, compare tips, and revile their employers.

Thence they proceeded to show each other the contents of their respective trays. Nehamah the black was the bearer of an appetizing square of strudel, two big honey cakes, a fish-shaped cake stuffed with ground nuts and sugar, and a slab of poppyseed cake rich with honey. Nehamah the red carried a fat *Hamantash*, black with poppyseed, two "cushion cakes," so called from their shape and softness, a golden cookie starred with black raisins, a slab of tart, and two cherub cakes. As any Kasrielevkite expert could have told you, the gifts were balanced to a nicety, both in respect of each other and of the relative social status of the senders.

Who would have thought that from this casual encounter of two servant girls would ensue a cause célèbre never to be forgotten in the annals of Kasrielevky? And who but a Kasrielevkite could understand, and even sympathize with, the circumstances? Beginning with loose, idle talk, the two Nehamahs, tired and hungry, as well as rebellious and envious, passed from the scrutiny of each other's trays to the consideration of conspiracy. What would be the harm, they asked, if an equal quantity of sweetmeats were removed from each tray, leaving the balance where it had been? Thus, if the strudel disappeared from the tray of Nahamah the black, and the golden cookie from the tray of Nehamah the red, the gifts of Zlota the wife of Reb Isaac and of Zelda the wife of Reb Yossie would still be perfectly matched. One could go further: if a honey cake faded from the tray of Nehamah the black, accompanied by a cushion cake from the tray of Nehamah the red, the equilibrium would still remain undisturbed. And was it not more fitting that the said strudel and honey cake and cookie and cushion cake should go to the feeding of the stomachs of the Nehamahs rather than the vanity of their employers?

Said and done; which showed they were only two foolish servant girls; for they left two fatal considerations out of the count. Zelda the wife of Reb Yossie and Zlota the wife of Reb Isaac would remember what they sent, but see only what they received. There was, moreover, the unalterable status established and maintained throughout the years.

Thus it was: Nehamah the black brought her depleted shipment to Zelda, the wife of Reb Yossie, who uncovered the tray, took one glance, and uttered a shriek which woke from his afternoon nap her husband Yossie — Yossie the Washrag as the Kasrielevkites had named him because he was the most henpecked husband in Kasrielevky.

"Tell your mistress," hissed Zelda to Nehamah the black, "that I hope she lives till next Purim and doesn't get a nicer *Shalah Monot* than this from anyone in town."

Nehamah the red brought her diminished offering to Zlota, the wife of Reb Isaac, who uncovered the tray and almost fainted. She could not call to her husband, Reb Isaac, because he was not at home. One-a-year Isaac was *his* nickname, because every year, without fail, his wife brought forth a baby. That was the way of the Kasrielevkites; they gave a man a nickname and it stuck. Reb Isaac might live to the age of ninety, and cease to procreate at the age of seventy, but it would be One-a-year Isaac till the day of his death.

"Look at this *Shalah Monot*," gasped Zlota. "May all the nightmares of my life, and the nightmares of the lives of all my ancestors, be visited upon the heads of my enemies! Is this a *Shalah Monot* or a joke? Take this back to your miserable mistress, do you hear?" Wherewith the wife of One-a-year Isaac thrust out of doors Nehamah the red and sent her back to Zelda, the wife of Yossie the Washrag.

It would have been bad enough if One-a-year Isaac and Yossie the Washrag had been mere acquaintances. They were friends, which was odd enough since their two dry-goods stores stood side by side on the market-place and they were forever snatching away each other's customers. But they were friends. They lent each other a couple of roubles now and again, they came to each other's homes on Friday evenings for the Sabbath benediction, and in the winter they went into each other's stores to warm up at the stove or play a game of checkers. Their wives, too, were on friendly terms, exchanging pots and scandal, pouring out their hearts to each other, and taking counsel on their domestic problems. Friends have, of course, larger foundations on which to erect a quarrel than mere acquaintances. On the morning following this Purim, Reb Yossie the Washrag and One-a-year Isaac, well primed by their respective wives, opened their adjacent stores as usual and stationed themselves at their respective doors, each one waiting for the other to say "Good morning" in order that he might not answer. Customers being scarce that raw spring day, Reb Yossie and Reb Isaac stood there grimly, hour after hour, till their wives arrived.

"Isaac," said Zlota, acidulously, "why don't you thank your friend for the wonderful *Shalah Monot* he sent us yesterday?"

"Yossie," said Zelda, poisonously, "have you returned adequate thanks for the noble present you received?"

"I don't speak to a Washrag," announced Reb Isaac loudly.

"I wouldn't answer a One-a-year," responded Reb Yossie.

There you had it! The battle was joined. In less time than it takes to put on a prayer-shawl, the husbands were in each other's beards, the wives in each other's hair. The market-place came to life; half the town assembled to separate the combatants or to join in the mêlée. The air was filled with questions and answers: "*Shalah Monot*," "insult," "*Shalah Monot*," "fit for a beggar," "*Shalah Monot*," "*Shalah Monot*,""*Shalah Monot*." Before the day was over, One-a-year Isaac and Yossie the Washrag invaded the office of the prefect, Pan Milinievsky, to lodge charges of libel, assault and battery, and malicious slander. With them came their wives, relatives, acquaintances and enemies.

It is as shocking to report as it would be dishonest to deny that recourse to Pan Milinievsky the Gentile on matters connected exclusively with internal Jewish differences was only too frequent. Particularly was this true in the autumn, round the time of the festival of Booths and *Simhat Torah*, the Rejoicing for the Law. But no season of the year was exempt from such scandals. There could always be an explosion over precedence in the synagogue, over privileges denied or honors misplaced. Feivel, the son of Chantze Mirke, got the most coveted section of the Torah to read out on a Sabbath morning when obviously it should have gone to Chaim, the son of Leah Dvosse; Kiveh One-eye was called twice in one month to roll up the sacred Scroll, and Deaf Itzig not even once in two months. Pan Milinievsky, a Russian with a high forehead and a vast beard, had been prefect of Kasrielevky so long that he spoke Yiddish like a native and even understood something about the delicate problems of precedence and social status in the synagogue. A decent enough man, considering that he was a Gentile and an official; reasonable enough in the taking of bribes and, though an antisemite, devoid of viciousness. A trifle impatient, though, as he showed again on this occasion. For having tried for over an hour to get a word in edgewise between accusations and counter-accusations of Zlota, Zelda, Isaac, Yossie, and their partisans, he rose to his feet and roared: "Get out! Get out! The whole kit and kaboodle! Go to your rabbi!"

So the litigants and their partisans streamed toward the house of Reb Yozifel, the old and honored rabbi.

Patient, wise, long-suffering Reb Yozifel!

Reb Yozifel's home has been invaded by the tumultuous crowd turned away so unceremoniously by Pan Milinievsky. And here the scene was repeated, with this difference, that Reb Yozifel made no attempt to wedge in a word. He let the hours pass while the room resounded with the clamor of accusation and counter-accusation: *"Hamantash," "Shalah Monot,"* "insult," "beggarly," "Washrag," "One-a-year."

They quieted down at last and demanded judgment, which Reb Yozifel, as *Rab*, was bound to render. Never had he been known to fail in this duty, no matter how complicated or embittered the dispute. Indeed, Reb Yozifel was famous for his judgments — not less than for his sanctity.

But before judgment came the summation of the case, which Reb Yozifel began with a heart-broken sigh.

"We stand," he said, "on the threshold of the Passover, the great, the holy festival — the festival, it may be said, without an equal. Thousands and thousands of years ago our ancestors went forth from Egypt in freedom, and traversed the Red Sea dryshod. What a festival! What a sea! What a miracle! Forty years they wandered thereafter in the wilderness, having received the Torah at the foot of Sinai, that marvellous Torah in which it is written *ve'ohabto*, and thou shalt love, *le-re-eko*, thy neighbor, *komoko*, as thyself. Ah, what a Torah God gave us! And how shall we honor it? With quarrels, with foolish disputes, with vanities? Is it not a desecration to prepare thus for the Passover? Come, children, we have serious business before us. We must begin to consider what shall be done in this town of ours for the poor, who must celebrate the Passover like all the others. Have we yet made a list of what they need, in the way of eggs and potatoes and chicken-fat — not to mention *Matzot*, of course? But stay! There is a quarrel to be composed, a judgment rendered. Let us begin the summation once more. The Passover is approaching! The Passover! What a festival! Our forefathers went out of Egypt in freedom, and traversed the Red Sea dryshod. And after that they wandered forty years in the wilderness, having received the

Torah at the foot of Sinai! What a Torah! A Torah without an equal! Do you know what that means!..."

And so Reb Yozifel went on with his summation, in his
weak, sad voice, and one by one the partisans began to sneak
from the room; one by one they withdrew, and after them
the litigants, each one going thoughtfully and shamefacedly
home, to wonder what the excitement had been about, and
to prepare for the great and holy festival of the Passover.

Could King Solomon have done better?

PURIM GIFTS[3]

Samuel J. Agnon

When the season of Purim arrived, the bridegroom's
father in Rohatin sent the father of the bride at Brod gold
earrings and a pair of bracelets of pure gold, as befits the
wealthy, together with a honey cake plaited like a Sabbath
loaf, all of them as gifts for the bride. As generally happens
when there are two of the same name in a town and valuable
gifts are sent to one, to whom should they be delivered if
not to the wealthier of them. And so when these gifts were
brought to Brod for Reb Yudel Nathanson, to whom should
they be delivered? Surely to the famous and wealthy
Reb Yudel.

And Reb Yudel Nathanson was astonished at these gifts,
coming from he knew not whom and intended for he knew
not whom; for there was no point in sending bridal jewelry
to Reb Yudel Nathanson who was childless, the Merciful
One deliver us. He even began to reckon that somebody who
had borrowed money from him and never repaid his debt
had now repented but, being ashamed of himself, had put
his money in jewelry and repaid him to the value of his debt.
But his wife pointed out: When a man sends a gift to
another, he will send him something that will be of use;

there's no sense in sending a bald man a comb, or gloves to a man without hands. Which, he said, leaves the problem where it was. Well, said she, they are probably for Miriam and were sent in her name, Miriam being the daughter of Reb David Nathanson, Reb Yudel's brother, who had previously been married to the great Gaon Reb Zev Frankel, who had been the rabbi of the Tailor's Synagogue at Brod, but had been divorced following a quarrel; and Reb Yudel's wife thought that meantime she had been engaged to another man who had sent her these gifts for Purim.

So Reb Yudel sent to ask his brother: Has Miriam become engaged? No, his brother sent a message back. And is a match being arranged? He went on to ask again. No, came the answer. Then whose are these jewels and ornaments? Reb Yudel sent to ask him. Why, yours, came the reply. But I haven't any daughter, Reb Yudel sent to remind his brother. But it stands to reason, his brother sent to remind him: Your name's written on the packet and they don't belong to you; then how much less are they mine, whose name isn't written on the packet.

In that case, said Reb Yudel Nathanson at last, it would appear that there must be two Reb Yudel Nathansons in Brod, but I'm well known and the other one isn't. Well, tomorrow's Purim when a large number of people come to visit me; I'll ask them if they know of the other Yudel Nathanson and send the things on to him.

And on the morrow Reb Yudel Nathanson sat at the head of his table with a cloth spread and the table covered with all manner of dainties; and there were two big dishes before him, one full of silver coins and one of copper; and he was wearing his festival clothes and smoking his pipe and studying the tractate on Purim while people came in and went out; wardens of charity and householders who had come down in the world, may the Merciful One deliver us, and the poor and needy and tramps and loafers and Purim players and people wearing masks, with musical instruments and weird faces and foolishness. And they all danced and made merry in honor of Purim, while he poured each one out a glass of wine and treated them to the cakes known as Haman's ears; and when they were about to leave he would give each one something in accordance with his standing and ask him: Do you know the wealthy Reb Yudel Nathanson? And they would all answer: Is there anybody in Brod who doesn't know the wealthy Reb Yudel Nathanson, long life to him, and would point at him with their fingers. No, he would answer, I'm not speaking of myself but of somebody else with the same name, very wealthy, with a lot of money. No, they would respond, we've neither seen nor heard of such. For who would remind himself of the Hasid, when the talk was of wealthy folk, and particularly as Reb Yudel, the Hasid, was not called by his family name but was known as Yudel Student.

What did the wealthy Reb Yudel do thereupon? Began cross-questioning newcomers and trying to confuse them, asking: How much did you get this morning from the wealthy Reb Yudel Nathanson? No, not from me, but from the other fellow of the same name. And he asked again: Which of you will take Purim gifts to that wealthy Reb Yudel Nathanson? No, not to me but to the other one in town. And folk smiled, thinking he must be tipsy and no longer able to tell the difference between "Curst be Haman" and "Blest be Mordecai;" which is a fit and proper state to be in on Purim. So seeing that the line he was following did not accord with his self-respect, Reb Yudel desisted. Time will tell, said he to himself.

In brief, those went and others came, some for themselves, and some for others while others were going about for them, since more is received when you go round for others than when you come in, poor and ashamed, on your own behalf and have not the courage to make demands. Some wore Gentile garb, and some Gentiles there wore Jewish clothes. And not a single one of all these callers had reason for complaint against the generosity of Reb Yudel Nathanson.

Reb Yudel Hasid also went forth to collect for the poor, since there were poorer folk even than he; and he wished to make himself a pair of boots so that he should not suffer the fate of the barefoot saint who revealed himself after his demise wearing fine raiment and precious, but barefoot and unshod. Rabbi, his pupils asked him, how is it that your whole body is covered with such fine clothes while your feet are bare? My sons, said he, my body which carried out the commandments and performed good deeds has been garbed in fine array; but my feet which never ran to solicit alms for the poor have been left barefoot.

On the way Reb Yudel turned in at the house of Reb Yudel Nathanson, where he met Nuta who had come to rejoice the wealthy man's heart on the festival. And so it came about that Reb Yudel stood in the presence of Reb Yudel without the one knowing that the man he sought for was in his presence, and without the other knowing that the man in whose presence he was sought him; in order that greater things and yet more wonderful might come about.

And Reb Yudel asked Reb Yudel: Do you perhaps know Reb Yudel Nathanson; I'm not speaking of myself but of some other very wealthy Reb Yudel with a lot of money. Reb Yudel remembered the incident of the Reb Yudel he had met at the house of Tobiah of Polikrif and said to himself: Here you are, even so wealthy a man as this isn't alone but has others of the same name as wealthy as he. And he rejoiced at heart that the All-Present had made rich and poor equal in this, and that just as there are poor men of identical name and identical needs, so there are wealthy men of

identical name and identical wealth. But he did not have
the means of giving Reb Yudel the information, for he did
not know any other Reb Yudel who was as wealthy as this
Reb Yudel; so he answered: Would that all the Lord's people
were well-to-do. Meanwhile Nuta remembered that when
he had been traveling the roads with Reb Yudel, the Hasid,
and the king's constable had asked Reb Yudel his name,
he had answered: Nathanson's my name; and he was already wishful of pointing to Reb Yudel. But such is the
way of those in whose heart the quality of truth has no fixed
and permanent place; even when the truth lights up in their
heart, it is hard for them to utter it at the mouth. For
Nuta considered to himself: What it's good to tell a Gentile
it's no good telling Reb Yudel Nathanson. And so he
remained silent.

And in Brod there were many jokers known as "Brod
singers" who used to relate all the troubles of the time in
rhyme and made up mocking songs. In the ordinary way
they are held of small esteem by decent Brod folk, but at
Purim they mount in the general regard, for their songs are
approved by reason of the joyfulness required for Purim.
Now these singers came to Reb Yudel Nathanson; one was
dressed as a Hasid and one as a wagoner; the latter told the
tale of all that had befallen them on the way and the former,
putting his hand to his ear, sang in tune and rhyme....

Never has such laughter been seen as that of Reb Yudel
Nathanson when he heard the ballad of Reb Yudel Hasid;
the very walls of the house laughed with him. After he had
regained control of himself he dug both his hands into the
dish and took out much money and said, Reb Yudel, I
also wish to take part in that great injunction of bringing
the bride under the canopy.

Reb Yudel Hasid thought that the householder could

only be speaking to him, and held out his hand. But somebody else was ahead of him, and that was the other Reb
Yudel who had put on the clothes like Reb Yudel's. Reb
Yudel stood staring at his person and could see no difference between the other and himself, neither in face nor
in garb nor in movements. And to whom could Reb Yudel
be compared at that moment? To the two-headed man
whose father died. Said the two-headed man: I'm a firstborn
and so entitled to a double share, and my second head is
another person and also entitled to a share of the inheritance.
Not so, said his brothers, you're only entitled to two portions, one for yourself and one for your birthright. So they
came to King Solomon for a decision. And what did he
do? Poured boiling water over the one head, and the other
began yelling; and that showed at once that they could
be counted as a single head and there was only one portion
between them. But the two-headed man at least received
a double portion, for himself and his birthright, but Reb
Yudel got nothing at all. So Reb Yudel said to Reb
Yudel, Reb Yudel has taken Yudel's share and Yudel hasn't
had anything from Reb Yudel, and put his hand out once
again to Reb Yudel. Thereupon Reb Yudel Nathanson
put his finger to his nose and said, After I've given you all
that you have to come and ask for more? For Reb Yudel
Nathanson could not distinguish between Reb Yudel and
the one who had disguised himself as Reb Yudel. Even if
you and I had been there we couldn't have distinguished
either between Reb Yudel Hasid and Reb Yudel, the Brod
singer; and that was even more the case with Reb Yudel
Nathanson who knew nothing about Reb Yudel or the
Reb Yudel who was not Reb Yudel, but was dressed in
clothes like those of Reb Yudel. And so Reb Yudel could not
go and ask again. Never in my life, said Reb Yudel, have I
seen rich men equal to one another, but poor men are

always the same and equal, sometimes even to their very faces.

Once Purim was over, the poor folk returned home and arranged to expend their money on their Passover require-ments, and the people with masks took them off and went back to work, and the wardens went out to collect wheat-money for the poor. Blest be the All-Present, blest be He for not forsaking His children without mercy, and for pro-viding them with good wardens, and for setting loving-kind-ness in the hearts of Israel so that he who doth not need to take doth give. Two charity wardens came to Reb Yudel Nathanson, and he began to converse with them at length in the hope that from their words he would learn something about another Reb Yudel Nathanson. Had the wardens come to him last of all after passing through the city from end to end, they would not have had the wherewithal to answer his questions; and still more was it the case when he was the first in the town that they came to. So he gave them his contribution, wondering all that while that there should be another Reb Yudel Nathanson in town whom nobody knew, for whoever he might ask pointed to him and said: The only Reb Yudel Nathanson we know is the one in front of us.

So then Reb Yudel said to his wife: Well, it's customary that when one man receives a gift from another he returns something in its stead; whom do we have to return some-thing to? For since he had been through the town and had not found his namesake he was sure that the gifts must be for him. Not that he had any daughter, but he thought that the other man who sent the gifts must be a wag of some kind.

Since he has sent us, said he, bridal array, we must send a bridegroom's trappings in return. Well said, Yudel, said his wife. After all, these gifts are worth quite a little money; whether he's fooling us to the value of a little money or we're fooling him to the value of a little money, the presents at least are very nice. Had the gifts come to the house of Reb Yudel Hasid, Pessele would have put on the earrings and the bracelets, and her face would have been bright as the summer sun and her heart would have been happy; and father and mother, seeing, would have known their salvation was close to hand; but since they had come into the hands of Reb Yudel Nathanson they only served to remind him of his wife's sorrow and his own that they had no children and no hope of seeing any child of theirs a bride.

So Reb Yudel and his wife considered the gift they should send. What shall I send him? he asked. A watch and chain? Why, he must have one of his own and what use is mine to him? Is he a little boy beginning to study the Pentateuch that has to be dressed up with such toys? Should I send him an amber pipe? And supposing he doesn't smoke, the nice present will induce him to smoke, and what's more he may come to think that my gift gives him authority even to take snuff on the First Day of the Festivals; and so he'd be led into error through me. But I'll send the four volumes of the Turim. The sort of person, said Reb Yudel, who wants to try and joke with me must certainly lack such staid and serious and authoritative compendia of the Torah as the Four Turim.

So he took a set of the Turim printed at Medziboz and Polnoa, for the printing of which he had donated money and had been sent two sets bound in wooden boards with red vellum covers and copper locks, and his name and the name of the part in gold lettering on each volume and a gold edging to the leaves and a ewer embossed on the cover, Reb Yudel Nathanson being a Levite and the printers making the necessary symbol in his honor since the Levite pours water over the hands of the priest at the time of the benediction. For himself, however, he kept the edition of Venice, since the Venice type is pleasant to read; and shortly before Passover he sent the set of Turim to the Holy Congregation of Rohatin and wrote a letter to the bridegroom in good style, and with the book wished all that was best/ from the bride rejoicing and blest/ whose heart was ever true/ to the lad she hoped to view/ a youth so fine and such a gem/ whoever saw them both would know they were of blessed stock and stem. And Reb Yudel's wife also took a turkey cock, tied its legs together and sent it as a gift to the groom's mother.

The gifts came to Rohatin. The bridegroom took the four volumes, said the blessing of gratitude for living to see the day so worthwhile a thing happened to him, and uttered blessings and praise/ to God's wonderful ways/ in choosing him rather than another lad/ and giving him these four Turim, and best to be had/ be with me still, O Lord, as Thou hast been hitherto/ and in Thy Torah day by day I'll show what I can do. And he at once began studying the Laws of Passover, refreshing himself between chapters with the stomach of the turkey cock and its stuffed neck and its liver. And meanwhile Reb Yudel Nathanson put the entire matter out of mind so that he forgot all about it.

CHAPTER X

PURIM IN POETRY

THE BANQUET OF ESTHER[1]

YEHUDAH HALEVI (1086–1142)

WHILE copious flowed the banquet wine,
 The king addressed his lovely queen.
"But ask, and all thou wilt I'll give."
 'Her tears now supplicate him.'

"O king, my lord, I humbly crave
 My life, and more my people's life.
For we are sold to bitter foe
 'Since thou didst yield before him.'

"What other wish could now be mine,
 With violence so rank afoot?
Could I betray my kin to fangs
 'Of beast that would devour him?' "

The king cried out: "What subject this,
 Or who in all my broad domain,
Or who among my creditors
 'Dare ween you're sold to please him?' "

She spake, "This Haman fell, malign,
 Who voids his venom on my folk."
O woe unto the evil man;
 'His plotting shall undo him.'

27. ESTHER'S BANQUET   Painting

Rembrandt, 1660

The king in wrath his garden paced;
    Returned, sees Haman abject, vile.
    The very skies revealed his guilt,
        'And earth rose up against him.'

A faithful chamberlain said, "See
    His gallows made for Mordecai."
    The king cried out, "Hang Haman high!
        'The gallows loomed before him.' "

Queen Esther urged her people's plight;
    The edict dire must be annulled.
    For how could one smite Israel!
        'Unless God planned to heal him?'

Forthwith an edict was prepared
   To arm the Jews against their foes.
Good Mordecai in power grew;
    'The peace of God possessed him.

His people breathed fair freedom's air
   When he was made Chief Minister
With honors great, in Haman's place
    'Of power to succeed him.'

Then Persia's Jews in self defence
   Rose up to guard themselves from hurt.
Through Haman's machinations foul
    'His sons met death beside him,'

Parshandatha, Dalfon, Aspatha,
   Poratha, Adalia, Aridatha,
Parmashta, Arisai, Aridai, Vaizatha.
    'The earth would not receive him.'

Delivered from the yawning grave,
   The Jews hurled back each fell assault.
God's succor strong upheld the weak
    'And poor with none to aid him.'

Be this now writ indelibly
   That age to age may ne'er forget,
And he who reads may sing, "Let man
    'Rejoice when God protects him.' "

So feast, good friends, go eat and drink;
   Purim shall be your merry feast.
But in your joy seek out the poor
    'With gifts; do not forget him.'

From ancient time God's providence
   Has borne me o'er engulfing tides.
For this my spirit counsels me,
    'Thy hope is God; await Him.'

THE SONG OF WATER[2]

SOLOMON IBN GABIROL (1021–1069)

When the store of wine was ended
From my weeping eye descended
    Streams of water, streams of water.

From the meat the taste is wrested:
Not the best can be digested
With the board of drink divested —
    Saving water, only water.

Moses a pursuing nation
Doomed to watery damnation:
Now my host in emulation
    Slays with water, slays with water.

See, my song is changed to croaking
Like the frog in marshes soaking,
With my lips like his invoking
    Gods of water, gods of water.

May the house that with the hated
Element its neighbors feted
Be forever dedicated
    Unto water, unto water.

THE BALLAD OF EPHRON, PRINCE OF TOPERS[3]

IMMANUEL BEN SOLOMON OF ROME (1270–1330)

Come listen to a merry song about a merry wight —
The sovereign of all topers he, Ephron the prince that hight;
He strict forbade that any lad who aimed to live aright
    Should ever drink a drop — a drop of water!

When with his court he sate at board, they always brought
  him first,
A bowl of twenty flagons for to slake his royal thirst;
Then he'd fall to, and crunch and chew until you thought he'd
  burst —
  But never stop to drink a drop — of water!

Each morn Prince Ephron said his prayers before he broke
  his fast —
"Good Lord!" he'd cry, "My mouth is dry, my tongue and lips
  stick fast;
My throat's on fire, my heart's a pyre, my frame's a furnace vast,
  O, quench my flame with drink — but not with water!

"Make haste, dear friends, for love of god and my immortal soul,
And fetch me good old white wine in my lordly silver bowl;
O, that's the thing to heart a king and make a sick man whole —
  But spoil it not, O spoil it not, with water!"

Prince Ephron kept the sacred days of Israel's faith. At least,
If fasts him irked, he never shirked a single holy feast;
And on the Days of Penitence, was none, in West or East,
  That, more than he, kept gullet — free from water.

Tebet would make him whine and fret; through Tammuz he
  would bawl;
And sore he'd moan and fast he'd groan in Ab for Zion's fall,
Till by the ninth too weak he'd grown, to try to fast at all;
  Yet still he strict abstained — from drinking water.

Yom Kippurim his eyes went dim, with anguish of the soul,
So by the *Din* it was no sin to call for plate and bowl;
But down his cheeks in salty streaks the tears of guilt would roll,
  And once in every year, he tasted water.

Amends, indeed, he made full meed. Each month he'd keep Purim
The four cups he made forty — every night *Leyl Shimurim;*
Sukkot, Shabuot, *Kiddush* and *Habdalah* were good to him —
  Be sure his cup of blessing wasn't water!

Whene'er it rained or threatened rain, at home would Ephron stay;
"If clouds were wine-vats and their showers strong drink," he
    used to say,
"I'd hie me out the storms to flout, and bask in them all day —
    'But what's the use of 'ifs,' " he said — "or water!"

"If 'stead of brine, the waves were wine, of vintage fine," quoth he,
"I'd wish to be a Jonah's fish a'swimming in the sea;
None other Eden would I ask to all eternity —
    But for our sins God made the sea of water!

"For had He sent a flood of wine — in Noah's time, you know,
Our patriarch had built no ark, to be shut in, below;
In such a tide, Oh, none had died — but all cut up Didò —
    And that's why rivers, rains and seas are water!"

Prince Ephron (peace upon his soul!) lies sleeping in the dust
Until that day when, sages say, the sinful and the just
Shall rise to meet their due reward. Then, let us humbly trust,
    Nor he, nor we, shall crave in vain for water!

SATIRE FOR PURIM[4]

JUDAH LEB BEN ZE'EV OF CRACOW (1764–1811)

My gullet is parched and my palate is burned,
Earth hath not water to quench such a thirst.
My head is wine-sodden, my senses are turned;
Drained all my moisture, my vigor dispersed.

Weak grow my steps, my feet slip and are smitten.
Shorter my paces, my feet trip and are hidden.
The light from my eyes has fled with their feeling.
Then up rise the walls and about me revolve.
They totter, they shake, they reel and they quake.
Till I cry that I've drunk pure rolling and reeling.

Turn ye away! Leave me! I'd sleep,
And find rest and new strength in my bed.
Then when I awake, I'll seek and drink deep
Of the redness that's wine
And the wine that's deep red.

REB ABRAHAM[5]

ABRAHAM M. KLEIN

Reb Abraham, the jolly,
Avowed the gloomy face
Unpardonable folly,
Unworthy of his race.

When God is served in revel
By all his joyous Jews,
(He says) the surly devil
Stands gloomy at the news.

Reb Abraham loved Torah,
If followed by a feast:
A *Milah*-banquet, or a
Schnapps to drink, at least.

On Sabbath-nights, declaring
God's praises, who did cram
The onion and the herring?
Fat-cheeked Reb Abraham.

On Ninth of Ab, who aided
The youngsters in their game
Of throwing burrs, as they did,
In wailing beards? The same.

And who on Purim came in
To help the urchins, when
They rattled at foul Haman?
Reb Abraham again.

On all feasts of rejoicing
Reb Abraham's thick soles
Stamped pious metres, voicing
Laudation of the scrolls.

Averring that in heaven
One more Jew had been crowned,
Reb Abraham drank even
On cemetery-ground.

And at Messiah's greeting,
Reb Abraham's set plan
Is to make goodly eating
Of roast leviathan.

When God is served in revel
By all His joyous Jews,
(He says) the surly devil
Stands gloomy at the news.

ESTHER[6]

(Extract)

JEAN BAPTISTE RACINE (1639-1699)

AHASUERUS

Believe me, dearest Esther,
This sceptre, and the homage fear inspires
Have little charm for me; the pomp of power
Is oft a burden to its sad possessor.
In thee, thee only, do I find a grace
That never palls nor loses its attraction.
How sweet the charm of loveliness and virtue!
In Esther breathes the very soul of peace
And innocence. Dark shadows flee before her,

She pours bright sunshine into days of gloom
With thee beside me seated on this throne
I fear no more the wrath of adverse stars;
My diadem, fair Esther, seems to borrow
A lustre from thy brow that gods themselves
Might envy. Answer boldly then, nor hide
What urgent purpose leads thy footsteps hither.
What anxious cares perplex thy troubled breast?
Thine eyes are raised to heaven as I speak.
Tell me thy wish; it shall be gratified,
If its success depends on human hand.

Esther

O kindness reassuring to the heart
It honors! No light matter prompts my prayer.
Lo, misery or happiness awaits me;
Which it shall be hangs trembling on thy will.
One word from thee, ending my sore suspense,
Can render Esther happiest of queens.

If Esther has found favor in thy sight,
If ere thus wast disposed to grant her wishes,
Vouchsafe thy presence at her board to-day,
Let Esther entertain her sovereign lord,
And Haman be admitted to the banquet.
Then, in his hearing, I will dare to utter
What in his absence I must still conceal.

Ahasuerus

All shall tremble at the name
Of Esther's God. Rebuild His temple, fill
Your wasted cities; let your happy seed
With sacred triumph celebrate this day,
And in their memory live my name for aye!

SATAN AND HAMAN[7]

(After the Talmud)

PHILIP M. RASKIN

When the Persian Haman
    Thrilled and throbbed with joy,
At the gladsome prospect
    Israel to destroy;

Satan, likewise joyful,
    Brought to God the news,
Bade Him sign the verdict
    To destroy the Jews.

The Almighty answered:
    "Thy request is good,
But my seal, ere signing,
    Must be dipped in blood.

Bring some human blood, then,
    Shed by Jewish hands."
Forthwith sped old Satan
    Over sea and lands,

Searching every highway,
    Every cave and wood;
But, alas, he could not
    Find such human blood.

Then, to God returning,
    He brought back the tale:
"Cowards are Thy people,
    And of hearts too frail."

SONG OF THE MASK VENDOR[8]

I. D. Minzberg

Masks, masks, masks for sale!
Masks as cheap as words!
Guaranteed! They cannot fail
To make you free as birds:

Birds of prey, yes, indeed,
To swoop upon all weakness,
And clothe the nakedness of your deed
With robes of verbal meekness.

Masks, masks, masks for sale!
Masks for priest and layman!
Come one, come all, woman, male,
Teresh, Zeresh, Haman!

A mask for each and every station
In auto-or democracy!
A mask for people in every nation
Paying homage to hypocrisy.

Masks, masks, masks for sale!
Masks as cheap as cheap can be!
Your conscience wails? Let it wail!
Sell your soul and then be free!

CHAPTER XI

PURIM IN MUSIC

A. W. BINDER

DESPITE the fact that instrumental playing, singing and joy-making were forbidden to the Jew after the destruction of the Second Temple in Jerusalem, these restrictions were lifted, from almost the very beginning of the exile, on at least two occasions in the Jewish calendar year: on Simhat Torah and Purim. Joy became unlimited and uninhibited on these two holidays, the latter gradually approaching, often with official sanction, close to hilarity. The joyous spirit of Purim began with the reading of the *Megillah* (Book of Esther) in the synagogue and gradually reached into the home. As time went on, it extended into the *Purimspiel* and into the various parodies and songs which form an important part of the music which grew out of the celebration of this festival.

MUSICAL TRADITIONS AND THE *Megillah* READING

The reading of the *Megillah* is preceded by three benedictions, in a mode which is major and in which one immediately feels the joyous and carefree atmosphere of Purim.[1] The traditional manner of reading the *Megillah* is, like that of a letter or document,[2] animated and hasty. In oriental comunities it is read in almost *parlando* style[3], with melodic variations at half and full stops. The Dorian and Phrygian modes are used by some orientals, while the Ashkenazic

Jews use the system of cantillation based on the Dorian scale.[4] This mode is, however, embellished by borrowing from the cantillation of the Book of Lamentations and certain liturgical motives. These borrowings are primarily used to give expression to certain key phrases and sentences of the *Megillah*, to make them accord with the talmudic and midrashic interpretations of the text.[5] *Midrash Esther* 2.11, for example, tells us that the vessels used at Ahasuerus' feast were those taken from the Holy Temple when Jerusalem was captured by Nebuchadnezzar in 586 B.C.E. — therefore the melodic change from the joyous *Megillah* mode to the sad mode of Lamentations.

According to tradition, those additional phrases which depict the gloom and despair of the Jews are also to be chanted with motives from the cantillation mode of Lamentations.

At the beginning of Chapter 6.1 we are told of the sleeplessness which King Ahasuerus suffered on a certain night. According to *Midrash Esther* 10.1, God, the King of kings, also suffered sleeplessness on account of the terrible plight of his people in Persia. Therefore, the Ashkenazim chant this sentence with the elaborate melody used for *Ha-Melek* (The King) at the opening of the second section of the morning service on Rosh Hashanah and Yom Kippur. According to the musical tradition in some communities ויתלו את המן (7.10) is chanted in a joyous and exultant style.

These are some of the special musical detours made by the reader while reading the *Megillah*. The congregation which listens to the reading has its say, too, at these points, and recites these verses aloud before the reader.

These phrases were also either read by the congregation or sung to snatches of popular songs of the day.[6] Such congregational interruptions gave the Jews an opportunity to express their distaste for the many Hamans of their own day. The phrases were also sung to simple tunes, for the purpose of amusing the children.[7] Everything was done during the reading of the *Megillah* to make it happy and expressive of Israel's gratitude for past and future deliverances.

After the reading of the *Megillah* a special hymn, *Shoshanat Ya'akob*,[8] is sung to a joyous and sometimes even hilarious melody.

ORIGIN AND USE OF THE *Grogger*

Noisemaking at the mention of the name of Haman dates back to the earliest days since the *Megillah* reading became customary. In Deuteronomy 25.19 we are commanded "to erase" the name of Amalek who was the first enemy of the Jews after they left Egypt. And so we find that some oriental Jews write the name of Haman (who was supposed to be a descendant of Amalek) on a slip of paper and erase it at the mention of Haman's name, or they write it on the soles of their shoes and rub and stamp on it. But the practice of using the *grogger* at the mention of Haman's name, as we know it today, goes back to the thirteenth century in France and Germany.[9]

In view of the fact that the *grogger* is now classified among musical instuments as a percussion instrument, it should be interesting to trace its origin here.

The *grogger* is a combination of two primitive instruments: the "bull-roarer" and the "scraper."[10] The bull-roarer consisted of a long stick at the top of which was attached a string and at the end of the string a thin board. When this was twirled, it made a weird noise. The faster it was twirled the higher the pitch of the noise. The "scraper" consisted of notched shell, bone or gourd which was scraped with a rigid object. The *grogger* combines both these rattles.

28. *GROGGER*　　　　Silver

19th Century

Noisemaking of this kind was an old custom among primitive people at the outgoing and incoming of new seasons,
in order to scare away the evil spirits. Purim, which comes
at the beginning of springtime, most likely adopted the *grogger* from primitive practices at this period of the year.[11]
Many such primitive instruments have turned up among
children's toys.

It took the oriental Jews a long time to change their
practice of knocking two stones together and stamping
their feet at the mention of Haman's name. But today in

Palestine they have turned to *groggers* which they buy from the Ashkenazic Jews. In Persia, Jews still do not use the *grogger*. Children masque and go from house to house beating drums.[12] In Italy trumpets appear, when Jews on Purim circle round an effigy of Haman, while the trumpets are blown.[13]

MUSIC IN PARODIES AND THE PURIMSPIEL

Included in the joy-making on Purim were parodies which go back to the fourteenth century. These were usually composed according to patterns taken from the synagogue liturgy or from the popular songs of the day. These parodies were usually put to the melodies of the original songs or prayers. A parody on the Hanukkah hymn entitled מעוז צור לפורים (*Maoz Tzur for Purim*) by Gabriel Pollack,[14] to be sung at the table, is an interesting example. These parodies were full of the good humor of the festival, caricatures of the wicked characters in the *Megillah* and the idealization of its heroes. Many of these parodies were in the form of wine songs.[15]

The Purim *Rab*, who was a "take-off" of the local rabbi, was an important item in Purim parody. He would deliver a humorous sermon, in the style of the local rabbi, and sing the Purim *Kiddush*, which was a potpourri of several versions of the *Kiddush* for the holy days and the Sabbath.[16]

The birth of the opera in the sixteenth century immediately began to exert its influence on Jewish music in and out of the synagogue. We hear of cantors at this time indulging in excessive vocal pyrotechnics during the chanting of the service, in operatic style, to the delight of the congregation and the disgust of the rabbis. It was also at this time that the office of cantor and rabbi were divorced from each other in many of the large communities in Europe. Many communities wanted the cantor to possess a beautiful voice and to be able to sing some of the prayers with melodies taken from the popular songs of the day, no matter whether they were secular or sacred.[17] And so, when Purim came and joy and hilarity reigned, outside musical influences made themselves strongly felt, especially in the *Purimspiel*.

Operatic influence may be detected when we discover choral numbers used as *entre-actes* as well as epilogues in *Dus Purim Lied fun Yosef ben Binyomin*, found in Isik Walich's collection.[18] *Der Ashmadai Spiel* had two interludes which were sung by the chorus of Solomon's Suite. *Shoshanat Ya'akob*, the Purim liturgical hymn, usually ended all Purim plays and, during the seventeenth and eighteenth centuries, it was frequently arranged and sung for solo and chorus, in the operatic style of the period.

Acta Esther (Prague, 1720),[19] which we are told was looked over by the famous Rabbi David Oppenheim of that period and performed by his students, contains two songs in aria form[20] and calls for the accompaniment of כל מיני כלי זמר וחצוצרות (trumpets and all types of musical instruments). In *Hakmat Shlomoh*[21] we find a Death March for David and trumpets for the crowning of Solomon. Jacob Dessauer in Amsterdam in the eighteenth century calls for music by various composers in his *Purimspiel, Mordecai and Esther, The Greatest of Jews*.[22] Many popular melodies of the day must surely have been included.

Who were the participants in the *Purimspiel*? The musical accompaniment was done by the *Klezmer* (musicians of the town),[23] although in some cases, as in Bukowina, the *Purimspiel* was accompanied by Gentile musicians.[24] The acting was done by the *Lezim*[25] and *Badhanim* (folk minstrels) of the town and much of the singing was done by these as well as by the *Meshorerim* (choir singers).

MUSICAL CUSTOMS ON PURIM

Details of customs in the celebration of Purim vary not only from country to country, but from city to city and community to community.

Singing was the main means of individual and collective expression and was an aid to creating the joyous Purim spirit. The main singing was done during and after the Purim feast which took place a little before sundown on the day of Purim. Songs in the vernacular were permitted on this festival and in various parts of Europe and the Orient songs in Judeo-Italian, Judeo-Spanish and Judeo-German were sung.[26] In Persia, Purim songs could be heard in the streets of the Jewish quarter weeks before Purim.[27] In Amsterdam in 1804 humorous songs were circulated in the community before Purim in a Purim almanac. Solomon Doklar became famous for his "Purimiads" which were to be "read, sung and re-told."[28]

The hasidic sect, which was founded in the eighteenth century, developed its own manner and customs in the celebration of Purim. Hasidim found spiritual qualities in the hilarities of a Purim celebration. They, for example, believed that all of the Rebbe's prayers and requests were granted to him in heaven at the conclusion of his Purim dance. They also believed that the Divine Presence rested on a joyous and happy face, and took special advantage of this interpretation on the festival when joy was unlimited. They began in the synagogue by singing passages such as, ויתלו את המן, והעיר שושן, ליהודים, בלילה ההוא (Esther 7.10; 8.15; 8.16; 6.1) very elaborately and with a good deal of noise and enthusiasm.

Rabbi Levi Yizhok of Berditchev, of the early part of the nineteenth century, danced while he chanted על מקרא מגילה,

the first of the three benedictions preceding the reading of the *Megillah*.

Rabbi Abbush Maier of Sanz, who was extremely musical, composed a new melody for *Shoshanat Ya'akob* every year. His hasidim would gather at the *Shalosh Seudot* (third meal) on the Sabbath preceding Purim, and at that time he would teach them the new tune. This would, of course, be sung *ad infinitum* during the Purim celebration. The tune would again show up at the following Sabbath eve service in *L'kah Dodi*.

29. PURIM PLAYERS   Engraving

Megillah "with Herms"

On the night of Purim a flood of songs was released. At that time the *Shoshanat Ya'akob* held the center of attraction. Later they sang such Psalms as אשא עיני, שגיון לדוד, רננו צדיקים, לולא ד' (121, 7, 33, 124), and others.

Then there would also be songs, hasidic and others, in the vernacular. Hasidim would frequently entertain the Rebbe

and the other hasidim with a *Purimspiel* which was frequently accompanied by singing and even instrumental playing.

On the following day, Shushan Purim, joy and hilarity
were still unabated, reaching a climax at the *Minhah* (afternoon) service, when one of the hasidim would act as cantor.
He would first of all dress in a *Kittel* (white shroud used on
the High Holy Days) and chant the prayers with the serious High-Holy-Day melodies in burlesque style.

These were some of the ways in which the hasidim whose
credo it was to "serve God in joy," made joy unbounded on
this day, the most joyous of holidays.[29]

Purim Music in Israel

In Israel, Purim is celebrated in carnival style, particularly in Tel Aviv. On Purim eve one hears the *Megillah*
read throughout the streets surrounding the Great Synagogue over loud speakers for the benefit of those who cannot be accommodated in the synagogue proper. In the evening the whole city is a blaze of light in accordance with the
verse in the *Megillah* "And unto the Jews there was light
and joy." Mass singing envelopes the city. Choruses from
roof-tops join those in the streets. Here and there groups of
young people may be seen whirling about to the tune of a
Horah which the band coming down the street is playing.
On a platform erected on one of the main streets the characters of the *Megillah* sing and dance and entertain the crowds
till the wee hours of the morning.

Folk Songs

It is hard to visualize any Purim, no matter how far
back, without the singing of songs by the people. Unfortunately, our sources for Purim parodies,[30] which were indeed the first songs which were sung on Purim in both synagogue and home, do not give us the melodies. The Purim

folksong, as we know it, dates back to the sixteenth and seventeenth centuries; examples may be found in Isik Walich's collection[31] and in Elijah Kirchan's *Simhat ha-Nefesh* (Joy of the Spirit).[32]

Fundamental in Yiddish songs of Purim is the folksong which is based on the greeting *Gut Purim*,[33] with which Jews greeted each other on Purim and which the *Purimspielers* sang when they entered a home in which they were to perform. The folksongs then proceed to tell of the joy of the day, the revenge on Haman and Zeresh, his wife (purported to be a shrew), King Ahasuerus the drunkard, and the hero and heroine of the story, Esther the Queen and Mordecai the Prince. The songs also tell how the tables were turned on Haman, who plotted to destroy the Jews but who himself met with destruction. The latter subject is especially popular in folksongs, in view of the fact that Hamans were never lacking in Jewish life in every generation. In one song we are asked why we cannot have Purim every day in view of the ever present Haman.[34] Many songs tell also of the custom of the sending of gifts on Purim, and the special Purim delicacy, the *Hamantash*.[35]

Many of the Yiddish folk songs were the creation of the *Purimspielers*. Early Yiddish playwrights made use of the Purim theme. In Yiddish plays, such as *Ahasuerus* by A. Goldfaden, we find the popular folksong *Heint is Purim*. In Hurewitch's very popular play, *Ben Hador*, a stanza in the famous song *Min Hametzar* is devoted to the subject of Haman.

Little children, masked, went from house to house, rapped at the door and sang:

> Today is Purim,
> Tomorrow is none;
> Give me a penny
> And I'll be gone.

Variations came in the third line where children at various times and places substituted for the word "penny," "kopek," "groshen," "krepel," "Hamantash," etc.

The melodies of the Yiddish Purim songs lost their ghetto pathos on Purim and, since there were not too many joyous tunes in the Jewish folksong repertoire, such melodies had to be borrowed from foreign sources for these joyous texts.

Hebrew folksongs for Purim, as we have pointed out, began with the Hebrew parodies of the Middle Ages. Purim songs in Hebrew began to be composed even at the time when the first Purim was celebrated by the early Palestinian pioneers of 1881. Since then many songs have been composed for this important and happy Palestinian festival. These songs fall into three groups: 1. original poems with original melodies; 2. poems translated from Yiddish to the accompanying melody; and 3. parodies on Yiddish folksongs sung to the accompanying melody.

While the Hebrew Purim songs deal with all themes enumerated in the Yiddish folksong, there are a few additional ones to be found in these, as for example: the general "tipsy" feeling of carnival times, the description of the *Adloyada* in Tel Aviv, the costume colors, and the moods and pictures which the *Megillah* characters portrayed.

In the many children's songs which are sung in Israel, weeks before Purim, we find the idea of personalizing the *Grogger*, the *Hamantash* and the *Shalah Monot*. Purim is also idealized in a song such as *Pur Pur Purim*, in which birds and fishes, too, are pictured as celebrating the festival. One cannot say that Palestinian melodies are particularly Jewish in character. One thing, however, is certain — they are extremely rhythmical and vibrant, a new element in Jewish folksong, as compared to those of the ghetto.

Purim Songs in America

Too much originality has not been displayed in our own country, where a musical literature for Purim has been growing steadily. While many of the Purim lyrics by the late Samuel S. Grossman are good and admirably catch the spirit of Purim, the melodies for the most part are banal and undistinguished in character. The texts of our American Purim songs deal for the most part with the same subjects as those which we found in the Yiddish folksong. A number of attempts have been made to translate some of the Yiddish and Hebrew songs into English[36] in order to enable our children to catch some of the true Purim spirit. An attempt has also been made to utilize the cantillation mode of the Book of Esther in one English song[37] so as to accustom the ears of the younger generation with a branch of Jewish song unfamiliar to them. In American Sunday schools, hymns of faith and deliverance are also sung on Purim.[38] A favorite musical process on Purim, in Sunday schools, clubs, Hebrew schools and other gatherings, is to sing Purim parodies to popular American folk songs, nursery rhymes and songs of the day. We find Purim parodies set to *The Man on the Flying Trapeze, Tit-Willow, It Ain't Gonna Rain No More, Polly Wolly Doodle, Farmer in the Dell, A Bicycle Built For Two, London Bridge is Falling Down, Here we go Round the Mulberry Bush* and *Two Little Indians.*[39]

An attempt has even been made to make a Purim parody out of the popular comic opera, *The Mikado,* by Gilbert and Sullivan. This was done by Mabel H. Meyer and has been re-named *Ha-Ha Hadassah.*[40]

PURIM ART MUSIC

Serious musicians have not neglected the subject of Purim. At the head of the list of art creations on this subject is George Frederick Handel's first oratorio *Esther*, written in 1720. Two cantatas by Bradbury and Stoughton were composed in our country during the past century and two operas by the German Jewish composers, Jacob Knoller and Frederick Bloch, were recently composed. Operettas, too, by various composers, have been composed and an overture entitled *Esther*, to Grillparzer's *Esther*, is to be found by Eugene D. Albert. The author of this article has just completed a dramatic narrative with music, entitled *Esther, Queen of Persia*.[41]

All in all, Purim has made its contribution to Jewish music by the very joyousness of its nature which, better than anything else, the cantillation mode of the Book of Esther expresses.

CHAPTER XII

THE ESTHER STORY IN ART

RACHEL WISCHNITZER

THE *Megillat Esther*, the reading of which is an integral part of the Purim ritual, belongs to *The Holy Scriptures* and its illustrations can be readily connected in some way or other with the illustrations of the Bible by Christian artists. Just how close this relationship was, to what extent the *Megillah* illustrators were familiar with general trends in art, how consciously they knew what was going on in the workshops of the leading masters of their time and how skillfully they were able to assimilate contemporaneous artistic conceptions is a fascinating problem to study.

Not less important is it to obtain an insight into the traditional rabbinical interpretation of the characters of the Esther story as it was retold in the talmudic *Agada* and the medieval paraphrases, as well as in later popular Hebrew and Yiddish literature — including theatrical plays — and to find out to what extent this Jewish literature has influenced the illustration of the Book of Esther, particularly Jewish illustration.

AN EARLY PURIM PAINTING

The impact of rabbinical re-interpretation can be observed in a painting of the third century of the Common Era, a period when the Talmud was still in the making. The Esther story is portrayed in one of the scenes of the mural de-

30. *AHASUERUS, ON THE THRONE OF KING SOLOMON,*
AND ESTHER Wall Painting

Synagogue at Dura-Europos, 3rd Century

corations of the recently excavated synagogue at Dura-
Europos on the Euphrates (dated 245 C.E.).[1] There we
have Ahasuerus and Esther seated on their thrones, figures
familiar from the Bible. However there is a new point added
in the picture. The throne on which the Persian king is
seated is the ancestral throne of the Jewish kings, the throne
of Solomon (f. 30). Where did the painter get this motif?
Undoubtedly, it was contributed by a legend which has
come down to us in the *Targum Sheni* to Esther.[2] There are
no traces of such a representation of the throne of Ahasuerus
in Christian art. In fact, the idea of associating the Persian
king with King Solomon and his throne had originated in a
quite unique circumstance. The city of Dura was in Roman
hands. Previously it had been part of the Persian Empire.

The Jews of this city, as of other places in the Middle East overrun by Roman armies, hoped for the Persians to come back. Therefore, they were inclined to idealize Ahasuerus and projected upon him their pro-Persian attitude.

Dura was actually recaptured by the Persians shortly after the synagogue murals were painted. Whether a sufficient number of Jews survived the siege and destruction of the city to celebrate a merry Purim, we do not know.

In Medieval Art

Medieval Jewish book illustration was less politically minded and rather didactic and moralizing in character. In this sense it was related to Christian book illustration of the time, which was likewise set to educate the reader.

Because of this similarity in purpose, a miniature depicting Ahasuerus and Esther in an Ashkenazic Bible, dated 1238 (f. 31), has much in common with a picture in the *Hortus Deliciarum* (f. 32), the work of a German nun, Herrad of Landsberg, at the end of the twelfth century.[8] Both pictures show Ahasuerus sternly pointing to Haman hanging on the gibbet. There are differences of detail, of course, and it is worth noting that Esther in the German manuscript looks mildly interested in the procedure, while in the Hebrew codex she vigorously points to Haman and thus takes an active part in the demonstration of the punishment of the wicked. Perhaps we can see in this difference of behavior a difference in the social position of the woman in the German and Jewish family of the time. It may be due to a different evaluation of Esther's role on the part of the Jewish artist.

The Jewish picture has another particular feature, this one borrowed from the Midrash. Haman and his sons are hanging on a tree instead of a gallows. Obviously the artist

31. *AHASUERUS AND ESTHER; HAMAN AND HIS SONS*
     ON THE GALLOWS   Illuminated Manuscript

Hebrew Bible, 1238

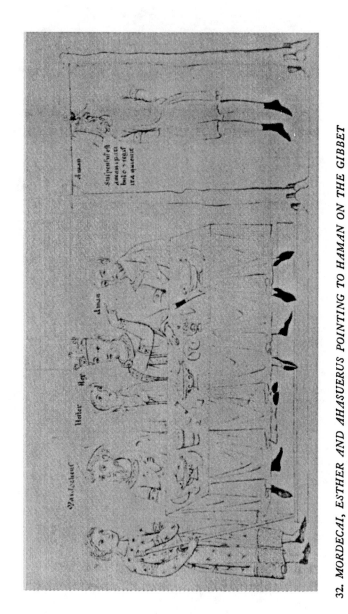

32. MORDECAI, ESTHER AND AHASUERUS POINTING TO HAMAN ON THE GIBBET

Hortus Deliciarum, 12th Century

was familiar with the legend about the competition of the trees for the distinction of being used as a gibbet for Haman.[4]

In a fourteenth-century Hebrew Bible, probably executed in Ratisbon,[5] the scene of "Mordecai's Elevation" reveals a familiarity with the talmudic passage, Megillah 16a. Haman is seen in the miniature lying on the ground instead of leading the horse (f. 33).

According to our talmudic source, Mordecai, exhausted by three days of fasting and unable to mount the horse unaided, used Haman as a footstool. The Talmud was no doubt inspired by contemporary customs of the Roman triumph, with the victor actually treading upon the vanquished enemy. In a relief on the Arch of Constantine in Rome, Trajan can be seen galloping over the body of a conquered barbarian. The Jewish author, however, in describing the humiliating episode, had pious scruples lest one might suspect him

33. *MORDECAI'S TRIUMPH*
Illuminated Manuscript

Hebrew Bible, 14th Century

of indulging in vindictive feelings. He, therefore, put in the mouth of Haman the words: *Rejoice not when thine enemy falleth, and let not thy heart be glad when he stumbleth* (Proverbs 24.17); whereupon Mordecai replied with great dignity that he was punishing an enemy of the people rather than a personal foe. To give the story a gayer touch, Mordecai added a rather ambiguously used scriptural quotation: *And thou shalt tread upon their high places* (Deuteronomy 33.29).[6] The double meaning of these words could not escape the reader.

In a similar spirit and again in agreement with Jewish legend, the daughter of Haman is introduced into a scene of "Mordecai's Triumph" in a fourteenth century prayerbook (a *Mahzor* of Leipzig University Library) where it illustrates a passage referring to Haman. We see her watching from a tower what is going on in the street and emptying a vessel of dish-water over the head of the leader of the

34. *MORDECAI'S TRIUMPH;*
HAMAN'S DAUGHTER
Illuminated Manuscript

Ashkenazic Mahzor, 14th Century

horse whom she takes to be Mordecai (f. 34). Realizing her mistake, she throws herself from the window.[7] Mordecai on his horse wears the royal crown on his head and his *Judenhut* on a streamer on his back, in true medieval fashion, for it was quite customary for a man to carry two headgears. On the page facing this, Mordecai is seen in the company of three children (f. 19, p. 131). This episode is described in *Yalkut Shimoni* II, 1057, where it is related how Mordecai, in his troubled mood, was comforted by some verses three school boys coming from class happened to recite.[8] The other figures are easy to identify. There is Haman waiting with his horse for Mordecai to go for a ride and, further to the left, Ahasuerus extending his scepter to Esther.

Jewish Influences on Christian Art

Rabbinical reinterpretation of the biblical Book of Esther was not exclusively restricted to Hebrew book illustration. There are quite a number of instances where the illuminator of a Christian book would use some feature of Jewish origin; but such influence was usually indirect, carried through Christian literary sources. There is, however, one Christian Bible, the Alba Bible, whose illustration shows a direct dependence on Jewish interpretation. The Bible, in the possession of the Duke of Alba in Madrid,[9] is a Castilian version of the Old Testament, compiled in 1422-30, by the Jew, Moses Arragel of Guadalajara, for the Franciscan Order of Calatrava. As a vassal of the order, Arragel could not possibly decline the job of revising the translation and providing the commentaries. However, he refused to supervise the illustration of the Bible, with the excuse that the Second Commandment would not permit him to do so. Since some Hebrew Bible illustration existed at that time in Spain, we have to assume that he either disapproved of it or simply wished to evade the responsibility for the illustration. However this might have been, he could not help it that a great deal of his vast knowledge of the *Agada* went into the creation of the miniatures owing to his year-long collaboration with the friars in the preparation of the texts.

The Jewish features in the illustration of the Alba Bible have never been thoroughly examined.[10] Since we are interested here in the Esther story, let us discuss the pictures which illustrate it. There is, for instance, the picture of Vashti endowed with a monstrous tail. Who would suppose that this point was taken from a Jewish source? And yet we learn from Megillah 12b,[11] that the Archangel Michael thus wished to ridicule the queen, and it appears from various talmudic references that Vashti deserved her fate because she had been unkind to Jewish children and had also opposed the rebuilding of the Temple.[12] It is interesting that the rabbis felt that whatever is recorded in the Bible must have some profound justification. The idea that Vashti's disgrace and deposition might have been undeserved was intolerable to them. In some instances Ahasuerus was blamed for treating Vashti so harshly. In others, he was excused on account of her bad character. She deserved her fate, and in order to account for her disappearance from the scene in the Bible the motif of her execution[13] was introduced in the Agada and turns up in later *Megillah* illustration.

To revert to the Alba Bible, the bedchamber scene follows entirely the midrashic story (f. 25, p. 165). The attending page, who is supposed to read the chronicles to the king, turns out to be a son of Haman. He tries to skip the passage where Mordecai's good services are recorded. But the Archangel Michael intervenes and the text is read by an invisible voice.[14] This is faithfully depicted in our Bible, with the Archangel emerging from behind the curtain and vigorously pointing to the passage in the book. In order to convey that the page holding the chronicles is a son of Haman, the artist has used the ingenious device of dressing him exactly like the two boys accompanying Haman — obviously his other sons — as he proceeds in the morning to the royal bedroom. On the right, Mordecai is seen stepping through the royal gate and trying to mount the horse. Haman offers his back as a footstool and Haman's daughter pours out her dishwater.

The most attractive scene of the Esther cycle in the Alba Bible shows Esther and Mordecai dictating letters to the Jews, with the scribe writing into a huge scroll (f. 17, p. 115).

THE ILLUSTRATED ESTHER SCROLL

The reader will ask at this point about the illustrated Esther Scroll. We have passed in review a synagogue mural,

.niniatures in Jewish medieval Bibles, prayerbooks and one or two Christian manuscripts. Our primary interest, however, is the illustrated scroll used at the Feast of Purim.

Synagogue scrolls were not illustrated. As for scrolls used for home reading on Purim, no medieval specimens have been found so far. It seemed at one time that the *Megillah* of the Kirschstein collection decorated in fifteenth century style might provide the missing link.[15] After closer examination of that scroll, however, this hope had to be abandoned. It was impossible to reconcile the decorative design of that scroll — too obviously imitating motifs from an often reproduced fifteenth-century *Haggadah* — with its illustration which is stylistically entirely out of tune. It is perhaps a hopeful sign that forgers have discovered the field of Jewish art.

The earliest specimens showing some design date from the sixteenth century. The *Juedisches Lexikon IV, 607,* has fortunately reproduced the fragment of a *Megillah* the location of which is unknown (f. 54, p. 430). It is the initial leaf of a scroll with the blessings for Purim, enclosed in engraved borders. The engraver, Andrea Marelli, is known to have been active in 1567–72 in Rome and Siena. Was he Jewish? The first name, "Andrea," makes it appear doubtful. Another sixteenth-century *Megillah* with engraved borders throughout its whole length was in the collection of H. Frauberger,[16] and is possibly in this country now.

We have in these two examples something new: Parchment-sheets with engraved framework, the text to be filled in by hand. Such sheets could be obtained at the print-seller's. Along with the prints, however,[17] handpainted *Megillot* were also in popular favor and in some cases the scribe himself may have designed the decorative framework of the scroll. A handpainted *Megillah*, produced in 1616 in Ferrara, has turned up recently in a private collection.

The earliest dated Purim scroll with engraved illustration is the one in the Jewish Museum in London, formerly in the Arthur Howitt collection in Richmond, Surrey, England. It is dated 1637, but bears no signature of the engraver. Whether the date is engraved or added by hand by the scribe who wrote the text is not known to me. Another complete copy of this print is in the collection of Mr. M. Zagajski in New York. It is not dated (f. 35). Cecil Roth holds that the Howitt scroll is possibly the work of Salom Italia, a Jewish engraver of Amsterdam of whom we have several dated and signed works.[18] In 1641 he engraved the portrait of J. J. Leon Templo, and in 1642 that of Manasseh ben Israel, the second a free version of Rembrandt's etching. There exists also a smaller *Megillah* with a similar, but rather sketchy design, signed *Salom Italia sculpsit*, and one is puzzled by the poor quality of the signed work. However this may be, as long as no other name turns up, we may associate this *Megillah* type with the name of Salom Italia, as its engraver and possibly also its designer.

The main features of the Salom Italia type of *Megillah* are: the standing figures of the characters of the Esther story in the intervals of the text columns, and in the lower border a running narrative cycle. The rich Italianate architectural framework of the text-columns is decorated with allegorical palmbearing female figures, masks and charming little landscapes with typical Dutch mills, ships, bridges and trees. The episodes of the Esther story confined to the lower border are necessarily small and do not show any longer the delight in the thousand details of the *Agada* of which the medieval illustrator was exceedingly fond, as we have seen. New ideas now influenced the conception of the pictures, ideas suggested by Esther plays and also by the great art.

This change of concept involved a stronger emphasis on the drama, on the logical sequence of the scene, with a proper beginning and a logical end. The standing figures of Ahasuerus, Vashti, Esther, Mordecai, Haman, his wife Zeresh, Harbonah and the other chamberlains — the selec- tion of figures and their number may vary — resemble the actors of a play who appear on the stage before the curtain is raised to make their bow to the audience and introduce themselves. The way the figures are placed in space, in an interior or in a landscape, reveals the impact of the paintings of the time widely popularized through engrav- ings.

A scroll produced by Salom Italia in 1649 (f. 36) shows the tendency to sacrifice as much as possible of the Italianate architectural framework so as to obtain more space for the figures. Here he introduces also an important feature of Dutch art — the still life. In this scroll we come to know Salom Italia as a draftsman. The *Megillah* (last found in the Rothschild Museum in Frankfort) is a pen-and-ink draw- ing signed and dated by the artist. The colophon is in Hebrew, but only a German translation has been pub- lished. It reads: "Designed and com- pleted by Salom, son of Mordecai of Italia, Amsterdam, the 19th of Adar 5409."[19] The date is 1649 of the Com- mon Era. To mention an interesting little detail: the crown of Esther is seen placed on a table beside the

Engraving

Salom Italia, 1637

35. *MEGILLAH*

young queen. This is not meant to show that she has not yet been crowned, as has been suggested, but simply betrays the desire of the artist to picture Esther in terms of contemporary portraits of royalty. In Van Dyck's portrait of Henrietta-Maria, Queen of England, the crown is placed exactly that way. In the medallion scenes which run on the lower border, the protagonists of the story are shown in "cavalier" costumes and poses of a very Dutch character. The action is seen expanding in the little pictures towards the rear, quite in the style of seventeenth-century realism.

The description of the scenes is all we have besides a photo of a portion of the scroll, which gives a suggestion of the fine quality of the design. It is regrettable that so little has been done to build up a photographic record of our art treasures.

A much-imitated engraved *Megillah* is the one with herms (tapering down pedestals) instead of the standing figures (f. 37).[20] Here we meet with the episode of Vashti's execution. A second row of pictures is introduced into the upper border, charming little landscapes with few figures and hills in the far distance. On the initial leaf, where the blessings are transcribed, the more important scenes are gathered around the text. Ahasuerus and Esther on the throne above are flanked by courtiers and court ladies. The gallows scenes follow underneath. On the bottom we have from right to left: "Mordecai Receiving Raiment from Esther's Messenger," "Mordecai Mounted on the Royal Horse Led by Haman," in the manner of van Dyck's equestrian portraits, and "Esther and Mordecai Writing Letters to the Jews." The last scene, an interior, with the table neatly laid with a damask cloth, betrays the influence of Dutch domestic scenes. Aert de Gelder in 1685 painted Esther and Mordecai sitting at a table quietly conversing (f. 1, p. 5). De Gelder's teacher, Rembrandt, pictured Ahasuerus, Esther and Haman sitting at a table together (f. 27, p. 199).

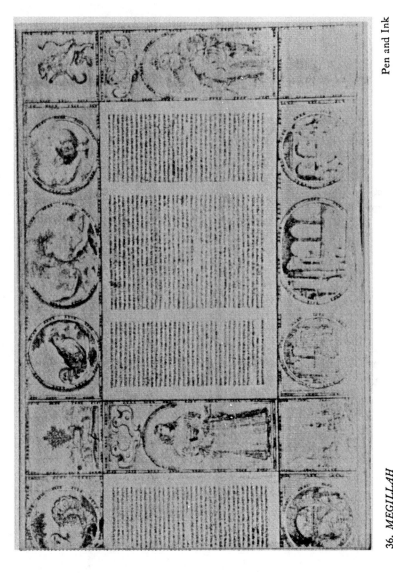

36. *MEGILLAH*

Salom Italia, 1649

Pen and Ink

OUTSIDE INFLUENCES ON JEWISH ART

The dependence of Purim scroll illustration upon contemporary art has not yet been realized and no attempt has been made so far to examine the material from this angle. If a Dutchman is not afraid to point out Italian in-

38. *MEGILLAH*   Drawing

A. Chaves, 1687

fluence in Rembrandt, why should we be reluctant to point out outside influence in our early Jewish artists who, after all, were pioneers in their fields? Very often they resorted even to direct copying, unable to recast their borrowings into something new.

Some years ago a *Megillah*, designed by Abraham or

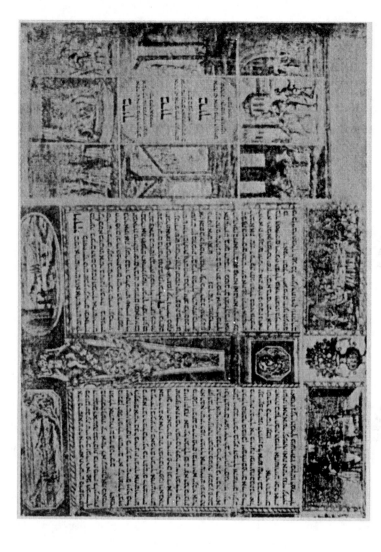

37. *MEGILLAH*　　　*17th Century*　　　Engraving

Aaron de Chaves, a Dutch Jew, was published in a Holland-Jewish review.[21] The scroll was produced in Amsterdam in 1687 (f. 38).

Checking the scene "Esther before Ahasuerus" — the only illustration in this scroll — with pictures of the Bible by M. Merian the Elder, I was not too much surprised to find that de Chaves had copied one of Merian's engravings (f. 14, p. 105). To escape the influence of the versatile Swiss engraver, whose various Bible editions flooded the book market of Europe, would not have been easy. A few years later, in 1695, the engraver of the Amsterdam Haggadah in a similar way used Merian's engravings as his models.[22]

These borrowings show that the Jews of Amsterdam had close contacts with the world around them. They knew what was taking place in the field of art and in book production. They may have known of Merian's German Bible editions which began to appear in 1625, or else they may have seen the Dutch edition of around 1650. To trace the channels of these influences and contacts through works of art means to add another set of references to the description of the cultural Jewish life of the period.

Bridal Chests and the Esther Story

In Italy the illustrated Esther scroll has a somewhat different background. Here the type was set by bridal chests (*cassoni*) decorated with paintings. These wedding chests, made for patrician families, were usually gifts of the mother to the bride. They used to be adorned with appropriate mythological or biblical scenes. Among the latter those glorifying the virtue of women were predominant. The Esther story was in special favor. Sometimes the front and two side panels of the chest were decorated with episodes from a single story. Thus little cycles originated. Among the chests decorated with Esther scenes we may mention the

one attributed to a painter of the school or workshop of
Botticelli. The side panels, "Esther on her Way to the Palace" (f. 24, p. 157) and "Mordecai's Triumph" (f. 15, p. 107)
are in the Liechtenstein Gallery in Vienna. The front panel
is in Chantilly. It exhibits the "Elevation of Esther" (f. 18,
p. 128). The king with the princes are in the royal loge in
the center, while the maidens, Esther and six others, walk
one by one down the hall in the foreground. Esther is the
one in the center making a curtsy. Mordecai sits near the
right pillar, resting his head on his right hand and holding
his left on a book. On the left Hegai, the keeper of women,
points to Esther, his choice, as she passes by. In the rear
there are two banquet scenes: the one on the left depicts
Ahasuerus' feast, the one on the right the banquet of Vashti
who is seen receiving the king's messenger. These rear scenes
have been interpreted as Esther's banquet.[23] This conception
is erroneous, since the rear scenes are intended, of course, to
recall to mind past, not future, events. And besides it is
easy to see that the guests at the left are men while those at
the right are women.

The relationship of the *cassoni* pictures to the type of
plays known as the *Rappresentazione Sacra*, among which
there were also Esther plays, was recognized by Schubring.
This relationship is interesting, as we have here a certain
convergence, for the Jewish illustration of the Esther scroll
was similarly dependent on theatrical plays. The painters of
the *cassoni* were apparently the earlier ones to make use of
the suggestions of the stage. The *cassoni* style, with its emphasis on magnificent architectural settings and its display
of large crowds, was in vogue throughout the Renaissance
period. It has influenced also book illustration.

In the recently published[24] Esther scroll of the Vatican
(cod. hebr. 533) we have an illustration of the Esther story
in the charming Italian *cassoni* style (f. 12, p. 96; f. 13,

p. 100). The format of the pictures which run in the lower border of the framework is similar. The conception of the crowds, banquets and architectural settings is in true Renaissance taste. We have here that fondness for courtly splendor, for out-of-door scenes with the figures moving in streets, squares and magnificent, colonnaded open courts so typical of the Italian Renaissance. The costumes in the pictures are adapted however to seventeenth-century fashions, and the elongated figures go somewhat beyond the Renaissance ideal.

The Vatican *Megillah*

The Vatican *Megillah* has inspired many versions. In some of them the figure scenes were changed, reduced and simplified, so that only the architectural framework of the text columns remained intact. Francesco Griselini, active in Venice around 1740, a non-Jewish engraver known from other Hebrew works supplied by him with engravings, has used the Vatican scroll as a model for his Purim scrolls. A parchment scroll engraved by him was transcribed by Loeb son of Daniel in 1748. The name of the scribe's place of origin was tentatively read as Goerz.[25] However, a comparison with another *Megillah*, the scroll of the Cincinnati Hebrew Union College, shows that the reading is not correct, for the scribe of this scroll, Arje Loeb son of Daniel, is obviously identical with the former, and he gives his place of origin as Guriia in Little Poland.[26] The Cincinnati scroll was made in Venice in 1748. Guriia is obviously Goray in the province of Lublin. The name of that town is listed in the *Yevreyskaya Encyclopedia* (VI. 684).

The Cincinnati *Megillah*

In the Cincinnati *Megillah*, it can be observed (f. 39) how an elaborate seventeenth-century type of decoration derived from the Salom Italia scroll-type was transformed into a naive, popular piece of work. Note the tiny figures in the medallions below, how every suggestion of depth is banned and the figures are set off from a black background and how the decorative elements, the doves and the grapes, the lions and the pinks, have outgrown the figures in scale. Note also the ample use of labels giving the names of the figures, a typical folk-art device in this late period.

The exquisite artistic effect is produced by the doll-like stiffness of the figures, the sharp contrasts of black and white and the soft half-tones of the surfaces shaded with cross-hatchings. The male figures characterized as orientals wear dashing headgear trimmed with tassels, high boots and cloaks with flying sleeves. Ahasuerus wears beneath his crown the linen coif of Venetian doges. The women wear the seventeenth-century hoop skirts, close fitting bodices and the fashionable Spanish mantilla. Ahasuerus, Vashti and Esther carry a scepter, Mordecai a book, Zeresh a fan, while Haman and the chamberlains swing a saber. Haman is the only man represented beardless. Respectability apparently required a beard. Haman wears a long mustache which stresses the cruel expression of his face. Busts, all labelled, adorn the upper border. Typical of the character of this folk-art illustration is the revival of interest in the Midrash and a sense for the burlesque. Here again Haman's daughter appears (f. 20, p. 140) on the tower pouring out dishwater, and in some versions of this much-copied scroll-type, Haman is seen stepping forward to gather the liquid in a drinking vessel.

In the course of time the popular *Megillah* type becomes predominant. The academic type deteriorates at the hands of untrained provincial copyists, such as Marcus Donath in Nyitra, Hungary, who etched a *Megillah* after the scroll "with herms" in 1834. A copy is in the Jewish Museum of Budapest.[27]

39. *MEGILLAH* 1748

Modern Illustrators

Among modern illustrations to the Esther book we may mention engravings by Henryk Glicenstein and the miniature set by Arthur Szyk. The Union of American Hebrew Congregations issued recently an abridged English translation of the *Megillah* on genuine parchment, in the format of the traditional scroll, designed and illustrated by Nelson Ronsheim (f. 55, p. 435). Pen-and-ink drawings by Mark Chagall, made for Bella Chagall's *Burning Lights*, depict the observance of Purim in Russia (f. 6, p. 58).

A great many Purim scrolls are intended for the younger generation and are illustrated in a fairy-tale style. Otto Geismar, in his amusing *Megillah* published in 1936 in Berlin (f. 40, p. 260), omitted the gallows scenes, probably for political reasons. As a matter of fact, I may mention that I had to rewrite my Purim article for the Berlin community weekly, at that very time, because the editor wished me to drop the references to Haman. The article appeared on March 8, 1936, under the innocent title: "The Little Source that Became a Stream." The subject matter was the Septuagint additions to Esther.

Ceremonial Rites in Illustrations

The actual celebration of Purim is a subject sometimes added to the historical picture-cycle of the *Megillah*. The "Purim rabbi" is portrayed in the chair imitating the preacher preaching a sermon in the synagogue; the exchanging of gifts is also depicted. More often represented are dancing couples, playing musicians and jesters.

The Purim service in the synagogue was pictured in a more impressive way in non-Jewish works, such as the well-known *Juedisches Ceremoniel* by P. C. Kirchner, published in Nuremberg in 1724 and other editions (f. 43, p. 325).

The lively, gesturing "Purim rabbi" is found in a hand-painted *Megillah* in the David Kaufmann collection at the Budapest Academy (f. 4, p. 52). The scene is preceded in this *Megillah* by the exchanging of gifts (f. 23, p. 151). A dancing couple is shown in the Cincinnati scroll (f. 51, p. 412).

THE PURIM JESTERS

The Purim jesters are best known from an engraving often reproduced in Jewish magazines. It shows the Purim players hopping with pots and pans, brooms, kettledrums and a hobby horse. This charming picture belongs to a set of engravings illustrating Jewish customs in the *Philologus Hebraeo-Mixtus* by the Protestant Dutch scholar Johan Leusden, printed in Utrecht in 1682 (f. 8, p. 69). The engraver was a Dutch artist, Johan van den Avele, who later emigrated to Sweden where he died in 1727. Where did the engraver get his conception of the Purim jesters? The answer is most amusing, for the model of the engraving actually was another very popular picture of the jesters — a woodcut known to us from the *Sefer Minhagim*. It shows three men disguised as harlequins, with the typical pointed shoes and two-horned fool's caps, making noise with all sort of instruments, the taller man carrying a huge beer-jug (f. 49, p. 364). Our picture is taken from the Amsterdam edition of 1723. However, the jesters and the whole cycle of illustrations of the *Sefer Minhagim* are found already in the Venice edition of 1593, printed at di Gara's press. A copy of this rare edition is in the possession of Prof. Judah Joffe in New York. Leusden took over the woodcuts of the *Sefer Minhagim* for the first edition of his *Philologus*, Utrecht, 1663. The jesters appear in this Latin work under the heading *De Feste Purim*. Then, following the general trend in taste, Leusden had the woodcuts redesigned and engraved by van de Avele for the second edition of his book. We have here a unique case of a seventeenth-century book of a Gentile illustrated with pictures borrowed from a Jewish book in the Yiddish language.

The jesters are found also represented in Purim scrolls. There is the charming little picture of five masked men in seventeenth-century costumes — two playing the mandolin, one blowing a horn, dancing a round dance — in a *Megillah* of the Bezalel Museum in Jerusalem (f. 47, p. 358). Eight figures in a round dance with the accompaniment of a music band — two violins, a flute, a horn and a contrebass — are seen in the *Megillah* "with herms" (f. 29, p. 216).

DECORATED PURIM PARAPHERNALIA

The paraphernalia for Purim are quite interesting. To begin with, there is the container of the Purim scroll. When special cases for the *Megillah* first were used, we do not know. In Bernard Picart's *Ceremonies and Religious Customs* (Amsterdam, 1723) the case of the Esther scroll is mentioned in the text, but not illustrated. A fine Purim-scroll case in wood, with incised inscriptions and some design, from Ratisbon, dated 1781, is illustrated in the *Juedisches Lexikon* (IV. 43). Silver cases, cast or with embossed work, are to be found in art collections. They still await dating and study. The *Megillah* is wound, in distinction from the Torah scroll, on a single roller, which is usually encased in the cylindrical container and provided with a handle at the bottom, outside the case. When the handle is turned, the parchment scroll is pulled out through a side slit of the cylinder. An interesting custom of Sephardic Jews was the presentation of engraved *Megillah* scrolls to bridegrooms. We illustrate a silver case last found in the collection of Ventura Vitalis in

Vienna, made by Baruch Dornhelm, a Jewish silversmith born in Lwow, Poland, in 1858, and active there and later in Vienna, where he died in 1928.[28]

The case is decorated with figure scenes: "The Crowning of Esther," "Esther before Ahasuerus," and other episodes of the Esther book (f. 21, p. 145).[29] The artist may have known the *Ze'enah u-Re'enah*, a Yiddish paraphrase of the Pentateuch, the Five Scrolls and tales from Talmud and Midrash, adapted for female readers. The Amsterdam edition of 1792 has among its woodcut illustrations "Esther before Ahasuerus," borrowed from an engraving in Merian's Bible. The silversmith, who incidentally worked also for the Polish clergy, no doubt had access to non-Jewish illustrative material and may have been familiar with the Bible with Merian's engravings.

Among the dishes especially used on Purim — *to send portions one to another and gifts to the poor* (Esther 9.22) — we may mention the eighteenth-century pottery dish, in the Musée de Cluny in Paris, with a charming "Triumph" scene (f. 26, p. 181). [There is an obvious error in the Hebrew spelling of the word אשר.] Another dish, about 1810, shows a man offering a cup of wine. Vine leaves and grapes appropriately decorate the rim of the plate.[30]

"Mordecai's Triumph" is found depicted also on pewter plates (f. 52, p. 416). A more common decoration of these dishes is that of fishes, the sign of the Zodiac for Adar, the Purim month (f. 7, p. 61). The dish is dated 1787.

Dated Purim pewter dishes are rare. There was one in the Cassel Museum, dated 1776.[31]

As food delicacies are an important part of the observance of Purim, it is not surprising that molds were made for forming cakes with appropriate symbols. The Jewish Theological Seminary has three wooden forms carved with Purim designs and the date, 1870, from Nemiroff, Russia.

The sign of the fishes is found also on Adar tablets called, *Misheniknas*, from the initial word of the saying: With the month of Adar begins the joyous season (Ta'anit 29a).

These wall tablets seem to have been chiefly in use in Galicia. On one such tablet, designed on paper, two men are seen drinking. Three wine bottles on the table convey the merry mood of the revelers. Besides the fishes, the lion of Judah and the stork, a fertility symbol like the fishes, make up the decoration (f. 45, p. 337).

Special Purim wine tankards were manufactured in Bohemia, with Hebrew inscriptions and appropriate decorations. An exquisite specimen of such a tankard, decorated with the scene "Mordecai and Esther before Ahasuerus" (f. 44, p. 335), and a cup with the figure of a "Purim rabbi" (f. 46, p. 349), in Bohemian glass with enamel decoration of the first half of the nineteenth century, belong to the collection of Dr. Ludwig Feuchtwanger, now in Jerusalem.

Very charming is also a Purim hand-towel with the merry Mordecai on a caparisoned horse, embroidered in cross-stitch on linen (f. 53, p. 419). The date is 1812.[32] Towels of this kind were objects of display rather than of practical use.

PURIM GREETING CARDS

Although the sending of handwritten congratulations on the occasion of Purim was customary in the nineteenth century, the custom of sending printed greeting cards has developed rather recently. In World War I, the National Jewish Welfare Board issued Purim greeting cards (f. 16, p. 110), reproduced in World War II, of which over two million were distributed to the Jewish members of the United States armed forces who sent them to their families and friends from all over the world. For Jewish servicemen stationed in China, the National Jewish Welfare Board printed an interesting card with the Purim symbols, Chinese lettering and a picture of a "coolie" pulling a rickshaw in which Queen Esther is seated (f. 10, p. 84). Other organizations and individuals have also issued greeting cards. A charming card published by the Furrow Press was designed by Temima N. Gezari (f. 41, p. 261).

The Grogger

And last, but not least, let us say a few words about the *grogger*. How modern Purim *groggers* look and are manufactured can be learned from an art-craft guide by Temima N. Gezari of the Jewish Education Committee of New York (f. 50, p. 393).

The late Benjamin Mintz had in his collection in Warsaw, which he was fortunate enough to bring over to this country, a Purim *grogger* in silver, made in the nineteenth century in Russia (f. 28, p. 212). It was of elaborate workmanship, complete with whistle, bells, a rattle and even a tiny golden Haman swinging inside. Hissing, stamping and rattling at the mention of Haman was a pleasant duty of the youngsters at the reading of the *Megillah* in and outside the synagogue.

Art Expresses Purim Joy

From this rapid survey of Purim and of artists — Jewish and non-Jewish — who have sought to embellish its ceremonial objects, we may learn a number of things: Jewish artists borrowed from Christian art-forms and techniques; Christian artists were influenced by Jewish art-conceptions;

and both caught the rollicking spirit of the festival and embodied it in caricatures that made the Jews rejoice and laugh. Thus the art of the draftsman and engraver, as well as of the painter, united with the art of playwright and poet to celebrate the joyousness of Purim.

BOOK THREE

Purim for Young People

... these days should be remembered and kept throughout every generation, every family ... that these days of Purim should not fail from among the Jews, nor the memorial of them perish from their seed.

ESTHER 9. 28.

CHAPTER XIII

STORIES FOR PURIM

THE STORY OF PURIM[1]

DEBORAH PESSIN
(age level six to nine)

LONG, long ago, in the land of Persia, there lived a king called Ahasuerus. Ahasuerus had a beautiful wife named Vashti.

One day, at a feast which Ahasuerus gave for his friends and courtiers, he decided to call his wife Vashti so that his friends could see how beautiful she was. So he sent a messenger, bidding her come before him.

Vashti did not wish to appear before the courtiers without her veil, for in those days women covered their faces in the presence of strange men. She knew that her foolish husband had drunk too much wine.

"Tell him I will not come," said Vashti.

The messenger left the queen's chamber and returned to the king.

"She will not come, your Majesty," he told the king, bowing low.

"How dare she say she will not come?" he shouted, his face red with anger.

Then Ahasuerus looked around at his friends and courtiers.

"What shall be done to a queen who does not obey the king?" he asked.

"You must send her away," said an adviser,"for if the women of Persia hear that Vashti does not obey the king, they will no longer obey their husbands."

"Well spoken," said Ahasuerus, and turning to the messenger, he told him to go to the queen and order her to leave the palace forever.

A New Queen Is Chosen

The next morning Ahasuerus was sorry that he had sent Vashti away. He called for his advisers who came and stood about him.

"I need a new queen," said Ahasuerus, "for I am very unhappy without a queen beside me."

The advisers thought for a long time. At last one of them said, "Your Majesty, I have a plan for choosing a new queen."

"What is it?" asked the king eagerly.

"Have your royal messengers ride through the land of Persia, and have them bring back the most beautiful maidens of the land. And you will choose the most beautiful among them to be your queen."

The king was delighted when he heard these words, and he sent for his messengers at once. A short time later, they mounted their swift steeds and rode off in all directions to bring back the most beautiful maidens of Persia.

In the city of Shushan, which was the capital city of Persia, there lived a Jewish man called Mordecai. With him lived his cousin, Esther, whose parents had died when she was a little girl. Esther was very beautiful. She had long black hair that hung in heavy braids to her waist, and clear black eyes filled with soft lights and deep shadows.

Now it happened that a messenger, passing her garden, looked in and saw her. Quickly he dismounted and spoke to her.

"Will you come to the palace with me?" he asked. "The king is seeking a new queen, and perhaps you will be chosen for you are indeed beautiful."

Esther ran into the house to ask Mordecai's advice.

"Yes, Esther," said Mordecai when he had heard the messenger's request, "you must go to the palace. Perhaps, if you become queen of Persia, you may some day help your people."

So Esther went to the palace of the king where she was led to a large chamber. Here there were many other beautiful maidens, weaving flowers and jewels into their hair and rubbing sweet oils and perfumes into their skin. They wore rich robes that glowed with threads of gold.

At last it was time for the maidens to appear before the king. Attended by slaves, they went to the throne-room, where the king sat, surrounded by his courtiers and advisers.

Slowly the maidens passed before the king, each maiden dressed in her finest robes, flowers and jewels twinkling in her hair. And each maiden seemed more beautiful than the other. Some looked like bright birds, swift and delicate, and some were like slender flowers swaying in the wind. Then came Esther, moving softly like a breath of summer. Her hair, black as the night, hung in two heavy braids to her waist, and her black eyes were like wells under a dark sky filled with light and shadows. The king gazed upon her and he was pleased.

"This is the maiden who shall be my queen," he said, rising and taking her hand.

And Esther became queen of Persia and sat beside the king.

After that, Mordecai would often come to the court-yard of the palace. Whenever he had something to tell Esther, he would send a message to her.

MORDECAI SAVES THE KING'S LIFE

One day, as Mordecai was sitting near the palace, he heard two men speaking in a strange language. Now Mordecai, who knew many languages, understood the speech of the men. He soon realized that they were planning to kill the king.

Mordecai sent a message to Esther at once, and Esther told the king of the plot. The conspirators were caught, and Ahasuerus had his scribe write in his book of chronicles that the Jew, Mordecai, had saved his life.

There was a very wicked man in the court of the king, whose name was Haman. Haman had a wicked wife, called Zeresh, and ten sons. Next to the king, Haman was the most powerful man in Persia. So powerful was he that everyone feared him. Whenever he passed through the streets of Shushan, everyone bowed down before him, for so the king had ordered his subjects.

One day, as Haman was walking up and down in the court-yard of the palace, he met Mordecai. To his surprise, Mordecai did not bow before him.

"Stop!" cried Haman. "Why do you not bow before me?"

"I bow before no one but God," said Mordecai, "for I am a Jew."

Haman fumed with anger. He rushed home and told his wife what Mordecai had said. And Zeresh became as angry as her husband.

"Why do you not have him killed?" she asked. "Get the king's permission to kill him and all the Jews."

For some time after that Haman went about plotting to get the king's permission to kill the Jews.

One night, it happened that the king could not sleep. He tossed and rolled on his couch and at last he sent for his scribe.

"Read to me," he said, "for I cannot sleep."

The scribe seated himself at the king's feet and read to him from the book of chronicles. He read the part that told of how Mordecai had saved the life of the king.

"Was Mordecai ever rewarded?" asked the king.

"No, your Majesty," answered the scribe.

Ahasuerus sent for Haman at once.

"Haman," said Ahasuerus, "What shall be done to the man whom the king delights to honor?"

Haman, of course, thought that the king meant him, and his eyes glowed with happiness.

"Let that man be dressed in the robes of the king," said Haman. "And let him be seated on the king's white horse, and let a nobleman, one who is high in the court, lead the horse through Shushan. Then let the nobleman cry aloud, so that all may hear: "Thus shall be done to the man whom the king delights to honor!"

"Excellent!" cried the king. "Mordecai is the man, and you, Haman, shall lead the horse."

Haman dared not show his anger to the king. Silently he turned away, biting his lips. And the king sent for Mordecai who was dressed in the king's own royal robes and seated upon the king's white horse. When this was done, the king sent for Haman. Trembling with rage, Haman led the horse upon which Mordecai sat through the streets of Shushan. People lined the streets, and gazed with amazement at the powerful Haman who was leading Mordecai and crying aloud: "Thus shall be done to the man whom the king delights to honor!"

WICKED HAMAN'S PLOT

After that Haman hated Mordecai more that ever. At last, when he had thought of a plan to have him killed, he hastened to the king.

"O king," he began, "there is a strange people living in this land."

"Who are they?" asked the king, who was busy drinking wine.

"The Jews," said Haman. "They follow strange customs, they have their own God. It is not good to have a people in a land which is different from all other people."

"What shall I do about them?" asked the king, emptying his glass.

"Have them killed," said Haman. "Here I have the decree all ready."

"Very well," said Ahasuerus, "give it to me."

And he put his seal on the decree.

When the Jews heard what had happened they grieved and mourned. And Mordecai, dressed in sackcloth, with ashes on his head, came and sat in the court-yard of the palace. Esther saw him and sent for him at once. When Esther heard the cruel news, her heart was filled with grief.

"What shall I do to help my people?" she asked Mordecai.

"You must go to the king and tell him that you are a Jewess, too."

"But how can I go," asked Esther, "when the king has not sent for me? No one may enter his throne-room, unless sent for by the king. Even the queen dare not appear before him. If he is displeased at my coming, he may have me killed."

"You must go to him," said Mordecai. "If the Jews die, you will die, too, with all your people."

"Tell the Jews of Shushan to fast and pray for three days," said Esther. "I and my maidens will also fast and pray. Then I will go to the king."

"We shall pray for you," said Mordecai, and he left her chambers.

For three days, Esther and her maidens fasted and prayed.

Then she arose from her couch, put on her finest clothes and went to the throne-room. She opened the door and walked in.

On his throne sat Ahasuerus, his scepter in his hand. He looked up and saw Esther at the door, her black eyes filled only with deep shadows. Then Ahasuerus raised his scepter to show that he was pleased at her coming. Esther came forward and stood before him.

"What is it," he asked, "that has made you risk your life in coming to me, unsummoned."

"I am giving a feast in your honor," said Esther, "and I would have you come. And you, too," she said, turning to Haman, who was standing at the king's side.

Esther Pleads For Her People

The next day Ahasuerus and the very proud Haman came to the queen's feast. When the king had eaten and drunk till his heart was gay, he turned to his wife and said, "Ask anything of me, my dear Esther, and it shall be granted, even unto half my kingdom."

Esther stared out of the window at the gallows that rose in the public square. Haman, following her gaze, wondered what it was that was troubling the queen.

"I ask only for my life," said Esther, turning to the king.

"Your life?" cried the king. "Who dares threaten your life?"

"This is the man who seeks to destroy me," said Esther, pointing to Haman.

"I?" cried Haman, falling to his knees before her. "I would protect your life with my own."

"The king has sealed a decree that all the Jews will be killed," said Esther. "I, too, am a Jew."

"I did not know," said the king.

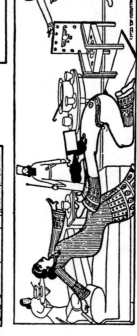

40. *MEGILLAH*

Otto Geismar

Pen and Ink

"And Mordecai," Esther went on, "the man who saved your life, is my cousin."

Haman groaned and hid his face in his hands. And the king walked back and forth in the room, his hands behind his back. Suddenly he looked out of the window and saw the gallows.

"For whom are those gallows?" he asked.

"Haman had them built for Mordecai," said Esther.

Trembling, Haman pleaded for his life. He swore he had not known that Mordecai was Esther's cousin. But the king was very angry. He shouted for his guards who rushed into the room.

"Have Haman hanged on the gallows he built for Mordecai", he said.

And Haman was led away to the gallows, but still Esther was unhappy.

"What of my people?" she asked. "Must they die?"

"I have sealed a decree," said the king sadly, "and I cannot recall it, for a king's word is law."

"Then have another decree sent out," said Esther, "a decree saying that the Jews may defend themselves if they are attacked."

41. *PURIM GREETING CARD*

Temima N. Gezari

THE JEWS ARE SAVED

The king sent out his new decree at once. His messengers, mounted on the swiftest of steeds, brought the news to all parts of Persia that the Jews might defend themselves if they were attacked. Then the king sent for Mordecai to take the place of Haman in his court. When the Jews heard that Mordecai now stood beside the king and was his chief adviser, they sang and danced for joy in the streets of Persia.

And since that day, each year, on the 14th day of Adar, the day when the sorrow of the Jews of Persia was turned to great joy, the Jews throughout the world have celebrated the holiday of Purim.

HOW K'TONTON MASQUERADED ON PURIM[2]

Sadie Rose Weilerstein
(age level four to six)

"Father," said K'tonton,* "when you were a little boy, did you dress up on Purim and wear a mask?"

"What a question!"

"And did you go to other people's houses and sing songs?"

"Of course!"

"Could I dress up and masquerade?"

"A little fellow like you, K'tonton? You would be left behind under a doormat. But I'll make you a *grogger*. That will be better than masquerading."

K'tonton's father took out a pen knife and a bit of wood and made him a beautiful noise-making *grogger*.

"Ras! Ras! Ras!" went the *grogger* as K'tonton whirled it about.

"It's nice to have a *grogger*," said K'tonton, "but not so nice as masquerading on Purim. I'd better talk to Mother."

Mother was in the kitchen rolling out *Imberlah*. She lifted K'tonton to the table.

"Could I masquerade on Purim?" asked K'tonton.

---

*K'tonton was a tiny boy, no bigger than your thumb.

"You?" said Mother. "Listen to the child! Haven't I lost you enough times already? But I'll tell you what I'll do. I'll make you a little *Hamantash* all for yourself. See! I've been pounding the poppy seeds." She pointed to a brass mortar on the table.

"Oh," said K'tonton, "poppy seed with honey?"

"Honey, of course," said Mother. "What else? Now sit still, K'tonton. I'll be back in a minute."

Off Mother went. K'tonton crossed his legs and waited.

"A minute is a long time," he said after a while.

He sat still again.

"I guess it must be two minutes. I guess it must be nine minutes. I guess I'll just get up and take a look at that poppy seed."

Up the side of a sack of flour he ran. Now he could see deep down into the mortar. He could see the pounder leaning against the side.

"That's a good slide," said K'tonton. He loved sliding down things. "I'll slide down and take a taste of that poppy seed. Mother wouldn't mind just a little taste."

The next minute his legs were over the top of the pestle and he was sliding down. A thought popped into his head. "I must stop before I reach the bottom. I might get stuck." But he couldn't stop. He was going too fast. Blimp! He was in poppy seed up to his waist.

And there was Mother's voice coming toward him. "Where's that K'tonton? I can't seem to keep track of him today. Well, I'll have to make the *Hamantashen* without him."

K'tonton felt the mortar lifted and turned over. The next moment he was tumbling head over heels into a big bowl with poppy seed all around him. You couldn't tell which was poppy seed and which was K'tonton.

"Mother! Mother!" K'tonton began, but a stream of

honey was flowing over him. The words caught in the honey and stuck fast.

And now a big wooden spoon came down into the bowl. It picked K'tonton up. It tossed him! It chased him! Round and round went K'tonton with the wooden spoon close behind. It caught him at last. It lifted him up into the air. It set him down in the middle of something soft. Dough! A flat piece of dough! K'tonton was being made into a *Hamantash!*

"I must speak! I must call!" thought K'tonton. "My voice! Where is my voice?" It was gone. By the time it returned, he had been slipped into a pan and was being carried off.

A *Hamantash!* That meant he would be put into an oven, a fiery furnace like Abraham and Daniel's companions. And God would not save him as He had saved Daniel's companions and Abraham. Had he not disobeyed his dear Mother?

"Dear God," K'tonton prayed, "save me from the fiery oven even if I don't deserve it."

A voice was speaking. K'tonton pressed his ear to the hole in the *Hamantash* and listened.

"I'll leave the cakes on the shelf here to rise." The pan was lifted. Then all was still.

Then he wasn't to be put into the oven, not for a little while at least. He might yet escape. But how? He tried to move. His arms were stuck fast to his sides.

"I'll eat my way out," said K'tonton. He ate and he ate and he ate. He ate so much he felt he could never look at honey or a poppy seed again. The hole grew bigger and bigger. It grew so big he could stick his head out, and he could wriggle his hands loose, his arms, his legs. He was free.

Far, far below was the table. K'tonton shut his eyes tight and jumped — safe into the middle of the sack of flour.

But his troubles were not yet over.

Creak, creak, came a step across the floor.

"Mother!" thought K'tonton. "I must hide until I get this poppy seed washed off."

He slipped onto a plate and hid behind a pile of *Imberlah*.

Mother's voice came nearer. "Father," it said, "I'm going to take this *Shalah Monot* to the new little boy next door. He has been sick in bed ever since they moved in. Poor little fellow! The sweets may cheer him up a bit."

She threw a napkin over the plate.

"Look after K'tonton, Father," she said. "He's somewhere about."

She lifted the plate and was off. And there was K'tonton in the *Shalah Monot* dish with cakes and candies and *Hamantashen* all about him.

"I wonder what is going to happen next?" he thought.

He was so tired he snuggled down at the bottom of the dish and shut his eyes. In another minute he was asleep.

"What has happened? Where am I?" said K'tonton when he opened his eyes a little later.

He peered cautiously over the side of a *Hamantash* and looked about. He was in a strange room. The dish was lying on a table near a bed, and on the bed lay a young boy propped up with pillows. Such a pale, unhappy looking little fellow! He was staring soberly at the *Shalah Monot*, at the cakes, the Purim candies, the *Hamantash*, but he did not taste a thing and there wasn't a smile on his face. Something hurt inside of K'tonton.

"One oughtn't to look like that on Purim," he thought. "Purim is a good day, a day of gladness and feasting, a day of sending gifts to one another. The *Megillah* says it is."

K'tonton forgot that he was supposed to be hiding. He forgot he was covered with poppy seed. He forgot that he was dusted with flour. He knew only that he had to make that little boy smile. He stepped from behind the *Hamantash* and bowed low.

The boy's mouth opened and his eyes grew as big as saucers.

"The inside of a *Hamantash* came alive!"

He stared hard.

"It must be a toy," he decided. "I suppose there are springs inside." He reached out his hand to feel, but K'tonton sprang back.

"I'm not a toy," he said. "I'm not the inside of a *Hamantash*, though I was inside one," he added truthfully. "I-I —." It was then that the great thought dawned on him — "I'm a Purim masquerader and I'm dressed up in poppy seed and I've come to other people's houses, to your house, to sing Purim songs."

At that he lifted his shrill voice and began to sing:

"Happy, happy Purim,
Happy Purim day!"

For a minute the boy sat perfectly still and stared. Then he threw his head back and laughed. Such a happy, jolly, hearty, rollicking laugh, a regular Purim laugh! Ha, Ha, Ha, Ha, Ha, Ha! Ho, Ho, Ho, He, He!

"What could have happened?" cried the little boy's Mother, who was in the next room. "I haven't heard David laugh in weeks."

She hurried into the bedroom and K'tonton's Mother followed her. There was David laughing and clapping his hands; and there in the middle of the *Shalah Monot* dish, black with poppy seed, dusted with flour, was a wee little fellow singing and dancing away.

"K'tonton!" cried his Mother. "How did you get here? What does this mean?"

"I-I'm the inside of a *Hamantash*," said K'tonton. "I'm in other people's houses. I'm masquerading as you did when you were a little girl."

"Please let him stay, please," begged David. "We're having such a jolly time."

So K'tonton's Mother hurried home and fetched him a clean little suit and blouse and scrubbed him and dressed him in his holiday clothes.

K'tonton's Father came too. He brought a *Megillah* with him and sang them the whole story of Purim, all about the King and Mordecai and the wicked Haman, and how good Queen Esther saved the Jews. K'tonton ran along under the words in the *Megillah* — to keep the place, you know — and every time he came to the name of the wicked Haman he whirled his *grogger* — Ras! Ras! Ras!

Then they sang songs and ate the cakes and *Imberlah* and *Hamantashen*; and everybody had such a happy time that no one thought of scolding K'tonton at all.

TEL AVIV[3]

Libbie L. Braverman
(age level seven to nine)

What a crowd there was in the streets of Tel Aviv! The twins and their parents had just arrived in Tel Aviv for Purim. They were on their way by bus to *Rehob* Ahad Ha-Am where the Gordon family lived.

"Are you sure the Gordons will have room enough in their house for all of us?" asked Tamar.

"Oh, yes, indeed," answered Imma. "I made these arrangements a long time ago. I knew, at Purim time, Tel Aviv fills up with visitors. People come even from America. Every hotel is filled."

"We're lucky that the Gordons invited us. Wouldn't it be nice to ask Ari Gordon to Nahalal for his summer vacation?" asked Tamar.

"Yes," answered Imma. "We'll let David invite him."

Tel Aviv was decorated with flags, huge signs, and palm branches.

"Look at the arches over the streets," cried David as they rode along. "Tel Aviv is all dressed up for the parade."

"Yes," answered Abba. "The arches have electric lights in them and will be lit for the carnival."

"What is that man doing way up on top of that building?" asked Tamar.

"He's putting some electric light bulbs in a huge crown," said Abba.

"That must be Queen Esther's crown," cried Tamar.

"Yes," answered Abba. "Many tall buildings have Queen Esther crowns placed on their roofs for the festival. Every evening they are lit up. The whole city is a network of twinkling lights at night."

When the family arrived, their friends, the Gordons, were waiting at the door to welcome them.

Tel Aviv Becomes Shushan

At last it was *Ereb* Purim. Hotels and stores were decorated with flags and large banners. Thousands of visitors from all parts of Palestine and other lands crowded the streets of the city. They came from many parts of the world: Egypt, Turkey, Poland, Switzerland, England, Germany and even from America. Yet they all seemed to belong to this great pageant. Hundreds of Arabs from nearby Jaffa and thousands of Jews from the neighboring colonies continued to pour into Tel Aviv. Some were hastily making last minute purchases in preparation for the big day.

Others were promenading through the city, enjoying the colorful decorations and the excitement, losing themselves in the crowds. Traffic rules were forgotten as the city was jammed to overflowing.

Mr. and Mrs. Gordon and their guests were on their way to the synagogue to hear the reading of *Megillat Esther*.

"Look!" said David, gazing with surprise at a street sign. "I thought this was *Rehob* Allenby."

"Yes," explained Mr. Gordon. "It was *Rehob* Allenby. Its name has been changed for Purim. It is now called Shushan *ha-Birah*. Other streets have had their names changed for Purim too. These names are all taken from the Book of Esther."

"Tel Aviv really becomes Shushan then," said David delightedly.

Just then, the siren of the fire department sounded. It was immediately picked up by the shrill factory whistles and by the boats in the harbor.

The electric crowns on the tops of the buildings burst into light. Over their heads, a network of gaily-colored lights strung across the streets twinkled merrily. The children stood still and watched.

"Hurry," said Abba, "we must get to the synagogue in time to hear the reading of the *Megillah*."

"You needn't hurry," Mr. Gordon laughed. "We probably won't be able to get in anyhow."

"Oh," said Tamar disappointedly, "what will we do?"

"Don't worry, Tamar. There is an amplifier outside the synagogue and another in Mograbi Square."

They joined the huge crowd that jammed the street in front of the Great Synagogue. The crowd grew still as they listened to the chanting of the story of Esther.

When it was over, the crowd surged toward Mograbi Square. From the Opera House the melody of *Shoshanat*

Ya'akob, the traditional Purim song, was heard. Then the band struck up the newest Purim melody. A hush fell over the audience that stood in front of the newly built Persian palace.

The pageant had begun. The old, old story came to life again before their eyes. Esther was chosen queen. The villain Haman planned to destroy the Jewish people. Unafraid, Esther appeared before the king. She outwitted Haman and brought deliverance to her people.

The play was over. The amplifiers carried the band's Purim melodies to every corner of the city. The people could no longer stand still. Soon their feet were keeping time to the music. The band struck up the popular *Emek, Emek*. With their arms on each other's shoulders, men and women, old and young, merrily danced the *Horah*. Thus began a night of festivity in the city.

But it was now long past the children's bedtime. Unwillingly, they left the gay carnival. Forcing their way through dancing and singing throngs, they finally reached home. In spite of the noise, the children were soon fast asleep.

THE ADLOYADA

The next morning David opened his eyes first. Through the window he saw green trees and blue sky. He tried to recall something very important. He knew that something very exciting was going to happen. What was it? Oh, now he remembered, and he hastily jumped out of bed.

"Wake up, Ari! Hurry!" he called, shaking his friend. "Today is the day of the *Adloyada*."

They dressed quickly and went out on the porch. Wagons filled with children were clattering through the streets on their way to the children's celebration.

"Come, hurry, or we'll be late!" Ari urged. "I am in a play that my school is giving at the Civic Center."

In a few minutes, the children were ready and were on their way to the Civic Center.

Huge banners bearing the names of Tel Aviv's schools were flying in the air.

"Over there the Herzliah School is assembling," said Ari. Here are the kindergarten schools, and here is the Bialik School. These boys marching by belong to the Ahad Ha-Am School. There is the banner of my school, Balfour. This is where we sit."

"Look at that *Menorah* over the water tower, Ari," cried David.

"That is the electric *Menorah*," he explained. "We have another on the roof of the Great Synagogue."

"We light a large Hanukkah *Menorah* at home in Nahalal, too," said Tamar.

"A *Menorah* is lit in every home and is placed in the window," continued Ari. "It is really a very pretty sight to see all the lights twinkling from so many windows in our city. But what's even nicer is the Children's Light Parade. We carry candles and lighted torches and march through the streets to the Civic Center."

"That must be lovely," exclaimed Tamar.

"It certainly is," answered Ari, "but still I like Purim better. It's much more fun."

Soon the mayor of Tel Aviv mounted the platform. He welcomed the boys and girls to the Carnival and told them that this was the biggest children's celebration of the year. Eight thousand children were present. The program opened with a short reading from the *Megillah*. This was followed by a Purim play in which Ari took the part of one of the wicked conspirators. Then all the children joined in the

singing of Purim songs. The twins knew all the songs and
sang along with the others.

Prizes were then awarded for attendance and good work.
Proudly, Ari marched up to the platform when his name
was called. Then the mayor announced the names of the
three healthiest children of the city. They were two boys
and one girl who had been born and brought up in Tel Aviv.
He finished his talk by saying that one of the most important slogans of Palestine is, "A healthy mind in a healthy
body."

Later, the children formed circles and danced the *Horah*.

When the twins and Ari joined their parents, Mr. Ben
Ami said, "We must find a good place to watch the parade
of the floats."

"I have an excellent place in mind," said Mr. Gordon.
"Some of my friends live at the corner of *Rehob* Allenby and
Rehob Nahlat Binyamin."

"There is no *Rehob* Allenby now, Dad. You mean Shushan
ha-Birah," cried Ari.

"That's right," laughed Mr. Gordon, "but do let's hurry."

What ordinarily was a five-minute walk took them fully
a half hour today. The lunchrooms were crowded to the
doors. Many people were eating their lunch in outdoor cafes
right on the sidewalks. Others were looking for a good spot
from which to watch the parade. Although the parade was
fully an hour off, every place, every corner, every roof and
every porch was jammed full of people.

They were finally settled on the porch of their friends'
home.

"Abba," said Tamar, "this is the first time in all my life
that I have ever seen so many people in one place."

The policemen were busy directing traffic and the Mac-
cabiah athletes were helping to keep order.

With the first sound of the loud speaker, the noise began to subside. The mayor led the procession, followed by the other officials of Tel Aviv. As they passed each group, they were greeted with applause and cheers, *"Hedad! Hedad! Hedad!"*

Then the parade of the floats began. The first float was a miniature city of Tel Aviv, showing its growth. The next one carried a huge box, the *Keren Kayemet* box. A sign on it read, "Every Cent for *Keren Kayemet* Adds More Land to Jewish Palestine."

The Mikveh Yisrael float, which was next in line, was entirely covered with fruit and vegetables. In the center stood several boys, each one holding a farm tool in one hand and, with the other, pointing proudly at the produce of his own school.

"Look at that one!" cried Ari. "It s a small wine cellar. It looks exactly like the one we saw at Rishon le-Zion."

"It is the one at Rishon le-Zion," answered his father. "Let's see, what does it say? 'The Second Largest Wine Cellar in the World.' "

"Which is the first, Abba?" asked David.

"The largest wine cellar in the world is in Bordeaux, France," replied Abba.

"There is an orange float," cried Tamar. "Look at the big oranges, and lemons, and grapefruits! They make my mouth water."

"Those grapevines look as though they are growing right there on the floats," said David.

"Kenu Tozeret ha-Arez" (Buy the Products of Palestine!), Tamar read on the next float. On it were displayed a great variety of the products of the land. One float showed corn and wheat grown on the Emek farms. Not to be outdone, the mountain farmers exhibited olives and almonds.

Groups of masked revelers capered and pranced through the crowd. Big sausage-like balloons sailed by. Grotesque figures poking fun at Haman, Hitler and other enemies of Jews appeared next.

A group of dark Yemenite Jews marched by. They represented the children of Israel entering Canaan.

A burst of children's laughter was heard when a float rolled by, filled with merry, smiling children. Their *Gannenet* (kindergarten teacher) was with them. This was the first time the *Gannenet* really earned her name, for the children were dressed like a garden of flowers. This float was labeled "Products of Palestine."

The procession was over much too soon for the children.

"I'm sorry it's over," said David.

"All good things must come to an end sometime," said Imma.

"Yes," said Ari. "And overnight the magician of the Persian palace will turn Shushan back again to Tel Aviv."

THE MAGIC GROGGER[4]

Levin Kipnis
(age level seven to nine)

One Purim eve, just before sunset, grandfather was sitting on a stool examining his *Megillah*. Before the stove stood grandmother, blowing at the fire, raising clouds of smoke and preparing all kinds of cakes and cookies.

Suddenly Haggai, their little grandson, came running in.

"Grandfather, it's almost time to go to the synagogue to hear the *Megillah* read. And I haven't a *grogger*."

Grandmother peered out from a cloud of smoke.

"Haggai is right," she said. "How will he beat Haman without a *grogger?*"

"It's time to make one, then," said grandfather.

So grandfather, who was handy with tools, took his sharp penknife. It was an old penknife, but it shone as though it had just come out of the factory. He picked out a smooth piece of wood from a box and began to work. He cut and hacked away, the splinters flying in all directions. Haggai danced about, trying to catch the splinters.

"Stop dancing about," said grandfather. "While I make your *grogger*, you study your lessons."

Haggai took his grandfather's old Bible out of his bag and opened to the book of Joshua.

"And it came to pass after the death of Moses. . ."

Grandmother stood at the stove listening, her eyes filled with tears of joy. Grandfather listened, too, but he did not stop his work for a moment.

Haggai read one chapter, two chapters, three, four, five. And grandfather worked away on the *grogger*. He put together small pieces of wood, big pieces, narrow, wide thick wheels, sharp rollers, smooth rollers.

Haggai reached chapter six and his voice rang out like a golden bell, "Jericho was shut in," just as his grandfather was finishing the *grogger*. The wheels were put together, a screw here, a nail there, and the *grogger* was finished!

"And the people shouted," read Haggai.

At that moment the *grogger* shouted, too. The voice of the *grogger* shook the air. For this year grandfather had made the most wonderful *grogger* of all. On top was a little blue and white flag, and while all *groggers* have only one wing, this *grogger* had two wings.

Haggai closed the book in the middle of chapter six and even grandmother left her *Hamantashen*. Grandfather rose happily from his work, like a conqueror. He tucked his *Megillah* under his arm and the three went to the synagogue.

There Haggai's *grogger* became famous. It made more noise than any other *grogger* in the city. As its wings turned, the synagogue became a thundering mountain and Haggai might have been a messenger from Joshua sent to throw down the walls of Jericho.

When the three returned home again, they happily ate their Purim meal.

"Tomorrow," said Haggai, "I'll dress in blue and purple, like Mordecai, because my *grogger* conquered Haman."

Grandfather smiled, then sighed and said, "Yes, Haggai, Haman was killed, but there are other Hamans, many others. In Germany. . .Rumania, Poland. . ."

That night Haggai lay in his bed, tossing from side to side. Suddenly his *grogger* came and stood beside him.

"Haggai, why aren't you asleep?"

"Oh, dear," said Haggai, "one Haman was hanged and now there are so many others."

"Yes," answered the *grogger*, "but they'll all be punished. You should be happy because it's Purim. Tomorrow there's that big celebration in Tel Aviv."

"How can I be happy," said Haggai, "when Jewish children are suffering in other lands?"

"Why don't they come here?" asked the *grogger*.

"I wish they could," sighed Haggai.

The *grogger* jumped about in great excitement. "Why not?" it asked. "You can bring them, Haggai, if you're brave."

"How can I bring them?" smiled Haggai.

"Listen," said the *grogger*. "Take me outside. Spread my wings, then sit upon me and fly off. Together we'll fly over foreign lands and bring all the Jewish children here. But don't forget to take provisions, not cakes and goodies, but rockets and flares to light the way."

"Hurrah!" cried Haggai.

And he tumbled out of bed, took the *grogger* out of doors, and it spread its wings. The flag became a propeller and, as the wings were gently lifted from the ground, Haggai sat between the wings and rode up to the sky on his airplane.

Over hill and vale he flew. The propeller whirred. In a minute, they had soared over the sea and were in foreign lands.

Haggai threw down some rockets. They fell to earth like great falling comets, like arcs of bright lightning. In every land, the children of Israel came out into the streets, men and women, old and young, children with their *groggers* in their hands. They all stood gazing up at the sky where Haggai sat on his *grogger* in a pillar of light.

"Listen," called Haggai, "Listen, dear children of Israel.

"How long will you live oppressed in these lands?

"Arise! Be brave and leave the lands that oppress you. Our land is waiting for her sons, her builders.

"Our land is beautiful. In the Valley of Jezreel a new life is blossoming. On the hills of Galilee the shepherd plays his flute. In Sharon the Hebrew worker rejoices.

"Why do you remain here, in the lands where Hitler oppresses you?

"Arise and come with me!"

As Haggai finished speaking, he lit a flare. Brilliant sparks shot out in all directions in great arcs of light. Below, the people stood gazing up. Only the children, boys and girls, turned their *groggers*, their eyes shining.

"We are free," they shouted, "we are free!"

Their voices were still ringing in the air when Haggai lit another flare.

"Whoever is brave," he cried, "come with me!"

The children answered, "We'll go singing to our land."

Then, from every land the children, in great columns, came marching. The earth trembled beneath their feet. On and on they went, while Haggai rode above them on his *grogger-*airplane.

When they reached the Mediterranean Sea, they stood on the shores and asked each other, "What shall we do now? How can we cross without ships?"

"We will cross," cried Haggai from his pillar of light. "We have no boats, but we have *groggers*. You will be the sailors. Don't be afraid. Sit on your *groggers* and ride out to sea. We'll reach port by morning."

"Hurrah!" shouted the children.

And they plunged into the sea astride their *groggers*. They whipped out their handkerchiefs and quickly tied them to the *groggers* for sails. The stars in the sky were the lanterns. Strong winds rose and spanked the sails. By morning the children had reached port.

Shouting with joy they jumped ashore and ran toward Tel Aviv. Down came Haggai on his *grogger*, down to earth, his eyes shut against the wind. His feet touched ground and he opened his eyes.

He was lying in his bed. Grandmother stood at the stove, blowing the fire. And grandfather, just home from synagogue, came into the room.

"Why are you lying there so quietly, Haggai?" he asked. "They're starting the Purim parade."

"Lying there quietly!" cried Haggai. He jumped out of bed.

"You are right, grandfather, I shouldn't be lying here. I have work to do, lots of work." Haggai pulled his shirt on over his head.

"I'll get my friends together, all of them. No, grandma. I've no time for breakfast. Well, maybe just one *Hamantash*. We have work. Trees to plant, fields to till." Haggai struggled into his jacket.

"We've got to have things ready when they come here. The land must be beautiful, every bit of it."

"When who comes, Haggai?" asked grandmother.

"The children of Israel, of course."

And Haggai dashed out of the house, his shirt tails flying, in search of his friends.

THE PURIM GUEST[5]

HERMANN SCHWAB
(age level seven to nine)

It was Purim, and everyone, old and young, was happy and in good spirits. Only one little house at the very end of the town was silent, and without joy. Purim seemed to have passed it by.

A poor woman lived here, with her two young children. She had been ill in bed for weeks, and if a few kind neighbors had not brought them a little food they would have fared badly.

But now, for some days, no one had been near them, and Purim had come and they had nothing in the house except some dry bread.

The poor woman lay in bed, feeling very unhappy, and the two little children sat beside her. They spoke to her about their school, and what the teacher had told them about Purim, about the wicked Haman and the good Mordecai, and the beautiful Queen Esther.

"And because God saved the Jews from Haman's wickedness, we celebrate Purim, our teacher told us," said the little girl. "And we eat and drink, and send gifts to each other, and give to the poor."

"Why haven't we anything good to eat on Purim?" asked the little boy, looking sorrowfully at the piece of dry bread in his hand.

"Because we are poor," said his mother, "and people have forgotten us."

The children saw their mother crying, and they too wept.

That afternoon a strange old man came through the town. No one there knew him, no one had ever seen him before. He wore a long cloak and carried a heavy stick, and his long white beard shook at every step he took.

He came to the little house and stood looking through the window into the tiny room where the mother was lying in bed, with her two little children at her side.

He nodded his head. Then he knocked at the door and walked in.

"Good Purim," he said. "I have walked all day, and I am tired and hungry. Can you give me some food?"

"Good Purim," answered the woman, speaking in a sad, faint voice.

The two children sprang up from their seats, and brought out all the dry bread that was left in the house, and gave it to the stranger.

And as he was eating, the mother told him their sad story, how she had been ill, and how poor they were.

And the old man listened and nodded his head.

When he had finished eating, he thanked them and prepared to go.

"You have been very kind," he said, "I shall always remember you. You gave me your last piece of bread. And I want you to remember me, too — as long as you live. I grant you three wishes. Each of you may have one wish, and they will be granted."

The mother and her children stared at the stranger. What had happened to the poor old man who had come to them, tired and hungry, wandering from town to town? He had grown so tall. He looked so fine and noble. His eyes shone, and his voice rang like a bell.

"I wish we could keep Purim properly, like all people," said the little boy.

"I wish I were well again," said the mother quietly.

"I wish we could always give to the poor," said the little girl.

The stranger placed his hand on the mother's head, and she was well. He struck the table with his stick, and it was covered with delicious food, choice fruit and sweet wine.

The mother and her children stared open-mouthed at the stranger. They thought they were dreaming.

"Who are you," cried the mother, "that you do these wonderful things?"

"I am Purim," said the old man. "I came to you because you had not forgotten me, though you are ill and poor. I came to try you. I asked you for your last crust of bread, and you gave it to me. I asked you for three wishes, and you thought of me. I shall never forget. Health, wealth and happiness will be yours always and Purim will be your happiest day."

Then the old man went out into the night.

The mother and her children sat down to the richly-laden table and ate and drank and celebrated that wonderful Purim.

And they lived happily ever after.

HOW ESTHER BECAME QUEEN[6]

Joseph Gaer
(age level ten to twelve)

Of all the Jewish holidays Velvel liked Purim best. He liked it because it came the day after the Fast of Esther, and a holiday after a fast is a double holiday.

In the morning Velvel went with his father to synagogue to listen to the happy voices reading the Book of Esther amid outbursts of red Purim-rattlers in the hands of gleeful boys.

From synagogue they came directly home, and Elka rushed them through the noonday meal.

A troup of gypsies, acquainted with the Jewish custom of almsgiving on Purim, came into the house, their leader playing a violin, another rattling wooden castanets, and a young girl dancing to their music. Reb Aaron dispatched them with a coin. Velvel followed the gypsies to the neighbor's house. But fearing that he might miss something at home, he hastened back, twisting his Purim-rattler triumphantly as he ran, coatless, through the street.

The "Purim-gifts" was another custom for which Velvel enjoyed the holiday. Toward the end of the day he delivered presents to relatives, who, in turn, compensated his trouble with candy, nuts and sometimes money.

"Are they all ready?" Velvel asked as he inspected the trays.

"Not yet. I haven't unpacked the candy, and the cake isn't cut yet."

"Esther," Grandma Libe called tenderly. "Come here, daughter!"

"What is it, grandma?"

"I want you to start cutting the cake."

Esther came over, expressing surprise at the honor conferred on her.

"Because your name is the same as hers in whose honor we have today's celebration," grandma said.

"Oh, Queen Esther!"

"Yes, child! Here, wet the knife first. That's the way! You know how Queen Esther cut the cake, don't you?"

"Which cake?"

"The cake that was made for her when she became queen. You remember how Queen Esther became queen, don't you?"

Velvel was aware that Grandma Libe wished to tell a story.

"You remember, don't you, that when King Ahasuerus divorced his wife Vashti, he began to look for a wife to suit his throne." Grandma Libe took the knife from Esther and began to cut the cake deliberately.

"How does a king like that, a king who rules over one hundred and twenty-seven provinces that stretch from sea to sea and from one end of the world to the other, how does he choose a wife for himself?"

"How?" Leah, who was also in the kitchen, asked.

"A king like that sends out three thousand three hundred and thirty-three messengers to every one of his provinces and he lets it be known in every language that Ahasuerus, King of Shushan, is looking for a bride to be made queen of his kingdom. And so he did. And in every province he appointed a judge to pick the most beautiful maidens. And the maidens that these judges found beautiful enough in face and form were sent to Shushan."

Every one in the kitchen was now listening to Grandma Libe's story. Elka quietly arranged the baked dainties, fruit and candy on the trays before her. And as is customary, she placed special gifts among the dainties.

"Did they go directly to the king?" Leah asked.

"To the king? Not so soon! First the king made them live for a year in a palace where they were fed dainty food and clad in the finest clothes. They bathed in purest perfumes. Hundreds of servants were at their command to wait on them. Whatever their hearts desired these maidens could ask for, and it was given them. You can imagine — any one of them might be the future queen!"

"Did many come?" Leah was eager to know.

"Many? All of Shushan was full of these beautiful maidens, filling all the palaces that were built for that purpose. They came from every province and from every city. Some came from the distant countries, seventy days away

from Shushan. On horseback and on camels they came to live
in the palaces, each one making greater demands than their
neighbors for things that would make them more beautiful."

"How long did that last?" Again it was Leah who asked.

"How long? It says it took exactly one year to pick the
most beautiful maidens, and one year to keep them in riches
and in luxury, to prepare them for the king to look
at.

"The day was set, and all the beautiful girls dressed and
perfumed themselves and made great demands. For instance, one girl who came
from where the red pepper
grows wanted to appear
before the king in a sled.
But it was in the middle
of the summer. What could
they do? They ordered four
black horses to be hitched
to a gilded sled, and they
spread in the streets thousands of sacks of salt, and
in that manner the girl
drove by near where the
king sat to judge the most
beautiful girl. Another girl
who had heard of it also
wanted to go in a sled, but
she wouldn't go on salt, she
said. She wanted to ride
on sugar. So, do you think

42. *ESTHER DOLL*

Created by Diana S. Forman

they did not do as she wanted? They did! They swept
the streets of the salt and spread sugar instead. Another
wanted to appear before the king in a boat. So what
did they do? They saw to it that there should be water,

and brought the royal boat and rowed her past the king's chair. And so many passed."

"And the king?" Leah asked.

"The king just looked at them, but he couldn't make up his mind. He thought to himself: 'Why should I say now I like this one or that one. Let me first see them all, then I will be able to tell which is the prettiest of all.' So he sat there with his court looking at them."

"And Queen Esther?" Velvel began to be anxious.

"I was just coming to that. As he sat there, he suddenly noticed a girl walking down the street. She was dressed in simple clothes, her hair combed neatly and covered by a veil.

" 'Who is that girl?' the king asked.

"But no one seemed to know who she was. So they sent messengers to run after her to tell her that the king wanted to speak to her. When the girl came up to the throne the king rose and asked:

" 'What is your name?'

" 'My name is Esther,' she answered.

"Then he wanted to know why she wasn't dressed in gold and silver and why she walked instead of coming in a carriage. And Esther told him that it was because she knew there were more beautiful girls in the kingdom and that she was not worthy of even being considered as a queen. When the king heard that, he raised the crown of purest gold and diamonds, especially prepared for the queen-to-be, and placed it on Esther's head. Then he turned to his officers and said:

" 'This woman I choose as queen of my kingdom. She is the most beautiful in my provinces. For no woman can be truly beautiful unless she is modest and chaste.'

"And he sent his messengers out to all the provinces to let it be known that King Ahasuerus had chosen Esther as his queen."

"And Mordecai?" Velvel asked.

"You'd better take this now to Aunt Hannah." Elka covered one of the trays with a napkin and made it ready for Velvel.

"Let grandmother finish the story first. It's early yet," Velvel sulked.

"No, child, it is time for you to go," Grandma Libe urged him. "I'll tell you the rest when you come back."

Velvel picked up the tray and started for the door. Then he turned and said, "And you'll not tell it while I'm away?"

Grandma Libe smiled as she replied, "No, I'll wait until you return."

PLUM JAM PURIM[7]

William Mordecai Kramer
(age level ten to twelve)

The streets are narrow now in Jung-Bunzlau, a little village in Bohemia, and they were even narrower in the year 1731 when on the narrowest street in the poorest section, David Brandeis and his wife and his son, Danny, had a little grocery store. The Jews and Christians called it a grocery store, although for the most part its shelves would have been empty but for the fine preserves and pickles that Mrs. Brandeis used to make. And although people called it a grocery store it was really the front room of the little house in which the three Brandeis lived.

Ever since Danny remembered, he had liked to eat his mother's preserves and, ever since he had been old enough to count, he had managed the store and sampled the sweets, while his mother worked in the kitchen preparing the fruits which Mr. Brandeis bought during daily trips to the orchards along the countryside.

You would think a fine-looking, strong, eighteen-year-old boy like Danny would be lonesome working in the little store each day, but it wasn't so. Danny loved to talk to the customers, and Danny loved to eat and what Danny loved best was the daily afternoon visit of Miriam, the rabbi's pretty daughter.

They would laugh together and their words were probably made sweeter by the sweet things they ate.

One day Miriam entered the store and said, "*Shalom*, Danny."

"*Shalom*, Miriam," he replied. And they talked and tasted of many things.

"I hear that Paul Prajak is making trouble for us Jews," Miriam said, "and that he would like to see us driven away from our homes here in Bohemia."

"Don't you worry, Miriam," Danny said gallantly. "I'll never let anybody hurt you."

"And I'll look out for you, Danny, even if I am only a girl," said Miriam as they both reached for the big jar, took gobs of plum jam on their fingers and blissfully ate.

While they were talking, the shop door opened and Pauline, the daughter of Old John the bookbinder, came in to make a purchase. Miriam admired the blonde hair of the pretty Christian girl and perhaps was a little jealous as Danny waited on her.

"Some jam, please," said Pauline, "I want the best you have. Paul Prajak is coming for dinner and my father says we must be nice to him." Miriam winced when she heard that name, but she said nothing.

"Here is my mother's best There are no finer preserves in all the world than my mother's plum jam." Saying this, Danny scooped out a measure of his favorite food from the big jar. He collected a copper coin and, as Pauline left, he called over to Miriam. Since they were going to talk some more he didn't put the cover back on the jam jar. And they talked and they tasted until Miriam had to leave for home.

The next morning, as David Brandeis and his son Daniel finished their morning prayers and removed the *Tefillin* from their arms, they heard a loud knocking on the door. Danny called out that he was "coming," but before he reached the door it was broken down revealing the town sheriff. "You are under arrest," he said, "all three of you. You are under arrest for selling poisonous food to Christians. You sold some plum jam to Pauline Kreska and, according to Dr. Ludvig, Old John the bookbinder, her father, has died." Then he led the Brandeis off to jail.

When Miriam heard the news, she rushed to her father, the rabbi, and told him that the charge was untrue. She explained how she and Danny had eaten from the same jar both before and after Pauline had made her purchase. The rabbi listened carefully to his daughter's words and asked who had been present at the bookbinder's home. Miriam answered him and he said that he would talk to Mr. Brandeis and others and see what could be done.

The Brandeis were imprisoned and the flies ate the rest of the jam in the little shop and they did not die; Miriam missed Danny and Danny missed Miriam; Mrs. Brandeis missed her freedom, though she missed her kitchen more; and Mr. Brandeis missed his drives to the country for fresh fruit, and the orchard-keepers missed his friendly smile.

They stayed in prison until one day their barred doors were opened and they were told that the rabbi had arranged through a friend of his in Prague, the capital, that they be given a trial. "It is time to go to court," the jailor said.

Everyone was in the courtroom. There was the sheriff on one side talking to Paul Prajak, in back was Pauline and her mother and near them was Dr. Ludvig, and on the other side was the rabbi with Miriam. "Who is the lawyer for the Brandeis?" asked the judge.

"If there is no objection, I will be," said the rabbi as the family nodded gratefully. "And I will call up my daughter as the first witness."

Miriam answered her father's questions, and blushingly (and therefore beautifully) she told the court how she had come to the little store and how she and Danny had talked and while talking they had tasted the plum jam. "Both before and after Pauline came we ate from the same jar," she said.

Then the rabbi called upon Mr. Prajak and asked what had happened at the bookbinder's home.

"What happened is that your Jews, old rabbi, have killed my friend John. You would kill us all and take away our business if you dared," said Prajak. "Bohemia would be better off without your kind." As Prajak left the stand, Dr. Ludvig was called to take the witness' oath.

The rabbi spoke. "Dr. Ludvig, you look like a worried man. Even when you returned those books of mine the day of Old John's death you seemed worried. But, of course, you were tired that day, for it was then you certified that the good bookbinder had died of poisonous plum jam. Yes, that must be why you seemed worried and didn't stay on at my house for our usual game of chess."

Dr. Ludvig did look worried as he sat in the witness chair.

The rabbi continued. "Or perhaps you were concerned about money that day. I remember how I tried to help you when you spoke of your fear of being imprisoned for debt. I wished that I had had the money. But since you are still free, dear doctor friend, it seems that Paul Prajak has relented and not called in the money he loaned to you, or taken your home and your horse instead."

Dr. Ludvig had played chess too long with the rabbi not

to know where this line of reasoning would lead. And, like the good chess player that he was, he admitted his defeat before the superior force of the rabbi's questions.

He told how he had been called to the Kreska's home and found them slightly ill of meat poisoning. It was something that would cure itself in the following hours. Only Old John, the bookbinder, who had been ill many years with a lung disease, could not stand the strain and it had caused his death.

Ludvig said that Prajak, with his hatred of the Jews, had made him falsely swear that death was due to the plum jam. "Swear or be in the debtor's jail."

Prajak was condemned to exile. The Brandeis were set free.

Then David Brandeis arose in the courtroom and crystals of joy streamed the length of his face as he said, "For me and my descendants I will write a Hebrew scroll and it shall be read each year on this day as the *Megillah* of a family Purim. Now and forever the Brandeis family shall call this day Purim Plum Jam, for on this day was averted an evil decree."

And in the little town of Jung-Bunzlau that night the Brandeis held Purim Plum Jam amidst the sound of *groggers* and the reading of a fine Hebrew scroll.

It was as David Brandeis said, "Prajak is our Haman and the good rabbi is our Mordecai."

And as Danny continued, "And Miriam is my Esther, the queen of my heart."

HAMAN AND ESTHER IN POLAND[8]

LEOPOLD VON SACHER MASOCH
(age level thirteen to fifteen)

It was Shushan Purim. The entire town of Sandomir was in a state of lively commotion, and each and every one was doing his best to transform night into brightest day. All windows were illuminated; houses were gayly decked with lamps and colored lanterns. At the windows sat fair young Jewesses and smiling matrons, in superb fur-trimmed cloaks, laughing, jesting, eating dainties. In the streets, merry young fellows, in long caftans, were bent on mischief and fun. The masquerade was at its height.

A party of Jewish youths, costumed as Little Russian peasants, serenaded their friends with Little Russian songs, to the accompaniment of flutes, violins and violoncellos. Others, dressed as bears, dealt terror and confusion among the groups of girls leaning in doorways. A more ambitious band played the farce of Ahasuerus. Esther, arrayed in royal velvet and ermine, a gold paper crown on her head, was borne aloft by four slaves; then followed the King Ahasuerus, in his scarlet mantle, behind him Monderish (Mordecai) with his huge turban, and last though not least appeared the distinguished figure of Haman. This last was of course the principal personage. A tall, battered hat sat audaciously on his head, several sheets sewed together served him as princely raiment, and with the aid of his stilts, he moved nimbly about through the crowd like some ghostly giant. His great false nose, with its three enormous crimson warts, would intrude occasionally into the second-story windows of the smaller houses and provoke terrified screams from the young girls, followed by endless jest and merriment. Haman was impersonated by none other than Laktef Wilna, the handsomest, strongest, boldest, lightest-hearted young Israelite in all Sandomir, where Israelites there were not a few.

The deafening noise of drums, tin lids, saucepans and trumpets announced the approach of the royal party. Despite the cold, windows were opened, and black eyes, lighting rosy faces, peered down the street to watch the advent of the merry crew; though, truth to tell, Laktef

Wilna, cutting his mad pranks with the most solemn air in the world, gained the lion's share of attention.

Mrs. Pfaumenbaum opened her casement but for an instant; that was long enough, however, for Haman to send in his greeting in the shape of an old slipper, and disappear with a laugh. To Mrs. Zuckerspitz, wrapped in her sable *Kazabaika* (cloak) and leaning out of her window, with the idea of being seen as well as of seeing, he gravely presented a large gingerbread hussar which, strange to relate, sent the color flying over her pretty cheeks. To little Miss Greenwald, whose slender proportions were generally discussed and exaggerated, he swore that he had just unearthed a bridegroom for her and sedately handed her a scrawny herring. At Johnathan Schmeikes', where half-a-dozen young girls had gathered for the merrymaking, he sent a mouse flying into the room, and shook with laughter as he watched the girls jump on tables and chairs and scream with horror, until the little mar-joy had betaken its trembling self into a friendly hole in the wall.

Cracking a joke with one, playing the merry-andrew with another, Laktef Wilna finally reached a long, narrow street, and paused before a wretched dwelling whose walls were falling in like a badly built house of cards. Behind its worm-eaten doors and broken windows lived about thirty Jewish families, its two floors divided each into a dozen rooms. Latkef's attention was attracted by one of the windows whose deficiency in glass was made good by an old stocking, and looking into the room, about the size of a diminutive poultry-house, beheld a girl in a patched calico gown. She was crying bitterly. Laktef's Shushan Purim had vanished in an instant; for like all jolly young fellows, his heart was as compassionate as his spirits were high, and the sight of tears was more than he could endure.

He listened, standing in shadow and leaning his great nose against the pane. The end of a candle, in the hollow of a potato, cast a feeble light about the tiny room. In an old armchair, of which Time had ravaged one of the feet, sat a man with folded hands. Upon his face there brooded a boundless sadness. He was wrapped in a shabby caftan, while upon his gray head rested the inevitable *Yarmulka* (skull cap).

The occupants of the room were Toby Fishthran, a poor blind tailor who had done patching in his time, and his daughter Esther. Young Wilna had recognized them at a glance.

"Do not cry, Estherka," said Toby, gently; "it ruins the eyes. What would become of us if you too could not work?"

"What is the good of working, father," said the girl with a sob, "when God has forsaken us?"

"God forsakes not the humblest of His creatures," replied the old man. "He tries us often, but He forsakes us never."

"But we have been tried more than all the others put together, and we have not sinned more than the rest. Have I not worked from dawn till night? And I have not even been able to heat the room for my poor blind father, nor to make cakes that the poorest of the poor have on Shushan Purim."

"We do not want cakes," cried Toby; "can we not hear all the music and laughter below in the streets?"

"It makes my heart break to hear them laugh," said the girl, and again she began to weep, but gently that her father might not hear her.

Haman had seen enough. He hurried off on his stilts, suddenly metamorphosed into seven-league boots.

The son of well-to-do parents, he could readily have aided the wretched family by throwing a handful of money into the room; but that would not have afforded him the fun he wanted, and, to him, pleasure-giving lost half its charm could he not add a dash of deviltry to it. He instantly decided that by playing a few innocent pranks on the rich, he could most admirably come to the assistance of these poor creatures, and, suiting the action to the thought, he hurried off to Jainkef Jeiteles', a lumber merchant. There, leaning over the wall, behind which was a large shed filled with wood, he pulled out a number of logs and threw them over his back to Mordecai, his friend Teitel Silberbach, whom he had enlisted in the service, and then the two scampered off to the Fishthrans'. Reaching the house, young Wilna descended from his stilts, and the conspirators tiptoed to Esther's door, where they noiselessly arranged a fine pyramid of logs. This accomplished, Haman again scoured the streets in quest of his next commission. Peering into Johnathan Schmeikes' kitchen, he discovered two great plates of smoking cakes on the window-seat. The cook's back was turned. In a trice the cakes had vanished, and off darted the rogue, with never a thought to his conscience. Mordecai, still crowned with his monstrous turban, climbed the stairs without a creak of his boots, knocked three times at Esther's door and fled rashly.

As Esther rose to open the door, Laktef, on his stilts, pulled the stocking from the window-hole, threw the cakes in the room, replaced the stocking, and drew back into the friendly shadow of the rain-pipe.

"Father," cried Esther, as she opened the door, "here is some wood! Who could have brought it?"

"Wood!" exclaimed Toby. "You are dreaming!"

"There were three knocks at the door," said the girl, nervously; "and when I went to see who it was, what should I find but this wood! And such wood! It is magnificent! Shall I take it?"

"Don't stand so long talking about it, my child. Bring it in, bring it in!"

"But, father dear, this is like magic!" She carried the logs inside, piled them behind the stove, threw one of them into the smouldering fire, and soon a fine blaze cheered and warmed the room with its ruddy glow. Esther had dried her eyes.

"What are these cakes? Father! What is the meaning of all this?"

"Cakes!" repeated the blind man, with an incredulous air and yet with a visible tremor of joy. Esther put one in his hand, and father and daughter began eating with avidity.

"They are hot from the oven," cried the girl. "There is no question about it, father, this is a miracle."

"You see, Esther, God has not forsaken us. Our benefactor is none other than the Prophet Elijah; he witnessed your tears, and brought you these presents for Shushan Purim."

"You are right, father; it must have been the Prophet Elijah," returned the girl, in an awe-stricken voice, and she joined her prayers to her father's.

"But if he were present and saw our poverty," sighed Esther, "why did he not send some clothes and a pair of shoes to my poor blind father?"

"What do I want with clothes," said Toby with a smile, "now that we have a comfortable, warm room? He should indeed have brought some for you, my child; for you have to run the streets all day, in the cold and snow, with a thin dress and broken shoes."

"Don't ask for too much, father dear. Remember I have my shawl."

"If the Prophet Elijah wished to," said the blind man recklessly, "he could clothe you like a princess and cover you with a sable cloak."

"O father!"

"If praying will bring it, let us pray. I will ask for a sable cloak for you."

"Stop, father; he will be angry, and the wood will disappear."

"Well, well, I'll not ask for sable; but it must be a cloak for you, at all events."

"What is the good of asking, father? Be sensible!"

"A cloak lined with fur, that you will not feel the cold," continued the old man imperturbably.

Laktef Wilna had listened eagerly to this conversation; and, laughing from the very depths of his good kind heart, off he went on his stilts to transform the part of Haman into that of Elijah. Haman's nose, however, was still a conspicuous feature; it brushed by doors and windows, helping the eyes to keep a sharp lookout, and restrained not the arms from intruding into chambers and carrying off whatever the Prophet Elijah might deem needful.

Winkelfield, second-hand dealer, had hung a pair of red boots enticingly before his door, proudly conscious of their selling qualities, as they had been purchased from a gentleman. Haman took them *sans ceremonie*. From Sprintze Veigelstock — who was rich and could spare it — he stole a black satin caftan. From Freudenthal's daughters he purloined a dress and a pair of shoes. Where was he to find a fur coat? A happy idea! The maskers had gathered in a body at Mrs. Zuckerspitz's and the revelry was at its height. The pretty hostess had flung her *Kazabaika*, lined and trimmed with sable, on a chair by the window. The sash had been slightly raised; the desperate marauder pushed it gently open and made off with his booty.

A few minutes later, he knocked at Esther's window.

"It is the blessed prophet," said Toby, in a solemn whisper. "Open for him!" Esther raised the sash, then ran and hid behind the stove and closed her eyes. When she opened them there lay the caftan, *Kazabaika*, dress, shoes and boots.

"Father," she cried, "he has brought us everything we asked for." She reverently closed the window, then, hurrying to her father, took off his old caftan, threw the new one about him, tried the dress and shoes on herself and, finally, with a cry of delight that was half a sob, slipped into the magnificent *Kazabaika*.

"What a miraculous godsend!" exclaimed the blind father. "You must look like a princess. Estherka, come close to me." He could not see his princess, but he could feel the velvet and fur with his trembling hands.

"My child, this is sable," he breathed in a state of nervous excitement. "The good prophet hearkened to my petition; he has brought you for Shushan Purim a sable cloak. Ah, see how God cares for us in His loving-kindness! Now that the merciful prophet has blessed us with so many gifts, he should bring forward a handsome young man for my little Esther's husband."

The girl put her hand over the old man's mouth. "Be quiet, father, else everything will disappear as miraculously as it has come."

The mischievous young prophet outside peered closely through the pane and, seeing Esther in her fine dress and magnificent cloak, muttered, "She's a pretty girl; and what a heart, as brave as pure! I wonder she has not found a husband."

At the same moment, the object of his reverie turned to the old man and said, "Who would have me, father, a poverty-stricken girl like me?"

"Listen," whispered Toby; "you ought to try your luck, Estherka, for Shushan Purim, and spread a net."

"A good idea," she answered, with a merry laugh. "I'll go out in the street and set a trap to catch a husband. But suppose it should be an old man or a hunchback?" and, her eyes twinkling with fun, she pulled three long black hairs from her braid, and twisted them in and out, murmuring some cabalistic words the while.

Laktef watched this snare-setting, and, laughing in his sleeve, said softly: "Wait a bit, little one, and you'll capture the wariest bird in the whole *Kehillah* (community)."

While Esther was preparing to start on her adventure, Haman descended from his stilts, gave his hat, mantle and nose to Mordecai, drew back into the shadow and succeeded in stepping into the net just as the little schemer was about seeking refuge in the housedoor. The snare had done its work, but the girl was caught as well; for, as she turned, a pair of strong arms clasped her waist, and a pair of lips sealed hers with a kiss. She tore herself loose and, with a beating heart, fled up the narrow stairs.

The following morning, Mrs. Zuckerspitz bewailed her sable cloak, Veigelstock mourned the loss of his caftan, and the second-hand dealer wept tears of regret over the missing boots; when, like the *deus ex machina*, young Wilna appeared and explained all.

"I took your *Kazabaika*," he said to the pretty coquette, "to give it to a poor girl; she believes that the Prophet Elijah made her a present of it, but I will return it."

"No, no!" she exclaimed. "For that matter it was an old one, and my husband will be only too happy to give me another. You have performed a charitable action for me, and I am your debtor."

From all his other victims he met with a similar reception; for the pious Jew knows no greater joy than that of giving to the poor.

The same day, old Wilna paid a visit to Toby Fishthran, and formally demanded pretty Esther's hand for his son.

THE FIDDLER[9]

LUDWIG PHILIPPSON
(age level thirteen to fifteen)

Now everyone knows that the *Metim* (the Dead) visit synagogues at midnight in order to say their prayers, but not everybody is aware of the fact that they also come there to celebrate Purim and to have a good time.

But my good old grandfather happened to learn about it from a trustworthy witness, and I am going to tell you the story that Karpel the Fiddler told to him.

Once there lived in our town a little gray-haired man named "Karpel the Fiddler." You could always see his fiddle hanging upon the wall of the garret in which he lived; but, although he used to grin at it every morning and evening, no one could ever coax him to take it down.

But on the evening of Purim, when all the Jewish houses were illuminated by many big candles; when the tables groaned under their weight of veal and steaming punch-bowls; when brightly-dressed figures marched through the streets, muffled up in cloaks, and rushed in to every Jewish home to sing their Purim songs — at this festival season, says my grandfather, we could see our little man going from house to house with his fiddle in his hand. Wherever he entered, with his greeting of "Good Purim, good Purim to you, dear people!" he was welcomed by a shout of joy: "There's our Karpel with the fiddle! A hearty welcome to you! Play for us, Karpel!"

To begin with, the old man would wipe the perspiration from his face, and smooth the hair straight back from his forehead; then he would draw the bow across his violin and play with all his might. He knew only three tunes; these he played over and over again, although not always in the same order! After every melody his host would force a glass of punch upon him. In a little while, he would be so light-hearted and merry that he would become confused until he seemed to be playing all three at the same time. His listeners nearly split their sides laughing; until at last when their ears were almost deafened with this concert, they would shriek: "Stop, Karpel — for the love of Heaven, stop playing!" But such interruptions never disturbed old Karpel. Sometimes a guest would hold one of his arms, while another seized him by the other elbow; but as soon as his arms were free, he would continue his confused music, until at last his pockets were filled with cake and he was laughingly pushed out of the house with an invitation to play his three tunes "next Purim!"

Once out in the street, Karpel would shake his head, empty his pockets to make room for another filling, enter the next house which was giving a Purim party, and start his noisy show all over again.

Now, everyone treated Karpel so generously that, when he came out into the street, his head was quite dizzy. Or, perhaps, it was the fault of the moon, which seemed to be dancing in the sky, as though celebrating its Purim with the stars. Karpel ran after the moon and tried to catch her, but he noticed that all the houses were standing upside down and that they seemed to be using their chimneys for legs, and were dancing too! Poor Karpel tried to dodge between them; but suddenly one large red-brick house grew fretful and kicked him with one of its chimneys. He fell sprawling upon the ground, and, as he was drowsy by this time, he decided to fall asleep.

But how could he do so when, as soon as he closed his eyes, a very brilliant light flashed upon his lids! He sat up with a start and, behold, in front of him stood a large building, its countless windows blazing with lights. Suddenly the great doors were flung open; within, Karpel caught sight of two or three figures, who kept winking and beckoning to him; he could not resist their invitations and, taking up his fiddle, he went up the stairs. He found himself in a large hall, crowded with people; some nodded to him, and he recognized them as old acquaintances who had been dead for the last ten or twenty years; then, he drew near to shake hands with them — but they were off in a moment and, when he saw them, they appeared at a great distance.

Suddenly the guests at this strange Purim ball formed two long rows, making a lane for him to pass. A moment later, he found himself in a splendid hall, the walls of which were of marble, covered with gold-framed mirrors, lighted with huge numberless candles, and draped with garlands of flowers. At one end stood a high throne, with a covering of red velvet and gold fringes; on the steps crouched golden lions with eyes of carbuncle, while under the golden canopy sat King Ahasuerus with Queen Esther at his side. Karpel looked around to find the Grand Vizir, Mordecai, but he is forbidden to have a share in all Purim enjoyments, as a punishment for having neglected the study of the Torah after becoming the governor of the Persian kingdom. For a long time, Karpel stood motionless, staring at the king's high crown and Esther's glittering robes. But at last King Ahasuerus raised his heavy scepter and beckoned the fiddler to come to him.

"Karpel," began Ahasuerus, "I am very glad to see you here in our midst, and hope your health is good and that you have had a merry Purim. Now, we want you to fiddle to us as well as you can, for the dead can not play any instruments. I have a great desire to hear dance music, for I have missed the musicians who used to play for me when I was ruler over Persia. Take your fiddle and play."

Karpel was a little frightened at first, for he had never met a king before in his whole life; but he soon took heart, seized

his violin and fiddled merrily. As soon as he began to play
the first tune, King Ahasuerus stretched his kid-gloved left
hand to Queen Esther and, after descending the steps of the
throne, they danced together, dressed in their long velvet
cloaks, the trains of which were borne by four pages, who
also danced behind them. (Now, don't ask me how they
managed it! I am telling you the story just as I heard it from
my grandfather.) A long line of courtiers dressed in splendid
attire danced after them; the faster he fiddled, the wilder
did they dance and, if he paused for breath, they would cry
out to him to continue. His three melodies were already
played, and he began from the first; again he went through
them; again he started anew; yet this gave no trouble to
Karpel, nor to Ahasuerus nor to Esther.

At last the king stopped dancing and Karpel stopped
playing. "My good Karpel," asked the king, "don't you
know any other tune but these?"

"No," answered Karpel. "Don't you like them?"

"They are very nice, my dear Karpel; but my chief court-
singer will sing my favorite melody to you and then you
will play it to us."

The king winked and the chief court-singer came up; he
was a tall, thin man in a black silk turban and girdle, and
he had a dark pointed mustache, which gave him a fierce
expression. He stood erect in front of Karpel and opened
his mouth very wide. Karpel pricked his ears to listen; he
could hear nothing, but suddenly he began to feel as if a new,
strange tune was being poured into his soul. He lifted up
his bow, drew it across the violin, and new tunes issued from
it, making a melody he had never heard before. Ahasuerus
smiled to hear his favorite tune again, and the whole company once more took up their whirling dance to the fiddling
of the new melody.

Many hours passed, and still none of them seemed to feel

tired from dancing; but all at once both Ahasuerus and Esther stopped dancing and lifted up their faces, as though they felt something strange in the air. Then the king muttered: "I scent the morning air; we must make haste. Karpel, you have been amusing our Majesties with your music; now you shall have your reward!"

Obeying a gesture from the king, the treasurer, a fat, important-looking man, came up with a large bag full of gold. The king, dipping into the bag, filled Karpel's pockets, until the fiddler felt too heavy to move from the spot. A moment later, a keen draught of air passed through the windows and doors; and the lights were blown out, and Karpel found himself sitting in the street, rubbing his eyes and still holding his fiddle.

Gradually the figures he had seen and all that he experienced that night became clearer to him. He recollected how he had entertained the *Metim* (the Dead), how kind and merciful Ahasuerus had been to him, and how the court-singer had taught him a fourth tune — and the gold the king had stuffed into his pockets! He jumped up and felt his pockets. Yes, they were crammed full — but with broken slices of cake — the gold was gone. . . Karpel began to wonder whether the great King Ahasuerus had played a Purim trick upon him. Hastily he took up his fiddle and raised his bow. The new melody sounded so lovely to his delighted ears, that he kept playing it over and over again and comforted himself for the loss of the gold, as he realized that at last he knew how to play more than three tunes.

Everyone was astonished the next Purim, when Karpel made his rounds and delighted them with his new melody. "Where did you pick up this pretty tune, Karpel?" they cried. But Karpel only nodded his head, without saying a word. But to my grandfather, who had always been very kind to Karpel and who had given him his Sabbath meals, he entrusted this mystery, telling him how he had learned it from King Ahasuerus's chief court-singer on that remarkable Purim night. My grandfather laughed at the beginning, saying: "Karpel, it was only a dream, for if it were true, where is the gold?" But Karpel always answered: "Rabbi Joseph, as sure as I am alive, it is all true. King Ahasuerus transformed the gold into crumbs of cake, but I know that I played before him or how could I have ever learned this fourth tune?"

Now, my grandfather could not answer this argument, and he was the wisest man I ever met. And so he at last decided that Karpel's story must be true. If my grandfather believed it, I cannot doubt it, for how could I be wiser than my grandfather?

CHAPTER XIV

POEMS FOR PURIM

PURIM[1]

SARA G. LEVY
(age level four to six)

READY FOR PURIM

I'M happy, I'm happy, I'm happy as can be,
For Purim is coming as everyone can see.
My costume is finished, my mask is all done;
I'm ready, I'm ready, I'm ready for the fun!

PACKING SHALAH MONOT

What is this I'm packing, can you see?
A box of *Shalah Monot* it must be.
Now isn't this the way — "Oh yes," we say —
To celebrate Purim, a happy holiday.

BAKING A HAMANTASH

Pat-a-cake, pat-a-cake,
Baker's man,
Bake me a *Hamantash*
Fast as you can!
Roll it, and fold it,
And make corners three;
Make one for mommy, for daddy and me!
Pat-a-cake, pat-a-cake,
Nice baker's man,
Bake me a *Hamantash*
Fast as you can!

MERRY PURIM[2]

LEVIN KIPNIS
(age level four to six)

JESTER: Ding, dong, dell,
             I have a cap and bell —
             And now we bring a Purim play,
             A tale of old to tell.

AHASUERUS: One, two, three,
             Ahasuerus you see,
             With crown of gold and scepter, too,
             I enter merrily.

BOYS: Each and every one of us
             Wears a golden crown,
             We are all the mischievous,
             That king of great renown.

ESTHER: Queen Esther is my name,
             My crown's a golden flame;
             My uncle is brave Mordecai,
             The Jew who rose to fame.

GIRLS: Each and every one of us
             Wears a golden crown,
             For we are Esther, virtuous,
             That Queen of wide renown.

MORDECAI: O, I am Mordecai;
             My blue robes match the sky.
             Groggers and sweet *Hamantash*
             I'll give you by and by.

CHILDREN: Blessed be Mordecai,
             His blue robes match the sky,
             Groggers and sweet *Hamantash*
             He'll give us by and by.

HAMAN: I'm Haman bold, of course.
         I've brought along a horse.
         I'll lead the noble Mordecai
         Without the least remorse.

BOYS: He's Haman bold, of course,
         He's brought along a horse,
         He'll lead the noble Mordecai
         Without the least remorse.

ALL: Purim is a day of frolic;
         Merrily we sing and rolic.
         Purim's jolly, Purim's bright,
         Purim's crowded with delight.
         Purim is a day of gladness;
         Purim's gift will banish sadness.
         Today we raise our voices high:
         Blessed be Esther and Mordecai.

WHAT SHALL SHE BE[3]

SADIE ROSE WEILERSTEIN
(age level seven to nine)

Let me see! What shall she be?
What shall our little Judy be?
She'll have to be something on Purim Day,
It's the only proper Purim way.
Shall she be a king with a golden crown?
Or the king's white horse trotting up and down?
Haman, perhaps, with a horrid frown,
Or a Purim Jester, a jolly clown?

NO

I won't be a king with a golden crown!
I won't be a horse trotting up and down!
I won't be a clown, a Purim Jester!
I won't be anything but ESTHER.

OH!

What shall we do? What shall we do?
Judy wants to be Esther, too;
So do Ruthie, and Ann, and Hester.
All the girls want to be Queen Esther.
What shall we do? What shall we do?
Judy wants to be Esther, too.

LET HER!
WHAT COULD BE BETTER?

One Haman's enough to plot and pester;
But there's no such thing as too much Esther.
She saved the Jews and they all blessed her,
Let every girl be another Esther.

ABOUT PURIM[4]

MIRIAM MYERS
(age level seven to nine)

I love this merry Purim time;
    I know the story, too;
And if you don't mind listening,
    I'll tell it all to you.

Well, many, many years ago,
    'In Persia, far away,
The King Ahasuerus lived
    And ruled with royal sway.

There was a lovely Jewish maid,
    And Esther was her name;
The king soon chose her for his wife,
    So queen she then became.

Her cousin's name was Mordecai,
    A good and pious Jew,
Who loved Queen Esther very much
    And to the king was true.

Now Haman, the king's favorite --
    A very wicked man —
Just wanted to kill all the Jews
    And formed a cruel plan.

But Mordecai let Esther know;
    At once she told the king,
Who, when he heard the wicked plot,
    Was mad as anything.

"Oh, no, the Jews shall all be saved,"
    Ahasuerus said;
And Haman and his wicked sons
    Were hanged till they were dead.

MYER'S MASQUERADE[5]

ELMA EHRLICH LEVINGER
(age level seven to nine)

David, David, come and see
What my mother made for me:
Funny suit of red and green,
Funniest hat you've ever seen!
Won't I be the queerest sight,
When I sing tomorrow night:
    Heint is Purim, morgen is ois
    *Git mir a groshen, und varft mir arois!**

    *"Today is Purim, tomorrow it's o'er
    Give me a penny, and show me the door!"

I shall be a jolly jester;
Sister Ruth will dress as Esther;
Mother's skirt and cloak she'll wear,
And shining things upon her hair;
And Sam is Haman — Dave, his nose
Will be a foot long, I suppose.

Come and mask on Purim night!
Mother'll help you dress right.
You can be a Persian king,
Soldier, slave, or anything;
Buy a mask and come along,
And help us sing our Purim song:
    Heint is Purim, morgen is ois
    Git mir a groshen, und varft mir arois!

WHY I LIKE PURIM[6]

ELMA EHRLICH LEVINGER
(age level seven to nine)

Now I like Hanukkah a lot,
    And Sukkot in the fall,
And Pesah, but I think that I
    Love Purim most of all.

Maybe it's 'cause I like to watch
    My mother when she bakes;
And help her pound the shiny stuff
    She puts in Purim cakes.

The kitchen air smells awful sweet;
    I just won't go away.
Till she gives me a *Hamantash*
    And sends me out to play.

Then father takes us all to *Shul*,
    Me, mother and the boys;
It's more fun than the reg'lar days,
    'Cause I can make a noise.

At home, we put on mother's clothes —
    Her oldest ones, I mean;
And cousin Rachel dresses up
    And tries to act a queen.

For then we give our Purim play
    And laugh and dance and cheer;
Say, don't I wish that Purim came
    'Bout twenty times a year!

BLESSING FOR PURIM[7]

JESSIE E. SAMPTER
(age level ten to twelve)

Before Reading the Book of Esther:

ברוך . . . על מקרא מגלה

Blessed art Thou, O God, our King,
The Lord of life and everything,
Whose word has hallowed Israel's soul,
And bade us read Queen Esther's scroll;
(Because her courage and her faith,
When God had pity in old days,
In exile saved us all from death
And let us live to sing His praise.)

PURIM IN PALESTINE[8]

JESSIE E. SAMPTER
(age level ten to twelve)

Flowers in the crannies
    And vines that trail the walls,
And down among the lemon trees
    The piping Bulbul calls!

It's springtime here at Purim,
  The very heart of spring,
With days that shine but do not burn,
  When gardens bloom and sing.

We're putting up a scaffold
  In the cruel old-fashioned way,
But we're only going to hang on it
  A curtain for our play.

Don't bother hanging Haman,
  Nor hating anything,
When we're planning for our festival
  In Palestine, in spring.

We're glad that Haman hated,
  And we're glad that he was hung,
Because it's fun that Purim brings
  When you're a Jew and young.

We hold no grudge against him,
  And we're glad he lived and raged,
Because without old Haman, how
  Could Purim plays be staged?

FOR PURIM[9]

ZALMAN SHNEOUR
(age level ten to twelve)

Oh, Haman lived in Shushantown,
  And he was most oppressive;
He wore a blue and purple hat,
  Three cornered and impressive.

Knock, knockers, knock; knock, knockers, knock;
And rattlers, rattle, rattle;
For Haman and his sons were hanged
Upon a tree like cattle.

With Mordecai was Haman grieved,
And swore in his vexation
To hang him on the gallows high,
And wipe out all his nation.

Knock, knockers, knock; knock, knockers, knock;
And rattlers, rattle, rattle;
For Haman and his sons were hanged
Upon a tree like cattle.

He sent out letters: "Rise and slay
The Jews that they all perish,
The thirteenth day of Adar-month" —
The Purim-day we cherish.

Knock, knockers, knock; knock, knockers, knock;
And rattlers, rattle, rattle;
For Haman and his sons were hanged
Upon a tree like cattle.

But on that day a miracle
God wrought, and sent salvation,
For we were saved, but Haman was
Effaced from His creation.

Knock, knockers, knock; knock, knockers, knock;
And rattlers, rattle, rattle;
For Haman and his sons were hanged
Upon a tree like cattle.

In memory of the cornered hat
Of Haman so ambitious,
We eat a cake resembling it,
A *Hamantash* delicious.

Knock, knockers, knock; knock, knockers, knock;
    And rattlers, rattle, rattle;
For Haman and his sons were hanged
    Upon a tree like cattle.

ESTHER TODAY[10]

ELMA EHRLICH LEVINGER
(age level ten to twelve)

You have all heard the story of Esther
    Who pled for the Jews long ago;
Who rescued our race from destruction,
    Who delivered our brethren from woe.
Do you think when you read of her courage,
    So great for a girl to display,
And her simple, unfaltering devotion,
    That an Esther is needed today?

We need women, real mothers in Israel,
    Who love their faith dearer than life,
Who will teach Israel's faith to daughters
    And arm worthy sons for the strife.
For enemies, deadly as Haman,
    Are still eager our people to slay;
And to battle with falsehood and error —
    An Esther is needed today.

Let us then do our duty as she did,
    Trusting God to the last — unafraid;
Let us never be traitors or cowards
    When our people beseech us for aid;
Forget not that He knows His people;
    That He will protect us always —
And remember to fight for Him gladly,
    If Esther is needed today.

PURIM[11]

C. David Matt
(age level thirteen to fifteen)

Come, quaff the brimming festal glass!
  Bring forth the good old cheer!
For Esther's Feast has come at last —
  Most gladsome in the year.

And now, when hearts beat glad and free,
  Come gather all about,
And tell once more how, long since, He
  Did put our foe to rout.

Full oft has beauty ruled a land,
  And held its sceptred sway;
Full often foiled th' avenging hand
  And bade oppression stay.

But ne'er did beauty so avail
  As when fair Esther's charm
'Gainst vengeful Haman did prevail
  To 'fend the Jews from harm.

So all the dire impending woe
  That hovered o'er their head
Did light upon their ruthless foe
  And ruined him, instead.

And thus, throughout the ages long,
  In every land and clime,
They chant an old thanksgiving song
  E'er mindful of that time.

Yea, Israel's Guardian never sleeps —
  No slumber to His eye! —
But loving watch He ever keeps
  Upon His flock from high.

DIALOGUE STANZAS[12]

GRACE AGUILAR
(age level thirteen to fifteen)

*Composed for, and repeated by, two dear
little animated girls, at a family celebration
of the Festival of Purim, 1845.*

"Come forth, sweet sister! leave your book, we have no task
    to-day,
The flowers, and birds, and sunny sky, invite us forth to play;
Oh! think what joys, what happy hours, this long'd-for day
    we share,
And let us hunt for spring's sweet flowers, to wreathe our mother's
    hair.
Come, we have days enough to read, sweet sister, come with me,
Away with such grave looks and thoughts! To-day is but for glee."

"A little while and I will come — I only want to know
What pass'd upon this very day — a long time ago;
Our mother told us a sad tale — that thousands were to die,
E'en little children, sister dear — as young as you or I.
And all because a cruel foe swore vengeance on our race,
That from the noble Mordecai no homage could he trace."

"But we were saved, sweet sister; death was averted then,
Our mother told us Esther came, and there was joy again:
She was so lovely, and so good, the king could naught deny,
And so she sent fleet messengers, that Israel should not die.
There! I have told you all the tale — you need not read it now,
Come, dearest! to our birds and flowers — and clear that thoughtful
    brow."

"Sweet sister! let me think a while, and then I'll merry be.
Should we not think a grateful thought e'en in our sunny glee.
It was not only Esther's words — but Israel's God was there.

The king of Persia's heart to turn His chosen ones to spare.
And we should bless Him, sister dear, that He protects us still,
And such kind friends bestows on us, to guard us from all ill."

"Yes, yes, sweet sister, you are right, not only is to-day
For idle mirth, and noisy games, and merry thoughtless play.
We'll love our mother more and more, and all our dear kind friends,
And grateful be that hours of dread no more our Father sends;
That we may sport amid the flowers as happy as a bee,
And cruel foes can never come to mar our childish glee."

"See, see! I'm ready, sister dear — I've put the book away;
Come while the sun so brightly shines, we'll weave our garland gay.
What joy! — what joy! this happy day shall see us all together,
E'en those dear friends, whom time and space so long from us
    did sever;
Oh! many, many happy years still spare us to each other.
Sweet sister, come! I'm ready now — the garland for our mother."

BOOK FOUR

Purim Joy

The Jews had light and gladness
and joy and honour.

ESTHER 8. 16.

CHAPTER XV

PURIM PRANKS

PURIM, undoubtedly the festivity *par excellence* in the Jewish year, has given birth to curious capers and strange pranks. Many of these antics, otherwise unknown in the sober and earnest course of Jewish life, were borrowed from non-Jewish neighbors who observed similar festive occasions at the season of Purim.

The unrestrained joy which the Jews found in celebrating Purim is quite understandable, for Haman was to them the type of Jew-baiter with whom they were unfortunately too well acquainted, and his undoing represented a prophecy of what they hoped would happen to their own oppressors. Therefore, they gave themselves freely on that day to all kinds of merrymaking. They permitted themselves to make sport of some of the things which they otherwise held sacred and to relax those rigid disciplines of life to which they were normally accustomed.[1]

The carefree, joyous nature of the festival, with its hilarity and levity, found expression long centuries ago, in the days of the Talmud and the Geonim, and not only, as is commonly thought, in comparatively recent times. Embellishments, to be sure, were added later by the Jews of the ghetto, as well as subsequently, but the gay excitements of Purim are rooted in the distant past.

The celebration of Purim naturally revolved about Haman's downfall and especial glee was found in its commemoration. Indeed, from his downfall developed many of the strange customs and antics which were seemingly devised

to fulfill the commandment: *Thou shalt blot out the rememb-*
rance of Amalek,[2] of whom Haman was a descendant, and
from the other biblical statement: *The name of the wicked*
shall rot.[3] Similarly, a deduction as to the treatment of Haman
was made from the verse: *Then it shall be, if the wicked*
man deserve to be beaten, והיה אם בן הכות הרשע.[4] Since the
final letters of the first three words spell Haman and the next
words imply that he should be beaten,[5] the burning in effigy
of Haman and his "beating" became popular Purim pastimes.

THE BURNING OF HAMAN IN EFFIGY

The burning of Haman in effigy originated apparently in
Babylonia and Persia during the period of the Talmud and
the Geonim. An account of such early Purim pranks, con-
firming the *Aruk*,[6] was reported by Professor Louis Ginzberg
from a Gaonic Responsum which was found in the Genizah
(repository for torn and outworn sacred books) in Cairo:

> Four or five days before Purim the young men make
> an effigy of Haman and hang it on the roof. On Purim
> itself they build a bonfire into which they cast the effigy,
> while they stand around joking and singing, at the same
> time holding a ring above the fire and waving it from
> side to side through the fire. The purpose of the ring is
> not stated by the Gaon, but it may be assumed that the
> effigy was suspended from it. The Aramaic word for
> this ring is: משוורתא "the jumper," and the same word
> is used for "stirrup."[7]

Other explanations for the use of the ring are that it "was
used by the young men as a means of swinging over the
bonfire,"[8] and that it was a revolving wheel ofttimes used
to produce the spark for primitive bonfires.[9] The Talmud
also speaks of a "stirrup (a ring suspended from a frame)

thrust over a bonfire on Purim."[10] Rashi explains that on
Purim the children used to jump over a hole in the earth
with a bonfire burning in it.[11]

According to Kalonymos ben Kalonymos, the Italian
Jews of the Middle Ages "made merry round a puppet representing Haman, which was set on an elevation, amidst shouts
of vengeance and blowing of trumpets. This custom was
called *Ira*, which is the Italian for vengeance."[12] A unique
practice of Jewish fathers and sons in Italy was to conduct
sports tourneys "in which the boys fought on foot with nuts
as pellets, while their fathers rode on horseback through the
streets, flourishing wooden staves and, to the blast of horns
and bugles, tilted at an effigy representing Haman, which
was subsequently burnt on a mock pyre."[13]

An odd custom was practiced in Frankfort-on-the-Main
during the eighteenth century. A house of wax was made,
with costumed wax figures of Haman, his wife Zeresh and
two guards. The house and its occupants of wax were
placed on the reader's desk in the synagogue, in full view of
the entire congregation. When the reader started the reading of the Scroll of Esther, the house and its occupants were
set afire.[14]

A nineteenth-century Russian Jewish traveller, Joseph
Judah Chorny, reports the continued observance of the custom of the burning of Haman in effigy by the Jews of
Caucasus, although they do not do it publicly.[15] Chorny
describes this practice in these words: "On Purim, when the
men return home from reading the Scroll of Esther in the
synagogue, the women prepare a black piece of wood in the
kitchen by the fire. When the man comes into the room he
asks his wife what it is, and she says, 'It is Haman.' At
once the man gets angry and begins to scream at his wife
that she should burn it. After kicking it, they all throw it
into the fire."[16]

BEATING OF HAMAN IN THE SYNAGOGUE

As long as Jews felt fully at home in their synagogues, they gave vent there to emotions expressive of their varying moods on the awe-inspiring days of atonement and repentance as well as on the festive days of rejoicing. Purim was no exception. That is why the rabbis then tolerantly sanctioned a degree of indecorous conduct in the synagogue, during the reading of the *Megillah*, which was expressed in the beating of Haman when his name was read.

In several European countries, in the thirteenth century, the established custom for children was to draw the name or figure of Haman on two smooth stones or pieces of wood and to knock them against each other until the inscription was obliterated.[17] Another technique that was in vogue was the writing of Haman's name on the soles of shoes. The people would then stamp their feet at every mention of Haman during the reading of the *Megillah*. Leon de Modena (1571–1648) wrote that in Venice the Jews, while reading the *Megillah*, would "clap their hands at the name of Haman, as a testimony of their utter abhorrence and detestation."[18]

An engraving of a Purim service in a synagogue, published in Nuremberg in 1724, shows a number of the congregants holding what appear to be hammers. A more sedate and dignified manner of "wiping out" the name of the wicked Haman was employed by Jews in the Sephardi synagogue in London during the early part of the nineteenth century. They would write Haman's name on pieces of paper and, whenever it was read from the *Megillah*, they would erase it with a rubber.[19]

To avoid delay and confusion by constant interruptions at the reading of the name of Haman, the custom in Egypt was to allow the beating of Haman only at the reading of the names of his ten sons and at the end of the *Megillah*.[20]

The beating of Haman was not a universally accepted practice, and in some communities it was considered a flagrant violation of synagogue decorum. Fear of the possible

43. *PURIM AT THE SYNAGOGUE*   Engraving

I. G. Puschner, 18th Century

hostile reactions of Christians was also an important factor in urging its restricted use.[21] Differences of opinion as to its propriety were sharp in certain congregations and sometimes resulted in violent quarrels. Synagogal regulations were enacted prohibiting any noises during the reading of the *Megillah*. In 1783, the *Ma'amad* (Board of Trustees) of the Spanish-Portuguese congregation in London ruled that anyone making a disturbance was to be evicted from the synagogue.[22] In 1866, the *Kehillah* of Rogasen in the province of Posen, Poland, promulgated a set of rules concerning synagogue demeanor and included the prohibition against using Haman *groggers* on Purim.[23]

The ancient custom of blotting out the name of Haman is effectively served today by the use of rattlers or *groggers* and the stamping of feet. Fifty-four times Haman's name is read in the *Megillah*, and fifty-four times the reading is interrupted with resounding noise, and then again when the names of his ten sons are read.

MASQUERADING AND MASKS

Masquerading on Purim originated about the end of the fifteenth century among the Jews of Italy, who observed and imitated the carnival practice of the Lenten season which occurs about the time of Purim. From them it spread to all countries where the Jews lived.

Since masquerading often took the form of men and women wearing the clothes of the opposite sex, many rabbis frowned upon it, for the Bible states: *A woman shall not wear that which pertaineth unto a man, neither shall a man put on a woman's garment*;[24] others, however, sanctioned this exchange of clothing to enhance the joyousness of the festival.[25] Needless to say, it was the opinion of the more lenient rabbis that was generally accepted.

A Jewish folklorist found justification for masquerading in the talmudic passage: "Where is Esther [אסתר] found in the Torah? It is written, And I will surely hide [הסתר אסתיר] My face from you."[26] To him this was sufficient proof of the propriety of masquerading on Purim, as well as of hiding one's face with a mask.

The first known reference to the wearing of masks on Purim is found in 1508. In masquerading, people did not always wear masks. The mask was probably a much later invention, as people became more sophisticated and felt somewhat ashamed of their burlesque dress and the childish tricks their "characters" were supposed to perform. Thus, to avoid recognition by their neighbors and friends and to achieve greater freedom of joyful expression, they covered their faces with masks.

The popular costumes usually employed were those that portrayed the characters in the Book of Esther.

While the masses of the people disguised themselves by wearing costumes that imitated the clothes worn by the Purim characters, some of the great Jewish scholars, looking askance at this custom, sought to imitate the Talmud, Haggadah, prayer book and other literary works through humorous parodies. (The parodies which also belong to the realm of Purim antics are treated fully in Chapter XVI.) It will suffice here to mention that in our days a literature of parodies is being created in Israel. Much of this literature is found in periodicals and pamphlets. These parodies which usually appear for Purim do not deal exclusively with the festival; they also treat of such subjects as the current political situation of Israel.

RESTRICTIONS ON PURIM PRANKS

Some of the Purim escapades that annoyed, interfered with, or harmed others in the community brought about restrictions in their practice. In the general patent that Frederick the Great of Prussia issued on April 17, 1750, for the "protection" of the Jews in the observance of their religious practices, there is a proviso that "they must refrain from all improper excesses in their festivals, particularly during the so-called Haman or Purim festival."[27]

Sometimes Prussian barons were annoyed by the excessive hilarity on Purim that frequently ended in quarrels. To prevent such occurrences, the Baron of Sugenheim, a small town in Franconia with a Jewish population of twelve householders, when issuing a constitution for the local Jewish community in 1756, stipulated that "no one shall dare mask himself or run around in clown's garb or with candles and torches on Purim, under penalty of a florin to be paid the civil authorities."[28]

On June 10, 1823, the Grand Duke Carl Friedrich promulgated an edict whose purpose was the regulation of the Jews in the Duchy of Saxe-Weimar. Some of the clauses of the edict were concerned with the disorder in the synagogue, and one specifically forbade "Haman beating" on Purim.[29]

In Egypt it was an old custom that on Purim boys would ride around the streets of the Jewish quarters on horses, camels and donkeys, in remembrance of the triumph of Mordecai whom the king caused *to ride on horseback through the street of the city*.[30] Because of the danger lest the riders dash about in the crowded quarters and injure someone, this symbolic practice was abolished.[31]

The rabbis condoned certain practices on Purim upon which they ordinarily frowned. The custom of "stealing" the *Afikoman* at the Passover *Seder* is of course well known and was sanctioned by the rabbis; the lesser-known practice of "stealing" food on Purim was also permitted. "Every dish that the boys take from one another, even without permission, for the purpose of rejoicing on Purim, from the hour of reading the *Megillah* until the Purim meal, is not considered a theft or a robbery and they are not subject to the jurisdiction of the court."[32]

Dancing, especially the "Dance of Death," was an accepted Purim pastime from the fourteenth to the seventeenth centuries.

The *Purimspiel*, the most characteristic form of amusement on this holiday, is treated in Chapter XVII.

THE REVIVAL OF PURIM PRANKS

Well may it be asked today: Where are the Purim pranks—bonfires, parodies, masquerades, plays and other delightful and amusing antics — that formerly heralded the festival? Israel Abrahams answers this query thus:

"It is unquestionable that Purim used to be a merrier anniversary than it is now. The explanation is simple. In part, the change has arisen through a laudable disinclination from pranks that may be misconstrued as tokens of vindictiveness against an ancient foe or his modern reincarnations. As a second cause may be assigned the growing regrettable propensity of Jews to draw a rigid line of separation between life and religion, and wherever this occurs, religious feasts tend towards a solemnity that cannot, and dare not, relax into amusement. This tendency is eating at the heart of Jewish life, and ought to be resisted by all who truly understand the genius of Judaism."[33]

Fortunately, this tendency of which Israel Abrahams complains, is being arrested in the more normalized and freer atmosphere of the *Yishub* in Israel. There the revival of the positive features of the joyous Purim spirit can be seen today in Tel-Aviv where the Jewish community is unhampered in the expression of its Jewish feelings and spirit.

CHAPTER XVI

THE HISTORY OF PURIM PARODY IN JEWISH LITERATURE[1]

Israel Davidson

PARODY, satire's most powerful weapon, though of hoary antiquity in classic literature, is not so ancient in Hebrew literature. While the Bible abounds in various forms of satire, it does not contain a single example of parody. Nor is this form of satire to be found in the apocryphal literature, even if we choose to regard imitation as a species of parody. For only that kind of imitation can be said to border on parody which ridicules the original, or treats it in a spirit of playfulness. But the apocryphal literature, though largely imitative, aims neither at playfulness nor at ridicule. On the contrary, it holds the original in high esteem.

In the Talmud, we would naturally expect to find the art of parody adequately represented. For the ancient rabbis had a keen sense of humor and often manifested it in the course of their educational and religious work. Some of them, for instance, were in the habit of prefacing their lectures with humorous remarks, others brought their native wit into play in their religious controversies with the Sadducees and the *Minim* (Infidels), while those who were conversant with Roman matters satirized the tyranny and the profligacy of the Caesars. Withal, there is in the Talmud very little that may be called pure parody, and even the number of its travesties is too small to merit more than passing notice. In the few instances where the rabbis travestied the subleties of the schools, they did so at the risk of bringing reproach and ill-favor upon themselves. The talmudists were fond of puns and conceits, especially etymological puns. They also indulged in what may be called *imaginary* compositions, as for instance, the edict of Haman and the prayers of Mordecai and Esther. But as no one will allow the term parody to take on so broad a meaning as to embrace these forms of literature, we must not look for the beginning of parody until we reach a much later period in the history of Jewish satire.

It is only in the twelfth century, that we first meet with parody in Jewish literature. Those, therefore, who see in parody a sign of literature's decay, will find their theory shaken by this fact. For the twelfth century was the golden age in Jewish literature, having such authors as Judah Halevi, Abraham and Moses ibn Ezra, Maimonides and Harizi among its representative men.

It was probably in the same century that Menahem ben Aaron wrote the *Hymn for the Night of Purim*, which was embodied in the *Mahzor Vitry*. It parodies the *Hymn for the First Night of Passover* by Meier ben Isaac, imitating it more in form than in diction. The parodist, apparently, has no other aim than to dress a wine-song in the garb of a religious hymn. The burden of the song is that on Purim one must throw off all care and anxiety. "This night (of Purim) is a night for drunkards, a night for wine drinking and rejoicing... On this night all creation is intoxicated... and woe betide the man who should put forth his hand for the bitter water. The day of Purim is a day of feasting and drinking and merrymaking." But in order to make our happiness complete, we must remember the needy, and share our luxuries with those that are in want of them.

During the next seven decades the art of parody was neglected, and when it began again to flourish, it did so no longer in the Iberian Peninsula but in Provence and in Italy.

PARODY IN PROVENCE AND IN ITALY
IN THE FOURTEENTH CENTURY

Parody was first developed into a distinct branch of literature in Provence and in Italy. Traces of it are already found in Provence as early as the twelfth century. The hymn of Menahem ben Aaron, who undoubtedly was a native of southern France, is an example. In the thirteenth century, we find an anonymous parody of the *Azharot* of Rabbi Elijah ha-Zaken, also a wine-song — which Prof. Schechter regards as "one of the jolliest and wildest parodies for the feast of Purim" — preserved in a *Mahzor* by a French copyist of the name of Benjamin (fl. cir. 1276), and the satiric utterances of the *Zohar* against the Talmud couched in the form of homilies. . .

It was not until the middle of the first half of the fourteenth century, that parody became a distinct branch of Hebrew literature. Between 1319 and 1332 three parodies were written which raised this form of satire into an art. In the *Masseket Purim* of Kalonymos ben Kalonymos, and the anonymous *Sefer ha-Bakbuk ha-Nabi* (Book of the Prophet "Bottle") and *Megillat Setarim* (Scroll of Secrecy), parody attained to an individuality of its own. Whatever else they may have accomplished, they certainly made parody to be recognized as an art worth cultivating for its own sake. For the first time men of such great renown as Kalonymos and Levi ben Gershon ventured to deal with the Talmud playfully. The numerous anecdotes and various customs that cluster about the jolly season of Purim are related in the solemn language of the *Tannaim* and *Amoraim*. That it was in no

way meant as a disparagement of the original, need hardly
be said. None but the obdurate fanatic could fail to see the
humor of it. The *Masseket Purim* concludes with the following words:

> Wherefore does this tract close with the chapter, "We
> Are Not to Read" (אין קורין)? Because we are not to
> read this treatise except when it is neither day nor
> night. For it was written in mere fun, to amuse people
> on Purim. He who reads this treatise is none the worse
> for it than if he read books on medicine, and similar
> topics, which prove beneficial to the body and harm-
> less to the soul.

Similarly, we find in the *Megillat Setarim* that, "wherever
the name of the deity is mentioned in it, no sacredness
should be attached to the name." And again:

> What is meant by the Scroll of Secrecy (*Megillat
> Setarim*)? Translate it the Scroll of Purim. But why did
> they call it the Scroll of Secrecy? Because the pious
> men of old handed it down in secret to their pupils and
> did not make it known to any one unless he was pos-
> sessed by a good spirit and under the influence of wine.

These parodies, therefore, meant nothing more than that
the Talmud, like any other great work of literature, had to
pay the penalty for its popularity. Still, the more conservative elements were indignant and looked upon these
parodies as vile profanations. Their antipathy for this class
of literature in general was perhaps intensified by passages
like the following:

> Rabbi Abraham was wont to say: "I have a tradition
> from my great grandparents, that whoever has no share
> in the pleasures of this life will have no share in the
> pleasures of the future life; but he who enjoys this life
> will likewise enjoy the life to come."

Again:

> Children are taught on Purim. What are they taught?
> To fight one another... so that, if they live to see the
> days of the Messiah, they will be skilled in the tactics
> of war and will fight the battles of the Lord.

Otherwise, the satire of the *Masseket Purim* is inoffensive.
It ridicules the drunkard and the glutton, laughs at the
miser, and reproaches the idler and the professional men-
dicant; but nowhere is the state of society attacked in as
wholesale a manner as in the *Touch Stone*. Occasionally we
meet with a grotesque passage, as the story of the glutton
who doffed his clothes and dived into a bowl of soup to look
for his portion of meat. We also learn, in passing, some customs connected with the feast of Purim of which no mention
is found anywhere else. We read, for instance, that people
rode on horseback through the streets with pine branches
in their hands, or made merry round a puppet representing
Haman, which was set on an elevation, amidst shouts of
vengeance and blowing of trumpets. This custom was called
Ira, which is the Italian for vengeance. The custom of
giving Purim gifts to children was just then introduced into
the Jewish community of Rome. Dances and games, chiefly
the game of chess, were usual forms of amusement. As to
eating and drinking, Kalonymos enumerates twenty-seven
dishes which the Greeks called *Oinomeli*. Occasionally, he
betrays a knowledge of hygiene. He also takes the opportunity of praising the Italian women for cleanliness, and
offers an explanation for the practice of usury prevalent in
his day throughout Western Europe.

The heterogeneity of the contents of the *Masseket Purim*
does not detract from its merits as a parody of the Talmud.
For it copies the original, not only in style and diction, but
also in the manner of bring together dissimilar subjects into

one discussion; and the skill with which the ancient texts are imitated tells how thoroughly saturated the author was with talmudic lore. In the opening chapter it parodies the first chapter of the Treatise *Shekalim*, but it soon passes to

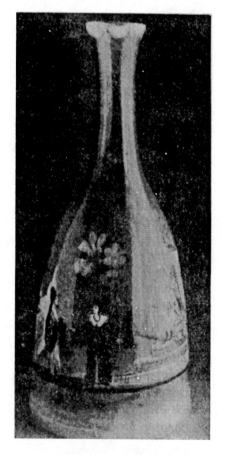

44. *PURIM WINE TANKARD*
Hand-Painted Glass

19th Century

other talmudic passages, and is for this reason more of a
travesty of the talmudic style than a parody of any particular talmudic text.

No less clever and skillful is the *Megillat Setarim* of Levi
ben Gershon. It opens with a parody of the first Mishnah
of Abot, giving the *Drunkard's Chain of Tradition*, as the
original gives the chain of Jewish tradition:

> Ha-Bakbuk (The Bottle) received the Laws from Karmi
> (Vineyard) and handed it down to Noah, and Noah
> handed it down to Lot, and Lot to the brothers of
> Joseph, and they handed it down to Nabal the Carmel-
> ite, and he to Ben-hadad, and Ben-hadad to Belshazzar,
> and Belshazzar to Ahasuerus, and Ahasuerus to Rabbi
> Bibi (Rabbi Drunkard).

It has a number of clever puns and exegetical parodies, and
its style approaches that of the halakic midrash. Renan and
Neubauer think "it possible, that Levi (ben Gershon)
abridged the parody of Kalonymos, cutting out the Roman
names and taking away the local color to adapt it to the
community of Provence." This assertion, however, is without foundation and not warranted by the contents of the
parodies. The very plan of the *Megillat Setarim* proves its
independent origin. For it is a talmudic parody in the
double sense of the word. Like the parody of Kalonymos,
it imitates the diction and style of the Talmud, but, in
addition, it also copies the structure of the halakic midrash.
Just as these midrashim have the Bible for their framework,
so does the *Megillat Setarim* take for its framework a Bible
of its own — the *Sepher ha-Bakbuk ha-Nabi*. It may also
be pointed out, as additional proof of the independent origin
of the *Megillat Setarim*, that its humor is quite different
from the humor of the *Masseket Purim*. The humor of
Kalonymos, as we have seen, approaches more the grotesque,

and his satire is directed against the scum of society: the drunkard, the idler, the beggar and the miser. The humor of Levi ben Gershon, on the other hand, is a species of wit, and his satire is directed against no one in particular. On the contrary, he occasionally laughs at himself and is the target of his own jokes. He delights in exegetical parodies, in puns and in anachronisms. Kalonymos is fond of coining names to fit the subject under discussion. Thus, he has Rabbi Idler, Rabbi Beggar, Rabbi Miser take part in the discussions, each defending his own particular habit. Levi ben Gershon, on the other hand, mostly uses his own name, "Levi," and a few from the Talmud.

Another point of interest, found in *Megillat Setarim*, is the account of the custom, which seems to have been prevalent in some localities of Provence, to appoint a master of ceremonies for Purim. This personage was dubbed "King." What his functions were is not stated, except that on the first day of Adar the master of cere-monies invited all his towns-men to his home and hand-ed over his staff of authority to another man, who in turn assembled the people to his home and gave the staff

45. *ADAR TABLET*   Drawing
19th Century

over to another, and so on, until the staff went the round of the community. On the 16th day of Adar, the staff was returned to the master of ceremonies and the people once more gathered in his house. From such meager data it is difficult to draw definite conclusions, but it is not unlikely that this custom, in some way, took its origin from the *Feast of Fools*, or the Carnival, and later gave birth to the Purim plays of the seventeenth century and the Purim Rabbi of more modern times.

The *Book of the Prophet Bottle* (Sefer ha-Bakbuk ha-Nabi) is a parody without satiric motive. Jean de Plantevit found a cabalistic significance in it, seeing in the name Karmi (כרמי) an allusion to the Jewish Messiah, and in Beeri (בארי) to the Gentile World. But this naiveté was already ridiculed by Bartolocci, who recognized the humor of the book. How far the author succeeded in being humorous is another question. The language of the Prophets is cleverly imitated, but the humor is not very pronounced. The Jewish people, says the parodist, were divided in their allegiance between the Vineyard (Karmi) and the Well (Beeri), an allusion, it would seem, to intemperance and abstinence. The Bottle (*Bakbuk*) was the inspired prophet, sent to turn the people to the worship of the Vineyard, which after many trials he succeeded in accomplishing, hinting thereby, that the Jewish people were no ascetics.

With the satires of Kalonymos, parody completed its first period of growth, and entered upon a period of decay that lasted almost three centuries. From the middle of the fourteenth century to the middle of the seventeenth, there was almost a total disappearance of humor from Jewish literature. As the age of codes and casuistry, of extreme, unhealthy seclusiveness, it lost all taste for poetry and the beautiful in literature. Romances of any kind were condemned, and writings such as Immanuel's were put on the *Index*. In a word, the age was hostile to humor in general and especially opposed to the humorous treatment of sacred texts.

The Decline of Parody from the Middle of the Fourteenth Century to the Middle of the Seventeenth

During the three centuries, from the middle of the fourteenth to the middle of the seventeenth, we search in vain after parodies of importance. With few exceptions, all the parodies of this period are only parts of other compositions. In the fifteenth century a few independent parodies are found, but most of these are ascribed to this period only by conjecture.

The earliest parody of this period is the work of a Samaritan priest, who sets forth the messianic doctrine of his sect in the style in which the deluge is described in the Bible (Genesis 6. 13–8.11).

Next in point of time is a group of parodies found in each of three manuscripts of the first half of the fifteenth century. Who the author was cannot be ascertained, but that he was a native of Provence is quite certain from the frequent use which he makes of the Provençal language. The first of these parodies consists of a series of thirty-two Resolutions, or By-Laws (*Haskamot*), pertaining to the Purim-King. The opening resolution is that this King, being the ruler over the Vineyard Community, is to be regarded as the supreme ruler of all potentates. The next resolution demands that the Purim-King should place all other kings under a solemn oath to observe the Laws of the Prophet Bakbuk (The Prophet of the Bottle). The other resolutions deal with the various fines and assessments imposed upon the community for the benefit of the King. The resolutions are preceded by an anathema on those who disregard them and followed by a benediction on those who observe them. Contrary to our expectations, they do not help us to discover what the functions of the Purim-King were. The second of these

parodies is a wine-song in the form of a hymn; and the third
and last of these parodies is a fragment of a talmudic travesty,
which adds this much to our knowledge about the Purim-
King, that it was his duty to entertain his townspeople with
music and serve them with refreshments during his reign.

Further mention of the Purim-King is found in an anonymous *Masseket Purim*, which was perhaps written in
Provence during the fifteenth century. According to this
talmudic travesty, every Jewish town elected a Purim-King
a month before Purim and invested him with full power
over the lives and property of his subjects. The most interesting feature of this parody, however, is that it gives a
biblical origin for the game of dice.

> Rabbi Shigaon (Lunatic) said: "Behold I am almost
> seventy years old and I was never privileged to under-
> stand why dice should be played on Purim, until Rabbi
> Badai (Fiction) expounded (the passage in Esther 9.27):
> *The Jews ordained and took upon them* (קִימוּ וְקִבְּל
> היהודים עליהם). Here קִבָּל is written instead of קִבְּלוּ.
> This [strange spelling] is to indicate the spots on the
> six sides of the die in their proper order. *Hirek* points
> to the side with one spot; *Sheva* to the one with two
> spots; *Kibbuz* to the three spots; the *Kibbuz* and the
> *Hirek* to the four spots; the *Kibbuz* and the *Sheva* to
> the five spots, and the *Kibbuz*, *Hirek* and *Sheva* to the
> side with six spots."

In the same passage mention is also made of the game of
cards (שחוק הצורות), the game of chess (נרדשיר) and a game
of tables (שחוק השלחנות), which is undoubtedly the game
of backgammon. The parody closes with an imitation of
the *Kaddish* which turns the prayer for the dead into a eulogy
of good living.

There is also a number of parodies whose style and subject

matter, as well as the age of the manuscript in which they are found, justify us in ascribing them to the sixteenth century. A *Purim Sermon on Wine*, written by a man named Meier, is described by N. Brüll as *ein humoristischer Purim Traktat*.

To the same group belongs a wine-song modelled after the Spanish version of the hymn *Ha-Mabdil*. As this version was already well known in the latter part of the thirteenth century, the parody might have been composed even as early as the beginning of the fourteenth century, but its subject matter stamps it as a product of the latter part of the sixteenth. The following translation preserves the metrical system of the original.

> Here's to him who flings aside
> The cup of penitence at Purim tide,
> And flees the hermits with drunkards to bide
> Howling through the night.

> Red wine I prize as meed,
> White wine is good in time of need,
> But the water-drinker I hate, indeed,
> As the dense darkness of the night;

> I cry, and tears I shed
> If on water I am fed;
> O, for twenty measures of sparkling red
> To quench my thirst to-night.

> Your praise, my friends, aloud I'll cry
> If ne'er the wine in my cup go dry.
> With brimful jugs of beer we'll try
> To get drunk to-night.

A holy deed I teach you, hear!
Men of wisdom, incline your ear!
Keep your house of water clear,
   'Tis as bad as the night.

Summon courage, men of lore,
For Noah's sake, the Righteous of yore,
Who planted vineyards, unknown before,
   To drink by day and night.

This wine-song evidently grew out of the custom of making the fourth meal on Sabbath an occasion for much feasting and carousing.

The Revival of Parody From the Middle of the Seventeenth Century to the Close of the Eighteenth

The revival in the art of parody began in the last quarter of the seventeenth century. What seems to be the earliest parody of the period dates from the year 1679. It bears no title, but it imitates the style of *Letters of Credentials* and concerns itself with the feud between two factions. It may perhaps have reference to some political communal events of that period, but the enigmatic language in which it is couched defies all interpretation.

To the same period may also be ascribed a parody of an *Almoner's Credentials*, entitled *The Humorous Letter for Purim*, addressed to the "mighty in drink," asking them to extend their hospitality to the bearer, for whose name a blank space is left in the body of the letter. To all appearances, this parody has no historic significance, nor does it have exceptional literary merit. . . .

The true revival of parody must be attributed to such works as have seen the light of day. It is, therefore, a noteworthy incident that, just as in the first period of its growth, parody reached its culminating point in the *Masseket Purim* of Kalonymos, so it began its revival in the latter part of the seventeenth century with a new parody of the same name and character. The *Masseket Purim* of the seventeenth century, however, is not only of unknown authorship, but in its fifth and final version, it is the composite of several authors. Like some popular legend that grows in variety of incident and narrative as it is carried down the stream of generations, so this talmudic travesty grew in matter and changed in form as it passed from one ambitious copyist to another. In its earliest version, this parody is more midrashic than talmudic in character. There is very little of the halakic element in it, while the agadic preponderates. In the second version, however, it not only grows in substance, but also assumes a different form. It preserves its agadic aspects and in addition assumes also the halakic. It has the true ring of talmudic argumentation, though its diction is not as archaic as it should be. The third version is but a slight modification of the second, and the fourth is an inexact copy of the third. But the fifth and last version again presents a radical change in substance and form. In it, the element of agada is much reduced, and the halakic passages much amplified. The arguments are put more compactly, the language is more concise, and the diction approaches nearer to the diction of the Babylonian Talmud. In addition, it is also augmented with parodies of the three best known talmudic commentaries, namely, Rashi, Tosafot and the *Novellae* of Rabbi Samuel Edels. This version, made by a number of Polish *Bahurim* (young men) in the beginning of the eighteenth century, caught the fancy of the people. Though it was not published until 1814, it must have been copied and circulated quite extensively. It has certainly superseded the *Masseket Purim* of Kalonymos in popularity, and today is by far the most widely known parody.

In the first version, the parody has only one theme — the praise of wine:

> Said Rabbi Bakbuk (Bottle): "Whosoever drinks wine on Purim, and becomes as intoxicated as Noah the Righteous, will be protected the rest of the year from the evil effects of bad water. You may learn this from Noah the Righteous. For when the deluge came and drowned the whole world, even the giants, there remained no one in the world, excepting Noah, his wife and children and those who were with him in the ark — all because he was destined to plant a vineyard and become intoxicated on Purim."

> Rabbi Hamram (Wine Dealer) said: "Why did the eyes of Isaac our forefather grow dim sooner than those of any other Patriarch? Because all his life he busied himself with nothing but digging wells, as it is told in the Pentateuch, and never planted even one vineyard. . . ."

The same note runs through the whole parody. It is one long eulogy of wine and those who drink it to excess on Purim.

In all later versions, however, the parody broadens out, and by means of talmudic methods deduces from the Bible a number of fantastic laws for Purim, retaining all the while the seriousness of tone for which the talmudic discussions are noted. In the manner of the first Mishnah of Pesahim, the parody begins:

> MISHNAH: On the eve of the fourteenth (of Adar), water should be searched for and removed from houses and from courtyards. All places where water is not

usually kept need not be searched. — GEMARA: Where is the biblical authority for this law? It is found in the Scriptures: *So shalt thou put away the bad from the midst of thee* (Deuteronomy 13.6), and nothing is bad but water; for it is written: *the water is bad* (II Kings 2.19).

In the same humorous strain it is deduced from the Bible that on Purim we must avoid a stream and, if rain fall, must remain indoors. Occasionally the humor turns into the grotesque, as in the following instances:

> When Rabbi Hamram drank wine on Purim and a drop fell on the ground, he fell on his knees and licked it off with the dust and all.
> When Rabbi Shakran (Drunkard) went to sleep on the night of Purim, he suspended a bag of wine over his head, from which the wine dripped through a puncture into his mouth.

But the most humorous feature of this parody is undoubtedly the relation which it establishes, in talmudic fashion, between well-known historic events and the day of Purim. Thus, the deluge came upon the earth, because that generation drank water on Purim. The night on which Lot was intoxicated by his daughters (Genesis 19.33) was Purim, and so was the day on which Esau sold his birthright to Jacob, and the day on which Joseph made himself known to his brothers. Similarly, the day on which Miriam, the sister of Moses, died was Purim; for, since it is said: *and there was no water for the congregation* (Numbers 20.2), it must have been Purim. The generation that died in the desert will have no share in the future world because they drank water on Purim; and, finally, the day on which Sisera fled to Jael's tent (Judges 4.17) was Purim, and she killed him, because he asked for water.

To sum up, this parody is a fair specimen of scholastic wit.
Thought not fancy, subtlety not imagination, pervade it.
Its humor does not flow from the spring of life, as true humor
should. It is the work of recluses, who have no eye for the
real, no sense for the tangible. It is the product of a school
that delighted in play on words and attached as much importance to names of things as to things themselves.

Closely associated with the preceding parody, both in
printed copies and in manuscripts, are a number of wine-
songs in the form of hymns, the theme of which is that on
Purim it is our duty to drown our sorrows in wine and song,
abstain from all manual work and do nothing but dance
and carouse, give full freedom to our expressions and indulge
even in profane language — in a word, we may let folly rule
the day.

From these we pass on to the parodies of the eighteenth
century. Early in that century the *Burlesque Testament*, or
the parody of the Ethical Will, and the parody of the Requiem came a good deal into vogue. The Ethical Will figured so prominently in Jewish literature of the Middle Ages
that the parodist could not but encounter it in his search
after literary models; while the parody of the Requiem,
though logically it should have followed the Will as the next
and final episode in the human drama, really preceded it by
a few centuries, as can be seen from the parody of Judah
ben Isaac ibn Shabbetai.

What seems to be the earliest effort in this line is a collection of parodies by David Raphael Polido, published in 1703
under the title of *Commemoration of Purim*. Haman is described as lingering in prison, awaiting execution. Meanwhile he calls his family to his side and reads them his testament. In language which parodies in part the Blessing of
Jacob (Genesis 49) and in part the Ten Commandments,
Haman admonishes his children to live peacefully among

themselves and to unite in their hatred against the Jews. He also advises them to have no mercy on the poor, to abstain from the practice of charity, because it is profitless, to threaten their creditors with violence if they importune and, on the other hand, to give their debtors no rest if they refuse to pay promptly. Finally, he urges them not to steal from the poor, because they possess little that is worth stealing. Such, according to the parodist, are the Ethics of Haman.

The liturgic parody, which in this collection follows the *Burlesque Testament*, is hardly worth the name of literature. It consists of curses and maledictions hurled at the head of Haman, the symbolic enemy and oppressor of the Jewish people. The several parodies of the Requiem, with which the collection closes, are no better. They all abound in word play, but are sadly deficient in ideas. Euphony is mistaken for thought, and paranomasia for humor. The one passage in the book which may be called humorous is where Haman requests his family to pension the parodist, that he may buy new clothes every Purim. We can see, as it were, the face of the poor, shabby scribbler brighten up as he labors over his puns, amused at his ingenuity in telling people what he needed without asking them for it.

Similar to Polido's parody, not only in name but also in contents, is the *Book for the Commemoration of Purim*, by M.C-i of Modena, which is perhaps the pseudonym of Malachi Colorni, who flourished in that town in 1781. It is written in the Aramaic dialect and is an attempt to present Haman's downfall in dramatic form. The parody draws a good deal upon the Midrash and the *Targum Sheni* of the Book of Esther. And though its literary execution, as a whole, is not much better than that of Polido's parody, some of the individual parodies embodied in the *Burlesque Testament* are better than the rest. Such, for instance, are the *Epitaph on Haman's Tomb* and the *Lamentation of Haman*.

On the whole, however, it must be admitted, that from a literary point of view all these parodies are very poor. They represent the efforts of mediocre minds, and are not only void of the brilliancy of original invention, but are also without the lustre of clever imitation.

To the early period of the eighteenth century belongs also what may be considered the earliest specimen of Yiddish parody. It has been embodied in a Yiddish Purim play, the earliest printed copy of which appeared in Frankfort in 1708, under the title: *Ein schon neu Achaschwerosch Spiel.* Recently there appeared *Dus Pirimspiel,* which is a new version of the Yiddish play, based on the collation of two copies, independently drawn by two professional Purim players, both of which point to a more ancient source.

The parodies found in these versions of the Purim play are very quaint and deserve to be reproduced on that account alone, but they defy all efforts at translation. In one of these, Mordecai is represented as the Father Confessor to Queen Vashti. Before she is led away by the executioner, Mordecai comes to administer the last rites. "Repeat the Confessional after me," he says, "word for word," and thereupon he recites the blessing which Jacob pronounced upon the children of Joseph (Genesis 48.16), but every word of that passage is so translated — or rather mistranslated — into Yiddish, that, as a result, we have a string of nonsensical phrases extremely funny, though in parts somewhat vulgar.

Again Mordecai appears in the character of a *Shadkan,* or professional match-maker, on which occasion the Jewish marriage formula is parodied in quite a witty fashion. There is also a prayer by Esther, which is a clever imitation of the style of the *Tehinot* (Prayer for Grace), and in Schudt's edition of the Purim play there is also a funny, but vulgar parody of the *Selihot*.

In connection with the parodies in the Yiddish Purim plays, mention must also be made of the *Kiddush le-Purim*, or the parody of the formula for the blessing over the wine, with which these performances always wound up. It is similar in character to the English *Tom-O'-Bedlam*, or the French *Coq-à-l'âne*, but its construction is peculiar to itself. It is formed by attaching to one biblical phrase, ending with a certain word, another which begins with the same word, continuing the same process through a long rigmarole of meaningless phrases taken from all parts of the Bible.* One of the cleverest of these parodies was published together with *Dus Pirimspiel* mentioned above. Like the play itself, this liturgic parody very likely had its origin in the early part of the eighteenth

46. *PURIM WINE CUP*
Hand-Painted Glass

19th Century

century and is a product of Jewish folklore in Poland and Lithuania, where many versions of it are current among the students in the *Yeshibot*.

In 1792 an anonymous travesty of the marriage contract appeared in Judeo-Spanish, entitled *The Marriage Contract of the Daughter of Haman*, and in the following year, Isaac

* See page 355.

Israel of Hamburg wrote a satire on the professional match-maker in the form of a parody.

Another representative of the last part of the eighteenth century, and one who deserves a place among the best of literary parodists, is Judah-Loeb Bensew of Cracow. His *Order of Penitential Prayers for Purim*, or, as it is more often called, *Satire for Purim*, is a hymnal for the worshippers of Bacchus, a Book of Devotion for the lovers of wine and music. In language that vividly recalls the characteristics of the *piyyutic* style, the parodist describes the thrilling incidents in the history of Purim and the tragic end of the ill-fated Haman. He depicts in glowing colors the manner of celebrating the feast of Purim prevalent in his day, and gives two sketches of the drunkard that are masterpieces of style and humor and easily compare with Immanuel's famous *Song on the Chief of Drunkards*. Satiated and feeling the effects of intoxication, the drunkard falls into a peniten-tial mood and gives expression to his feeling in the following manner:

> How can I open my mouth or lift mine eye.
> Confused is my tongue from the tumult of wine,
> Also the light of mine eyes is gone from me,
> I am like one weapon-wounded . . .

His wine-song is likewise one of the best in Hebrew litera-ture. Hebrew poets of all times have occasionally indulged in sounding the praises of wine: Gabirol, Moses ibn Ezra, Harizi and Immanuel, even Menahem de Lonzano did not disdain to compose a wine-song in honor of Purim. But the wine-song of Bensew has the additional interesting feature, that it is a parody of a religious hymn. And although it is encumbered with rhymes and acrostics, and is obliged to follow the original poem which it parodies, it nevertheless has an easy style and shows no sign of labor or unusual effort.

The history of parody in the eighteenth century closes with a new literary form — the *Zohar* parody. *The New Zohar for Purim*, by Tobias Feder, though of uncertain date, and unearthed more than seven decades after the author's death (1817), is undoubtedly one of Feder's youthful productions, and therefore belongs to the literature of the eighteenth century. In the language and phraseology of the Canon of Cabala, Feder sounds the praise of wine. Wine, he says, is the elixir of life, the source of perfect happiness, the power that opens the gates of love in heaven and on earth. It holds the key to the mysteries of the Universe. Whoever abstains from it will not see the day of resurrection, but he who indulges in it freely, will share the good of this world and of the world to come. Drawing upon some of the biblical narratives, the parodist continues in the same strain. Wine, he says, brought the curse of Noah upon the head of Canaan, and played an important part in the episode of Lot's daughters; it procured for Jacob the blessing of his father, and brought Haman to his ignominious death.

The literary execution of the *New Zohar for Purim* must be pronounced excellent, even though we notice in it a lack of unity and occasionally meet with repetitions. For, aside from the fact that it was the first attempt to parody the style and diction of the *Zohar*, we must bear in mind that it was most likely written at long intervals, which made repetition and looseness of construction almost inevitable.

There is a free flow of humor in the *New Zohar for Purim*, and one is almost tempted to believe that, in praising the drunkard, Feder was indulging in fun at his own expense. For it is well known that he was strongly addicted to drink and that liquor put him in the best mood for writing. But for this very reason, perhaps, his humor is of a low order, and at times even vulgar and obscene in its allusions. The poverty under which Feder labored all his life seems to have infected his writings. The uncouth habits contracted during a life of wandering and begging appear occasionally in his works, and are especially noticeable in this parody because it was not intended for the public eye, and therefore not purged of its objectionable elements.

However, if we overlook this single objection, we may consider the *New Zohar for Purim* even superior, in some respects, to most of the parodies of the eighteenth century. For, unlike most of them, it shows considerable satiric power. It is not mere word play, but the expression of a strong purpose. This purpose was to ridicule the wonder working rabbis of the Hasidim, who had so abused the system of hermeneutics that the text of the Bible became in their hands an instrument of folly and a tool for fraud. Adopting, therefore, the language and style of the *Zohar*, with which these rabbis were most familiar, Feder proceeded to show that he could find a text for anything and everything imaginable — obscenity not excepted. In other words, he proved once more that, in citing Scripture, the Devil is never at a loss. The *New Zohar for Purim*, then, in as much as it deals with phases of contemporary life, may be regarded as the forerunner of the satiric parody, or the connecting link between the old parody and the new, between the parody that is merely entertaining and the parody that seeks to correct error and stamp out evil. For only few of the parodies of the preceding centuries have any bearing on contemporary life and might have been written in any age and in any land, while the parodies of the nineteenth century are the direct product of the times and reflect intellectual movements in general and the progress of Jewish thought in particular.

EXAMPLES OF PURIM PARODY

מתוך „הגדה לליל שכורים"

The *Haggadah for the Night of Drunkards* by H. Sommer-
hausen is one of the cleverest parodies in Jewish literature.
When reading the following excerpts it would be well to
compare them with the passages of the Passover Haggadah
that they imitate.

אֱכוֹל וּשְׁתֵה, שְׁתֵה וָאֱכוֹל   שְׁתֵה וָאֱכוֹל, אֱכוֹל וּשְׁתֵה

עַד לֹא תֵדַע בֵּין יָמִין לִשְׂמֹאל.   וְכָל מַכְאוֹב־לֵב הָלְאָה זָרה

מגביהין כוס תשיעית

כְּהָא חַמְרָא דְשַׁמְפַּנְיָה דִי שָׁתוּ אַבְהָתָנָא בְּכָל אַתְרָא
וְאַתְרָא, כָּל דְּצָמֵי יֵיתֵי וְיִשְׁתֵּי, כָּל דְּאִית לֵיה דִּינָרָא בְּכִיסֵיה
יֵיתֵי וְיִזְבּוֹן. הָשַׁעְתָּא הָכָא לְשָׁעָה הַבָּאָה בְּבֵיתָא דְמִשְׁתַּיָה,
הָשַׁעְתָּא הָכָא, לְשָׁעָה הַבָּאָה שִׁכּוֹרִין.

וכאן הבן שואל:

מ ה   נ ש ת נ ה   היום הזה מכל הימים. שבכל הימים פעם אנו
עוסקין במלאכה ופעם אנו אוכלין, היום הזה כולו אכילה ושתיה.
שבכל הימים אנו שותים מים או שכר או יין, היום הזה כולו
יין. שבכל הימים לחם לבב אנוש יסעד, היום הזה אין פחות
בישראל בלי סעודת מלכים. שבכל הימים אנו אוכלים כדי שובע
ושותים לצמאון, היום הזה כולנו זוללים וסובאים ושכורים.

א מ ר   רבי   בקבוק הנטופתי: הרי כבר שמחתי בשמחת־פורים
זה שבעים שנה ולא זכיתי שתעשה סעודת פורים שלשה ימים ושלשׁה
לילות.   עד שדרשה בן־יינא סבא, שנאמר: מיגון לשמחה ומאבל

ליום־טוב. מה יגון ואבל שלשה ימים ושלשה לילות ככתוב: וצומו
עלי ואל תאכלו ואל תשתו שלשה ימים לילה ויום, כן שמחת יום־
טוב.

ב ר ו ך המקום ברוך הוא שנתן המגלה לעמו ישראל ברוך הוא.
כנגד ארבעה בנים דברה המגלה אחד חכם ואחד שוטה ואחד תם
ואחד שאינו יודע לשתות:

ח כ ם מה הוא אומר מה העדות והחקים והמשפטים לעסוק בהם
יומם ולילה הלא טוב לנו שבת על סיר הבשר או לכת אל
בית־המשתה. ואף אתה אמור לו מי שיושבים בסעודה של פורים
אין נפטרין עד הפסח ממקומן:

ש ו ט ה מה הוא אומר מה שמחת פורים לכם אשר לא ראיתם
לא המן ולא מרדכי לכם ולא לו ולפי שהוציא את עצמו מן הכלל
כפר במגילה ואף אתה הקהה את שניו ואמור לו וכל זה איננו שוה
לי ולא לו. אילו היה שם היה נתלה:

ת ם מה הוא אומר מה זאת ואמרת אליו סעודת פורים היא וכל
המתעסק בה זוכה ליהנות מסעודה של לויתן:

ו ש א י נ ו   י ו ד ע   ל ש ת ו ת את פתח לו את הפה שנאמר הרחב
פיך ואמלאהו ונאמר ולמדה את בני ישראל שימה בפיהם:

י כ ו ל מראש חדש מפני שנאמר והחדש אשר נהפך להם תלמוד
לומר להיות עושים את שני הימים האלו. יכול מעלות השחר תלמוד
לומר מיגון לשמחה. לשמחה לא אמרתי אלא בשעה שהכוסות מזוגין
לפניך:

מתחלה היו מתענים שלשה ימים ואוכלים יום אחד ועכשיו
מתענים יום אחד ואוכלים עד אין קץ ואין תכלית, עד שיכלה הבשר
מהשולחן והיין מהכוס והפרוטה האחרונה מהכיס: ואם ימי תענית

וחגים מבוטלים, ימי הפורים יהיו לעד קימים. שנאמר וימי הפורים
האלה לא יעברו מתוך היהודים וזכרם לא יסוף מזרעם.

ב ר ו ך שומר יינו במרתפו כל השנה לכבוד פורים ברוך שחשב
ומנה וספר את החביות שלא יגזלו ממנו. שבכל השנה השתיה רשות
ובפורים חובה לשתות שנאמר והשתיה כדת עד שישתכר ויישן
ובחלומו יראה שיש לו רכוש גדול.

ו ה ו א היין שעמד לאבותינו ולנו כי ברצות המקום לזכות את
ישראל הרבה להם סעודות של מצוה וכוסות של ברכה. קדוש
והבדלה. מילה ופדיון הבן. ובר מצוה וארוסין וסעודת נשואין
וברכת מעין חתום. אשרי אלה שזוכים לכולם וכוסם בידם.

קְדוּשָׁא רַבָּא לְפוּרִים

This famous parody of the *Kiddush* was a favorite introduction to the Purim *Seudah*. It is composed of verses from
the Bible and the prayer book strung together, with the
last word of the first verse becoming the first word of the
second verse, and so forth. Each verse is sung with its own
peculiar melody.

יוֹם הַשִּׁשִּׁי וַיְכֻלּוּ הַשָּׁמַיִם (בראשית ב, א, קדוש לליל שבת)

הַשָּׁמַיִם מְסַפְּרִים כְּבוֹד (תהלים יט, ב, פסוקי דזמרה לשבת)

כְּבוֹדוֹ מָלֵא עוֹלָם מְשָׁרְתָיו שׁוֹאֲלִים זֶה לָזֶה אַיֵּה (קדושת מוסף שבת)

אַיֵּה שָׂרָה אִשְׁתֶּךָ (בראשית יח, ט)

אִשְׁתְּךָ כְּגֶפֶן פוֹרִיָּה בְּיַרְכְּתֵי בֵיתֶךָ (תהלים קכח, ג)

בֵּיתֶךָ וּבִשְׁעָרֶיךָ. וְהָיָה אִם־שָׁמוֹעַ תִּשְׁמְעוּ אֶל־מִצְוֹתַי אֲשֶׁר אָנֹכִי
(דברים ו, ט; יא, יג, קריאת שמע)

אָנֹכִי ה' אֱלֹקֶיךָ אֲשֶׁר הוֹצֵאתִיךָ מֵאֶרֶץ מִצְרָיִם ‹עשרת הדברות, שמות כ, ב›

(מ)מִצְרַיִם גְּאַלְתָּנוּ ... וּמִבֵּית עֲבָדִים פְּדִיתָנוּ ... וּמֵחֳלָיִים רָעִים
וְנֶאֱמָנִים ‹נשמת›, שחרית לשבת›

וְנֶאֱמָנִים וְנֶחֱמָדִים לָעַד וּלְעוֹלְמֵי עוֹלָמִים, עַל אֲבוֹתֵינוּ וְעָלֵינוּ ‹‹אמת
ויציב›, תפלת שחרית›

עָלֵינוּ לְשַׁבֵּחַ לַאֲדוֹן הַכֹּל ‹עלינו לשבח›

הַכֹּל יוֹדוּךָ וְהַכֹּל יְשַׁבְּחוּךָ וְהַכֹּל יֹאמְרוּ אֵין קָדוֹשׁ ‹תפלת שחרית לשבת,
ברכת יוצר›

קָדוֹשׁ קָדוֹשׁ קָדוֹשׁ ה' צְבָאוֹת מְלֹא כָל־הָאָרֶץ ‹ישעיה ו, ג, קדושה›

(ו)הָאָרֶץ הָיְתָה תֹהוּ וָבֹהוּ וְחֹשֶׁךְ עַל פְּנֵי תְהוֹם וְרוּחַ אֱלֹקִים מְרַחֶפֶת
עַל פְּנֵי הַמָּיִם ‹בראשית א, ב›

מַיִם רַבִּים לֹא יוּכְלוּ לְכַבּוֹת אֶת הָאַהֲבָה ‹שיר השירים ח, ז›

אַהֲבָה רַבָּה אֲהַבְתָּנוּ ה' אֱלֹקֵינוּ ‹‹אהבה רבה›, תפלת שחרית›

ה' אֱלֹקֵינוּ לֹא לִידֵי מַתְּנַת בָּשָׂר וָדָם ‹‹רחם נא›, ברכת המזון›

דָּם צְפַרְדֵּעַ כִּנִּים עָרוֹב דָּבֶר ‹הגדה של פסח›

דֶּבֶר וְחֶרֶב וְרָעָב וְיָגוֹן ‹‹השכיבנו›, תפלת ערבית›

וְיָגוֹן וַאֲנָחָה בְּיוֹם מְנוּחָתֵנוּ וַהֲרִיאֵנוּ ‹‹רצה והחליצנו›, ברכת המזון של שבת›

וַהֲרִיאֵנוּ בְּבִנְיָנוֹ וְשַׂמְּחֵנוּ בְּתִקּוּנוֹ, וְהָשֵׁב ‹‹מלך רחמן›, מוסף לרגלים›

וְהָשֵׁב אֶת הָעֲבוֹדָה לִדְבִיר בֵּיתֶךָ ‹‹רצה›, תפלת שמונה עשרה›

לִדְבִיר בֵּיתֶךָ וּפִנּוּ אֶת הַהֵיכָל וְטִהֲרוּ אֶת מִקְדָּשֶׁךָ וְהִדְלִיקוּ
נֵרוֹת בְּחַצְרוֹת קָדְשֶׁךָ וְקָבְעוּ ‹‹על הנסים, בימי מתתיהו›

יְמֵי פוּרִים אֵלֶּה לִשְׁתִיָּה וּלְשִׂכָּרוֹן לְשִׂמְחָה וּלְשָׂשׂוֹן, זֵכֶר לִיצִיאַת
מִצְרָיִם. כִּי בָנוּ בָחַרְתָּ וְאוֹתָנוּ קִדַּשְׁתָּ מִכָּל הָעַמִּים וּדְבָרְךָ אֱמֶת וְקַיָּם
לָעַד. בָּרוּךְ אַתָּה ה' אֱלֹקֵינוּ מֶלֶךְ הָעוֹלָם בּוֹרֵא פְּרִי הַגָּפֶן.

CHAPTER XVII

THE HISTORY OF PURIM PLAYS

Jacob Shatzky

THE history of Purim plays cannot yet be fully and satisfactorily told. Shrouded by the silence of centuries, ignored by the historians of Jewish cultural life, these products of Jewish histrionic talent have become better known only in the last three decades of our century because of the scholarly works of the new generation of East European historians.

The Badhan — First Purim Player

The prototype of the Purim players is discernible in the *Badhan*, the Jewish wedding jester and his mono-dramatic performances. This unique buffoon was the carrier of solemnity and frivolity and justly had claims to be looked upon as a professional performer. The oldest texts of Purim repertory consist of parodistic monologues, sketches impersonating some popular characters and types in Jewish communal life and vivid impersonations of local worthies. In addition to these themes, there were also morality plays in the form of dialogues between Good and Evil, Summer and Winter, Learned and Ignoramus; these served as interludes. Besides the jesters, the ghetto enjoyed the primitive amusements supplied by clowns, ventriloquists, circus acrobats and similar performers hired for the day's delight.

Purim King and Rabbi

The "Purim King" was another memorable character of communal fun who usually reigned from about two weeks before Purim until its end. Still in vogue in many communities is the custom of appointing a "Purim Rabbi" in *Yeshibot*, undoubtedly imitating the Catholic "jester-Pope" who holds sway during the carnival season. The first selection of such a "Rabbi" is generally attributed to the students of the *Yeshibah* of Volozhin. The "Rabbi" would wittily mimic and subtly criticize the venerated masters of the talmudical academies. The lectures and sermons of the impersonator were studded with cleverly phrased biblical and talmudical allusions.

Earliest Purim Plays

The earliest Purim plays thus far recorded were performed in Germany. In the Jewish communities of Germany these plays were known already in the fifteenth century, although the oldest unpublished text is dated 1697. Since this text is a copy procured by the renowned Hebraist, Johann Christopher Wagenseil (1633–1705), the original must have been much older. From Germany the Purim plays migrated, together with the emigrants, to Poland and there became the

47. PURIM JESTERS

Megillah

basis for a new development, adjusted to the local interests and surroundings of the new environment.

In Germany the Purim plays had been performed in many communities over the course of centuries. In some of these communities they were still an attraction as late as 1850, when, however, they fell into disuse. Purim plays in many communities attained such wide popularity that even the Christian population eagerly attended them. Such was the case in Frankfort-on-the-Main in the eighteenth century, in Fürth, Berlin, Prague and other cities. In Frankfort-on-the-Main the play excited such great curiosity among the Christian community that, in the year 1713, two soldiers were employed to keep the crowds off. Similar popularity attended the Purim plays in the Italian ghettos, where they were performed in a Jewish-Italian patois. In Gorizia, Italy, the municipality prohibited (in 1767) non-Jews from attending the Jewish Purim plays.

FOLKLORIZATION

In the course of centuries the original of the Purim play underwent considerable changes. The texts themselves became folklorized, that is, they were filled with contradictory elements, such as different linguistic styles, anachronistic remarks and inconsistent actions. This resulted from the fact that some players memorized their own parts and later reconstructed the play to fit the parts in with other players who remembered their lines. Hence the disruption of the sequence of incidents as compared with the texts printed, the interpolation of casual interludes and the diffusion of different techniques of theatrical art in the same performance. The desire to get around to as many houses as possible in order to collect gifts, for which the performance was mainly intended, was also a justifiable excuse to divide one scenario into two or more plays.

Purim — The Theatrical Season

Since Purim allows merrymaking, not only in private homes, but also within the synagogue, this day of rejoicing enlarged the possibilities of histrionic activities. Purim became the Jewish theatrical season, which in some communities lasted fourteen days.

Although in some places plays were given on Hanukkah and Passover, the Purim play overshadowed them, because it was the original form of such divertissement and was intimately and characteristically associated with that holiday.

Like other folk literature the Purim play defies exact definition. The problem of evaluating the playing is also very complicated. There were no reviewers in those days and the occasional remarks of the Christian witnesses were derogatory rather than constructive or informative. That the players came from the humblest levels of the Jewish population is a certainty. This can be inferred from the social criticism that some of the plays occasionally contain, in which a pronounced dissatisfaction is expressed with the leadership of the Jewish communities. This does not, of course, exclude the participation of the learned and the scholarly, since some parodistic elements in these plays reveal wide familiarity with Hebraic lore and literature. No doubt there were *Yeshibah Bahurim* (students of the *Yeshibah*) who gave expression to their normally inhibited animosities against the learned aristocrats by writing and playing witty parodies and satires about them. Purim was considered a day in which merrymaking was justifiable; it was just like the Roman Saturnalia.

Elements of the Purim Play

The pattern for the Purim play was the German play of the Reformation period which was so abundant in biblical themes, including the Esther story. The Jewish adaptations of the original German texts did not prove popular with the Jewish Purim mummers, because their spirit was not really Jewish and the entire text was too serious and was written in too solemn and theological a language. What made the Purim play so endearing and beloved was not its literary quality, but the opportunity it provided, through naive dialogue, simple, even primitive, song often of borrowed melody, and crude but frank action, to give vent to suppressed feelings and hopes heightened by current suffering. Here was a realm of freedom where the Jew could be assured of ultimate triumph over his enemies.

Gray and prosy was the life of the Jewish common man. The Purim spectacle lifted him above the level of his tedious and often depressing environment. None of the writers of Purim plays left his name to posterity. He did not know such a concept. He was as simple and unassuming as his speech. His imagery was limited in range. His humor was also not of a high level. No wonder that the Jewish notables of Frankfort in 1713 prohibited further performances of the Purim play. The obscene humor was shocking to them, and a historian of the Frankfort ghetto, the non-Jew Schudt, verifies the accusations of the Jewish notables and justifies their action.

The Purim play, so widespread and popular in Poland, Russia, Lithuania, Galicia, Rumania and other countries in Eastern Europe, had its basic source in the story of Haman and Esther. This was not the only theme for a theatrical performance on Purim, but it was the most popular and suitable. The story of Joseph in Egypt, or David and Goliath, enjoyed no less popularity. In all, more than a dozen plays, based on biblical themes, were in the repertory of the Purim players. Of these only a few complete texts from Germany and Eastern Europe are preserved.

PURIM PLAYS AND *Commedia dell' Arte*

The Purim play printed in 1708 in Frankfort-on-the-Main has a title reminiscent of similar titles of the Italian *Commedia dell' Arte*. It reads in English as follows:

> A beautiful new Ahasuerus Play, composed with all possible art! Never in all its lifetime will another be made so well, with such pretty and beautiful lamentations in rhyme. We know that whoever will buy it will not regret his purchase, because God has commanded us to be merry on Purim. Therefore have we made this Ahasuerus play enjoyable and beautiful. Therefore you householders and boys had better come quickly and buy this play from me; you will not regret the cost. If you read it, you will find that you have value for your money.

48. *PURIM PLAYERS*   Engraving

Megillah "with Herms"

The title-page of the text of 1718, printed in Amsterdam, assures the buyer that this is a Purim play "done in a new fashion, like an opera, and compiled from the *Targum Sheni*, the *Midrash*, the *Yalkut* and other *Midrashim*. And it is set in such a way that it deserves to be played by real comedians."

The technique of self-presentation of the acting character bears witness to this. Haman, for instance, introduces himself in this manner:

"Haman I am named. In gluttony and debauchery I am an adept."

King Ahasuerus addresses the audience:

"God bless you, ladies and gentlemen, one and all. I am named Ahasuerus. And I prepared a great feast for all, rich and poor. The Jews didn't eat, but they drank."

The finale of the chorus goes as follows:

"Here we stand around the purse. To ask you for ducats would be too much; we will be content with thalers."

The last phrase evidences the domestic environment in which the play was performed, when a collection followed.

The most popular texts preserved and actually performed are much simpler in their technique, than those printed in the eighteenth century. Fragments remained in the folk-memory, sometimes not more than a few rhymes or rudimentary parts of a play. These elements gave impetus to newly developed variations, less impressive in structure, but more vivacious in spirit, light-hearted and flexible. From over fifty folklorized texts saved from total oblivion by Jewish folklorists, one learns more about the technique of a Purim play, than from literary documents of preceding centuries. Some of these plays have a very superficial connection with the Purim holiday. Only the introductory remarks and the appeal for gifts in the concluding lines link them with Purim.

COMICAL INTERLUDES

The traditional Purim play was, as a rule, interspersed with comical interludes. The comic characters of the interludes were not connected structurally with the play. The comical dialogues were often supplied by the Fool. He was the audacious collector of gifts when the performance was over. Originally his function in the play was to be the protagonist of the people's complaints. He became so beloved and popular a character that an anonymous playwright produced a double of him. Thus Mordecai, the protagonist of justice and righteousness, became in some of the plays the Fool Mondrish, or the "Smart Alek," who dispelled the dramatic tension by his buffoonery. Other types of Fools were developed as independent characters; they were not incorporated into the narrative body of the play; they lived their own existence to such an extent that, when detached from the play, the play gained in tempo, and those who played the Fool became known as characters in and of themselves. Thus the character of the charlatan-doctor, widely popular in Poland, was originally an amusing part of an interlude. Later he developed into a character in himself, a take-off, in low burlesque manner, of a doctor-impostor. One could very easily establish the links between the *Commedia dell' Arte* and the type of the charlatan-doctor.

49. *PURIM JESTERS*   Woodcut
Sefer Minhagim, 1723

Of course, the plays presented by itinerant groups of mummers, who visited house after house, had obvious structural defects. Since both elements, the dramatic as well as the ludicrous, were indispensable to the play, no one could expect a just and adequate presentation of the subject. Exceptions to the rule, of course, there were, and they confirm the general opinion. There were plays consisting entirely of solemn drama leading to a moral lesson; or out-and-out burlesque plays in which pathos gives way to mockery.

PRIDE BEFORE A FALL

The general motive underlying the Purim play is similar to that prevailing in the Christian folk-dramas. Pride comes before a fall — hence a dramatic lesson in morality and righteousness. The man on the street likes stereotyped, monolithic characters, symbols of moral values. Subtle psychology is alien to him. Drama demands not only a vivid, but also a cultivated and enriched imagination. None of the texts of the Purim plays makes pretensions to literary style, though some of them have beautiful lyrics and even very effective dramatic dialogues. Just as in the *Commedia dell' Arte*, the plot of this kind of Purim play was known to each member of the "troupe," but the dialogue was left chiefly to be improvised at the moment. Like every folk-drama, the Purim play possessed values which the audience recognized and appreciated. It compensated for the naiveté of construction by its definite charm of ignoring time and place. The delighted listener did not notice the prevalent incongruity, the anachronism in customs, the bizarre amalgamation of contradictory elements.

He liked it not less than the casual performer did. The Jewish mummer, like the Italian actor of the *Commedia dell' Arte*, wanted only to arouse laughter. It was the end and aim of his entertainment. The "happy end" of the Purim story was the goal. The mummers took care not to offend the sacred canon of the Scroll of Esther and made such concessions to decorum as would bring them popularity. Since the Purim play made no great demands on acting ability, the actors had to be versatile in their use, not of difficult histrionic tricks, but of quick readiness of technique. Thus, the Purim play opened wide opportunities for such techniques as were within the ability of the amateur performer. The *Yeshibah Bahur*, for example, could expand the travesty by exhibiting his versatility and his intimacy with the Holy Scriptures and other learned books. The artisan, playing a robust Haman or a giant Samson, could give a performance of physical exuberance and grotesqueness. This method of playing evolved more by accident than by conscious and systematic design. It often delighted the performer as well as the audience. Suddenly brought before the tempting task of performing, one discovered talents of which he himself had not been aware. The improvised nature of the performance, in addition to its local flavor, gave to the old material a strange new vitality, and to the performer a new and unexpected opportunity.

This sort of entertainment was frankly justified in the course of time by its material rewards as well as by giving the multitude what they liked.

A Source of Income for Charity

In the organized society of Jewish communal life the Purim play achieved also another purpose. It became a source of income for deserving and popular charitable institutions. In Poland, for instance, the most eminent members of a local charitable society performed on Purim for the benefit of their organization. This was no more the traditional Purim play. It was as a rule a folk play, extolling the virtue of giving charity and publicizing the particular society they represented. It was more like a morality play with some humorous interludes. The buffoonery displayed by the *Gebirim* (wealthy men) of the town was sumptuously rewarded by the people whom the mummers visited. Thus, the idea of a Purim play was adapted to new needs and new social purposes.

Unfortunately, descriptive pictures, such as sketches or photographs, are almost not extant. Some etchings and drawings of the seventeenth and eighteenth centuries give a vague picture of the techniques of the mummers. More illustrative material is preserved from the nineteenth and twentieth centuries. There is not sufficient, however, to reconstruct the scenic history of the Purim plays and the histrionic techniques of the mummers.

Given an opportunity, some of the Purim players might have become actors. In Holland, for instance, the first professional Jewish actors on the stage had been formerly casual Purim players. The same was true in Russia and Poland. The first Yiddish actors, who came into prominence through the pioneering efforts of Abraham Goldfaden (1840-1908) to build a Yiddish theater, were Purim players. Some of the best dramatic traditions of the Purim play were adopted by Goldfaden and later by other eminent Yiddish playwrights.

The buffoonery of the Jewish *Commedia dell' Arte* has had a deep influence upon the modern Yiddish theater. It may even be traced to the first performances of the Habimah and the Moscow Yiddish State Theater.

Our efforts to reconstruct, from the dismembered parts of salvaged rudimentary fragments of Purim plays, a complete and adequate theory in form and technique have thus far not been satisfactory. But, the very effort in that direction testifies to the valuable cultural treasures that await discovery in this primitive folk-drama. There is still the possibility of reconstructing an interesting play based upon the extant texts, and by worthy presentation resurrect a forgotten chapter in Jewish cultural history.

CHAPTER XVIII

PURIM CURIOSITIES

BIBLE STUDY

THE Book of Esther is the only book in the Bible which does not mention God's name. Rabbi Hai Gaon explained this omission by saying that Mordecai knew that the Persians would copy it and he did not want His name used for idolatrous purposes.

Paradoxically, the *Additions to the Book of Esther* in the Apocrypha, which was not considered divinely inspired, included a prayer by Esther in which the Lord's name is found.

In sharp contrast to all the other biblical books, Palestine is not mentioned in the Book of Esther. The only reference to the relationship of the Jews of Persia with their ancient homeland is that Mordecai is described as one *who had been carried away from Jerusalem with the captives*. . . (Esther 2.6).

The Book of Esther is the only book of the Bible which contains the following words:

Tebet, the tenth Hebrew month (2.16).

Kasher, meaning "fit" (8.5).

Patshegen, a Persian word meaning "copy of the writing" (3.14; 4.8; 8.13).

Pur, a Persian word meaning "lot" (3.7; 9.24).

Karpas, a Persian word meaning "cotton" (1.6).

Ahashteranim, a Persian word meaning "the king's service" (8.10; 8.14).

All the letters of the Hebrew alphabet are found in verse 13 of Chapter 3 of the Book of Esther.

NUMEROLOGY

Mishteh (banquet) occurs twenty times in the Book of Esther, which is equal to the total of all the other times it is found in the rest of the Bible.

The longest verse in the Bible is Esther 8.9, which has 43 words in Hebrew and 90 words in English.

GEMATRIA — NUMERICAL EQUIVALENTS

The talmudic admonition that on Purim one should drink until he knows not the difference between "Blessed be Mordecai" and "Cursed be Haman" is questioned by the folklorist. He points out that the numerical value of the Hebrew letters of the phrases ברוך מרדכי "Blessed be Mordecai" and ארור המן "Cursed be Haman" amounts in each case to a total of 502.

Some commentators have placed "the King," המלך, and "Haman," המן, on the same level for the numerical value of the letters in both words is 95.

NOMENCLATURE

NAMES FOR PURIM

At one time Purim was known as Mordecai's Day, in honor of the hero of the Book of Esther.[1]

"The Sweet Festival," or *Id El Sukar*, was the name by which Purim was known to the Moslems of Jerusalem during the period of the Turkish regime. On this day the lead-

ing Moslems of the community were eager recipients of
Purim gifts of pastries and sugared candy sent by the chief
rabbis of the Ashkenazic and Sephardic communities as well
as by other Jewish dignitaries. If, by accident, a prominent
Moslem failed to receive his anticipated present of sweets,
he considered himself affronted.

ESTHER TOWNS

In the states of Missouri and Louisiana there are towns
called Esther. In the latter state there is also a town known
as Estherwood.[2]

QUEEN ESTHER STREET

Queen Esther Street is found in the heart of the all-
Jewish city, Tel Aviv, Israel.

PURIMS OF OTHER PEOPLES

IN INDIA

In India there is observed a festival which, by strange
coincidence, greatly resembles Purim and which usually
occurs on the 14th day of Adar. Celebrated in the open
with much festivity, the Jewish stranger may err in believing
he is observing his own Purim. In the cosmopolitan city of
Bombay, one can see, on the eve of Purim, multitudes
dressed in costumes and masks, particularly in pink and red
colors. On the day of Purim, there is a great procession in
which a wooden image is borne aloft on which the wrath of
the spectators is mercilessly wrought. When the procession
reaches a certain quarter of the city, a ceremony of burying
the image in a special hole begins amidst much Oriental

levity and with song. The image is a symbol of an enemy, such as Haman. The Bombay *Times* has printed articles dealing with this festival. Its origin is not clearly known, but it is evidently in memory of a miracle that saved the Indians from some impending peril.

Apropos, the Jews of India are wont to say that the only difference between Jew, יהודי, and Indian, הודי, is the letter י.[3]

THE KANARINSTI TRIBE

Israel ben Joseph Benjamin, in his *Travels of Israel*, gives interesting information about the Kanarinsti tribe in Eastern India. This tribe differs from the other tribes in the area in that it does not have a faith of its own. The tribesmen observe the traditions of their neighbors, particularly those of the Jews. On Purim they take two wooden pictures of men and they bang one against the other until one is smashed to smithereens. The broken image serves as a reminder of Haman and the remaining one recalls Mordecai. Their anger is not abated until they hang the remnants of Haman on a tree.[4]

AMERICANA

PURIM ASSOCIATION OF NEW YORK

"With a few young men imbued, as was Myer S. Isaacs, with the desire to celebrate the Purim festival in a refined way that should fittingly represent the social side of New York Judaism, he founded the Purim Association in 1861, that for forty years was so popular and useful, and not only enabled the citizens to have a yearly entertainment that was a protest against extravagance and impropriety in public amusements, but by means of its charitable appeals was a great benefactor to many deserving causes."[5]

"Annually the Purim Association invokes the aid of the citizens of New York on behalf of some well-deserving charity, and the financial success of the Purim balls furnishes the best proof that the appeals are not in vain. The ever-ready response of the people testifies to the deep interest of the community in maintaining all institutions which alleviate suffering and improve the condition of the needy and deserving poor."[6]

In 1886, the Association donated ten thousand dollars, the profit of the Purim Ball, to the Montefiore Home.[7] Mt. Sinai Hospital was also a beneficiary and, in 1900, $1,000.00 was contributed for a Life Bed in the name of the Association.[8]

The annual Purim balls were held in some of the largest auditoria of the city, such as Madison Square Garden and the Academy of Music. On the occasion of the observance in 1883, the Association published a Purim Gazette, a souvenir journal, with appropriate articles and advertisements as well as regulations that were to be "strictly enforced by order of the committee." Among these regulations were:

> No one will be admitted on the floor before midnight, unless in mask.
> Ladies wearing hats or bonnets, unless in fancy costume, will not be admitted on the floor.
> All masks must be removed at one o'clock.

This affair was reported in the *American Hebrew* of March 16, 1883, as follows:

> The grand fancy-dress ball of the Purim Association at the Academy of Music last night was a brilliant success. The festivities opened at 10:30 with an elegant tableau.
> On a lofty throne covered with rich drapery and glittering with Eastern decorations, were seated the

good Queen Esther, accompanied by the Prince and Princess Carnival, attended by brilliant retinues in gorgeous costumes. The robes of the royal personages represented were the richest ever seen in this country; that of Queen Esther was claimed to be a correct copy of the original, whatever may have been the source of authority on this interesting point.[9]

QUEEN ESTHER LADIES SOCIETY

In 1882, there was founded in New York the Queen Esther Ladies Society, which held annual balls on Purim for a number of years.[10]

HADASSAH FOUNDED ON PURIM

"Some while before Henrietta Szold visited Palestine she joined a study group of young women, the remnants of a Zionistic society called the Hadassah Circle. 'We met weekly and read papers, and the Zionist Federation looked upon us as organizers of strawberry festivals.' This was the group her mother had in mind when, revolted by the fly-infested children of Jaffa, she urged a program of practical work. Upon the return to New York, she proposed that the circle drop its paper-reading and make itself responsible for a specific piece of health work among the women and children of Palestine. 'A responsibility that requires funds for its execution,' she insisted, would insure life and vigor to the group. Moreover, the idea of a nation-wide organization of women Zionists was in the air.

"Preliminary agitation, discussion and meetings resulted in the gathering of a handful of women in the vestry rooms of Temple Emanuel in New York on Purim of 1912. They constituted themselves the Hadassah Chapter of a national organization to be known as the Daughters of Zion. The Feast of Purim, on which the meeting was held, made the name of Hadassah almost inevitable, for the word, which means 'myrtle,' was the Hebrew name of Queen Esther; and eventually it supplanted the 'Daughters of Zion.' Thirty-eight women subscribed as members. Miss Szold spoke on the need of a 'definite project,' and shortly after that she was elected president.

"Purim of 1912 was not only the birthday of Hadassah but of Miss Szold's life-work. Thereafter, for many years, the organization of Hadassah chapters and the financing and execution of its program became her paramount interest."[11]

In 1945, Hadassah, having grown from a roster of 38 to 125,000 members, published a play entitled *A Two-Fold Celebration* to mark its thirty-third birthday and the festival of Purim. By Purim, 1948, its ranks had skyrocketed to 250,000, including a Junior Hadassah membership of 25,000.

PURIM IN WORLD WAR II

Nazis Banned Purim Observance

The observance of Purim in Poland in 1941 was reminiscent of the Jewish holidays during the time of the Inquisition, when Jews of Spain and other countries gathered in basements and on attics to serve their God in hiding, lest the watchmen of the despotic rulers catch them at their prayers.

For Hitler had banned the reading of the Scroll of Esther (the story seemed familiar, though the parallel with his own career was not yet fully drawn) and had forbidden all *groggers* and other noisemakers at the mention of Haman.

All synagogues were ordered closed and barred for the day in the whole of Nazi-occupied Poland.[12]

Esther Story Read in English Shelters

Purim was celebrated in the traditional manner by the reading of the Scroll of Esther in London and in provincial centers underground in the air shelters. The daily press editorialized on the holiday. The *Evening Standard* wrote, "The story of Purim foreshadows the end of Hitler."[13]

The Habonim, a Jewish youth organization of England, issued a warning to its leaders about making noise during the reading of the *Megillah*. "This year the usual rattles must not be used. They are illegal because they are used as an important A.R.P. signal."[14]

Palestine Abandoned Purim Holiday in *Struma* Protest

Purim, traditionally associated with gaiety in Palestine and with special public affairs, was passed over in silence as a result of the official decision of the *Vaad Leumi* to cancel all Purim festivities and functions throughout the *Yishub* in view of the tragedy of the *Struma*, on which 750 Rumanian Jewish refugees lost their lives as the British Government refused them admission to Palestine.

Memorial services for the victims of the *Struma* were held by Jewish communities throughout Palestine as the Fast of Esther was proclaimed by the Chief Rabbinate.[15]

The Prophecy of Hitler

In a speech by Hitler on January 30, 1944, he said that, if the Nazis went down to defeat, the Jews could celebrate "a second triumphant Purim."[16]

PURIM FEAST, 1946

On October 16, 1946, ten sons of the Haman of our own day, Nazi chieftains, were hung on gallows at Nuremberg, Germany, as a punishment for monstrous crimes committed against humanity. According to an American eyewitness correspondent, when the foremost, of these antisemites, Julius Streicher, was led to the scaffold, he shouted: "Purim Feast, 1946." Little did he know that Purim commemorates not the hanging of his predecessor Haman, but the saving of the Jews.[17]

MISCELLANY

The 14th of Adar, on which Purim is generally celebrated, never occurs on the Sabbath. The Jews of Jerusalem who observe the 15th of Adar, which does occasionally fall on the Sabbath, have then a peculiar situation on their hands. They celebrate a "three day Purim" — on Friday, the 14th, the *Megillah* is read; on Saturday, the 15th, the blessing "who wrought miracles" is recited; and on Sunday, the 16th, the Purim meal takes place.

Although, according to Rabbi Jose the Galilean, *Hallel* was composed and sung by Mordecai and Esther when the Jews were saved from Haman,[18] it is not recited on Purim.

On Purim in 1870, one of the earliest Jewish colonies of modern Palestine, Mikveh Israel, famed for its agricultural school, was founded.

The *Congrega* of sixty of the Jewish community of Rome issued, in 1702, a long series of regulations, called *Pragmatica*, governing the conduct of the people. Therein, strange as it may seem, the sending of Purim gifts, unless of things cooked, is prohibited, "it being especially prohibited to send as gifts confections of any kind, or any other sort of candies."[19]

"The issue between Stoecker's and my party," said Paulus Cassel, a converted Jew, but still a Jew at heart, "is the question of Hamanism or Humanism."[20]

"In the month of Shebat the Samaritans hold the Feast of Purim. Among the Jews this feast is held in the month of Adar... The Samaritans hold Purim in the previous month, on the three last sabbaths in the month, to commemorate, not the deliverance of the Jews by Esther, but the mission of Moses to deliver the Israelites out of Egypt. They have a particular service for the day, which lasts for about six hours, comprising the history of the event as recorded in the law, with prayers, and blessings, and songs interspersed. The object of the feast is to bear a lively record and remembrance of Moses' gracious mission and the circumstances connected therewith. There is no authority in the law, as the priest observed, for holding this feast.

"In reply to my objections to the name of the feast, Amram (a Samaritan priest) would have it that the signification of 'Purim' was not 'lots' or 'portions,' but 'rejoicings.' "[21]

CHAPTER XIX

PURIM WIT AND HUMOR

TRUE REPENTANCE[1]

A JEW was seen by his neighbor eating a hearty meal in a public place on the Fast of Esther. The latter took him to task, saying:

"Even weak and elderly people do not eat on the Fast of Esther except to satisfy their pangs of hunger, and then only in private. I am amazed that you, a young and healthy person, should eat publicly on this fast day."

"I am not observing this fast," the accused replied, "because I believe that Mordecai was not justified in refusing to bow down before Haman, disobeying his command and jeopardizing the lives of the Jews of Shushan."

On the following day the neighbor noticed that the Jew was enjoying the Purim *Seudah*, eating *Hamantashen* and drinking wine as was customary on Purim. Again he protested vehemently, and said:

"If you favored the appeasement of Haman and violated the Fast of Esther, how is it that you partake of the Purim *Seudah* which commemorates the downfall of Haman?"

"Indeed, my actions may seem strange to you," the Jew replied. "Yesterday I was in full accord with Haman; but upon listening to the reading of the *Megillah* last night, I realized that Mordecai had acted properly. So I repented of my error and I decided to observe the Purim feast today."

HANUKKAH AND PURIM[2]

The Gerer Rabbi (Isaac Meir of Ger) explained why a special feast is ordained for Purim, but not for Hanukkah. On Purim we celebrate the annulment of the royal edict to destroy the body; therefore we partake of an enjoyable meal in order to give pleasure to the body.

On Hanukkah we were rescued from a decree which would have destroyed our soul. Therefore we chant the *Hallel* and gratify our soul.

OVERCOMING ISRAEL'S ENEMIES[3]

The Kobriner (Moses of Kobrin) was accustomed to command his Hasidim to give Purim gifts to each other and to pay for the messengers by a special donation to the poor of Palestine.

"This is the best way to strike at Haman," said the Rabbi.

AFFLICTING THE MIND AND THE BODY[4]

Said Rabbi Bunam: "Purim is greater than Yom Kippur. On Yom Kippur we are ordered to starve our bodies, but on Purim the Talmud enjoins us to imbibe more than usual, thereby starving our minds.[5] The affliction of the mind is greater than the affliction of the body."

THE DAY AFTER PURIM[6]

On the day following Purim, the Porissover (Jacob Zevi) would call the poor to his home early in the morning and distribute money to them. He gave as his reason the following: "Because it is a special *Mizvah* to make gifts to the poor on Purim, every one neglects this *Mizvah* on the next day; and I deem it an excellent deed to perform a neglected *Mizvah*."

NAPOLEON, THOU WILT FALL[7]

On the eve of Purim, 1812, when the Maggid of Kosnitz, in reciting the Book of Esther, reached the words *napol tippol, fall thou wilt surely fall* (Esther 6.13), which Haman's wife and his friends addressed to him, he interrupted himself and exclaimed: "Napoleon *tippol*" (Napoleon, thou wilt fall). He paused for a while; then he resumed the recitation of the *Megillah*.

RICHES ON PURIM

A bridegroom was being interviewed by his rich prospective father-in-law who asked, among many other questions, the amount that he earned. The poor young man answered, "I earn ten rubles a day." Satisfied that his daughter would have the comforts to which she was accustomed, the bride's father consented to the marriage.

In due course the wedding ceremonies took place. Following the wedding, the father-in-law was astonished to learn that his new son-in-law was not employed and, in great anxiety, he asked him, "Why are you not working? You informed me that you earn as much as ten rubles a day!"

"I did not deceive you," the son-in-law reassured him. "I am an experienced *Shalah Monot* messenger and I receive large gratuities for my services. On the one day of the year when I work, I earn at least ten rubles."

A BOTTOMLESS PIT[8]

A Hasid was privileged to have as a guest of honor, for his Purim *Seudah*, a distinguished grandson of a sainted Rebbe. When the wife of the Hasid placed the traditional *Kreplah* on the table, the guest took one and said:

"I am taking one to recall our God who is One Alone in the heaven and on earth."

He then took two and said:

"I am taking two to recall Moses and Aaron."

He then took three and said:

"I am taking three to recall the three patriarchs — Abraham, Isaac and Jacob."

He then took four and said:

"I am taking four to recall the four mothers in Israel — Sarah, Rebekah, Rachel and Leah."

He continued in the same manner until he finally reached twelve *Kreplah* and said:

"I am taking twelve to recall the twelve tribes of Israel."

The host, seeing that the guest's appetite was not yet satisfied and that he was prepared to continue devouring *Kreplah*, hastened to summon his wife.

"Leah, come quickly and remove the plate of *Kreplah*, as I suspect that the Rebbe may desire to recall the six hundred thousand Israelites who went forth from Egypt."

A Weak Memory[9]

A rich man forgot to send a Purim gift to his son's *Melamed* (teacher). Although the latter sent him a gentle reminder through the pupil, he still neglected the customary present for the teacher.

Shortly after Purim, the *Melamed* told the pupil to ask his father this question:

"Why did Abel kill Cain?"

The pupil obediently did as he was instructed and on the following day the father came running angrily to the teacher and shouted·

"Ignoramus! How can you ask such a question? It was Cain who killed Abel."

"Is that so?" the *Melamed* retorted quietly. "Such an ancient episode you can remember, but to send a Purim gift to your son's teacher, although I reminded you only a few days ago — that you could not remember!"

TIT FOR TAT[10]

When Meir Leibush Malbim was the rabbi in Herson, he had many antagonists among the elders of the city who sought by every possible means to make his life miserable.

Once, on Purim, one of his enemies, a rich and insolent man, sent him a Purim gift on a tray covered with a white napkin, according to the usage of the day. When the Malbim removed the napkin, he found on the plate a baked confectionery in the shape of a pig. He smiled and thought to himself: "How affectionate are my townsmen for they spare food from their own mouths and send it to their rabbi!"

To fulfill the commandment of "sending portions" and to reciprocate in kind, the Malbim took a picture of himself and placed it on the plate, covering it with the napkin. He gave it to the messenger to return to his congregant with a note which read:

"You were kind enough to send me a likeness of yourself, and so I am sending you one of me."

MORDECAI THE LINGUIST[11]

In the days of Nicholas I, when the Russian government sought to introduce the Jews to secular culture, Rabbi Moses Landau, a Jewish scholar and well versed in many other fields of learning, was one of the first Jews to accept the government's plan. Moreover, he became a strong advocate of spreading "Enlightenment" and used every opportunity to preach this program to Jewish communities.

One day he assembled the people of his city in the synagogue and spoke to them about the religious duty to learn the language of the land, citing proofs from the Bible and the Talmud to show that their ancestors approved the study of foreign tongues. He quoted profusely from the Book of Esther, saying:

"It is well known that the miracle of Purim was made possible because Mordecai heard the plotting of Bigthan and Teresh, who sought to kill King Ahasuerus, and reported it to Queen Esther. If Mordecai had not been able to understand the language of these two chamberlains, the series of events that led to Purim would not have occurred and the Jews would have been annihilated. . . ."

"You are mistaken," interrupted one of the Jews of the congregation. "What you say proves that the Jews did not know the language of Persia. The two chamberlains, Bigthan and Teresh, spoke unhesitatingly in the presence of Mordecai which shows they had no reason to suspect that he understood them."

An Open Book or an Open Hand[12]

One Purim, Rabbi Joseph Saul Nathanson of Lemberg saw a rich scholar sitting in the *Bet ha-Midrash* and studying the Talmud. The rabbi approached him and unceremoniously took away the volume in which the rich man was engrossed.

"Today your place is not in the House of Study before an open book," chided Rabbi Joseph Saul. "You should be at home before a plate full of money to dispense charity with an open hand to the poor who come to you."

LOTS[13]

The teacher explained to the class that *Pur* means "lot" and *Purim* is "lots." As a homework assignment the pupils were instructed to look up the meaning of "lots."

The next day the teacher asked the class what they learned about Purim. Abraham raised his hand and was called upon to recite. In a well-rehearsed tone he said:

"LOT, the nephew of Abraham, had LOTS of LOTS, and LOT had a LOT of trouble with his wife, and what a LOT was hers! We expect to have LOTS of fun on Purim."

MASQUERADING

Why is the Day of Atonement called in Hebrew *Yom Ki-Purim*, a day like Purim? The similarity between the two days is based on the fact that on both days it is customary to masquerade. On Purim, Jews masquerade and don the costumes of non-Jews. On the Day of Atonement, they masquerade as pious Jews.

THE PURIM TO COME

While Hitler was delivering one of his infamous speeches in a large hall in Munich at the start of the Nazi ascent to power, he could not help but notice that a man in the front row was making facial contortions of derision and joy marked with an occasional outburst of laughter.

The man's behavior resulted in bringing confusion to Hitler in the midst of his antisemitic invectives and causing annoyance to the *Fuehrer*. When the speech was concluded, Hitler in great ire sent for the one who disturbed him and indignantly inquired who he was.

"I am a Jew," he said innocently.

"Then you should be taking my address more seriously," warned Hitler. "Do you not believe that I will fulfill my threats to bring about the destruction of the Jews?"

"You should be aware," the Jew replied, "that you are not the first antisemite who sought to destroy us. You may recall that the great Pharaoh of Egypt sought to enslave the Jews. To commemorate his defeat and our redemption, we eat tasty *Mazot* and observe the festival of Passover. Haman was another enemy of ours who brought about his own downfall. The delicious *Hamantashen* we eat and the jolly festival of Purim recall our deliverance from him. While listening to your venomous diatribe, I wondered what kind of delicacy would the Jews invent and what kind of holiday would they establish to celebrate your downfall."

PURIM FOLK PROVERBS

On Purim everything is permissible.

Today is Purim, tomorrow it's o'er;
So give me a penny and show me the door.

Twilight on Purim means pitch darkness on Passover. (Whoever cannot afford to pay for the simple needs of Purim will be in much worse circumstances for Passover with its costly requirements.)

Purim drives dull care away.

After a Purim meal no dog goes hungry. (The remnants of the Purim meal suffice plentifully for the dogs.)

On Purim no one says: "Thank you." (As it is commanded to give charity on Purim, the poor do a favor to their well-to-do brethren by accepting it.)

All year drunk, and on Purim sober!

It will last as long as from the Fast of Esther to Purim.

Less out of "the love of Mordecai" than of "the hatred of Haman."

On Hanukkah and Purim the poor become rich.

Not on every Purim does a miracle happen.

When Purim comes, one forgets all troubles.

CHAPTER XX

PURIM PARTIES AND PROGRAMS

LIBBIE L. BRAVERMAN

THE festival of Purim provides a perfect example of a holiday that is bound up traditionally with the past, but whose celebration can be modern and be readily integrated in American life.

Too often, Jewish holiday observance remains in the realm of unreality, something theoretical that is observed only in the school, something to be celebrated by children, but to be discarded when they become adults.

Upon Jewish parents rests the responsibility to reintroduce some of our traditions, customs and ceremonies into their homes today. They must make Judaism a living reality in conduct and in practice. Too often parents have been responsible for undermining standards of Jewish behavior, impoverishing Jewish life in their failure to give it substance through home practice and observance. If we are to stand for the ideals and aspirations that are cherished by our people, we must give tangible evidence of our approval of the Jewish way of life as worthwhile and significant. Otherwise it becomes empty and meaningless. Jewish life has to express itself in the home, in the religious school, in the synagogue and in the Jewish center. The home is the initiator, the roots from which grow the activities that relate to the holiday. If there is no observance in the home, the holiday has no fundamental reality and becomes a meaningless gesture. Holidays assume reality only when they are observed. Holidays take on the flesh of vitality when they are transformed into practice. This weaves the pattern of Jewish living.

The holiday of Purim richly lends itself to just such treatment — Purim, the holiday that treats of the perennial problem of the Jewish people. In every generation, in every land, tyrants have sought to destroy us, yet these tyrants again and again have themselves been destroyed, while the Jewish people remains to carry on its tradition, so witnessing to its indestructability. Purim becomes another story of the triumph of right over might.

This holiday is the essence of joyousness and gaiety. Every member of the family is included. Essential in the joyous celebration of this holiday is long-range planning so that the excitement of anticipation pervades the atmosphere weeks in advance. Purim is the holiday for the exchange of gifts, for giving to the poor, for festivities, for parties, for masquerades.

THE HOME CELEBRATION

The home can do much to create the atmosphere of the approaching holiday, so that it assumes importance in the lives of the members of the family.

Everything should be done to the house to herald the approaching holiday.

Decorate the house colorfully. Masks, the Purim characters, crowns, *groggers*, offer a variety of choice.

The Invitation

The invitation to the Purim affair can take the shape of a *Megillah* or a mask, or a *grogger* or a *Hamantash*. An informal invitation is most appropriate for this gay festival.

Perhaps you would like to use a rhyme. If you cannot think of a better one, the following will serve the purpose:

On Purim 'tis proper to mask and be gay;
Let's celebrate Purim the traditional way,
With fun and refreshments and plenty of games —
Just knock — then be silent — don't give your right names;
Beware — we'll be masked — but don't let that scare you.
We tell you this secret just to prepare you.

. . . .

Signed

The time.	*R*eply to address above.
	*S*end or bring a
	*V*ery inexpensive
The place.	*P*urim present.

Ask everyone to come masked and to bring an inexpensive gift in the tradition of *Mishloah Monot*. State in your invitation that this is the price of admission. As the guests arrive, have them place the gifts in an enormous *Hamantash*, which will be opened and the gifts distributed immediately after the *Seudah* (meal).

THE PLACE CARDS

The place cards can carry out the same theme as the invitation. The *Hamantash* or the mask are the simplest to make. If you are talented artistically, make a stencil of a Purim scene: Haman leading Mordecai on the king's horse; Esther before the king; the banquet for three; or use a cut-out of any one of these scenes.

BEFORE SEUDAH FUN

Animated Megillah Reading: — If you are ambitious and have guests who are talented, you might attempt reading a shortened account of the *Megillah* and intersperse it with Purim songs. An animated *Megillah* reading, which requires no scenery and little costuming, can readily be presented with a little previous rehearsing. Complete with production directions and music is *Animated Megillah Reading* by Nathan Brilliant and Libbie L. Braverman.[1]

Some folks prefer planned games. Each of these games should have Purim significance. Here are a few suggestions:

Talk-Fest: — Have two contestants face each other in the center of the ring. When you say "Go," they start talking on some subject connected with Purim. Here are a few simple rules: (1) Talk so that all can hear. (2) Do not use the hands. (3) Say as much as possible with more nonsense than sense.

At the end of sixty seconds, call "Stop!" The guests select the winner.

Dressing Queen Esther or Mordecai: — Prepare clothes-pins or lollipops and plenty of small strips of colored paper, small ribbons and thread. The one who can dress Esther or Mordecai to look most like the historical character is the winner.

A Debate: Resolved that a Doughnut is Better than a Hamantash:— Prepare samples of each. Select two people who have the "gift of gab" and can rise to such an occasion. Allow them five minutes to prepare their arguments. Each might pass around a sample of their assignment and let the audience be the jury and render a decision by acclamation.

Quiz Games: — Quiz games based on the story of Esther and the Purim celebration can be informative, stimulating and entertaining. Many variations are possible, giving them freshness and dramatic interplay. Have the questions and answers prepared in advance. The winning boy may be crowned as King Ahasuerus and the triumphant girl as Queen Esther.

Who Am I? — Pin on the back of each guest the picture of some Purim object or personality (crown, *Megillah*, gallows, Mordecai on horse, Queen Esther, the king). Each member of the party must then find out what he is by questioning the other members. He can only ask questions that can be answered by "yes" or "no", such as "Am I useful?" "Am I human?" "Am I a hero?" "A villain?" "Animate?" "Inanimate?" As soon as the person guesses what he is the picture is removed from his back and pinned where the guest, too, can see it.

AFTER SEUDAH FUN

If you want to go to the trouble of pencil and paper games, here are some that go a long way toward making the guests do a little thinking too.

Guess What? — A box on the table contains cards. On each of those cards is the name of one of the Purim characters or objects. Each player takes a card, writes a four-line rhyme about the name on the card, without mentioning the name, and puts the rhyme into the box. Later the rhymes are read and other guests guess what is being described.

Shushan Post Office: — Since Purim is the Feast of Lots, we have the drawing of lots. Write the name of each player on a slip of paper and put them all into a box. Each guest draws a name from the box. He then writes a humorous letter to that person and deposits it in the Shushan Mail Box. Have the mail distributed at any convenient time.

Jumbled Words: — Give a list of jumbled words found below, under column I, to each one of your guests who must write the correct word alongside the jumbled one. Allow ten minutes for the game. The winner is the one who has the largest number of correct words. The answers listed in column II are for you only.

I	II
Lathash Moon	Shalah Monot
Manah Hats	Hamantash
Dearmico	Mordecai
Thangbi	Bigthan
Shauerusa	Ahasuerus
Theres	Esther
Tisvah	Vashti
Gillhame	Megillah
Erggorg	Grogger
Wallsog	Gallows

Making Words: — Take such long words as Ahasuerus, Hamantashen or Mishloah Monot. A prize is given to the person making the most three or more letter words, using just those letters, within a five-minute time limit.

CHILDREN'S GAMES

Purim Magic Music: — Send one of your guests out of the room. Hide a *grogger* or any other Purim object. Call the player in and tell him to follow the directions of the music to find the *grogger*. If he approaches the *grogger* (which must not be hidden in impossible places) the music grows louder. When he is farther from the *grogger*, the music grows fainter. If a piano is not available you can sing Purim songs.

50. *GROGGERS*   Painted Cardboard

Designed by Temima N. Gezari

Choosing Queen Esther's Seamstress: — Give each girl at your party a needle and a yard of thread. Don't have the thread too thick or the needle's eye too small. Line the girls up and tell them to walk to the front door and return while threading their needles.

Choosing Queen Esther's Butler: — Have each boy place a handkerchief over his arm just as the waiters do in restaurants. The object of the game is to hold an imaginary tray for two minutes without laughing. The one who keeps the straightest face the longest is the winner.

Mordecai's Horse's Tail: — Mordecai is mounted on a horse without a tail. Each guest is provided with the missing tail. Blindfold the players. The one who can affix the missing tail closest to where it belongs is the winner.

THE REFRESHMENTS

Whether your guests sit down for the *Seudah* or whether the party is buffet style, the table decorations should be carefully planned and the refreshments invitingly served, in as attractive a setting as possible.

The centerpiece could very well be the large *Hamantash* in which the gifts have been placed. You might prefer a scene from the Purim story, using dolls, in appropriate costumes, or painted figures made of ply wood or even out of cardboard. "The Maidens Appearing Before the King," or "The Banquet Scene," both make attractive centerpieces and allow for creativity and colorful treatment.

No matter how elaborate or how modest the *Seudah*, the menu should include *Hamantashen*. Cookies cut in the shape of Purim objects may be the contribution of a more ambitious hostess. A fruit salad representing Queen Esther's Crown (pineapple with almonds for jewels) or Haman himself (a pear punctuated with raisins or cherries to make face and body) make for tasty refreshments in addition to their being attractive and meaningful.

The exchange of gifts, the reading of the rhymes and the delivery of the letters by the Shushan Postmaster, all tend to highlight the close to a delightful get-together on this Purim festival.

SHUSHAN NITE

We are frequently confronted with the problem of relating the celebration of the Jewish festivals to teen-age groups. The night-club idea appeals to them with its opportunities for taking the spotlight and exhibiting their talents in the field of music, drama and dancing.

The Shushan Nite Club is made to order for them. The tables are arranged around a dance floor which will also be used for the floor show. A huge caricature of Haman can be drawn in colored chalk on the dance floor. In this manner the traditional biblical injunction, "to eradicate the memory of Amalek," can be followed literally, for, after a few dances, the caricature is well on its way to oblivion.

Decorations should be *purimdig*. The suggestions made later in this chapter offer a variety of choices.

Hostesses greet the guests as they arrive and seat them at the tables. Waitresses, dressed in *Hamantash* aprons, serve the refreshments. Dancing to the recordings of the country's best orchestras is continuous. Then, at a given signal, the lights are lowered, the "spots" turned on and the show begins. A resourceful master of ceremonies can do much to make for a successful evening.

Recruit the acts for the floor show from the talented members of the group. The master of ceremonies supplies continuity. He may take the part of the Jester as he presents the entertainment before the King and Queen of Persia; or he may work up a modern version of the old Purim story, encouraging the crowd to hiss the villain and applaud the heroine. It is important to keep the staging simple with very few properties, and costumes that just suggest the characters (crowns for the king and queen, a moustache and three-cornered hat for Haman, a skull-cap for Mordecai). To add to the hilarity of the occasion, the young people may come masked and in costume.

Surely Purim is the costume holiday. A costume parade can be a part of a carnival but also may constitute, in addition to singing, the entire Purim celebration. The following is a list of suggestions for costumes:

1) Characters of the Purim story: Esther, Mordecai, the King, the Jester, Vashti, Haman, Zeresh, the conspirators, *Purimspielers*.

2) Animated symbols characteristic of Purim: *Magen David, Megillah, Hamantash, Grogger*.

3) Different kinds of Jews: Yemenites, Hasidim, *Haluzim*.

4) For groups: Esther and her Maidens; The Banquet Scene; Haman Leading Mordecai on a Horse; Vashti Banished.

Try to get everyone to come in costume. Even urge them to mask and unmask after the parade is over.

Prizes may be awarded for the best group costume, for the finest costume, the most beautiful, the most original, and even the most traditional.

The music for the parade is important, for music that is really marching music, whether it be rendered by a recording or a band, will greatly enhance the occasion. Be sure that the participants are widely spaced so that there will be an opportunity for the audience to view each participant.

THE PURIM CARNIVAL

Purim lends itself readily to a community celebration. It may sound like an enormous undertaking, but the resultant satisfaction of conducting a community celebration compensates for the trouble and energy expended.

The Purim carnival is an excellent medium for the celebration of Purim. The Palestinians developed this striking form of celebrating the folk-holiday and, in the good old days before the war, "went to town" with it. Folks came from hill and valley, from town and village, to celebrate in the all-Jewish city of Tel-Aviv. They called it the *Adloyada*, derived from the talmudic recommendation that on this day one should drink *ad d'lo yoda* — till one does not know the difference between *Baruh Mordecai* (Blessed be Mordecai) and *Arur Haman* (Cursed be Haman). In other words — Make Merry!

In Israel, the entire family celebrates. Shops and schools are closed and everyone makes merry. The carnival procession through the streets of Tel Aviv, in which people from Dan to Beersheba participate, features floats that portray progress in agriculture and in industry and caricatures that poke fun at government policy, prominent people and even the characters in the Purim story. This is the spirit that we must try to capture for our carnival. How can this be done?

Let your planning for the Purim carnival be quite ambitious even though you may be compelled by the limitations of the situation to settle for less.

Seek out people in your community, those who belong to the same synagogue or center. Choose people who have children, who would be willing to go to some trouble to carry out such a community project — for this project is primarily for the children. Be fully prepared with a complete blueprint for a carnival before you present the plans to the committee. Be prepared to accept suggestions for additions and eliminations, always bearing in mind your ultimate goal, so that you know where you are heading and allow nothing to divert you from your main objective, namely, the celebration of the holiday.

If your celebration is in the school, enlist the aid of the rabbi and the principal of the school and the teachers for your committee; if in the community center, be sure that the director and the club leaders are included in the plans from the very beginning. Appoint a chairman who coordinates activities and prevents overlapping. Select committees for housing, decorations, booths, publicity, entertainment, the purchase of merchandise and prizes. Although what follows need not necessarily be the order of procedure, here are a number of suggestions that should be considered by the members of the carnival committee.

INVITATIONS

For the first announcement of the carnival distribute an attractive invitation, humorous and in the spirit of Purim. A simple announcement will do, but if the invitation takes the form of a scroll, a *grogger* or a *Hamantash*, it will command more attention. Word the text to paraphrase the language of the *Megillah*, and illustrate with Purim symbols. Make sure that clearly and prominently stated on the invitation is the date and place of the coming event. Here is a suggested invitation in the style of the *Megillah*:

> It has been decreed in the name . . . ., that the Feast of Esther shall be observed this year, with joy and merriment by . . . . (name of organization), and it is further decreed that all good members of the

.... (name of organization), and with them all their friends, shall assemble on Purim, which is the ..... day of the month .... in the year ....., and make merry at the Purim Carnival. It is further decreed that for all the good times, there be no charge so that all may come and make merry while recalling the great deeds the Lord has performed in days of yore for the children of Israel and which He will again repeat in His own good time.

DECORATIONS

Appropriate for the carnival project are such suggested names as: "Streets of Tel Aviv;" "Palace of Shushan;" or "Adloyoda."

When the central theme has been chosen, it must be carried out in the decorations by every booth operator, every side-show producer and every other person involved. Booths may be arranged in rows and aisles named after Tel Aviv streets. Street signs may be printed in Hebrew and mounted on the streetcorners. It is wise to strive for general effects, executing the decorations on a large scale, without getting lost in details. Only the large general effects count.

Purim is rich in many symbols and the Purim motifs may contribute largely to making the carnival colorful. Huge murals painted in bright colors can be assembled as the co-operative venture of a number of groups, each of whom undertakes one unit of the mural. The scenes may depict the Purim story, caricatures of famous personalities, and Israel in industry, agriculture or education.

There are other large effects that can be produced if the murals seem to be too ambitious an undertaking. Select phrases from the Book of Esther and print them decoratively

on large posters or banners. Caricatures of Hamans throughout our history are good subjects to be drawn in charcoal on
brown wrapping paper. Huge palm trees can be very effectively made out of crepe paper — brown for the trunks,
and shredded green for the leaves. Colored-light festoons,
hung from the center and radiating to the corners of the
hall, contribute inestimably to the carnival mood. Crepe
paper (sewed on cords to prevent stretching) may just as
effectively be strung across the room.

Booths may reflect the outstanding architectural features
of Israel. Some booths could represent the modern archi-
tecture of Tel Aviv, while others could emulate the dome
structure of the old city of Jerusalem. But don't be frightened. The building materials are not concrete or even stucco,
but just lathes and paper.

Publicity

The task of presenting the carnival to the public is of
major importance and should be in the hands of an
experienced committee. The invitation described above is
the first announcement of the Purim carnival. Then begins
the work of creating interest, arousing curiosity in the event
and stimulating participation and attendance.

Posters should be placed in prominent places in the lobby
and on the bulletin boards of the building. Mimeographed
posters on 9" x 12" colored construction-paper, changed
each week, will maintain interest in the carnival. An enlarged reproduction of the invitation, an illustration of a
scene from the Book of Esther, or caricatures of kings, queens
and jesters make good poster material. Always bear in
mind that the function of the poster is to attract attention,
especially to the time, place and nature of the event.

Another good publicity stunt is to send bands of *Purim-*

spielers from class to class and from club to club, distributing circulars and reciting verses to publicize the coming event.

The English-Jewish papers will accept a story two weeks prior to the event and one week before, if each story stresses a different phase of the carnival. Pictures are important. Include as many names of workers as space will permit. For the daily press, other angles should be pointed up, such as a general story of the carnival, the committees and booth operators, the cast of the Shushan Theater and a description of some of the side-shows and booths.

Pictures of children playing at Haman's Stunts, or at Ten Pins, or a picture of the murals taken by newspaper photographers are good publicity and attract attention.

BOOTHS AND SIDE SHOWS

Haman's Bowling Alley: — Prepare a set of wooden ten-pins shaped to represent Haman's ten sons. Paint the figures in bright colors and have small name-tapes on each. Mount a 7 or 8 ft. runway on two boxes and decorate the runway with crepe paper or bunting. Set up the ten-pins like a regular bowling game. The players take turns rolling the ball down the alley to upset the pins.

Spell Purim: — On a fairly large sized board, print the letters for the word "Purim" and underneath each letter print its numerical equivalent.

מ	י	ר	ו	פ
40	10	200	6	80

Screw a hook underneath each of the letters. Toss rings at the hooks from a suitable distance. To win a prize, the players must attain at least 250 points.

Mishloah Monot for Galilee: — An ambitious group might undertake to make a paper-maché relief map of Israel and paint it. Toss pennies onto the map. If a penny lands in the Sea of Galilee (Kinneret) a prize is awarded. All pennies pitched are then dropped into a Jewish National Fund box.

Feeding Haman: — Any one of these games is a game of skill, using "poor" Haman as the target. The head of Haman is constructed out of beaverboard and stands about 5 feet high. His mouth is wide open and he is fed rubber balls. Or he can have a hook for a nose and rings or quoits will hook him. Another stunt is to throw darts at his moustache.

Casting of Lots: — A painted wheel is divided into twelve parts, each one named for one of the Hebrew months. The wheel is turned and, if it stops at Adar, the player wins. The game may be varied by permitting the players to choose any other month, preferably their month of birth.

Hit the Poppy: — Hitting the poppyseed part of a huge beaverboard *Hamantash* with darts is a popular game with the boys. Paint the poppyseed center black. Each player is allowed three chances with darts, which can be easily made out of a pin, a stick and a feather. If the point of the dart lodges in the black, the player wins. The prize for a dart that strikes the poppyseed can very well be a genuine luscious and delicious *Hamantash*.

Balloon Barrage: — Paint toy balloons to represent the characters in the Purim story. Toss darts to puncture.

Shushan Theater: — Entertainment based on the story of Purim makes good theater for children and adults. A dramatic club can conduct this side show. There are many good Purim plays to choose from but the play must be short and good comedy. Schedule at least four performances. If two plays are presented, alternate them, thus giving each cast "time off" to enjoy the carnival too. Signs and barkers announcing curtain times will help bring the audience. Allow them to cheer the hero and hiss the villain so that the audience also will be given a chance to participate.

Marionette Show: — If a group is interested in marionettes, or if it is possible to engage marioneteers, have them enact the Purim story, seriously or humorously. Marionettes or puppets are always attractions. The show should be short.

Purimspielers:— The *Purimspielers* offer gifted children an opportunity to exhibit their talents. It is really a vaudeville show with a competent master of ceremonies to supply the continuity. Instead of the traditional gong used for the amateur hour, how about using a *grogger*? Be sure to have a pianist ready and that he has the music well in advance. Rehearsal before the performance is a must to ensure smooth running of a show.

Purim Shadowgraph: — All you need is a white sheet for a screen and a spot light. The action takes place between the spotlight and the screen where the characters of the Purim story appear while they pantomime the action. A voice tells the story. There is ample opportunity for humorous situations. Suggested subjects: King Banishes Vashti; Esther Crowned Queen; Mordecai Overhears Conspirators; Mordecai on King's Horse with Haman Leading; Esther Appears before the King; Esther Denounces Haman.

Persian Peep Show: — Shoe boxes, each portraying another phase of the Purim story, satisfy the curiosity of large and small.

Vashti's Photo Gallery: — A talented person or persons can conduct this booth. The photo gallery might offer to cut silhouettes (black paper mounted on white cardboard) or actually sketch with crayon the subject who is willing to pay for the art. A real photography studio could be set up by amateurs. They might have on hand masks of Purim characters to be donned for the pictures. Guests in costumes would be anxious to have their pictures taken.

Change Your Personality: — The only equipment necessary for this side show is a make-up box. Give people a choice as to what they want to be: a character in the Purim story; a character from the Bible; etc. It's fun, but beards are expensive.

Yemen Fortune Telling: — Someone who is alert can be "clairvoyant," if the youngsters are observed as they come to have their fortunes told. School work, music lessons, Hebrew studies, attitude toward parents, what the future holds, are subjects of great interest to such a "clientele." The same results can be discerned by a handwriting "expert." A sense of humor and a quick wit are important assets for these stunts.

Shushan Magician by Appointment to King Ahasuerus: — Feats of magic performed by amateur magicians might include magic-writing or mind-reading or just magic out of someone's chemical set. This is always popular with children.

Shushan Post Office: — Anyone who appears at the Shushan Post Office window receives a greeting card in rhyme. These rhymes are divided into different categories, for big boys, for little boys, for big girls, for little girls and for adults. As an additional attraction a dainty *Hamantash* may accompany each greeting card.

Tot Lot: — Here's where the little tots who need rest and quiet may find it; and older brothers and sisters and weary parents may "park" their little ones. Purim stories, games, the singing of songs or even some handwork, under the supervision of a kindergarten teacher or an arts and crafts instructor, will keep the youngsters busy and happy.

Shushan Café aboard the S. S. Tel Aviv: — The Shushan Café is a project made to order for young people who are ambitious and reliable. They will surely have many of their own ideas. Here are a few suggestions which they may accept, modify or reject. Decorate the room to simulate the deck of the good ship *S. S. Tel Aviv*. Place tables and chairs around the "deck." Dainty sandwiches in the shape of *Hamantashen* make delicious eating. Tea or orange juice served with cake or *Hamantashen* will surely be appreciated. Girls and boys share in the preparation of the food and in serving the guests. The girls, wearing three-cornered hats and aprons in the shape of *Hamantashen*, and the boys, wearing hats in the shape of *groggers*, help to carry out the Purim motif. If you have tea, invite the rabbi's or president's wife to pour. This adds dignity to the occasion. Co-opt some of the talents of the *Purimspielers*. Be sure there is a piano in the room. A fortune teller reading poppyseeds, instead of the usual tea leaves, may be available at an additional charge.

Vashti's Dance Palace: — Rope off a section of the hall for Vashti's Dance Palace. An orchestra is preferable but equally enjoyable is dancing to the recordings of famous dance bands. Palestinian and Jewish folk dances will be likewise enjoyed. A dance troupe as a special attraction can present Purim dances.

Shushan Shmooser: — The Shushan Shmooser gives a journalism group an opportunity to make a contribution. The paper should be mimeographed and a charge made even if it is as little as one cent. A good way to increase circulation is to number every copy sold. The lucky number wins a prize at the end of the carnival. It can be published in the format of a *Megillah* by pasting the end of each page to the next.

Pattern it after a daily newspaper with headlines, news items and editorials.

Here are a few headline suggestions:

> Queen Esther Victorious
> Vashti Defies King
> Authority of All Husbands Endangered
> Tanglefoot, the Dancer, Strikes for Raise
> Premier Haman Exposed
> Haman Raised Again
> Haman Escorted by Mr. Moose
> Beauties of 486
> Miss Shushan of 1949 Elected Today
> Mordecai Foils Plot to Kill King

A column of brickbats, headed *Mishloah Monot* and featuring local personalities, will create interest.

The weather report could read as follows: Shiftless Estherly winds, accompanied by Vashtily changing temperature.

Queen Esther Contest: — There are several ways of running the Queen Esther Contest. One is to have each club or class elect a Queen Esther, who appears at the carnival to parade before the entire assembly. Have the crowd indicate popularity through applause. A ribbon badge carrying the legend "Queen Esther of 1949" may be her reward. The winner is crowned Queen Esther of the carnival and is seated on a throne, all the other Queen Esthers becoming maidens in her court.

Another method of selecting the queen is to sell votes at a penny a piece. The votes are collected, sorted and tabulated. The winner is announced at the end of the carnival and similarly "crowned." It is advisable to prepare the ballot in advance. It can be printed or mimeographed and then distributed or sold at the carnival.

Esther's Pool: — Esther's Pool is just another name for the popular fish pond, and is an absolute must for the little ones, who will probably return to "fish" several times during the carnival. Cover an open doorway with a sheet about two-thirds of the way up. Decorate it with colored paper fish, bubbles and blue wavy paper to represent the sea. The "fish" are inside the room and have been wrapped in advance and placed in separate boxes or bags labelled "little girls," "little boys," "big girls," and "big boys." When the fisherman arrives, he is given a fishing pole. He tosses his line over the sheet into the room. To the hook at the end of the line, a "fish" is attached by someone hidden in the next room and the youngster goes off happy with his prize.

Mishloah Monot for Mother and Dad: — There must be at least one booth for the sale of merchandise. Gifts for mother and dad give you an opportunity to dispose of contributions made by some of the members of the committee, who offer such items as handkerchiefs, pipes, cigars, etc. Women may have hand-made aprons, potholders, towels, etc., that bring good revenue. This booth or booths (depending on the amount of space you have) should also display Israeli products, art and ceremonial objects, Jewish books and miniature *Megillot*.

Knick Knack Knook:—The Knick Knack Knook is an excellent name for the booth where such merchandise as *groggers* and other noisemakers, paper hats, serpentine and balloons are sold.

SUGGESTED ORDER OF THE DAY

2:45 P. M. — Movies in auditorium (for purpose of assembling crowd)
3:10 P. M. — Purim songs
3:15 P. M. — Queen Esther parade on stage
3:30 P. M. — Adjourn to carnival hall
4:45 P. M. — Costume parade and finale of carnival

MINIATURE FLOATS PARADE

We have heard of the Mardi Gras in New Orleans with its floats parade, and we have seen pictures of the Tournament of Roses in Pasadena. But the less well-known floats parade of the Tel Aviv *Adloyada* is the source of inspiration for a Purim Miniature Floats Parade. It provides a rare opportunity for creative self-expression.

The Purim Miniature Floats Parade should enlist the participation of young and old. If the project originates in the school, the children should co-opt the interest and active assistance of the parents. If adults undertake this project they should make sure that children of clubs and classes are involved.

A series of committees may want to undertake responsibility for the various phases of the parade. The procedure as to decorations, ushering, planning, program, publicity, can very well follow the outline given for the Purim carnival. Much depends on the enthusiastic launching of the floats parade in order to arouse the interest and imagination.

In order to make sure that there is some uniformity in the floats submitted and in order to prevent mishaps, the following rules are set down to guide the committee:

1. Floats should be substantially built yet light enough to be carried.

2. Mount the float on a coaster wagon, kiddy car or anything else on wheels.

3. Dolls and puppets, furniture, etc., used in the construction of the floats should be securely fastened to prevent their falling during the parade.

4. To create a harmonious total effect, children drawing the floats should be dressed in costume to carry out the theme of the float. There should be no speaking parts. No children should stand on or sit in the floats.

5. There is no such thing as a parade without music. An orchestra, of course, is preferable, but recorded marches played over a public address system will serve.

6. Judges should base their decisions not only upon the art and content of the float but on the age level as well. A primary child's entry cannot be judged in the same categoi y as that of a fifteen-year old.

Suggestions For Floats

The story of Purim
> The Banishment of Vashti
> The Crowning of Esther
> Mordecai Refusing to Bow to Haman
> Mordecai Overhears Conspirators
> Esther Before the King
> Haman Leading Mordecai on Horse
> Queen Esther's Banquet

Other Purim Ideas
> *Purimspielers*
> Caricatures of Purim Characters
> International Queen Esther Beauty Contest
> Crime Does Not Pay
> *Mishloah Monot* Messengers

Current Events

Reproductions of buildings, such as Hebrew
University
Onward to Palestine
A New Exodus
The Eternal Haman
S. S. *Tel Aviv*
Jaffa Oranges — All Juice
Spirit of Tel Aviv
Israel Reborn

Suggested Order Of The Day

1. Assemble in auditorium, or wherever the floats will parade.
2. Community singing of Purim songs.
3. A short talk by an invited guest.
4. A short dramatization of the Purim story.
5. The floats parade.
6. Floats are returned to runway for exhibition.
7. Judges submit their decision.

CHAPTER XXI

PURIM DANCES

Dvora Lapson

THE dance among all peoples and religions has held an important place in religious and communal ceremonies. Even in the Bible there are traces of such ceremonial dances, as when Miriam led the women of Israel "with timbrels and with dances" (Exodus 15.20). Thus they celebrated the going forth from Egypt. Even King David, rejoicing at the return of the Ark, "danced before the Lord with all his might" (II Samuel 6.14). And the prophet Jeremiah describes the restoration of Israel to their desolate homeland as a time when all shall dance with joy, "both young men and old together" (Jeremiah 31.13). It is but a natural expression of happiness for Jews to turn to the dance on Purim, the season of their escape from destruction.

Since Purim is a festival of carnival, the dances used in the celebration of this joyous season have always been gay in spirit and of a folk — sometimes even primitive — character. According to the Talmud, the Jews of Babylonia observed the custom of burning Haman's effigy to the accompaniment of singing and dancing around a fire. A characteristic movement of the fire-dance was the leaping of children with a hoop through a bon-fire. Sometimes the hoop was suspended over the fire and boys would jump through it. Similar pantomimic dances were developed during the Middle Ages. Kalonymos ben Kalonymos, in

411

his *Tractate Purim*, states that dancing on Purim is permissible provided the men and women dance separately.

Hasidim expressed themselves in dance on Purim in a manner different from that of the rest of the year. On the Sabbath and other holy days their dances were of a spiritual character; on Purim, however, they had a more earthly quality. There was more finger-snapping, hand-clapping and shoulder-grasping. Partners would dance opposite each other, rather than in a circle, which was the usual formation. In some hasidic *Shtiblah* (gathering places) it was traditional to perform the "Mill Dance." A group of Hasidim would

51. *A DANCING COUPLE*

Megillah, 1748

arrange themselves in a circle on the floor, lying on their backs, with their feet towards the center and holding the hands of their neighbors. In this formation they would all try to move themselves like a wind-mill, dragging each other along, to the great delight of the onlookers.

In our own time in Israel, dancing is an integral and important part of the Purim *Adloyada* in Tel Aviv. In this carnival, which draws great multitudes of jubilant pilgrims to Tel Aviv, dancing has served from the very beginning as its core and chief attraction. Troupes of dancers present special performances in honor of the festival. The masses of celebrants give vent to their joyous feeling by folk and social dancing not only in public halls and private residences but even in the city's busiest thoroughfares.

In the United States children in Jewish schools and young people and adults in synagogues and Jewish centers utilize the dance in Purim celebrations. The dance formation described below, expressive of the spirit of Purim, is intended for use on such occasions.

PURIM HASIDIC DANCE

(For music and words see חג פורים, in Music Supplement)

Dressed in long coats of solid colors, with white collars and cuffs and skull caps from which earlocks extend, the Hasidim stand in a semi-circle around the Rebbe, who might wear a white coat and have a piece of fur around his skull-cap. The Rebbe holds a *Megillah* in his hands and reads or chants a short part of it. All the Hasidim respond to the names as they are mentioned in the *Megillah*. Esther's name is greated with "ah", Mordecai's with shaking head or uplifted arms; Haman's name is greeted with turns of *groggers* which the Hasidim take out of hidden pockets.

When the reading of the part of the *Megillah* is ended, the Rebbe and Hasidim form a circle and start singing and dancing.

Part I. On phrase 1 they extend both hands upwards right, upwards left, down, then straight up, out to the right side and left side and turn around in place.

On phrase 2, they all join hands in circle and take 2 steps to the right and on *rash, rash, rash*, stamp 3 times; 2 steps to the right, then 3 stamps on *rash, rash, rash*; 2 steps to the right, then 3 stamps on *rash, rash, rash*; 5 steps to the right on *bo-ra-a-sha-neem*.

Part II. On phrase 1 each one (except the Rebbe) faces his partner and makes the same gestures as in Part I, with the addition of snapping of fingers each time hands are extended. On phrase 2 each one grasps his partner's right shoulder and repeats steps of Part 1, phrase 2, changing to left shoulder.

Part III. Phrase 1, same as Part 1, phrase 1, but clap hands each time. Phrase 2, repeat as Part I, phrase 2.

CHAPTER XXII

PURIM DELICACIES

THE commandment in the Book of Esther to observe
Purim as *days of feasting and gladness, and of sending
portions one to another, and gifts to the poor* (Esther 9.22)
gave rise to the creation of many delicacies especially for
this festival. The traditions of both *Seudat* Purim (Purim
meal) and *Mishloah Monot* (sending of portions) resulted
in the introduction of new dishes in the Jewish home. On
the occasion of the *Seudah*, the Jewish housewife had an
opportunity to demonstrate her culinary ability. The
portions that were exchanged as well as the gifts to the
poor customarily included various types of eatables. Kalonymos ben Kalonymos, the Italian Jewish parodist who
lived in the fourteenth century, in his *Masseket Purim*,
lists twenty-four meat and pastry dishes that "were told to
Moses on Mount Sinai, all of which one must prepare on
Purim."

The Purim culinary art developed differently in the
different lands where Jews resided. The most popular of
the Purim dishes still in vogue today are the *Hamantashen*
and *Kreplah*.

The tri-cornered *Hamantashen*, baked dough filled with
poppyseeds, derives its name from a combination of the two
German words — *Mohn* (poppy seed) and *Taschen* (pockets).
Because of the association of this cake with Purim, its
original name, *Mohntashen*, was revised to *Hamantashen*,
recalling the enemy of the Jews in the Persian empire.
Some have interpreted the three-cornered delicacy as sym-

bolic of the three cornered hat said to have been worn by Haman while he was prime minister. More recently it has become a common practice to fill the *Hamantashen* with prunes.

Another favorite Purim dish is *Kreplah*, triangular pieces of dough filled with chopped meat. Purim shares *Kreplah* with two other significant days in the Jewish calendar — the eve of the Day of Atonement and Hosha'ana Rabba. The folklorist cleverly gives the following reasons for their popularity: *Kreplah* are eaten on those days on which there is "beating." On the eve of the Day of Atonement men are flogged with forty stripes. Willow branches are beaten on

52. PURIM DISH   Pewter

19th Century

Hosha'ana Rabba. During the reading of the Book of Esther on Purim, Haman is beaten whenever his name is mentioned. Support for the above explanation is derived from the biblical phrase הכה תכה, "Thou shalt surely smite." The phrase is interpreted as an abbreviation of: הושענא, כפור, המן, תאכלו כרעפליך הרבה, "On the days of Hoshana, Atonement and Haman, thou shalt eat many *Kreplah*."

In some places it is customary to eat cooked beans with salt, usually called *Nahit* or *Bub*. This vegetarian dish is in remembrance of Esther's diet, while she lived in the court of Ahasuerus. This, it is told, was limited to beans and peas so as not to violate the dietary laws. Daniel did likewise while in the court of Nebuchadnezzar (Daniel 1.12).

Those who were more punctilious in the observance of Purim were accustomed to eat turkey, which literally translated from the Russian means cock of India, and in Hebrew, *Tarnegol Hodu*. The eating of the "cock of India" is therefore in remembrance of Ahasuerus "who reigned from India unto Ethiopia" and was a foolish king. The turkey is generally considered the most foolish among fowl.[1]

The place of honor on the table set for the Purim *Seudah* is given to the *Keylitsh*, an exceptionally large, braided loaf of white bread, decorated with raisins. The top of the *Keylitsh* is braided with long strands, wide and high in the middle and narrow and low at both ends.

HAMANTASHEN (PARVE)[2]

DOUGH

4 cups of flour
2 heaping tsp. baking powder
¾ cup sugar—¼ tsp. salt
grated rind of lemon or orange
4 eggs
⅓ cup (generous) oil

MOHN (poppyseed) FILLING

¼ lb. poppy seed
½ cup sugar
½ cup raisins
2 tbsp. honey
1 egg
¼ tsp. cinnamon
1 tbsp. grated orange rind

PRUNE FILLING

1 lb. sweet prunes
3 thin orange slices
½ cup chopped walnuts
rind and juice of ½ lemon
¼ cup sugar
1 tbsp. oil
dash nutmeg

Sift all the dry ingredients into a bowl, break the eggs into the center, add the oil, and stir well. Mix all together and knead lightly until smooth. Roll out one-eighth of an inch thick. Cut into 3½ inch rounds. Put a heaping teaspoon of the filling in the center, draw up two sides and then the third across and pinch the edges together, to form a three-cornered pocket. Bake on a greased baking sheet in a fairly hot oven (375 degrees) for about half an hour, until nicely browned.

MOHN FILLING: Clean the *Mohn* carefully, wash with boiling water and drain. Add a cup of water, cover closely and allow it to steam for two or three hours on a very low flame. Add a little water if necessary. Drain, grind, using the finest knife of the food chopper, or pound in a mortar until grayish in color. Mix with the rest of the ingredients, and fill the dough.

PRUNE FILLING: Cook the prunes and the orange slices in a small amount of water until they are tender and the water has evaporated. Stone the cooked prunes and chop them together with the rest of the ingredients. Fill the dough.

KREPLAH

DOUGH	FILLING
1 egg	½ lb. beef
⅛ tsp. salt	1 slice onion
⅔ cup flour (about)	salt, pepper, cinnamon to taste
	1 tsp. chicken fat (if meat is cooked)
	1 egg

Run the meat — and you may use either all cooked or half raw and half cooked meat — through the food chopper together with the onion. Add the other ingredients and mix well. Now mix the egg, salt and flour and knead until elastic. Roll out thin and cut the sheet of dough into two inch squares. Put a small ball of the meat in the center of each square, fold one corner over diagonally forming a triangle and press the edges firmly together. Work quickly or the dough will become too dry. Let the *Kreplah* stand

53. *PURIM TOWEL* Cross-Stitch Embroidery

1812

for about ten minutes, then drop them into boiling soup and cook for half an hour. They may also be cooked in boiling salt water and drained. Sprinkle with a little chicken fat and either serve that way or slip into a hot oven to brown.

VERENIKES

These are really another species of *Kreplah*. They are made of the same dough, but cut round and slightly larger than *Kreplah*. They may be filled with chopped meat, chopped liver, mashed potatoes, kashe or cheese. To close them bring the edges of the circle together to form a center ridge and pinch them like a pie crust. Boil in salted water for half an hour, drain and serve hot with chicken fat or butter.

In the spring try filling them with stewed, pitted cherries mixed with a little cornstarch. Cook them in the cherry juice and serve hot in the juice. Or, instead of cooking them, brush well with shortening, bake in a hot oven, and serve in the cherry juice.

NAHIT

Soak one pound of chick-peas overnight. Drain and cook in salted water until tender. Drain, add pepper and serve hot or cold.

BOOK FIVE

Commemoration of Purim

Therefore do the Jews make the
fourteenth day of the month Adar
a day of gladness and feasting, and
a good day, and of sending portions
one to another.

ESTHER 9. 19.

CHAPTER XXIII

PURIM IN THE SYNAGOGUE

SHABBAT ZAKOR

THE Sabbath preceding Purim is known as *Shabbat Zakor* (Sabbath of Remembrance) and is the second of a series of four special Sabbaths announcing the approach of Passover. The names of these Sabbaths, derived from the additional portions of the Torah read as the *Maftir*, are: *Shekalim, Zakor, Parah* and *Ha-Hodesh.*

The additional biblical portion (*Maftir*) that is read on *Shabbat Zakor* deals with the Amalekites, from whom Haman reputedly was descended and is a fitting prelude to the festival of Purim. In the Talmud of Jerusalem[1] Rab says: "Why is it necessary for the portion of *Zakor* to be said before Purim? Because it is written *And these days shall be remembered and kept* (Esther 9.28). Their remembrance shall precede their observance, i.e., they should remember the deed of Amalek before celebrating the festival of Purim."

Shabbat Zakor derives its name from the first word of the portion which reads: *Remember (Zakor) what Amalek did unto thee by the way as ye came out of Egypt; how he met thee by the way, and smote the hindmost of thee, all that were enfeebled in thy rear, when thou wast faint and weary; and he feared not God. Therefore it shall be, when the Lord thy God hath given thee rest from all thine enemies round about, in the land which the Lord thy God giveth thee for an inheritance to possess it, that thou shalt blot out the remembrance of Amalek from under heavens; thou shalt not forget* (Deuteronomy 25.17-19). The significance of this passage is pointed out by some rabbis who considered its reading to be a biblical commandment, for it enjoined Israel through the generations to "remember what Amalek did;" and this, despite the fact that the reading of the Law itself was first instituted by Ezra the Scribe. This passage, furthermore, described the cruel and treacherous conduct of the Amalekites who later were regarded as the prototype of all who persecuted the Jews in whatever lands and at whatever times they lived.

Since Haman is called "the Agagite" (Esther 3.1), the prophetical portion read on *Shabbat Zakor* (I Samuel 15. 1-34) tells about the battle of King Saul and Agag, king of the Amalekites. Josephus likewise calls Haman "by birth an Amalekite."[2]

The special *Piyyutim* (hymns) recited on *Shabbat Zakor* in the morning and additional services are for the purpose of preparing the worshippers for the festival of Purim. The hymns (יוצרות) and poetical insertions (קרובות) describe the wickedness of Amalek and Haman. Most of these poems are ascribed to Eleazar ha-Kaliri, the most prolific writer of liturgical poetry for synagogue use.

Before the reading of the Torah, Sephardic congregations recite a special *Piyyut* composed by Judah Halevi, telling in poetical style the story of the Book of Esther. Its first part is an alphabetical acrostic. The last line of every stanza is a biblical quotation concluding with the Hebrew word for "to him."

On the afternoon of *Shabbat Zakor* in the old city of Jerusalem, it is the custom for the rabbi to deliver a special sermon. In Persia and other communities, *Targum Sheni* is read. In Salonica this special Sabbath bears its own particular imprint with a different name – Sabbath Pullarius. This Latin name describes a pyramid-shaped cake especially prepared for this occasion.[3]

FAST OF ESTHER

The Fast of Esther is observed on the 13th day of the month of Adar, the day before Purim. Although other fast days falling on the Sabbath, except the Day of Atonement, are postponed to Sunday, if the 13th of Adar occurs on a Sabbath, so that the fast shall not conflict with Purim which falls on Sunday, it is advanced to the preceding Thursday, because it is forbidden to fast not only on the Sabbath but also its eve, Friday, lest the preparations necessary for the Sabbath be interfered with.

This fast is named after Esther for it was she who said: *Go, gather together all the Jews that are present in Shushan, and fast ye for me, and neither eat nor drink three days, night or day; I also and my maidens will fast in like manner; and so will I go unto the king, which is not according to the law; and if I perish, I perish* (Esther 4.16).

The original practice was to fast for three days, as was done by Esther and the Jews of Shushan. Although the intent was to emulate Esther, "the three days of fasting for Purim were not kept consecutively but separately on Monday, Thursday and Monday."[4]

To lighten further the burden of fasting, the one-day fast was instituted.

Although Esther, Mordecai and the Jews of Shushan fasted during the month of Nisan, the Fast of Esther is observed on the eve of Purim because of the later prohibition of fasting during Nisan. The 13th day of Adar was chosen, according to some rabbis, because it was *the day that the enemies of the Jews hoped to have rule over them; whereas it was turned to the contrary, that the Jews had rule over them that hated them* (Esther 9.1). The day of the defeat of Israel's enemy was considered an occasion for fasting and mourning rather than for rejoicing. The 14th of Adar, therefore, is truly observed in commemoration of the salvation of the Jews and not on account of the destruction of their enemies.

Adar 13, the day of the Fast of Esther, was also the day on which Judah the Maccabee decisively defeated the Syrian general, Nicanor, in the year 160 B.C.E. This day was observed for some time as a day of rejoicing.[5] In Tractate Sofrim,[6] however, it is written: "Our Rabbis in Erez Israel were accustomed to fast after Purim because of Nicanor and his friends." We see therefore that Adar 13 was not observed as the Fast of Esther until after the Day of Nicanor had fallen into disuse. The Fast of Esther was not instituted at an early date. It is first mentioned by Rabbi Aha of Shabah, who lived in the eighth century and who explained *the thirteenth was the time of gathering* (Esther 9.8), as implying a day of prayer and fasting.

Special penitential prayers (*Selihot*) are recited on the Fast of Esther in addition to those regularly said on all other fast days. The portion of the Torah (Exodus 32.11-14; 34. 1-10) read on other fast days is also read.

Persian Jews, unlike some Jews elsewhere, adhere very strictly to the observance of the Fast of Esther.

MAHAZIT HA-SHEKEL

When the New Moon of Adar occurs on the Sabbath or, if it occurs on a weekday, on the Sabbath before it, synagogues observe *Shabbat Shekalim*. The extra pentateuchal selection (Exodus 30.11-16) read on this Sabbath recalls the tradition of bringing on the first day of Adar in the days of the Temple "half a shekel for an offering to the Lord." Rabbi Levi in the name of Rabbi Shimon ben Lakish[7] explained this practice as a precaution of the Almighty for averting the evil plan of Haman who offered *Shekalim* on the 13th of Adar (Esther 3.9). The present custom of *Maha-zit ha-Shekel* is derived from this source.

The half shekel (*Mahazit ha-Shekel*) was originally collected as an atonement during the annual census, from every Israelite, rich and poor alike, "twenty years old and upward" (Exodus 30.11-15). The period for the payment of this tax for the Temple fund was from the first day of Adar[8] to the last day of the month. From the first of Nisan onwards only the funds thus collected could be used for purchasing public offerings in the days of the Temple. After the destruction of the Temple, the payment of the shekel dues was continued by the Jews in the Diaspora. Messengers would collect the funds and bring them to Palestine for the support of the talmudical academies and their poor students.

In addition to recalling the shekel dues collected during the month of Adar towards the purchase of public sacrifices in the Temple, the present usage of *Mahazit ha-Shekel* is a reminder that, as Haman offered King Ahasuerus a substantial sum of money for the Jews, it is necessary for them to redeem themselves.

While originally the value of the shekel was twenty *Gerahs*, today it is considered equivalent to the standard currency of the country where Jews reside. In America half a dollar is equal to the *Mahazit ha-Shekel*. In some synagogues it is customary for the worshippers to give three half dollars before the reading of the *Megillah* on Purim night, as both "half shekel" and "offering" (*Terumah*)are written thrice in the biblical passages that treat of this subject (Exodus 30. 11-15). The money thus collected is distributed to the poor.

The shekel has become a symbol of Jewish national currency, and the Zionist movement has universally introduced it as the basis for affiliation, giving the privilege of electing delegates to the World Zionist Congress.

TRADITIONAL SERVICE FOR PURIM

On Purim the following prayer of thanksgiving, which includes a brief summary of the Purim story, is inserted in the
Amidah of the evening, morning and afternoon services immediately after "We give thanks unto Thee. . ." (מודים
אנחנו לך). It is also added to the grace after meals before the
paragraph beginning "For all this. . ." (ועל הכל).⁹

עַל־הַנִּסִּים וְעַל־הַפֻּרְקָן וְעַל־הַגְּבוּרוֹת וְעַל־הַתְּשׁוּעוֹת וְעַל־
הַמִּלְחָמוֹת שֶׁעָשִׂיתָ לַאֲבוֹתֵינוּ בַּיָּמִים הָהֵם בַּזְּמַן הַזֶּה:
בִּימֵי מָרְדְּכַי וְאֶסְתֵּר בְּשׁוּשַׁן הַבִּירָה כְּשֶׁעָמַד עֲלֵיהֶם הָמָן הָרָשָׁע.
בִּקֵּשׁ לְהַשְׁמִיד לַהֲרֹג וּלְאַבֵּד אֶת־כָּל־הַיְהוּדִים מִנַּעַר וְעַד־זָקֵן טַף
וְנָשִׁים בְּיוֹם אֶחָד בִּשְׁלֹשָׁה עָשָׂר לְחֹדֶשׁ שְׁנֵים־עָשָׂר הוּא חֹדֶשׁ אֲדָר
וּשְׁלָלָם לָבוֹז. וְאַתָּה בְּרַחֲמֶיךָ הָרַבִּים הֵפַרְתָּ אֶת־עֲצָתוֹ וְקִלְקַלְתָּ אֶת־
מַחֲשַׁבְתּוֹ וַהֲשֵׁבוֹתָ גְּמוּלוֹ בְּרֹאשׁוֹ וְתָלוּ אֹתוֹ וְאֶת־בָּנָיו עַל־הָעֵץ:

We thank Thee also for the wonderful deliverances,
the triumphant liberation, the providential comfort
and the wars which Thou hast wrought for our fathers
in the days of old, at this season.

Then in Shushan the fortress in the time of Mordecai
and Esther, the wicked Haman rose up and sought to
despoil, slay and utterly extirpate all the Jews, young
and old, women and babes, in one day, the thirteenth
day of Adar, the twelfth month. But Thou, through
Thy great mercy, didst frustrate his counsel and sub-
vert his designs, causing them to recoil on his own head,
until he and his sons were hanged on the gallows.

According to the Sephardic ritual, Psalm 22 is recited
preceding the evening service. This psalm, which begins
with "My God, My God, why hast Thou forsaken me?," is

said to have been recited by Esther in the hour of her distress.

The *Megillah* is read on the eve of Purim, following the evening service, and again in the morning after the reading of the Torah.[10] For laws concerning the *Megillah* see pages 143–150.

The Scroll of Esther is spread open and folded to give the effect of a letter, simulating the "letter of Purim" (Esther 9.29). The following blessings are chanted before the reading of the Megillah.

בָּרוּךְ אַתָּה יְיָ. אֱלֹהֵינוּ מֶלֶךְ הָעוֹלָם. אֲשֶׁר קִדְּשָׁנוּ בְּמִצְוֹתָיו וְצִוָּנוּ
עַל־מִקְרָא מְגִלָּה:

בָּרוּךְ אַתָּה יְיָ. אֱלֹהֵינוּ מֶלֶךְ הָעוֹלָם. שֶׁעָשָׂה נִסִּים לַאֲבוֹתֵינוּ בַּיָּמִים
הָהֵם בַּזְּמַן הַזֶּה:

When reciting the following blessing in the morning service, one should have in mind the fulfillment of the duties of sending portions, gifts to the poor and the Purim meal.

בָּרוּךְ אַתָּה יְיָ. אֱלֹהֵינוּ מֶלֶךְ הָעוֹלָם. שֶׁהֶחֱיָנוּ וְקִיְּמָנוּ וְהִגִּיעָנוּ לַזְּמַן
הַזֶּה:

Blessed art Thou, Lord our God, Ruler of the universe, Thou hast sanctified us by Thy commandments, and ordained on us the reading of the Scroll of Esther.

Blessed art Thou, Lord our God, Ruler of the universe, who wrought wonderful deliverances for our fathers in days of old at this season.

Blessed art Thou, Lord our God, Ruler of the universe, that Thou hast given us life and sustenance and brought us to this happy season.

54. MEGILLAH

Andrea Marelli, 16th Century

Engraving

After reading the Scroll of Esther, the following blessing, expressing thanks to God for espousing the cause of Israel, is chanted.[11]

בָּרוּךְ אַתָּה יְיָ. אֱלֹהֵינוּ מֶלֶךְ הָעוֹלָם. (הָאֵל) הָרָב אֶת רִיבֵנוּ. וְהַדָּן אֶת דִּינֵנוּ. וְהַנּוֹקֵם אֶת נִקְמָתֵנוּ. וְהַמְשַׁלֵּם גְּמוּל לְכָל אֹיְבֵי נַפְשֵׁנוּ. וְהַנִּפְרָע לָנוּ מִצָּרֵינוּ: בָּרוּךְ אַתָּה יְיָ הָאֵל הַנִּפְרָע לְעַמּוֹ יִשְׂרָאֵל מִכָּל צָרֵיהֶם. הָאֵל הַמּוֹשִׁיעַ:

> Blessed art Thou, Lord our God, Ruler of the universe. Thou hast contended for us and defended our cause, avenging us by bringing retribution on all our mortal enemies, and delivering us from our adversaries. Blessed art Thou, Lord God, the Redeemer, who deliverest Thy people Israel from all their adversaries.

This popular Purim hymn is a eulogy on Mordecai and Esther.[12] The Sephardic ritual includes only from "accursed be Haman" until the end.

שׁוֹשַׁנַּת יַעֲקֹב צָהֲלָה וְשָׂמֵחָה. בִּרְאוֹתָם יַחַד תְּכֵלֶת מָרְדְּכָי. תְּשׁוּעָתָם הָיִיתָ לָנֶצַח. וְתִקְוָתָם בְּכָל דּוֹר וָדוֹר. לְהוֹדִיעַ שֶׁכָּל קֹוֶיךָ לֹא יֵבשׁוּ וְלֹא יִכָּלְמוּ לָנֶצַח כָּל הַחוֹסִים בָּךְ: אָרוּר הָמָן אֲשֶׁר בִּקֵּשׁ לְאַבְּדִי. בָּרוּךְ מָרְדְּכַי הַיְהוּדִי. אֲרוּרָה זֶרֶשׁ אֵשֶׁת מַפְחִידִי. בְּרוּכָה אֶסְתֵּר בַּעֲדִי. וְגַם חַרְבוֹנָה זָכוּר לַטּוֹב:

> The lily of Jacob rejoiced and was glad when Mordecai was seen in the purple. Thou hast ever been Israel's salvation, and their hope in every generation, to make known that all who hope in Thee shall not be discomfited, neither shall any be confounded who put their trust in Thee. Accursed be Haman who sought to destroy me; blessed be Mordecai the Jew; accursed be Zeresh, the wife of him that terrified me; blessed be Esther my protectress; and may Harbonah also be remembered for good.

A special liturgical poem for Purim, *Meorah* (מאורה), is inserted in the morning service before "With abounding love" (אהבה רבה). The name of the author, Samuel, is found in an acrostic.

In each blessing of the *Amidah* of the morning service, excepting the fifteenth, a *Keroba* is inserted. *Keroba* is the name of a religious poem composed for the reader to say when he repeats the *Amidah* while standing near (קרוב) the reader's desk. The *Kerobot* for Purim are also called *Kerobez*.[13] The author of these special *Kerobot* for Purim is Rabbi Eleazar ha-Kalir. These poetical selections recount the story of Esther with midrashic embellishments. The first words of each passage comprise the verse: *And the king loved Esther above all the women, and she obtained grace and favour in his sight more than all the virgins; so that he set the royal crown upon her head, and made her queen instead of Vashti* (Esther 2.17). In addition to these *Kerobot*, a poem of five alphabetical parts with an acrostic of the name of the poet is inserted at the twelfth benediction.

During the morning service of Purim three men —a Cohen, a Levi and an Israelite — are called up to the reading of the Torah. The portion of the Torah that is read consists of the last nine verses of Chapter 17 (verses 8–16) of the Book of Exodus,[14] which describe the battle with Amalek and the proclamation of an unceasing war against him and his descendants among whom Haman was included.

While a minimum of ten verses is required for the reading of a pentateuchal portion, the single exception to this prescribed minimum is permitted on Purim[15] as the above nine verses are a complete unit. To compensate for this incompleteness, the last verse is repeated.

Although the *Hallel* (Psalms of Praise) is recited on Hanukkah, it is omitted on Purim. The former holiday commemorates the outcome of the battle of Hellenism against

Judaism, while Purim recalls the escape of the Jews from an impending physical danger. Other reasons are given for the omission of *Hallel* on Purim. The *Megillah* is considered a paean of praise to God, and its reading, therefore, fully replaces the *Hallel*.

Tahanun (Prayers of Supplication) are not said on Purim.

The *Musaf* (additional service), usually included in festival prayers, is omitted, as it is added only on those festivals for which the Torah ordained the offering of an additional sacrifice.

REFORM SERVICE FOR PURIM[16]

EVENING SERVICE FOR SABBATH BEFORE PURIM

Reader: On this Sabbath of Remembrance, when we recall Amalek, and all the foes who have ever threatened our existence, let us dwell on the power of faith and devotion which has preserved us to this hour. Many are the enemies that have risen against us, but trusting in Thee, O God, we have not been dismayed. Imbue us with the faith of former generations of Israel. Give us courage and steadfastness that, like Mordecai, we may bend the knee to Thee alone. Uphold us that, like Esther, we may walk undaunted in the path of loyalty. When adversity and sorrow come upon our people, may we face them manfully as trials of faith. Amid suffering and persecution may we continue to cling to thee and perform our appointed tasks in confidence and fortitude. Strengthen us to combat prejudice, injustice and oppression when they strike not only against us but against men of whatever race or belief. Let not divisions of blood and faith create distrust and strife. May we strive unceasingly for the triumph of truth and right over falsehood and wrong. Thus shall we be united in a true covenant of brotherhood and peace. Amen.

MORNING SERVICE FOR SABBATH BEFORE PURIM[17]

Almighty God and Father, on this Sabbath of Remembrance, we come before Thee with words of praise and thanksgiving for the providential care and guidance under which Thy people Israel has ever lived.

We remember today the darkness and gloom which enveloped Israel's life in the past. Painful trials and bitter struggles, torment of body and agony of soul have been his portion through the dreary centuries of fiery hatred and bloody persecution. But sustained by the undying hope that in the end right will triumph over wrong, good over evil, and love over hate, he has held aloft the banner of Thy truth.

We today, loyal to the memory of those heroic martyrs, come to thank Thee for the blessed assurance that the living hope born in the prophetic soul of Israel will not remain unfulfilled. Before the mighty onrush of Thy light and love, we shall yet see the forces of darkness, cruel Amalek and vindictive Haman, succumb and vanish. And though many a bitter experience may await us before prejudice and hate shall have vanished, still do we trust, as did our fathers, that in the end all barriers to brotherhood shall be broken down.

Grant us, we beseech Thee, the vision to see and the courage to do Thy holy will. Imbue our hearts with the fidelity of Mordecai and the devotion of Esther, that we may never swerve from the path of duty and loyalty trod by our fathers. Endow us with patience and strength, with purity of heart and unity of purpose, that we may continue to proclaim Thy law of love and truth to the peoples of the earth, until all men shall have learned to call Thee Father and know one another as brothers. Amen.

55. *MEGILLAH TITLE PAGE*

Nelson Ronsheim

MEGILLAH RITUAL FOR THE DAY OF PURIM[18]

(Blessings before Reading from Scroll)

Praised be Thou, O Lord our God, Ruler of the world, who hast sanctified us by Thy Commandments, and bidden us read the Scroll of Esther.

Praised be Thou, O Lord our God, Ruler of the world, who didst wondrous things for our fathers at this season in those days.

Praised be Thou, O Lord our God, Ruler of the world, who hast granted us life, sustained us, and permitted us to celebrate this joyous festival.

The following verses are read in a specially designed Scroll of Esther:[19]

Chapter 1.1,5-7, 15-17; Chapter 3.1-2, 5-6, 8-11; Chapter 4.1-17; Chapter 5.1-4; Chapter 6.1-11; Chapter 7.1-4; Chapter 8.3, 5-6; Chapter 7.7, 9-10; Chapter 8.15-17; Chapter 9.20-28.

After Reading of Megillah

Minister

God's promise unto the patriarchs has been our support through all the ages. As often as men rose against us to destroy us, the Holy One, praised be He, delivered us out of their hands.

The Roman legions, who laid waste the Holy Land and scattered us to the four corners of the earth, could not vanquish the soul of Israel. Amidst the ruins of a desolate land, the light of the Torah continued to shine. The storms of persecution could not quench it; the tyrannical decrees of cruel emperors could not smother it. The martyr's cry, as it ascended from the flaming pyre, kindled new zeal and steadfastness in the hearts of the oppressed, stirring them to resistance and heroic sacrifice.

Congregation

Unless Thy law had been my delight, I should then have perished in my affliction.

Minister

Through the dark ages of persecution, many rose against us, who, even as Haman of old, sought to drive us from our homes and crush our spirits. Inflamed by blind and heartless leaders, the Crusaders on their way to the Holy Land swooped upon the defenseless communities of Israel and with fire and sword wreaked vengeance upon a guiltless people. But the rage of the oppressor did not dim the faith of those whose trust was in God. They met unjust wrath with courage and confidence; and though many perished in rivers of blood, the devices of men of violence did not stand. The Lord heard the supplications of the wronged and afflicted, and delivered them from sorrow and distress. The murderous attacks on the innocent came to an end, and the cause of the righteous triumphed over the evil designs of the wicked.

Congregation

If it had not been the Lord who was for us, when men rose up against us, then they had swallowed us up alive. Praised be God who hath not given us as a prey to their teeth.

Minister

Often our enemies, bent upon the destruction of Israel and his faith, promised us release from oppression and bodily harm, if we would but surrender the beliefs and ways of the fathers. But the faithful sons of the covenant refused to deny their birthright. Neither the tortures of the inquisition nor the threats of cruel expulsion daunted their courage. They chose to take staff in hand and wander forth from Spain in search of new homes rather than prove disloyal to their God, their Torah, and their people.

Exalted in spirit, and transfigured by suffering, the exiles struck root in other lands, grew and prospered, and bore testimony to the strong faith that lived within them. They endured misery and pain, and in the end rose to new dignity and strength. They were tried and tested and found worthy of an even greater destiny. The nations that gave them refuge received fresh vision and strength from the exiles, and thus reaped a rich harvest from the good they had sown.

Congregation

Many there are that say of my soul: "There is no salvation for him in God." But Thou, O Lord, art a shield about me; my glory and the lifter up of my head. Salvation belongeth unto the Lord; Thy blessing be upon Thy people.

Minister

Not yet has the term of our suffering ended; even as our task in the world is still unfinished. In our martyrdom through the ages we have fallen prey to many a vindictive foe; but to none so virulent, so vengeful, so unspeakably cruel as the godless Nazis, whose wicked designs to exterminate our people came close to fulfillment. Millions of the sons and daughters of Israel sealed their faith with their blood. Innocent of any guilt save that they were of the seed of Abraham, they suffered fiendish torture and death at the hands of men who sought to enthrone the Moloch of ruthless force in place of God and His law of righteousness.

But God reigns supreme in the world; and Israel still lives. The fury of Nazi hatred and cruelty has abated; and while the blood of its myriad victims still cries out from the earth, the power of the tyrant is broken, and the rage of the heathen no longer strikes terror in the hearts of men. Those who defied the will of God and profaned His law have perished in defeat and infamy, leaving no memorial to bless their name. But the spirit of the martyred millions, whose heritage of faith pulsed in their veins, still lives and works among men, a perpetual benediction to all mankind.

Congregation

For the Lord regardeth the way of the righteous; but the way of the wicked shall perish.

Minister

Thou, O Lord, pleadest the cause of the just, and avengest the wrong of the innocent. The counsel of the heathen Thou bringest to nought; the devices of the crafty, Thou makest of no effect. When Haman, insolent in power and riches, rose up against us, Thou didst cause the devotion of Mordecai and the loyalty of Esther to triumph over tyranny and hate. The righteous were delivered out of the hand of the wicked, and those who sought to destroy were themselves destroyed.

We pray, Thee, O Father, that in the presence of cruelty and wrong our hearts remain steadfast and true. When evil men plot against us and seek to uproot us, let not despair drain our strength nor fear chill our faith. Teach us to meet enmity with courage and hope, and to battle against adversity with resolute will and unyielding self reliance. Keep alive within us the vision of our high purpose and noble destiny. Open our hearts to the cry of the persecuted and the despoiled. May the love and sympathy that brother feels for brother impel us to acts of service and sacrifice, so that the suffering and misery wrought by men may be alleviated, and the hope of the crushed spirit rekindled. Hasten the day when hate and strife shall cease to divide the family of men, and justice and love reign supreme in the world. Amen.

SHUSHAN PURIM

In "cities encompassed by a wall since the days of Joshua the son of Nun,"[20] Purim is observed and the Scroll of Esther is read on the 15th of Adar. This is done in accordance with the precedent established by the first celebration of Purim in Shushan: *But the Jews that were in Shushan assembled together on the thirteenth day thereof, and on the fourteenth thereof; and on the fifteenth day of the same they rested, and made it a day of feasting and gladness* (Esther 9.18).

In the unwalled towns, however, Purim is observed on the 14th of Adar (Esther 9.19).

Today, the Jews of Jerusalem, which is a walled city, celebrate Purim on the 15th of Adar. Elsewhere this day is called Shushan Purim and is observed as a half-holiday. On this day propitiatory prayers are not said and fasting is forbidden; *Al ha-Nissim* (We thank Thee for the miracles), however, is not recited.

PURIM KATAN

When Purim is observed in a leap year, that is, in the second Adar, then the 14th and 15th days of the first Adar are called *Purim Katan*. As on Shushan Purim, propitiatory prayers are not recited on those days and fasting and eulogizing at funerals are forbidden. The postponement of Purim to the second Adar is for the purpose of relating the redemption of Esther and the Jews of Persia closely to that of Moses and the Israelites of Egypt which is commemorated one month later on Passover.

MUSIC SUPPLEMENT

compiled by

A. W. Binder

I. LITURGICAL MUSIC

1. BLESSINGS BEFORE READING THE SCROLL OF ESTHER

Ad lib. (*Joyously*)   Traditional

ƒ Bo - - ruch a - toh——— A - do - noy E - lo -

he - nu me - lech ho - o - lom— a - sher kid - sho - nu b' mitzv-o-

sov— v' - tzi - vo - nu al mik - ro m' - gil - oh———

Bo - ruch a - toh——— A - do - noy E - lo -

he - nu me - lech ho - o - lom— she - o - soh ni - sim la - a - vo-

se - nu ba - yo-mim ho - hem baz-man ha - zeh———

Bo - ruch a - toh——— A - do - noy E - lo-

he - nu me-lech ho - o - lom— she - he - che - yo - nu v'-ki - y'-

mo - nu v' - hi - gi - o - nu laz - man ha - zeh———

בָּרוּךְ אַתָּה יְיָ אֱלֹהֵינוּ מֶלֶךְ הָעוֹלָם אֲשֶׁר קִדְּשָׁנוּ בְּמִצְוֹתָיו וְצִוָּנוּ
עַל מִקְרָא מְגִלָּה:

בָּרוּךְ אַתָּה יְיָ אֱלֹהֵינוּ מֶלֶךְ הָעוֹלָם שֶׁעָשָׂה נִסִּים לַאֲבוֹתֵינוּ בַּיָּמִים
הָהֵם בַּזְּמַן הַזֶּה:

בָּרוּךְ אַתָּה יְיָ אֱלֹהֵינוּ מֶלֶךְ הָעוֹלָם שֶׁהֶחֱיָנוּ וְקִיְּמָנוּ וְהִגִּיעָנוּ לַזְּמַן
הַזֶּה:

2. GENERAL CANTILLATION MODE OF THE SCROLL OF ESTHER

With gusto ... Traditional

f Va - ye - hi—— bi - me A - chash - ve - rosh
hu—— A - chash - ve - rosh—— ha - mo - lech
me - Ho - du v' - ad Kush—— she - - -
va v' - es - rim u - me - oh me - di - noh——

וַיְהִי בִּימֵי אֲחַשְׁוֵרוֹשׁ הוּא אֲחַשְׁוֵרוֹשׁ הַמֹּלֵךְ מֵהֹדוּ וְעַד־כּוּשׁ שֶׁבַע
וְעֶשְׂרִים וּמֵאָה מְדִינָה: א׃א

3. MUSICAL VARIATIONS IN THE CANTILLATION

Ve - che - lim —————— mi - ke - lim sho - nim. ——————

וְכֵלִים מִכֵּלִים שׁוֹנִים א:ז

Li - he - yos —— kol ish so - rer b' - ve -

so —— u - m' - da - ber kil-shon a - mo. ——

לִהְיוֹת כָּל־אִישׁ שֹׂרֵר בְּבֵיתוֹ וּמְדַבֵּר כִּלְשׁוֹן עַמּוֹ א:כב

V' - ha - na - a - roh a - sher ti - tav b' - e - nei

ha - me - lech tim-loch ta - chas Vash - ti va - yi - tav

ha - do - vor b' - e - nei ha - me - lech va - ya - as ken. –

וְהַנַּעֲרָה אֲשֶׁר תִּיטַב בְּעֵינֵי הַמֶּלֶךְ תִּמְלֹךְ תַּחַת וַשְׁתִּי וַיִּיטַב הַדָּבָר בְּעֵינֵי הַמֶּלֶךְ וַיַּעַשׂ כֵּן: ב:ד

A - sher hog - loh mi - y'ru-sho - la - yim im ha - go - loh

a - sher hog - l' - soh   im   Ye - chon - yoh——

me - lech Ye - hu - doh——   a - sher heg - loh

Ne - vu - chad - ne - tzar——   me - lech   Bo - vel.

אֲשֶׁר הָגְלָה מִירוּשָׁלַיִם עִם־הַגֹּלָה אֲשֶׁר הָגְלְתָה עִם יְכָנְיָה מֶלֶךְ־
יְהוּדָה אֲשֶׁר הָגְלָה נְבוּכַדְנֶצַּר מֶלֶךְ בָּבֶל: ב:ו

U - v - ha - gi - a   tor   Es - ther   bas A - vi-

cha - yil   dod   Mor - - - de - chay.

וּבְהַגִּיעַ תֹּר־אֶסְתֵּר בַּת־אֲבִיחַיִל דֹּד מָרְדְּכַי: ב:טו

Va - ye - e - hav ha - me - lech es Es - ther——

mi - kol ha - no - shim. Va - ti - so   chen—— vo-

che - sed l' - fo - nov mi - kol——   hab - su - los

va - yo - sem ke - ser mal - chus b' - ro - shoh——

Va - yam - li - che - ho ta - chas Vash ti—

וַיֶּאֱהַב הַמֶּלֶךְ אֶת־אֶסְתֵּר מִכָּל־הַנָּשִׁים וַתִּשָּׂא־חֵן וָחֶסֶד לְפָנָיו מִכָּל־
הַבְּתוּלוֹת וַיָּשֶׂם כֶּתֶר־מַלְכוּת בְּרֹאשָׁהּ וַיַּמְלִיכֶהָ תַּחַת וַשְׁתִּי: ב:י״ז

v'ho - ir Shu - shan— no - vo - choh

וְהָעִיר שׁוּשָׁן נָבוֹכָה: ג:ט״ו

U - Mor - de - chay— yo - da es kol

a - sher na - a - soh va - yik - ra Mor-de-chay es b'go - dov

va - yil - bash sak— vo - e - fer

va - ye - tze b'soch ho - ir va - yitz - ak—

z'o - koh g'do - loh— u - mo - roh—

וּמָרְדְּכַי יָדַע אֶת־כָּל־אֲשֶׁר נַעֲשָׂה וַיִּקְרַע מָרְדְּכַי אֶת־בְּגָדָיו וַיִּלְבַּשׁ
שַׂק וָאֵפֶר וַיֵּצֵא בְּתוֹךְ הָעִיר וַיִּזְעַק זְעָקָה גְדוֹלָה וּמָרָה: ד:א

Re - vach v' - ha - tzo - loh— ya - a - mod

la - y - hu - dim mi - mo - kom a - cher

v'at u - ves o - vich———— to - ve - du.

רוּחַ וְהַצָּלָה יַעֲמוֹד לַיְּהוּדִים מִמָּקוֹם אַחֵר וְאַתְּ וּבֵית־אָבִיךְ
תֹּאבֵדוּ ד:י״ד

V' - cha - a - sher o - va - d'-ti o - vo - d'-ti.

וְכַאֲשֶׁר אָבַדְתִּי אָבָדְתִּי ד:ט״ז

She - e - lo - si—— u - va - ko - sho - si——

שְׁאֵלָתִי וּבַקָּשָׁתִי ה:ז

V'chol zeh e - ne - nu sho - veh li——

וְכָל־זֶה אֵינֶנּוּ שׁוֶֹה לִי ה:י״ג

Ba - lay - loh ha - hu—— no - d'-doh——

בַּלַּיְלָה הַהוּא נָדְדָה שְׁנַת הַמֶּלֶךְ ו:א

sh'nas ha-me-lech—

Kach es hal-vush v' - es ha-sus ka-a-sher di - bar - to

קַח אֶת־הַלְּבוּשׁ וְאֶת הַסּוּס כַּאֲשֶׁר דִּבַּרְתָּ ו:י

Ti - no - sen li naf - shi bi - she - e - lo - si
v' - a - mi b'va - ko - sho - si.

תִּנָּתֶן לִי נַפְשִׁי בִּשְׁאֵלָתִי וְעַמִּי בְּבַקָּשָׁתִי ז:ג

Va - yit - lu es Ho - mon al ho - etz
a - sher he - chin — l' - Mor - de - chay —
va - cha - mas ha - me - lech sho - cho — choh

וַיִּתְלוּ אֶת־הָמָן עַל־הָעֵץ אֲשֶׁר־הֵכִין לְמָרְדֳּכָי נַחֲמַת הַמֶּלֶךְ
שָׁכָכָה: ז:י

La - ye - hu - dim — ho - ye -
soh - o - roh — v' - sim - choh v' - so -
son — vi - kor.

לַיְהוּדִים הָיְתָה אוֹרָה וְשִׂמְחָה וְשָׂשֹׂן וִיקָר: ח:טז

Ve - es Par - shan - do-so v'es Dalfon v'es Asfoso v'es Poroso
v'es Adalyoh v'es Aridoso v'es Parmashto v'es Arisay v'es Ariday
v'es Vaizoso.

פַּרְשַׁנְדָּתָא וְאֵת דַּלְפוֹן וְאֵת אַסְפָּתָא: וְאֵת פּוֹרָתָא וְאֵת אֲדַלְיָא
וְאֵת אֲרִידָתָא: וְאֵת פַּרְמַשְׁתָּא וְאֵת אֲרִיסַי וְאֵת אֲרִידַי וְאֵת וַיְזָתָא:ט:ז,ח,ט

4. SHOSHANAS YA-A'KOV* — שׁוֹשַׁנַּת יַעֲקֹב

Giocoso (♩=72)

A. W. Binder

mf Sho-sha-nas ya-a-kov tzo-ho-loh v'-so-me-choh bir-o-som ya - - chad te-che-les Mor-de-chay.

poco rit.

t'shu-o-som ho-yi-so lo-ne-tzach v'-sik-vo-som b'chol dor vo-dor. Sho-sha-nas ya-a-kov tzo-ho-loh v'-so-me-choh bir-o-som ya—— chad te-che-les Mor-de-chay l'-ho-di-a she-kol ko-ve-cho *p* lo ye-vo-shu v'-lo yi-kol-mu lo-ne-tzach

poco rit.

Kol ha-cho-sim boch—— kol ha-cho-sim boch. Sho—sha-nas ya-a—kov tzo-ho-loh v'-so-me-choh bir-o-som ya - - chad te-che-les Mor-de-chay.

*Complete with piano accompaniment in *A Purim Songster*, A. W. Binder,
Bloch Publishing Co., N. Y.

O - rur Ho - mon a - sher bi - kesh l' - ab' - di
Aru - rah Ze - resh e - shes maf - chi - di

mosso

Bo - ruch bo - ruch Mor - de - chay Mor - de - chay— ha - ye - hu - di
Bru - choh Es - ther mo - gi - noh ba - a - di Bru - choh Es - ther mo - gi - noh ba - a - di

Bo - ruch Mor - de - chay Mor - de - chay ha - ye - hu - di— Bo - ruch Mor - de - chay
Bru - choh Es - ther Es - ther mo - gi - noh ba - a - di— Bru - choh Es - ther

poco rit. *Giocoso*

Mor - de - chay ha - ye - hu - di.— *mf* Sho—sha - nas ya - a— kov tzo - ho -
Es - ther mo - gi - noh ba - a - di.—

loh v' - so - me - choh bir - o - som ya - -

chad te - che - les Mor - de - chay.

Largo

f V'— gam Char - vo - noh zo - chur la - tov v' -

Giocoso

gam Char - vo - noh zo - chur la - tov. Sho -

sha - nas ya - a - kov tzo - ho - loh v' - so - me - choh bir -

o - som ya - - chad te - che - les Mor - de - chay.

שׁוֹשַׁנַּת יַעֲקֹב צָהֲלָה וְשָׂמֵחָה

בִּרְאוֹתָם יַחַד תְּכֵלֶת מָרְדְּכָי.

תְּשׁוּעָתָם הָיִיתָ לָנֶצַח

וְתִקְוָתָם בְּכָל דּוֹר וָדוֹר.

שׁוֹשַׁנַּת יַעֲקֹב צָהֲלָה וְשָׂמֵחָה

בִּרְאוֹתָם יַחַד תְּכֵלֶת מָרְדְּכָי.

לְהוֹדִיעַ שֶׁכָּל קֹוֶיךָ

לֹא יֵבשׁוּ וְלֹא יִכָּלְמוּ

לָנֶצַח כָּל הַחוֹסִים בָּךְ, כָּל הַחוֹסִים בָּךְ

שושנת . . .

אָרוּר הָמָן אֲשֶׁר בִּקֵּשׁ לְאַבְּדִי

בָּרוּךְ בָּרוּךְ מָרְדְּכַי מָרְדְּכַי הַיְהוּדִי.

בָּרוּךְ מָרְדְּכַי מָרְדְּכַי הַיְהוּדִי (2)

שושנת . . .

אֲרוּרָה זֶרֶשׁ אֵשֶׁת מַפְחִידִי.

בְּרוּכָה אֶסְתֵּר מְגִנָּה בַּעֲדִי. (2)

בְּרוּכָה אֶסְתֵּר אֶסְתֵּר מְגִנָּה בַּעֲדִי (2)

שושנת . . .

וְגַם חַרְבוֹנָה זָכוּר לַטּוֹב. (2)

שושנת .

5. AL HA-NISSIM — עַל הַנִּסִּים

Allegretto spiritoso (♩ = 100)

Folk Melody

f Al ha - nis - sim v' - al ha - pur - kon v' - al ha - g'vu —

ros   v' - al —— hat - shu - os v' - al —— ha -

mil - cho - mos   she - o - si - so la - avo - se — nu

ba - - yo - mim ho - hem   baz - man ha - zeh.

עַל הַנִּסִּים וְעַל הַפֻּרְקָן וְעַל הַגְּבוּרוֹת וְעַל הַתְּשׁוּעוֹת וְעַל
הַמִּלְחָמוֹת שֶׁעָשִׂיתָ לַאֲבוֹתֵינוּ בַּיָּמִים הָהֵם בַּזְּמַן הַזֶּה:

6. BIMEI MORDECHAY — בִּימֵי מָרְדְּכַי

A. W. BINDER

Bi - mei Mor-de-chay v'-Es - ther b'- Shu-shan Ha - bi -
roh — ke-she-o-mad a - le-hem Ho-mon ho-ro - sho Ho-
mon ho - ro - - sho. Bi-kesh l' - hash-mid la - ha -
rog ul' a - bed es kol——— ha - y'hu - dim— es
kol ha-y'hu - dim mi - na - ar— v' -ad zo- ken

lu   o - so   v' - es   bo   nov   v' -

so-lu o - so   v' - es bo - nov——   al — ho— etz.

בִּימֵי מָרְדְּכַי וְאֶסְתֵּר בְּשׁוּשַׁן הַבִּירָה כְּשֶׁעָמַד עֲלֵיהֶם הָמָן הָרָשָׁע,
הָמָן הָרָשָׁע. בִּקֵּשׁ לְהַשְׁמִיד לַהֲרוֹג וּלְאַבֵּד אֶת־כָּל־הַיְּהוּדִים, אֶת־כָּל־
הַיְּהוּדִים, מִנַּעַר וְעַד זָקֵן טַף וְנָשִׁים בְּיוֹם אֶחָד בִּשְׁלשָׁה עָשָׂר לְחֹדֶשׁ
שְׁנֵים־עָשָׂר הוּא חֹדֶשׁ אֲדָר וּשְׁלָלָם לָבוֹז. וְאַתָּה בְּרַחֲמֶיךָ הָרַבִּים הֵפַרְתָּ
אֶת־עֲצָתוֹ וְקִלְקַלְתָּ אֶת־מַחֲשַׁבְתּוֹ וַהֲשֵׁבוֹתָ גְּמוּלוֹ בְּרֹאשׁוֹ וְתָלוּ אֹתוֹ
וְאֶת־בָּנָיו, וְתָלוּ אֹתוֹ וְאֶת־בָּנָיו, עַל־הָעֵץ:

II. HEBREW SONGS

7. MASSEKHOT — מַסֵּכוֹת

LEVIN KIPNIS
copyright

Folk Song

f Lich-vod Pu-rim ba-nos bo-nim, lis-mo-ach hey-noh bo-nu u-
la la la la la la la la la la la la la la la

ma-se chos al kol po-nim ish lo ya-kir o-so-nu.
la la etc.

הַיּוֹם פּוּרִים, מָחָר חָסַל   לְכְבוֹד פּוּרִים, בָּנוֹת, בָּנִים,

מִצְוָה הַיּוֹם לִשְׂמֹחַ.   לִשְׂמֹחַ הֵנָּה בָּאנוּ.

נָשִׁיר, נִרְקֹד, נִשְׁתֶּה, נֹאכַל   וּמַסֵּכוֹת עַל כָּל פָּנִים

וּנְמַהֵר לִבְרֹחַ.   אִישׁ לֹא יַכִּיר אוֹתָנוּ.

לַ-לַ-לָה...   לַ-לַ-לָה...

8. PUR PUR PURIM — פּוּר, פּוּר פּוּרִים*

Allegretto   M. NATHANSON

mf Pur pur Pu-rim Pu-rim mai chag shel sim-choh ad bli dai.

Pur pur Pu-rim yom hu tov chag shel sim-choh ad eyn sof. ad eyn sof.

דָּג בַּמַּיִם, עוֹף עַל גַּג,   פּוּר, פּוּר, פּוּרִים, פּוּרִים מַאי?

הֵם גַּם יוֹדְ־פּוּרִים חַג.   חַג שֶׁל שִׂמְחָה עַד בְּלִי דָי.

שׁוֹתִים יַיִן בְּכָל פֶּה,   פּוּר, פּוּר, פּוּרִים, יוֹם הוּא טוֹב,

שׁוֹלְחִים מָנוֹת זֶה לָזֶה.   חַג שֶׁל שִׂמְחָה עַד אֵין סוֹף.

* From *Manginot Shireynu*, M. Nathanson, Hebrew Publishing Co., N. Y.

9. HA-YOM PURIM LONU — הַיּוֹם פּוּרִים לָנוּ

JACOB FICHMAN
copyright

P. GREENSPAN
copyright

Scherzando (♩ = 80)

f Ha - yom Pu - rim lo - nu mo - chor yom chol. Ha-

yom Pu - rim lo - nu mo - chor yom chol. Eyl tzi - voh

ba - Pu - rim oz - ney Ho - mon e - chol— Eyl tzi - voh ba - Pu - rim oz-
es Es - ther bo - rech—
Mor - d'chay zo - chor—

FINE

ney Ho - mon e - chol. Eyl tzi - voh lis - mo - ach ha - yom ad b' - li dai.
es Es - ther bo - rech.
Mord— chay zo - chor.

D. S.

ul - vil - ti sh'cho - ach gam o - ni a - zai.—

הַיּוֹם פּוּרִים לָנוּ, מָחָר יוֹם חוֹל. (2)

אַל צְנָה בַּפּוּרִים׳ אָזְנֵי־הָמָן אֱכֹל. (2)

אַל צְנָה לִשְׂמֹחַ הַיּוֹם עַד בְּלִי דָי,

וּלְבִלְתִּי שְׁכֹחַ נַם עָנִי אֲנִי.

Repeat the song and substitute each time at asterick (*) one
of the following lines:

אֶת אֶסְתֵּר בָּרֵךְ.

אֶת מָרְדְּכַי זָכֹר.

אֶת הָמָן הַכּוֹת.

10. SOD SHEL PURIM — סוֹד שֶׁל פּוּרִים

LEVIN KIPNIS
copyright

MENASHE RAVINA
copyright

Allegretto (♩=72)

Has has y'-lo-dim a-ga-leh lo-chem sod
Has has y'-lo-dim a-ga-leh lo-chem sod

b'-Pu-rim es-cha-pes ey-lech l'-ves ha-dod.
es-cha-pes l'-yal-doh

va-a-sha-ne ko-li. Chag so-mey-ach. r r r...

poco rit.
mi a-ni u-ma sh'-mi chag so-mey-ach r r r....

a tempo
mi a-ni u-ma sh'-mi? Oz tik-ro— ha-do-doh
Lo So-roh ki Riv-koh

rit.   a tempo
heyn Sa-rah hi zos A-ga-leh oz po-nai
ya-a-neh ha-dod.

v'-etz-chak b'-chol peh lo So-roh lo Riv-koh hen

ye-led hu zeh- cha cha cha cha— chi chi chi-che che che

lo So-roh lo Riv-voh hen ye-led hu zeh.

אֲנַלֶּה אָז פָּנַי | .. חַג שָׂמֵחַ! רְרָרְ.. | הַס, הַס, יְלָדִים!
וְאֶצְחַק בְּכָל פֶּה: | מִי אָנִי וּמַה שְּׁמִי? | אֲנַלֶּה לָכֶם סוֹד:
„לֹא שָׂרָה, לֹא רִבְקָה, | חַג שָׂמֵחַ! רְרָרְ... | בְּפוּרִים אֶתְחַפֵּשׂ,
הֵן יֶלֶד הוּא זֶה! | מִי אָנִי וּמַה שְּׁמִי?" | אֵלֵךְ לְבֵית הַדּוֹד.
חָ, חָ, חָ, חָ, | אָז תִּקְרָא הַדּוֹדָה: | הַס, הַס, יְלָדִים!
חִי, חִי, חִי, חָה, חָה, חָה | „הֵן שָׂרָה הִיא זֹאת!" | אֲנַלֶּה לָכֶם סוֹד:
לֹא שָׂרָה, לֹא רִבְקָה, | „לֹא שָׂרָה, כִּי רִבְקָה!" | אֶתְחַפֵּשׂ לְיַלְדָּה
הֵן יֶלֶד הוּא זֶה!" | יַעֲנֶה הַדּוֹד. | נְאַשֶּׁנֶה קוֹלִי:

11. LA-Y'HUDIM — לַיְהוּדִים

לַיְהוּדִים הָיְתָה אוֹרָה (4)
וְשִׂמְחָה וְשָׂשׂוֹן וְשָׂשׂוֹן וִיקָר
לַיְהוּדִים הָיְתָה אוֹרָה
שִׂמְחָה וְשָׂשׂוֹן וִיקָר.

12. CHAG PURIM* — חַג פּוּרִים

Levin Kipnis
copyright

Gayly (♩ = 100)
(Phrase 1. **

Folk Song

Chag Pu - rim   chag Pu - rim   chag go - dol   hu   la - y'hu-dim

ma - sey-chos   ra - a-sho-nim   z'mi - ros   v' - ri - ku - dim.

) (Phrase 2.

Ho-voh nar-ee - shoh rash rash rash ho-voh nar - ee-shoh rash rash rash

Ho - voh nar - ee - shoh   rash rash rash   ba - ra-a - sho - nim.

חַג פּוּרִים, חַג פּוּרִים   חַג פּוּרִים, חַג פּוּרִים

זֶה אֶל זֶה שׁוֹלְחִים מָנוֹת.   חַג גָּדוֹל הוּא לַיְהוּדִים.

מַחְמַדִּים, מַמְתַּקִּים,   מַסֵּכוֹת רַעֲשָׁנִים,

תּוּפִינִים מִגְדָנוֹת.   זְמִירוֹת רְקוּדִים.

הָבָה נַרְעִישָׁה

רַשׁ, רַשׁ, רַשׁ.

הָבָה נַרְעִישָׁה

רַשׁ, רַשׁ, רַשׁ.

הָבָה נַרְעִישָׁה

רַשׁ, רַשׁ, רַשׁ

בָּרַעֲשָׁנִים.

---

* Piano accompaniment in *The Jewish Songster*, I. and S. E. Goldfarb, Brooklyn, N. Y.

** Phrases refer to "Purim Hasidic Dance," pages 413–4.

13. MISHLOACH MONOS — מִשְׁלוֹחַ מָנוֹת

Trans. by S. Ben-Zion

J. Engel

Moderato

mf

Esh ba - po - nim bo - a - yin zik, Ha - ko - va el ha - tzad, Otz-
Ba - ruch ha - boh hi - nai God boh, Mah yesh l'-cho kum p'soch! Li

dotz kach Yo - si ha - so - cher se - cho - roh lo ba - yod: Mo-
mam - ta - kim ba - a - lai zo - kon A - tu - yai poz - hai koch! Hoi,

nos mish - lo - ach lo mi - kol, He - och! Ha - bay - soh uf!— Lo
gad - yi gid - yi cha - ve - ri, Hi - nai esh - lach le - cho;— Rak

sus gam dog gam shor ha - bor, Ve - chu - lom no - fes - tzuf,—Sim-
es ha - sus ha - ni - cho li Hash - or hai kach l' - cho— Sim-

choh—   so - son—   b' - chag   ha - Pu - rim,   Sim-
choh—   so - son—   b' - chag   ha - Pu - rim,   Sim-

choh—   so - son——   b' - chag   ha - Pu - rim.
choh—   so - son——   b' - chag   ha - Pu - rim.

בָּרוּךְ הַבָּא! הִנֵּה גַּד בָּא—   אֵשׁ בַּפָּנִים, בָּעַיִן זִיק,
„מַה יֵּשׁ לְךָ? קוּם פְּתָחוּ"   הַכּוֹבַע אֶל הַצַּד,
—לִי מַמְתַּקִּים בַּעֲלֵי זָקֵן   אֵיךְדָּץ כָּךְ יוֹסִי הַסּוֹחֵר
עֲטוּיֵי פָז — הָא קַח!   סְחוֹרָה לוֹ בַּיָּד:
„הוֹ, גַּדִּי, גִּדְיִי, חֲבֵרִי   מָנוֹת מִשְׁלוֹחַ לוֹ מִכָּל,
הִנֵּה „אֶשְׁלַח" לְךָ;   הָאָח! הַבַּיְתָה עוּף!
„רַק אֶת הַסּוּס הַנִּיחָה לִי   לוֹ סוּס גַּם דָּג גַּם שׁוֹר הַבָּר
„אַךְ כָּל הַשְּׁאָר הָא סַח לְךָ."   וְכֻלָּם — נֹפֶת צוּף.
שִׂמְחָה, שָׂשׂוֹן בְּחַג הַפּוּרִים! (2)   שִׂמְחָה, שָׂשׂוֹן בְּחַג הַפּוּרִים! (2)

14. NES PURIM — נֵס פּוּרִים

J. KATZENELSON   A. W. BINDER

Con moto (♩=96)

1. Es haz-ke-nim al tish-o-lu v' - lo es ha - ba-chu-rim.
2. Bi - kesh—Ho-mon es ha-me - lech l'ha-kos es ha-y'hu-dim

Gam a-nach - nu kta-nim o - nu yod - im__ ma zeh Pur - im. A -
No-san che - rev lo .ha - me - lech, no - san lo gam g'du-dim __ . A -

chash-ve - rosh me - lech ti-pesh ti-pesh ho - yoh__ po - seh.
chash-ve - rosh me - lech ti-pesh do - vor__ zeh yo-du - a

Ma she Ho-mon zeh__ ho - ro-sho o-mer lo__ hu__ o - seh.
Ach __ ha __ mal - koh Es-ther pik - chit__ hi tz - nu - oh.

אֶת הַזְּקֵנִים אַל תִּשְׁאָלוּ, אֲחַשְׁוֵרוֹשׁ מֶלֶךְ טִפֵּשׁ, בִּקֵּשׁ הָמָן אֶת הַמֶּלֶךְ
וְלֹא אֶת הַבַּחוּרִים. טִפֵּשׁ הָיָה, פּוֹתָה. לְהַכּוֹת אֶת הַיְּהוּדִים.
נֵס אֲנַחְנוּ, קְטַנִּים אָנוּ מַה שֶׁהָמָן זֶה הָרָשָׁע נָתַן חֶרֶב לוֹ הַמֶּלֶךְ
יוֹדְעִים מַה זֶה פּוּרִים. אוֹמֵר לוֹ הוּא עוֹשָׂה. נָתַן לוֹ נֵס נְדוּדִים

אֲחַשְׁוֵרוֹשׁ מֶלֶךְ טִפֵּשׁ   אֶסְתֵּר, אֶסְתֵּר וְגַם מָרְדְּכַי   הֵם הִצִּילוּ אֶת הַיְּהוּדִים
דָּבָר זֶה יָדוּעַ.   שְׁנֵיהֶם הֵם חֲכָמִים.   מִידֵי הַבִּרְיוֹנִים.
אַךְ הַמַּלְכָּה אֶסְתֵּר, אֶסְתֵּר,   שְׁנֵיהֶם טוֹבִים וְרַחֲמָנִים   עַל כֵּן נִשְׂמַח וְגַם נִשְׁלַח
פִּקְחִית הִיא וּצְנוּעָה.   בְּרוּכִים לְעוֹלָמִים.   מָנוֹת לָאֶבְיוֹנִים.

15. PIZMON L'PURIM — פִּזְמוֹן לַפּוּרִים

Yiddish Folk Tune

Allegretto

f Si - su gi - lu, kol po - nim hatz - hi - lu lo - moh bo - u ha - shi - rim, ha - sim - choh ho - ri - ku-dim? K'vor hi - gi - a chag ha-Pu-rim chag Pu- rim so- me - ach, mar - nin — um - va - de - ach.

זְאֵב וָכֶבֶשׂ   בָּאנוּ, בָּאנוּ.   שִׂישׂוּ גִילוּ.
פָּרַח, עוֹף נָרְמֹשׂ   מִי יַכִּיר אוֹתָנוּ?   כָּל פָּנִים הַצְהִילוּ
קוֹף, שָׁפָן, נָמֵר, פַּרְפַּר,   עַל פָּנֵינוּ מַסֵכוֹת   לָמָה בָּאוּ הַשִּׁירִים,
דּוֹב, לַיִצָן, חָתוּל, עַכְבָּר   בְּתָפִּים וּבִמְחוֹלוֹת   הַשִּׂמְחָה, הָרִקּוּדִים?
כַּף מוֹחֵא, רוֹקֵד נָשָׁר.   נַסְעִיר נַרְעִישׁ אֶת הָרְחוֹבוֹת.   כְּבָר הִגִּיעַ חַג פּוּרִים.

(מקהלה)   (מקהלה)   (מקהלה)

אַף זֶהוּ חַג שָׂמֵחַ   אַף זֶהוּ חַג שָׂמֵחַ   חַג פּוּרִים שָׂמֵחַ
מָרְנִין וּמְבַדֵחַ.   מָרְנִין וּמְבַדֵחַ.   מָרְנִין וּמְבַדֵחַ.

III. YIDDISH SONGS

16. HEINT IZ PURIM* — הײַנט אִיז פּוּרִים

Gayly (♩=96)   A. GOLDFADEN

ƒ Heint iz Pur-im bri-der, S'iz der yom-tov grois.

Lo-mir zing-en lie-der, un geyn fun hoiz tzu hoiz. Lach

Mord-che-le lach, a yom-tov-'l mach, kinds

kind-er ge-denk-en dem nes. Zingt bri-der-lach, zingt, tantzt

frai-lach un shpringt, dem tei-er-en nes nisht far-gest.

Ho-mon iz a ro-sho, dos veist ye-der yid,
O-ber Got nish-ko-shoh, shveigt dem ro-sho nit,
Vart Ho-mon-ke, vart, du zei nit ge-nart
A nes hot ge-ton mit unz Got
Zingt kin-der-lach zingt, tantzt frei-lach un shpringt
Macht kin-der-lach gre-ser dem rod.

הָמָן אִיז אַ רָשָׁע, דאָס וויַיסט אִיעָדער אִיד,
אָבּער גאָט נִישקאָשֶׁה, שוויַיגט דעם רָשָׁע נִיט,
וואָרט הָמָן'קעַ, וואָרט, דו זײַ נִיט געַנאָרט
אַ נָס האָט געַטאָן מִיט אוּנז גאָט
זִינגט קִינדעָרלאַך זִינגט, טאָנצט פרייַלאַך אוּן שְׁפרִינגט
מאַכט קִינדעָרלאַך גרעָסעָר דעם ראָד.

* Piano accompaniment in *The Jewish Songster*, I. and S. E. Goldfarb, Brooklyn,
N. Y.

זֶה הַיּוֹם פּוּרִים .17

TUNE: Heint Iz Purim

זֶה הַיּוֹם יוֹם פּוּרִים
מַה־נָּעִים וּמַה טּוֹב,
זְמִירוֹת נְזַמֵּרָה
וְנִשְׂמַח עַד אֵין סוֹף,
שְׂמַח מָרְדְּכַי, שְׂמַח,
הַצָּרוֹת נָא שְׁכַח,
לָנֶצַח לֹא נִשְׁכַּח הַנֵּס.
הוֹי שִׁירוּ נָא שִׁיר,
כִּי בְּשׁוּשַׁן הָעִיר
הָמָן הָאַגָּגִי אָז מֵת.

הָמָן בֶּן הַמְּדָתָא
רָשָׁע הוּא כָל בּוֹ,
וְרִבּוֹן כָּל הָעוֹלָם
נְקָמָה עָשָׂה בוֹ,
זְכֹר הָמָן, זְכֹר,
נָפַלְתָּ בַּבּוֹר,
כִּי נִסִּים עָשָׂה לָנוּ אֵל.
וּבְכֵן פִּתְחוּ פֶּה,
וּנְזַמֵּר שִׁיר זֶה,
וּנְרַקֵּד כֹּה יוֹמָם וָלֵיל.

18. THIS IS PURIM, FELLOWS

TUNE: Heint Iz Purim

This is Purim, fellows,
A joyous holiday;
With songs and cheers and hellos,
Let's wend our merry way.
Laugh, comrades, laugh,
Eat hearty and quaff,
And marvel at God's wondrous way.
Sing, comrades, your songs;
Dance merry in throngs;
Remember that wonderful day.

Haman, wicked schemer,
His kind we've always known.
But God, the great Redeemer,
These fiends has overthrown.
Wait, Haman, oh wait,
Decreed is your fate,
Avenging and swift is His rod!
Dance, children, and sing,
Make larger your ring,
In happy thanksgiving to God.

English translation: A. M. Dushkin

19. SHLACH MONES — שלח־מנות

A. Rosset   J. Engel

Moderato (♩ = 66)

f Oig-lach blitz un bek-lach flam, Dos hit - el oif a zeit,
Plutz-ling ersht futz Cha-yim-el Die tier hot oif - ge-macht:

Loift klein Moi-she - le a - heim— Yom-tov-dig fer-shmeit. Er
A Gut Pu - rim Moi-she - le, shlach mo - nes dir ge-bracht!

hot shlach-mo - nes ein - ge-koift. Zvai tzu-ker-lach mit berd
Cha - yim - el mein cha - ve - ril, Ich hob a fish far dir,

Tei - be-lach mit foi - ge - lach, A fish - el un a ferd— Gut
Ch'gib dir oich die foi - ge - lach, Nor s'fer-del loz ich mir.— Gut

Pu - rim, Gut Pu - rim, Gut Pu - rim, Gut Pu - rim, Gut
Pu - rim, Gut Pu - rim, Gut Pu - rim, Gut Pu - rim, Gut

Pu - rim, Gut Pu - rim, Gut Pu - rim, Gut Pu - rim.—
Pu - rim, Gut Pu - rim, Gut Pu - rim, Gut Pu - rim.—

אויגלאך בליץ און בעקלאך פלאם,   פלוצלונג ערשט פוץ־חיימל

דאָס היטל אויף אַ זייט,   די טיר האָט אויפגעמאַכט:

לויפט קליין־משה'לע אָהיים   „אַ גוט־פּורים, משה'לע!

יום־טוב'דיג פאַרשמייט.   שלח־מנות דיר געבראַכט!"

ער האָט שלח־מנות איינגעקויפט: „חיימל, מיין חברל,

צוויי צוקערלאַך מיט בערד,   איך האָב אַ פיש פאַר דיר,

טײבעלאַך מיט פויגעלאַך,   כ'גיב דיר אויך די פויגעלאַך

אַ פישל און אַ פערד.   נאָר ס'פּערדל לאָז איך מיר."

גוט־פּורים, גוט־פּורים, גוט־פּורים!   גוט־פּורים, גוט־פּורים, גוט־פּורים!

20. HOP, MEINE HOMON-TASHEN! — האָפ מיינע המן־טאַשׁן!

Quickly (♩=100)

Folk Tune

f Yach-ne d'vo-she fort in shtot, Halt zich in ein - pa - ken;
S'geht a reg - en s'geht a shnai, s'ka-pet fun di de—cher,

Darf oif Pur - im koi - fen mon, Ho-mon - ta-shen ba - ken.
Yach-ne d'vo-she trogt shoin me, In a zak mit le - cher.

Hup, mei - ne Ho - mon - ta - shen Hup mei - ne

vei - se, Es hot mit mei - ne Ho - mon - ta - shen

grod pa - sirt a mai - se. grod pa - sirt a mai - se.

יאַכנע דוואָשע פאָרט אין שטאָט, ס'גייט אַ רעגן, ס'גייט אַ שניי,
האַלט זיך אין איין פּאַקן; ס'קאַפּעט פון די דעכער,
דאַרף אויף פּורים קויפן מאָן, יאַכנע דוואָשע טראָגט שוין מעל,
המן־טאַשׁן באַקן. אין אַ זאַק מיט לעכער.

האָפ מיינע המן־טאַשׁן,
האָפ מיינע ווייסע;
עס האָט מיט מיינע המן־טאַשׁן
גראָד פאַסירט אַ מעשׂה.

ניט קיין פּוטער, ניט קיין מעל, יאַכנע טראָגט שוין שלח־מנות
אויך פאַרגעסן הייוון; צו דער באָבע יענטע:
נאָר מיט מזל עס איז שוין גרייט, צוויי דרייַ שוואַרצע המן־טאַשׁן,
עס באַקט זיך שוין אין אייוון. האַלב רוי, האַלב פאַרברענטע.
האָפ מיינע המן־טאַשׁן... האָפ מיינע המן־טאַשׁן...

21. PURIM — פּורים

Z. GREENGLOZ   A. W. BINDER

Ma - me zogt: tzulib Ho-mon gor ho-b'n mir Pu - rim ye-den yor
Es is doch do a-zoi fiel Ho-mons oif der velt, oi ma-me zog

Un volt Ho-mon nit ge-ven volt nes— Pu-rim nit ge-shain
Zog far-vos iz Pu-rim ain - er Un far-vos nit ye-den tog.

Un volt Ho-mon nit ge - ven volt nes— Pu-rim nit ge-shain.
Un far -vos is Pu - rim ain - er Un far-vas nit ye-den tog.

מאַמע זאָגט – צוליב המן גאָר

מיר האָבּן פּורים יעדן יאָר;

און וואָלט המן ניט געווען –

וואָלט נס־פּורים ניט געשען.

עס איז דאָך דאָ אַזוי פיל המנ׳ס

אויף דער וועלט, אָ מאַמע, זאָג;

זאָג, פאַרוואָס איז פּורים איינער,

און פאַרוואָס ניט יעדן טאָג?

22. SHOSHANAS YA-AKOV — שושנת יעקב

Folk Song
arr. by A. NADEL

chay. Sho - chay.

Ho-men hot gi - volt di

yi-den uf - hen - gen Ho-men hot gi-volt di yi -den um-bren-gen,

Ho-men hot gi - volt di yi - den tun a tzo - roh iz er a-lian-ge-

vo - ren di ka - po - roh; Sho-sha-nas ya - a - kov
tzo ho loh ve - so - me - choh   bir - o - som ya -
chad   te - che - les Mor - de - chay.

che - les   Mor - de - chay.

שושנת יעקב צהלה ושׂמחה,

בראותם יחד תכלת מרדכי.

המן האָט געוואָלט די אידן אויפהענגען,

המן האָט געוואָלט די אידן אומברײנגען,

המן האָט געוואָלט די אידן טאָן אַ צרה,

איז ער געוואָרן די כפרה.

23. VER MIR ZEINEN — ווער מיר זיינען

Folk Song

$(\! = 66)$

mf
1. Ver mir zei-nen zei-nen mir   O - ber Yi-den zei-nen mir,
2. Ver mir zei-nen zei-nen mir   O - ber Yi-den zei-nen mir,
3. Ver mir zei-nen zei-nen mir   O - ber Yi-den zei-nen mir,

Vus mir tu-en   tu-en mir   O - ber   Pu - rim   fei - eren mir.
Vus mir tu-en   tu-en mir   O-ber die Me-gi - leh   lai - nen mir.
Vus mir tu-en   tu-en mir   O - ber Ho-mon-tash-en es - sen mir.

וועו מיר זיינען, זיינען מיר,   אָבער פּורים פירן מיר

אָבער יידן זיינען מיר,   אָבער די מגילה לייענען מיר,

וואָס מיר טוען, טוען מיר   אָבער המן־טאשן עסן מיר.

24. A GITN PIRIM — אַ גיטן פּירים

Ad libitum (♩=66) *Parlando*

Folk Song arr. by A. W. BINDER

A gi-tn pi-rim a gi-tn pi-rim, ma-ne li-be g'-vi-rim! Hant ho-b'n mir yoim ha-pi-rim

Vet ihr he-ren di groisse vin-dir, Vi got hot gi-hol-fn zai-ne

yi- di -she kin-der.

mf 1. — Hu-men is gi—ve-z'n
2. — Hu-men hot zich ge-zetzt
3. Far flucht zol   ver - en

shil - dik A - chash - ve - re - schen a   choiv
Shpi - len mit A-chash - ve - re - shen a   shach,
Ho - mon vus   iz   ge - vehn der   erg-ster,

hot er   im gi-zugt   di   t'li - ye iz u- fm hoif
Hot men ge-vor-fen goi - rel.   Oif der nek-ster   voch.
Ge-bensht zol zein Mor-de-chai, ge-bensht zol-zein   Es-ther.

REFRAIN *Mosso*

mf Zin-gen mir   tan-tzen mir Shoi - sha-nas yan - koiv;

Mosso

mf

f zin-gen   mir tan-tzen mir, shoi - sha-nas yan - koiv.—

f

אַ גיטן פירים, אַ גיטן פירים,

מײַנע ליבע גבירים.

הײַנט האָבן מיר יום הפירים

װעט איר הערן די גרױסע װינדער,

װי גאָט האָט געהאָלפן זײַנע ײדישע קינדער.

המן איז געװעזן שילדיג

אחשורוש'ן אַ חוב,

האָט ער אים געזאָגט: די תליה איז אױפן הױף.

זינגען מיר, טאַנצען מיר שושנת יעקב! (2)

המן האָט זיך געזעצט שפילן מיט אחשורוש'ן אַ שאָך,

האָט מין געװאָרפן גורל אױף דער נעקסטער װאָך.

פֿאַרפֿלוכט זאָל װערן המן, װאָס איז געװען דער ערגסטער,

געבענטשט זאָל זײן מרדכי, געבענטשט זאָל זײן אסתר.

IV. ENGLISH SONGS

25. GOD IS MY STRONG SALVATION*

Psalm 27

JAMES MONTGOMERY   A. W. BINDER

1. God is my strong sal - va - tion; Of whom shall I fear?
2. Place on the Lord re - li - ance, My soul, with cour-age wait,

In dark-ness and temp - ta - tion, My light, my help is near.
His truth be thine af - fi - ance, When faint and des - o - late.

Though hosts en - camp a - round me, Firm to the fight I stand;
His might thine heart shall strengthen, His love thy joy in-crease,

*From *Union Hymnal,* by permission of the Central Conference of American Rabbis.

When ter - ror can con - found me With God at my right hand?
Mer - cy thy days shall lengthen, The Lord will give thee peace.

26. IF OUR GOD HAD NOT BEFRIENDED*

EDWARD CHURTON   JACOB WEINBERG

f Allegretto

1. If our God had not be - friend - ed, Now may
2. Then the tide of venge - ful slaugh - ters O'er us
3. Praise to God, whose mer - cy to - ken Beam'd to

grate - ful Is - rael say, If the Lord had not de -
had been seen to roll, And their pride, like an - gry
still that rag - ing sea: Lo, the snare is rent and

* From *Union Hymnal*, by permission of the Central Conference of American Rabbis.

fend - ed   When with   foes   we   stood   at   bay,   Mad - ly
wa - ters,   Had   en - gulf'd   our   strug-gling   soul,   Those loud
bro - ken,   And   our   cap - tive souls   are   free.   Lord of

rag - ing, mad - ly   rag - ing,   Deem - ing our   sad lives their prey:
wa - ters, those loud   wa - ters,   Proud and spurn-ing   all con - trol.
glo - ry, Lord of   glo - ry,   Help   can come   a - lone from Thee.

27. GOOD PURIM*

S. S. Grossman

A. W. Binder

Very lively

f Good Pur - im! Good Pur - im—— Hap - py day of glad-ness, Good Pur - im Good Pur - im Drive a - way all sad-ness. Once a year filled with cheer Pur - im Pur - im Pur - im is here, A wel - come glad-some Pur - im! A wel - come glad-some Pur - im. On high a - loft let's raise our voic - es, The sky smiles soft when youth re - joic - es

Very broad

Wel-come glad-some glad - some Pur-im. Good Pur - im Good Pur - im—— Hap - py day of glad-ness Good Pur - im Good Pur - im—— drive a - way all sad - ness Good Pur - im.

* Complete with piano accompaniment in *A Purim Songster*, A. W. Binder, Bloch Publishing Co., N. Y.

28. ON PURIM*

Joyously (♩=80)   A. W. BINDER

1. Queen Es - ther so the scrip - tures say
2. And Ham - an was straight - way be - reft Of
3. But Ham - an's fam - i - ly was sad, Be -

Fast - ed and prayed for man - y a day; For
wealth ac - quired by fraud and theft; In
cause he had been ver - y bad, All

sempre staccato

Ham - an would her peo - ple slay On Pur - im.
fact he was quite bad - ly left, On Pur - im.
oth - er peo - ple were so glad On Pur - im.

Of her good deeds I need not tell, Nor—
Then Mor - de - cai the King did choose, To—
We're hap - py now that Pur - im's here, We—

how she did the ri - ots quell, Suf -
send glad ti - dings to the Jews, Who
all re - joice this time of year, Let's

fice to know she did quite well On Pur - im.
joy - ous - ly re - ceived the news On Pur - im.
shout a - loud that all may hear, It's Pur - im.

---

* Complete with piano accompaniment in *A Purim Songster*, A. W. Binder, Bloch Publishing Co., N. Y.

S. S. GROSSMAN   A. W. BINDER

1. I love the day of Pu - rim, When
2. We'll chase the haught - y Ha - man A -

all are gay and free, I love the day of
way from syn - a - gogue, We'll beat the naught - y

Pu - rim, With gifts for you and me. I
Ha - man, With grog and grog and grog. We'll

love to go to the syn - a - gogue To
cel - e - brate the — hol - i - day With

hear the Me - gil - lah read, To cheer for dear old
cheer and sing - ing then, And comes next year the

Mor - de - cai And clap off Ha - man's head.
fes - ti - val, We'll cel - e - brate a - gain.

REFRAIN

mf With a grogg, grogg, grogg, and a grogg, grogg, grogg! Look out,

Ha - man, we are af - ter you! With a

grogg, grogg, grogg, And a grogg, grogg, grogg! How dare you plot against a

* Complete with piano accompaniment in *The Jewish Year in Song*, A. W.
Binder, G. Schirmer, N. Y.

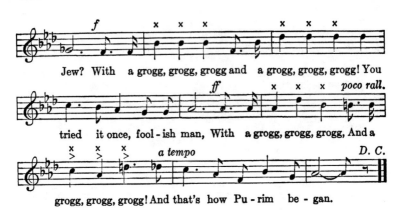

Jew? With a grogg, grogg, grogg and a grogg, grogg, grogg! You tried it once, fool-ish man, With a grogg, grogg, grogg, And a grogg, grogg, grogg! And that's how Pu-rim be-gan.

30. PURIM GREETING*

J. K. EISENSTEIN   J. K. EISENSTEIN

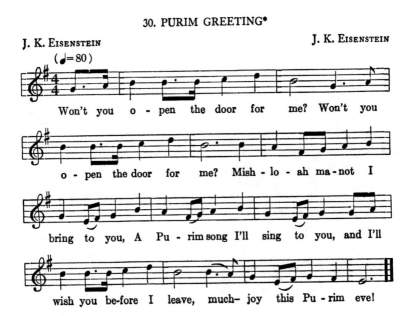

Won't you o - pen the door for me? Won't you o - pen the door for me? Mish - lo - ah ma - not I bring to you, A Pu - rim song I'll sing to you, and I'll wish you be-fore I leave, much joy this Pu - rim eve!

---

*Complete with piano accompaniment in *The Gateway to Jewish Song*, Judith Kaplan Eisenstein, Behrman House, N. Y.

31. A WICKED MAN*

MIRIAM MEYERS

Gayly (♩ = 96)

f Oh, once there was a wick-ed, wick-ed man, And
And Esth-er was the love - ly queen Of

Ha-man was his name, Sir, He would have mur-dered
King A-has-u - e-rus, When Ha-man said he'd

all the Jews Tho' they were not to blame, Sir.
kill us all, Oh, my how he did scare us.

REFRAIN

Oh, to-day we'll mer-ry, mer-ry be, Oh, to-day we'll

mer - ry, mer - ry be, Oh, to - day we'll

rit.   *Faster*

mer-ry, mer - ry be, And "nash" some "Ho-men-tash-en."

But Mordecai her cousin bold,	The guest of honor he shall be,
Said "What a dreadful chutzpoh,	This clever Mr. Smarty,
If guns were but invented now,	And high above us he shall swing
This Haman I would shoot, Sir."	At a little hanging party.
(CHORUS)	(CHORUS)
When Esther speaking to the King	Of all his cruel and unkind ways
Of Haman's plot made mention,	This little joke did cure him.
"Ha, ha," said he, "Oh, no he won't!	And don't forget we owe him thanks
I'll spoil his bad intention."	For this jolly feast of Purim.
(CHORUS)	(CHORUS)

* Complete with piano accompaniment in *The Jewish Songster*, I. and S. E. Goldfarb, Brooklyn, N. Y.

32. I LOVE THE DAY OF PURIM

S. S. Grossman

A. W. Binder
based on Megillah cantillation

Allegretto (♩=80)

1. I love the day of Pur-im so! For
2. — Have a part-y, Sing a song —
3. — Lots of fun and noise a-bout,

then to syn-a-gogue I go, And hear them read the
Turn the grog-er loud and long, Sh'-lo-ach mo-nos
Time to sing and laugh and shout — Queen and King to

sto-ry old Of Es-ther brave and Mor-decai bold.
give and take,__ Eat your Ham-an-tash-en cake.
ban-quet run__ Ha-man's lot is not much fun.

REFRAIN

O Pur-im, O Pur-im, Each Jew-ish girl and boy— cheer

Es-ther, cheer Mor-decai, On Pur - im day of joy.—

33. SONG OF THE PURIMSPIELER*

J. K. EISENSTEIN
Gaily (♩=72)   Hasidic Folk Melody

f Come and see our Pu - rim-spiel! Might-y won-ders we'll re - veal, of

Pu - rim, of Pu - rim, of— hap - py Pu - rim day.—

Get your groggers ready now, While the act - ors take a bow, And

put on their masks in— col - ors bright and gay.

See the me - gil - lah slow - ly un-wind-ing, And

out comes Es-ther danc-ing with the King, Ha-man the vil - lain and

Mor - de - cai the he - ro, Each one has his turn to dance and sing.

* Complete with piano accompaniment in *The Gateway to Jewish Song*, Judith Kaplan Eisenstein, Behrman House. N. Y.

V. PARODIES IN ENGLISH

34. IN SHU-SHU-SHUSHAN
TUNE: Polly Wolly Doodle

Moderately fast (♩=80)   RUFUS LEARSI

f Oh— Ha - man was a high and might - y bluff, In

Shu-Shu-Shu-shan long a - go, He or-der'd Mor-de - cai to

take his der - by off, In Shu - Shu - Shu - shan long a -

go. So we sing, So we sing, So we

sing and raise a row, For Ha - man, he was swing-ing While

Mor-de - cai was sing-ing, In Shu-Shu-Shu-shan long a - go.

But Mordecai sat and laughed in his face
In Shu-Shu-Shusan long ago.
So Haman swore he'd exterminate his race
In Shu-Shu-Shushan long ago.   (CHORUS)

Ahasuerus was a jolly little king
In Shu-Shu-Shushan long ago.
He ordered Haman to take a little swing
In Shu-Shu-Shushan long ago.   (CHORUS)

35. TEN LITTLE MAIDENS

Tune: One Little, Two Little, Three Little Indians

Briskly (♩=120) S. S. Grossman

f The King saw man-y lit-tle maid-ens, The King saw man-y

lit-tle maid-ens, The King saw man-y lit-tle maid-ens, He

loved them not at all One lit-tle, two lit-tle

three lit-tle maid-ens, Four lit-tle, five lit-tle,

six lit-tle maid-ens, seven lit-tle, eight lit-tle,

nine lit-tle maid-ens, He loved them not at all. The

King saw sweet little Es-ther, The King saw sweet little

Es-ther, The King saw sweet little Es-ther, and

loved her best of all. Ten lit-tle, nine lit-tle,

eight lit - tle maid - ens,   seven lit - tle, six   lit - tle,

five   lit - tle maid - ens,   four   lit - tle, three lit - tle,

two   lit - tle maid - ens, He loved her best of   all.

36. KING, O KING
Tune: London Bridge is Falling Down

Gayly   (♩=96)

f King, O King, O, save my life, save my life, save my life,

King, O King, O, save my life, Dear A - has - ue - rus.

2

I'll sure- ly save you, my dear wife, my dear wife, my dear wife

I'll sure - ly save you, my dear wife   my   dear Es - ther.

3

Why do you shake and trem-ble so, trem-ble so, trem-ble so,

Why do you shake and trem-ble so, my   dear Es - ther.

37. WHAT DO WE DO ON PURIM DAY?
TUNE: Here We Go Round the Mulberry Bush

What do we do on Pu - rim Day? On Pu - rim day, On
Pu - rim day? What do we do on Pu - rim Day? On
Pu - rim in__ the morn - ing? This is the way we car-ry the tray,
car - ry the tray, car - ry the tray, This is the way we
car - ry the tray Of Pu - rim Sho-lach Mo - nos.

38. A PURIM MELODY
TUNE: The Farmer in the Dell

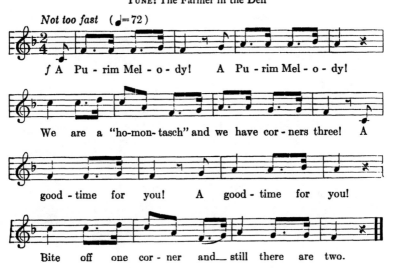

f A Pu - rim Mel - o - dy! A Pu - rim Mel - o - dy!
We are a "ho-mon-tasch" and we have cor - ners three! A
good - time for you! A good - time for you!
Bite off one cor - ner and__ still there are two.

GLOSSARY OF PURIM TERMS

ADAR — The twelfth month in the Jewish calendar which falls about March. Purim occurs on the fourteenth day of Adar.

ADAR SHENI (Second Adar) — In a leap year, which occurs seven times in a cycle of nineteen years, a thirteenth month, known as *Adar Sheni*, is added. During leap years Purim is observed in *Adar Sheni*.

ADLOYADA — A word recently coined in Palestine to designate the Purim carnival that takes place in Tel Aviv. The name is derived from the talmudic saying, "One should drink 'ad d'lo yada' (till one knows not) the difference between 'Baruk Mordecai' (Blessed be Mordecai) and 'Arur Haman' (Cursed be Haman)."

AHASUERUS — The king of Persia who plays an important role in the Book of Esther. He is usually identified as Xerxes I (485–465 B. C. E.).

AL HA-NISSIM (For the miracles) — A special prayer included in the Eighteen Benedictions and the Grace after Meals on Purim and Hanukkah.

BOOK OF ESTHER — One of the twenty-four books of the Bible which narrates the events leading to the establishment of Purim.

ESTHER — The heroine of the Purim story, originally called Hadassah.

ESTHER RABBAH — A midrashic commentary on the Book of Esther.

FAST OF ESTHER — See *Taanit Esther*.

GROGGER — Noisemaker used on Purim in the synagogue during the reading of the *Megillah* whenever the name of Haman is mentioned.

HADASSAH (Myrtle) — See Esther.

HAMAN — Minister of King Ahasuerus and villain of the Purim story.

491

HAMAN DREHER — See *Grogger.*

HAMAN KLAPPER — See *Grogger.*

HAMANTASH — A three cornered Purim pastry filled with poppy-seed. It derives its name from a combination of the two German words — *Mohn* (poppyseed) and *Tash* (pocket). The original name *Mohntash* was later punned as *Hamantash.*

MAHAZIT HA-SHEKEL (a half shekel) — It is customary on Purim to give to charity three half shekels.

MEGILLAH (Scroll) — Usually refers to *Megillat Esther* (Scroll of Esther) read on Purim during the evening and morning services.

MEGILLAT ESTHER — See *Megillah.*

MISHLOAH MONOT (Sending of gifts) — The practice of sending gifts to friends and to the poor on Purim.

MORDECAI — The hero of the Purim story and the cousin of Esther.

PIYYUT — Hymn.

PURIM (Lots) — The Feast of Lots or the Feast of Esther. The name of this minor historical festival is derived from the fact that Haman cast lots to discover the day most favorable to his plan for destroying the Jews.

PURIM KATAN (Small Purim) — When Purim occurs in *Adar Sheni* during a leap year, the fourteenth day of the first Adar is called *Purim Katan.*

PURIM RABBI — One who masquerades as a rabbi on Purim.

PURIMSPIELER (Purim player) — Purim players or actors would go from house to house to dance, sing and produce episodes of the Book of Esther.

RAASHAN — See *Grogger.*

SEUDAH (Meal) — The joyous observance of Purim is culminated in a festive meal at the conclusion of the day.

SHABBAT ZAKOR (Sabbath of Remembrance) — The Sabbath before Purim when the portion of the *Maftir* that is read begins with the words *Zakor...Amalek* (Remember... Amalek). Haman is considered a descendant of Amalek.

SHALAH MONOT — See *Mishloah Monot.*

SHALAH MONOT TREGGER (Messenger for sending gifts) — The messenger who carries the Purim gifts.

SHUSHAN — The capital of ancient Persia where the main events of the Book of Esther occurred.

SHUSHAN PURIM — The day following Purim, Adar the fifteenth. The holiday was celebrated on this day in Shushan as final triumph was achieved in that city then.

TAANIT ESTHER (Fast of Esther) — A fast day which occurs on the day before Purim, Adar the thirteenth.

TARGUM SHENI (Second translation) — A commentary on the Book of Esther.

VASHTI — Queen of King Ahasuerus, deposed for refusing to show herself to his guests.

ZERESH — The wife of Haman.

BIBLIOGRAPHY

GENERAL

ABRAHAMS, ISRAEL, Jewish Life in the Middle Ages, Goldston, London, 1896, chapter XIV, pp. 282–288.

ADLERBLUM, NIMA H., A Perspective of Jewish Life Through its Festivals, Jewish Forum Publishing Co., New York, 1930, pp. 69–73.

AGUILAR GRACE, The Women of Israel, Groombridge and Sons, London, 1872, pp. 335–368.

BRAVERMAN, LIBBIE L., and BRILLIANT, NATHAN, Let's Celebrate Purim, Euclid Ave. Temple, Cleveland.

DE HAAS, JACOB, Encyclopedia of Jewish Knowledge, Behrman House, New York, 1938. See Ahasuerus, Esther, Haman, Mordecai, Megillah, Purim, Shushan Purim.

DOB BER BEN SHNEUR ZALMAN, Sefer Shaare Orah, V-Hu Shaar ha-Hanukkah v-Shaar ha-Purim, Kapust, 5582.

DONIACH, N. S., Purim or The Feast of Esther, The Jewish Publication Society of America, Philadelphia, 1933.

EDIDIN, BEN M., The Festival of Purim, Jewish Life and Customs, Unit VI, Jewish Education Committee of New York, 1943.

———, Jewish Holidays and Festivals, Hebrew Publishing Co., New York, 1940, pp. 117–130.

EHRMANN, ELIESER L., Purim Ein Quellenheft, Schocken Verlag, Berlin, 1937.

EISENSTEIN, IRA, What We Mean By Religion, Behrman House, New York, 1938, pp. 132–135.

FINKELSTEIN, LOUIS, The Pharisees, The Jewish Publication Society of America, Philadelphia, 1940, vol. I, pp. 216–219.

FISHMAN, JUDAH LEB HA-KOHEN, Hagim u-Moadim, Mosad ha-Rab Kuk, Jerusalem, 1944, pp. 119–168.

GOLDIN, HYMAN E., Purim, A Day of Joy and Laughter, Hebrew Publishing Co., New York, 1941.

———, The Jewish Woman and Her Home, Jewish Culture Publishing Co., Brooklyn, New York, 1941, pp. 232–243.

GOODMAN, PHILIP, Purim Program Material for Youth and Adults, National Jewish Welfare Board, 1946.

———, Habanoth Manual, Women's Branch, Union of Orthodox Jewish Congregations, New York, 1937, pp. 52–60.

GORDON, ALBERT I., How to Celebrate Purim at Home, United Synagogue of America, New York, 1947.

GREENBERG, BETTY D., and SILVERMAN, ALTHEA O., The Jewish Home Beautiful, National Women's League of the United Synagogue of America, New York, 1941, pp. 27, 54–57, 71, 80, 103–108.

GREENSTEIN, JOSEPH, Purim, Mizrachi National Education Committee, New York.

GREENSTONE, JULIUS H., Jewish Feasts and Fasts, Philadelphia, 1945, pp. 135–170.

———, The Jewish Religion, Jewish Chautauqua Society, Philadelphia, 1915, pp. 109–114.

HARARI, HAYYIM, Moadim, Head Office Jewish National Fund and Omanut, Tel Aviv, 1941, vol. II, "Sefer Tebet, Shebat, Adar," third part, pp. 312–372.

HASTINGS, JAMES, Dictionary of the Bible, Charles Scribner's Sons, New York, 1899, vol. I, pp. 772–776, vol. IV, pp. 174–175.

IDELSOHN, ABRAHAM Z., The Ceremonies of Judaism, National Federation of Temple Brotherhoods, Cincinnati, 1929, pp. 34–37.

ISAACS, MIRIAM, and ROSMARIN, TRUDE-WEISS, What Every Jewish Woman Should Know, Jewish Book Club, New York, 1941, pp. 52–54, 88.

KAPLAN, MORDECAI M., The Meaning of God in Modern Jewish Religion, Behrman House, New York, 1937, pp. 360–368.

KASOVICH, ISRAEL, The Eternal People, Jordan Publishing Co., New York, 1927, pp. 245–249.

KESSLER, AHARON, Purim Program for Junior Clubs, National Young Judaea, 1945.

———, How to Arrange a Purim Program, National Young Judaea, New York, 1945.

KOSLEBIZ, DAVID, Hag ha-Purim, Curriculum Committee of the Hebrew Principals Association of New York with cooperation of the Jewish Education Committee of New York.

LEHRMAN, S. M., The Jewish Festivals, Shapiro, Vallentine and Co., London, 1938, pp. 137–151.

LEVINGER, ELMA E., Purim Entertainments, Union of American Hebrew Congre_ gations, Cincinnati, 1924. Also in her Jewish Festivals in the Religious School, Union of American Hebrew Congregations, Cincinnati, 1923, pp. 111–157; 351–448.

———, With the Jewish Child in Home and Synagogue, Bloch Publishing Co., New York, 1930, pp. 88–97.

MARENOF, SHELOMO, and LIBENZON, JOSEPH, Megillat Purim Shel ha-Ibri ha-Katan, Board of Jewish Education, Chicago.

MARKOWITZ, S. H., Leading a Jewish Life in the Modern World, Union of American Hebrew Congregations, Cincinnati, 1942, pp. 225–249, 300–304.

———, Purim, Adjusting the Jewish Child to His World, part V, Cincinnati, National Federation of Temple Sisterhoods.

MELAMED, DEBORAH M., The Three Pillars, Women's League of the United Synagogue of America, New York, 1927, pp. 129–133.

MOORE, GEORGE FOOTE, Judaism, Harvard University Press, Cambridge, 19' /, vol. I, pp. 244–246, vol. II, pp. 51–54.

NECHES, SOLOMON M., As At This Day, Bloch Publishing Co., New York, 1930, pp. 38–41.

R. B., Shay l-Ymey ha-Purim, Hamizrach, Jerusalem, 1946.

REINES, ISAAC JACOB, Sefer Orah v-Simhah, Wilna, 1898.

SAMUEL, MAURICE, The World of Sholom Aleichem, Alfred A. Knopf, New York, 1943, pp. 73–83, 90–101, 315–316.

SCHARFSTEIN, ZVI, Purim, Mikra l-Naarim, Shiloh, New York.

SCHAUSS, HAYYIM, The Jewish Festivals, Union of American Hebrew Congregations, Cincinnati, 1938, pp. 237–271.

SCHWARZ, JACOB D., Ceremonies in Modern Jewish Life, Union of American Hebrew Congregations, Cincinnati, 1937, pp. 19–30.

SOLTES, MORDECAI, The Jewish Holidays–250 Questions and Answers on Their Origin, Significance and Observance, National Jewish Welfare Board, New York, 1931, pp. 34–35, 72–74.

SPERO, SHUBERT, and WENGROVSKY, CHARLES, Special Purim Issue, Torah Umesorah, New York, 1946.

UNTERMAN, ISAAC, The Jewish Holidays, Federal Press, Philadelphia, 1939, vol. II, pp. 104–108.

———, The Feast of Esther, Jewish Publishing Co., Chicago, 1919.

WAXMAN, MEYER, A History of Jewish Literature, Bloch Publishing Co., New York, 1930, vol. I, pp. 15–17, 117, vol. II, p. 584, vol. III, pp. 527–528.

WEINSTOCK, I., Purim, Torah v-Abodah Library no. 3, Bachad Fellowship, London, 1943.

ZEVIN, SOLOMON JOSEPH, ha-Moadim b-Halakah, Mosad ha-Rab Kuk, Jerusalem, 1944, pp. 175–196.

B. B. Y. O. Program Guide, vol. XVII, no. 4 (January-February, 1945), Bnai Brith Youth Commission, Washington, D. C.

Bi-Yemey Mordecai v-Esther, Jewish National Fund, Jerusalem.

Habonim Purim Book, Habonim, New York, 1941.

Jewish Encyclopedia, "Ahasuerus," vol. I, pp. 284–285 (Gerson B. Lever and George A. Barton); "Esther," vol. V, pp. 232–241 (John D. Prince, Emil G. Hirsch, and Carl Siegfried); "Haman," vol. VI, pp. 189–190 (Max Seligsohn); "Megillah," vol. VIII, pp. 425–430 (J. Z. Lauterbach); "Mordecai," vol. IX, pp. 7–9 (Max Seligsohn); "Purim," vol. X, pp. 274–283 (Henry Malter and M. Franco).

Jüdische Feste Jüdischer Brauch, Ein Sammelwerk, Berlin, 1936, pp. 364–384.

Krobez le-Purim, Tel Aviv, 5693, 5694, 5695.

Pourim, édité par l'opej, Paris, 1947.

Pourim, Textes pour servir à la préparation de la fête, E. I. F., Paris, 1946.

Programme for Purim, Jewish National Fund, Jerusalem.

Purim, Holiday of Deliverance, Union of Orthodox Jewish Congregations of America, New York.

Purim, Holiday Series No. 2, Mizrachi Women's Organization, New York, 1942.

Purim, Library Bulletin, vol. II, no. 5 (February 1941), Jewish Education Committee of New York. Extensive bibliography.

Purim, Portfolios for Holy Days and Festivals, Board of Jewish Education, Chicago.

Purim Portfolio, Jewish National Fund Youth Department, New York.
Purim Program, Zionist Organization of America, Washington D. C., 1942.
Universal Jewish Encyclopedia, "Ahasuerus," vol. I, p. 137; "Esther," vol. IV,
    pp. 168–170 (Simon Cohen); "Haman," vol. V, p. 191; "Megillah," vol. VII,
    p. 438 (Rachel Wischnitzer-Bernstein); "Purim," vol. IX, p. 36–42 (Max
    Joseph).

I. THE ORIGIN OF PURIM

Haupt, Paul, "Purim," in Beitrage zur Assyriologie und Semitischen Sprach-
    wissenschaft, Band VI, Heft 2, J. C. Hinrichs, Leipzig, and Johns Hopkins
    Press, Baltimore, 1906.
Hoschander, Jacob, The Book of Esther in the Light of History, Dropsie College,
    Philadelphia, 1923.
Jampel, Siegmund, Das Buch Esther, Frankfurt a.M., 1907.
———, Esther und Purim im Lichte der Geschichte, Berlin, 1911.
Lewy, Julius, "The Feast of the 14th Day of Adar," in Hebrew Union College
    Annual, Cincinnati, vol. XIV (1939), pp. 127–151.
Stanley, Arthur Penrhyn, Lectures on the History of the Jewish Church,
    Scribner, Armstrong and Co., New York, 1877, Third Series, pp. 191–202.
Wolff, B., Das Buch Esther, J. Kauffmann Verlag, Frankfurt a.M., 1922.

II. SPECIAL PURIMS

Danon, Abraham, "Quelques Pourim Locaux," in Revue des Etudes Juives, vol.
    54 (1907), Paris.
Ginsburger, M., "Deux Pourims Locaux," in Hebrew Union College Annual,
    Cincinnati, vol. X (1935), pp. 445–450.
Roth, Cecil, A Jewish Book of Days, Edward Goldston, London, 1931, pp. 13, 17,
    50, 55, 60, 129, 144, 154, 184, 186, 196, 201, 248, 277, 281, 304.
———, "Some Revolutionary Purims (1790–1801)," in Hebrew Union College
    Annual, Cincinnati, vol. X (1935), pp. 451–482; "Supplement" to above in
    vol. XII–XIII (1937–38), pp. 697–699.
Zirndorf, Heinrich, "Imitative Purim," in Deborah, Cincinnati, numbers 35,
    38, 48–52, 1–3 (1893).

III. PURIM IN MANY LANDS

Chagall, Bella, Burning Lights, Schocken Books, New York, 1946, pp. 162–192.
Halevi, Menahem ben Shmuel, Mordecai v'Esther b'Shushan ha-Birah, Jerusa-
    lem, 5692.
Kobrin, Leon, A Lithuanian Village, Brentano's, New York, 1920, pp. 89–92.
Levin, Shmarya. Childhood in Exile, Harcourt, Brace and Co., New York, 1929,
    pp. 137–160.

SACHS, A. S., Worlds That Passed, The Jewish Publication Society of America, Philadelphia, 1928, pp. 227–235.

ZUNSER, MIRIAM SHOMER, Yesterday, Stackpole Sons, New York, 1939, pp. 51–55.

IV. PURIM IN THE BIBLE

ADENEY, WALTER F., "Ezra, Nehemiah and Esther,' in The Expositor's Bible, edited by W. Robertson Nicoll, A. C. Armstrong and Sons, New York, 1903, pp. 351–404.

CASSEL, PAULUS, Das Buch Esther, Berlin, 1878.

———, An Explanatory Commentary on Esther (trans. by Aaron Bernstein), T. and T. Clark, Edinburgh, 1888, in Clark's Foreign Theological Library, New Series, vol. XXXIV.

COHEN, MORTIMER J., Pathways Through the Bible, The Jewish Publication Society of America, Philadelphia, 1946, pp. 499–512.

DAVIES, T. WITTON, Ezra, Nehemiah, and Esther, vol. V of The Century Bible (Walter F. Adeney).

DRIVER, S. R., An Introduction to the Literature of the Old Testament, Charles Scribner's Sons, New York, 1894, pp. 449–457.

GOLDMAN, S., "Esther, Introduction and Commentary," in The Five Megilloth, Hebrew text, English translation and commentary, edited by A. Cohen, Soncino Press, Hindhead, Surrey, 1946, pp. 192–243.

HAUPT, PAUL, "Critical Notes on Esther," in Old Testament and Semitic Studies, edited by R. F. Harper, F. Brown, and G. F. Moore, University of Chicago Press, Chicago, 1908, vol. II, pp. 113–204.

KAHANA, ABRAHAM, Hamesh Megillot, Mekorot Publishing Co., Tel Aviv, 5690.

KIEL, C. F., "The Book of Esther" (trans. from the German by Sophia Taylor), in Biblical Commentary on the Old Testament, by C. F. Kiel and F. Delitzsch, T. and T. Clark, Edinburgh, 1873, vol. VIII, pp. 301–380.

MOFFAT, JAMES, A New Translation of the Bible, Harper and Bros., New York, 1922, pp. 559–568.

MONTEFIORE, CLAUDE G., The Bible for Home Reading, Macmillan and Co., London, 1900, Part II, pp. 385–407.

MOORE, G. F., The Literature of the Old Testament, Henry Holt, New York, 1913, pp. 133–136.

MOULTON, RICHARD G., The Literary Study of the Bible, D. C. Heath and Co., Boston, 1895, pp. 230–234.

———, The Modern Reader's Bible, Macmillan, New York, 1939, pp. 378–385, 1382–1383, 1559–1561.

PATON, LEWIS BAYLES, A Critical and Exegetical Commentary on the Book of Esther, in The International Critical Commentary, Charles Scribner's Sons, New York, 1908.

———, "A Text-Critical Apparatus to the Book of Esther" in Old Testament and

Semitic Studies, edited by R. F. Harper, F. Brown and G. F. Moore, University of Chicago Press, Chicago, 1908, vol. II, pp. 1–52.

RAWLINSON, GEORGE, "Esther," in *The Holy Bible with Commentary*, edited by F. C. Cook, Scribner, Armstrong and Co., New York, 1875, vol. III, pp. 469–499.

RHINE, A. B., The Essence of the Bible, Jordan Publishing Co., New York, 1930, pp. 423–435.

RYLE, HERBERT EDWARD, The Canon of the Old Testament, Macmillan, London, 1895, pp. 145–152, 210–218.

SAYCE, A. H., An Introduction to the Books of Ezra, Nehemiah and Esther, Religious Tract Society, London, 1885.

STREANE, A. W., The Book of Esther with introduction and notes, in *The Cambridge Bible for Schools and Colleges*, University Press, Cambridge, 1907.

ZEITLIN, SOLOMON, "An Historical Study of the Canonization of the Hebrew Scriptures," in *Proceedings of the American Academy for Jewish Research*, 1931–1932 (1932), pp. 132–134.

The Holy Scriptures, An Abridgment, The Jewish Publication Society of America, Philadelphia, 1931, pp. 718–734.

V. PURIM IN POST-BIBLICAL WRITINGS

BISSELL, E. C., The Apocrypha, Scribner's, New York, 1901, vol. I.

CHARLES, R. H., The Apocrypha and Pseudepigrapha of the Old Testament, Oxford, 1913.

GOODSPEED, EDGAR J., The Apocrypha, An American Translation, University of Chicago Press, Chicago, 1938, pp. 165–175.

OESTERLEY, W. O. E., The Books of the Apocrypha, Robert Scott, London, 1915, pp. 398–403.

TORREY, CHARLES CUTLER, The Apocryphal Literature, a Brief Introduction, Yale University Press, New Haven, 1945, pp. 57–59.

The Works of Flavius Josephus, Book XI, Chapter VI, Section 1–13.

VI. PURIM IN TALMUD AND MIDRASH

ALKABEZ, SOLOMON HA-LEVI, Sefer Monot ha-Levi, Venice, 1585.

BUBER, SOLOMON, ed., Sifre d'Aggadta Megillath Esther, Sammlung agadischer Commentare zum Buche Esther (*M. Abba Gorion*; *M. Panim Aherim*; *M. Lekah Tob*), Wilna, 1886.

——, Midrash Tehillim ha-Mekuneh Shohar Tob, Wilna, 1891, Psalm 22.

——, Midrash Lekah Tob, by R. Tobiah b. Eliezer, Wilna, 1884.

——, Aggadath Esther, Cracow, 1887.

EISENSTEIN, J. D., Ozar Midrashim, Resnick, Menschel and Co., New York, 1915, Part I (*M. Megillat Esther*; *Derosh l-Purim*; *M. Megillah*; *Halom Mordecai*; *Tefillat Mordecai v-Esther*).

ELIYAHU HA-KOHEN, Sefer Midrash Eliyahu, Warsaw, 1878.

GINZBERG, LOUIS, Legends of the Jews, The Jewish Publication Society of America, Philadelphia, 1913, 1928, vol. IV, pp. 365–448; vol. VI, pp. 451–481.

GOLDIN, HYMAN E., The Book of Legends, Jordan Publishing Co., New York, 1929, Part II, pp. 317–388.

HANDELZALZ, Y. A., Targum Sheni la-Am vela-Noar, Yalkut, Tel Aviv.

JACOB IBN HABIB, Ayn Yaakob, translated by S. H. Glick, Brooklyn, 5679, vol. II, 229–271.

MONTEFIORE, C. G., and LOEWE, H., A Rabbinic Anthology, Macmillan and Co., London, 1938, pp. 52–53, 97–101, 174–175, 679–680, 682.

POLANO, H., The Talmud, Frederick Warne and Co., Ltd., London, pp. 173–199.

POSNER, S., Das Targum Rischon zu dem Biblischen Buche Esther, Breslau, 1896.

RABNIZKI, Y. H., and BIALIK, H. N., Sefer ha-Agadah, Dvir, Tel Aviv, 5686, vol. I, book I, pp. 131–141.

RAPAPORT, SAMUEL, Tales and Maxims from the Midrash, George Routledge and Sons, E. P. Dutton and Co., New York, 1907, pp. 5, 76–77, 96, 118, 194–197, 204.

Helma de-Mordecai, in Bet ha-Midrash, V, 1–8, by A. Jellinek, Vienna, 1873.

In the Days of Mordecai and Esther (trans. from the German), Bloch Publishing Co., New York, 1928.

Megillah, translated into English with notes, glossary and indices, by Maurice Simon in The Babylonian Talmud, Seder Moed (I. Epstein), Soncino Press, London, 1938.

Midrash Megillath Esther, in Sammlung Kleiner Midrashim, by H. M. Horwitz, Berlin, 1881.

Midrash Rabbah Esther (trans. by Maurice Simon), in Midrash Rabbah, under the editorship of H. Freedman and Maurice Simon, Soncino Press, London, 1939.

Pirke de-Rabbi Eliezer (trans. by Gerald Friedlander), Bloch Publishing Co., New York, 1916, pp. 388–409.

Targum Rishon, in Hagiographa Chaldaice, by P. de Lagarde, Leipsic, 1837, pp. 201–223.

Targum Sheni, in Hagiographa Chaldaice, by P. de Lagarde, Leipsic, 1873, pp. 223–270.

Tractate Megillah, Babylonian Talmud, Wilna, 1895.

Tractate Megillah, Jerusalem Talmud, Krotoshin, 1886.

Yalkut Shimoni, Horeb, New York-Berlin, 5686, Esther, pp. 1051–1064.

VII. PURIM IN JEWISH LAW

ABRAHAM HA-YARHI, Sefer ha-Manhig, Lemberg, 1858, "Hilkot Megillah."

DANBY HERBERT, The Mishnah, translated from the Hebrew with introduction and brief explanatory notes, Clarendon Press, Oxford, 1933, pp. 201–207.

Eisenstein, J. D., Ozar Dinim u-Minhagim, Hebrew Publishing Co., New York, 1917, pp. 201–203, 335–337, 440, 464.

Ganzfried, Solomon, Code of Jewish Law, translated by Hyman E. Goldin, Hebrew Publishing Co., New York, 1927, vol. III, pp. 115–121.

Gartenhaus, Aaron, Sefer Taame ha-Minhagim, Torah Or Publishing Co., Brooklyn, New York, 1944, pp. 218–224.

Moses ben Maimon, Mishneh Torah, Amsterdam, 1702, "Hilkot Megillah."

Rabbinowitz, Joseph, Mishnah Megillah, edited with Introduction, Translation, Commentary and Critical Notes, Oxford University Press, London, 1931.

Laws and Customs of Israel, translated by Gerald Friedlander, Shapiro, Vallentine and Co., London, 1934, pp. 395–398.

IX. PURIM IN THE SHORT STORY

Asch, Sholom, "It Has Begun," in Kiddush Ha-Shem, The Jewish Publication Society of America, Philadelphia, 1926, pp. 95–106.

Bloch, Chayim, "Purim Joy and Tragedy," in The Golem, Behrman House, New York, 1925, pp. 173–183.

Gordon, Samuel, "Hindelah's Clothes Prop" and "The Mordecai of Serfs," in Strangers at the Gate, The Jewish Publication Society of America, Philadelphia, 1902, pp. 205–231, 369–390.

Kobrin, Leon, "The Feast of Esther," in A Lithuanian Village, Brentano's, New York, 1920, pp. 89–92.

Peretz, Y. L., "Whence a Proverb," in Yiddish Tales (translated by Helena Frank), The Jewish Publication Society of America, Philadelphia, 1912, pp. 73–79.

Sholom Aleichem, "Esther," in Jewish Children (translated from the Yiddish by Hannah Berman), Alfred A. Knopf, New York, 1922, pp. 178–186.

Zangwill, Israel, "The Purim Ball," in Children of the Ghetto, The Jewish Publication Society of America, Philadelphia, 1938, pp. 127–140.

X. PURIM IN POETRY

Friedlander, Joseph, The Standard Book of Jewish Verse, Dodd, Mead and Co., New York, 1917, pp. 333–348, 770–776.

Frug, S., Alle Shriften, Hebrew Publishing Co., New York, 1910, vol. I, pp. 181–206, 284–293.

Kohut, George Alexander, A Hebrew Anthology, Bloch Publishing Co., New York, 1912, vol. I, pp. 268–281.

XI. PURIM IN MUSIC

Binder, A. W., A Purim Songster, containing a tableau-ballade and other songs and hymns in English and Hebrew, Bloch Publishing Co., New York, 1929.

———, The Jewish Year in Song, G. Schirmer, New York, 1928, p. 16.

———, Esther, Queen of Persia, dramatic narrative with music for reader, congregation, choir and organ, Bloch Publishing Co., New York, 1949.

COOPERSMITH, HARRY, Songs of Zion, Behrman House, New York, 1942, pp. 186–194.

———, Songs of my People, Anshe Emet Synagogue, Chicago, 1937, pp. 178–190.

D'ALBERT, EUGENE, Esther, overture to Grillparzer's play, *Bote und Bock*, Berlin, 1888.

EISENSTEIN, JUDITH K., Gateway to Jewish Song, Behrman House, New York, 1939, pp. 96–111.

———, Music for Jewish Groups, National Jewish Welfare Board, New York, 1942, p. 36.

———, Festival Songs, Bloch Publishing Co., New York.

GOLDFADEN, A., Ahasuerus, operetta in Yiddish, Hebrew Publishing Co., New York, 1907.

GOLDFARB, ISRAEL and SAMUEL E., The Jewish Songster, Goldfarb, Brooklyn, New York, 1925, Part 1, pp. 52–72.

GUTTMAN, OSCAR, Purim Joy, Transcontinental Music Corp., New York, 1937.

HAHN, REYNOLDO, Esther, incidental music to play by Racine, Hengel and Co., Paris, 1905.

HANDEL, GEORGE FREDERICK, Esther, oratorio for chorus and orchestra (piano and organ), Novello and Sons, London, 1874.

IDELSOHN, ABRAHAM Z., Jewish Music, Henry Holt and Co., New York, 1929, pp. 36, 38, 65, 435–438.

KNOLLER, JACOB, Esther, opera in 4 acts, ms., New York Public Library, 1941.

MEYER, MABEL H., Ha-Ha-Hadassah, operatic parody on Gilbert and Sullivan's *The Mikado*, Bloch Publishing Co., New York, 1937.

NADEL, ARNO, Yonteff Lieder, Yüdischer Verlag, Berlin, 1919, part III.

NARDI, N., Songs and Plays for Purim (Hebrew), Tel Aviv, 1940.

NATHANSON, MOSHE, Shireynu, Hebrew Publishing Co., New York, 1939.

———, Manginot Shireynu, Hebrew Publishing Co., New York, 1939.

NAUMBOURG, S., Zemirot Yisrael, for choir and organ, choral responses for *Megillah* reading, H. W. Kaufman, Leipzig, 1847, part III, pp. 14–16.

PERLZWEIG, A., Megillat Esther, complete text and cantillation, George Rutledge and Sons, Ltd., London, 1923.

RABINOWITZ, MENASHE, ed., Nashirah, six Purim songs in Hebrew for voice and piano, Masadah, Tel Aviv.

RAUCH, MAURICE, Esther Hamalke, Yiddish cantata for tenor solo and mixed chorus with piano accompaniment, text by Wolfe Younin, Jewish Music Alliance, New York, 1946.

SLOUGHTON, ROY SPAULDING, Esther, cantata, White Smith Music Co., 1926.

SOLOMONOFF, D., Purim Spiel, one act with music, Goldenerhorn, Warsaw, 1927.

Ahasuerus Purim Spiel, old *Purimspiel* in Yiddish with music, edited by A. Litwin, music for voice and piano by M. Gelbart, Litterarisher Verlag, New York, 1916.

Cantata of Esther, words by Cady, music by Bradbury, Olivet Dotsan, Philadelphia 1890.
Hanukkah and Purim Service, reprinted from *The Sabbath School Hymnal*, by Isaac S. Moses, Bloch Publishing Co., New York, 1913.
Purim, Little Book of Jewish Songs, Hebrew Publishing Co., New York, 1928.
Purim Program Materials, Bureau of Jewish Education, Buffalo.
Purim Songster, Jewish Education Committee of New York, 1941.
Shire Purim, Zevi Stone, Brooklyn, New York, 1938. Texts of Hebrew, Yiddish and English songs with some melodies.
Union Hymnal, Central Conference of American Rabbis, Cincinnati, Third Edition, 1932, pp. 541–543.

XIII. STORIES FOR PURIM

BRAVERMAN, LIBBIE L., Children of the Emek, Furrow Press, Brooklyn, New York, 1937, pp. 76–84.
BURSTEIN, ABRAHAM, "Advice as to Names," in *The Ghetto Messenger*, Bloch Publishing Co., New York, 1928, pp. 236–240.
CALISCH, EDITH LINDEMAN, "The Story of a Brave Queen," in *Bible Tales for Young People*, Behrman House, New York, 1934, vol. II, pp. 124–133.
COHEN, LENORE, "Esther Loves Her People," in *Bible Tales for Very Young Children*, Union of American Hebrew Congregations, Cincinnati, 1936, Book II, pp. 208–219.
EAKIN, MILDRED, "Why the Jews are Happy at Purim," in *Getting Acquainted with Jewish Neighbors*, Macmillan, New York, 1944, pp. 86–89.
GAER, JOSEPH, "The Downfall of Haman," in *The Burning Bush*, Union of American Hebrew Congregations, Cincinnati, 1929, pp. 312–324; "How Esther Became Queen, in *The Magic Flight*, Frank Maurice, Inc. New York, 1926, pp. 49–59; "The Messenger from Shushan," in *The Unconquered*, Union of American Hebrew Congregations, Cincinnati, 1932, pp. 30–42.
GAMORAN, MAMIE G., "The Story of Esther" and "Many Purims," in *Days and Ways*, Union of American Hebrew Congregations, Cincinnati, 1941, pp. 96–104, 110–113; "A Crown for Queen Esther," "A New Friend," "The Megillah," "The Story of Esther," in *Hillel's Happy Holidays*, Union of American Hebrew Congregations, 1939, pp. 116–143; and "Esther," in *With Singer and Sage*, Union of American Hebrew Congregations, Cincinnati, 1930, pp. 271–290.
GERSON, EMILY GOLDSMITH, "A Modern Esther," "The Twins," and "The Band of Mordecais," in *A Modern Esther and Other Stories*, Julius H. Greenstone, Philadelphia, 1906, pp. 9–21, 41–49, 133–140.
GOLDIN, HYMAN E., "Purim," in *Holiday Tales*, Hebrew Publishing Co., New York, 1929, pp. 182–254.
ISAACS, ABRAM S., "The Happy Family," in *Under the Sabbath Lamp*, The Jewish Publication Society of America, Philadelphia, 1919, pp. 109–123.

Ish-Kishor, Sulamith, Children's History of Israel, Hebrew Publishing Co., New York, 1933, vol. III, pp. 12–19.

King, Marian, Amnon: A Lad of Palestine, Behrman House, New York, 1945, pp. 51–54, 69–74, 80–94.

Kohanski, Alexander S., Queen Esther, Asko Press, Lewiston, Maine, 1946.

Leonard, Oscar, "Kind as a Father," in *Americans All*, Behrman House, New York, 1945, pp. 95–100.

Levinger, Elma Ehrlich, "The Purim Players," in *In Many Lands*, Bloch Publishing Co., New York, 1923, pp. 72–78; "The Purim Pussy," in *Jewish Holyday Stories*, Bloch Publishing Co., New York, 1918, pp. 107–120; "A Day In Shushan" and "A Star For a Night," in *The Tower of David*, Bloch Publishing Co., New York, 1924, pp. 99–105, 106–114; "The Spring of Myrtle" in *Playmates of Egypt*, The Jewish Publication Society of America, Philadelphia, 1920, pp. 77–98; "The Cry of the Children," "Purim and the Twins" and "A Disappointed Joke," in *Tales Old and New*, Bloch Publishing Co., New York, 1926, pp. 96–101, 103–107, 115–124; "Esther, a Star of Good Fortune," in *Great Jewish Women*, Behrman House, New York, 1940, pp. 67–74.

Lurie, Rose G., "A Second Purim," in *The Great March, Post-Biblical Jewish Stories*, Union of American Hebrew Congregations, Cincinnati, 1939, Book II, pp. 103–115.

Mindel, Nissan, Complete Story of Purim, Merkos l'Inyonei Chinuch, Brooklyn, New York, 1944.

Silber, Mendel, Scripture Stories, Behrman House, New York, 1918, vol. II, pp. 209–223.

Silverman, Althea O., "Habibi and Yow Celebrate Purim," in *Habibi and Yow*, Bloch Publishing Co., New York, 1946, pp. 72–82.

Soares, Theodore Gerald, Heroes of Israel, University of Chicago Press, Chicago, 1908, pp. 351–363.

Solis-Cohen, Emily, "In Shushan the Capital," in *David the Giant Killer*, The Jewish Publication Society of America, Philadelphia, 1908, pp. 51–70.

Trager, Hannah, "The Festival," in *Festival Stories of Child Life in a Jewish Colony in Palestine*, E. P. Dutton and Co., New York, 1920, pp. 169–186.

Weilerstein, Sadie Rose, "How Mother and Daddy Were Fooled," in *What Danny Did*, Bloch Publishing Co., New York, 1932, pp. 44–48; "Eight Days Fun All in One," in *What the Moon Brought*, The Jewish Publication Society of America, Philadelphia, 1942, pp. 88–98.

Zeligs, Dorothy F., "Purim," in *The Story of Jewish Holidays and Customs for Young People*, Bloch Publishing Co., New York, 1942, pp. 126–145.

Most Purim issues of the following periodicals have appropriate stories: *Haboneh*, *The Jewish Child*, *World Over*, *Young Israel* and *Young Judaean*.

PURIM PLAYS

(min. = minutes; m = male; f = female; numbers in parenthesis indicate age level)

ARONIN, BEN, The Purim Pinocchio or Pincus Pinocchio, the Purim Puppet, Bloch Publishing Co., New York. 6 scenes, 25 min., 5 m, 1 f, (8–13). Children play the parts of puppets.

———, The Purim Wizard of Oz, Bloch Publishing Co., New York. 1 act, 30 min., 8 m, 1 f, (8–13), operetta. Depressed by Jewish sorrows, Dorothy seeks the State of Happiness. Mordecai, the Wizard of Oz, puts her mind at rest.

———, and COOPERSMITH, HARRY, In the Name of the King, Anshe Emet Synagogue, Chicago. 25 min., 20 m or f, (12–16). A humorous operetta.

BACHRACH, KALMAN, The Fall of Haman, New York. 2 scenes, 15 min., 9 m, extras, (12–16). A timely comedy.

BREVDA, MOSES, What is Purim? Bloch Publishing Co., New York. 1 act, 20 min., 12 m, 5 f, (10–13). The story of Purim is unfolded through a simple dramatization.

BRILLIANT, NATHAN, and BRAVERMAN, LIBBIE L., "Animated Megillah Reading," in *Religious Pageants for the Jewish School*, Union of American Hebrew Congregations, Cincinnati, pp. 76–87. 30 min., 9 m, 1 f, (10–13). A dramatization parelleling an abridged *Megillah* reading.

BURSTEIN, ABRAHAM, After the Play Was Over, Bloch Publishing Co., New York. 1 scene, 30 min., 6 m, 5 f, (8–13). Comical episodes backstage after a Purim performance.

———, Casting of Lots, Bloch Publishing Co., New York. 1 act, 20 min., 8 m, 4 f, . (11–14). A comedy with an occasional serious note.

CORWIN, NORMAN, Esther, Columbia Broadcasting System, New York. A radio dramatization, 30 min., 6 m, 2 f, extras, chorus, (adults). The story of Esther modernized.

DAGUT, HARRY, "A Purim Play," in *A Friday Night Book*, Soncino Press, London, pp. 149–166. 3 scenes, 40 min., 3 m, 1 f, extras, (14–18). A modern interpretation of how Ahasuerus and Esther fell in love.

DREW, LIZA BARRETT, Courage is their Badge, American Jewish Committee, New York. A radio dramatization, 30 min., 15 m, 1 f, (adults). The courageous defiance of the Danes against a modern tyrant in the liberation of their Jewish brethren against the background of Purim.

EPSTEIN, AARON, Shushan Short Wave, Furrow Press, Brooklyn, New York. 2 scenes, 30 min., 9 m, 2 f, extras, (14–18). A simulated radio broadcast from Shushan.

FIERMAN, MORTON, FINE, ALVIN, and NODEL, JULIUS, Shushan Review, A Musical Comedy, Union of American Hebrew Congregations, Cincinnati. 2 scenes, 25 min., 8 m, 7 f, (10–14). Two children "wake up" at the court of Ahasuerus and enjoy exciting experiences.

FLAX, DOROTHY ELLIN, It Happened in Elam, Union of American Hebrew Congregations, Cincinnati. 8 scenes, 50 min., 9 m, 4 f, extras, (14–18). The Purim story in rhyme.

GROSSMAN, SAMUEL S., The Purim Players, Julius H. Greenstone, Philadelphia. 1 act, 35 min., 8 m, 5 f, (12–16). The Purim story in rhyme with musical numbers.

HEKTIN, SHOLOM, Without Haman, Hebrew Education Committee for Labor Palestine, New York. 2 acts, 30 min., 12 m, 5 f, extras, (12–15). The children of Haluzim in the Valley of Jezreel enact the story of Purim with a modern touch.

KESSLER, HARRY, The Would-Be Dictator, Young Judaea, New York. 6 scenes, 30 min., 18 m, 5 f, (13–17). A play for Purim on a timely subject.

KIPNIS, LEVIN, Purim Time is Here (English translation by Deborah Pessin, Yiddish translation by Yudel Mark, music by Harry Coopersmith), Jewish Education Committee of New York. 5 min., 4 m, 1 f, extras. A dramatized Purim song.

KRAFT, LOUIS, A Daughter of Her People, National Jewish Welfare Board, New York. 1 act, 30 min., 2 m, 3 f, (13–17). A modern Esther intervenes on behalf of her people.

LEISER, JOSEPH, The Belle of Shushan, Union of American Hebrew Congregations, Cincinnati. 3 acts, 40 min., 6 m, 4 f, extras, (12–16). A dramatic version of the Purim story.

LEONARD, OSCAR, The Spirit of Purim, Union of American Hebrew Congregations, Cincinnati. 1 act, 40 min., 8 m, 5 f, (11–14). A fairy play which includes a *Purimspiel.*

LEVINGER, ELMA EHRLICH, A Purim Present, Bloch Publishing Co., New York. 1 scene, 20 min., 10 m, (11–14). The play takes place at a Young Judaean meeting.

———, Star of Judah, Union of American Hebrew Congregations, Cincinnati. 5 acts, 1 hour, 3 m, 2 f, (13–17). The Purim story in biblical language.

———, The Pageant of Esther, Union of American Hebrew Congregations, Cincinnati. 11 scenes, 1 hour, 5 m, 2 f, extras, (adults). An elaborate pageant.

LINSKY, FANNIE B., A Purim Fantasy, Union of American Hebrew Congregations, Cincinnati. 1 act, 30 min., 4 m, 1 f, extras, (10–14). A symbolical play in poetic form.

MAIZNER, HENRIETTA, The King Chooses a Queen, or The Royal Queen Contest, Bloch Publishing Co., New York. 3 scenes, 20 min., 5 m, 7 f, (13–16). A humorous account of the selection of a queen by Ahasuerus.

MASEFIELD, JOHN, Esther, Macmillan Co., New York. 4 acts, 90 min., 5 m, 3 f, extras, (adults). An adaptation of the classic play of Esther by the great French dramatist Racine.

MEYER, MABEL H., Swing High, Swing Low, Swing Purim, Let's Go! Bloch Publishing Co., New York. 1 act, 45 min., 6 m, 3 f, extras, (14–18). An up to date version of the Purim story in rhyme which can be produced with or without popular swing melodies.

NATHAN, HORTENSE, and LEOPOLD, JEANETTE, A Purim Cantata, Union of American Hebrew Congregations, Cincinnati. 4 acts, 40 min., 7 m, 2 f, extras, (12–16). The Purim story is unfolded through clever dialogue and song.

NEUMANN, HAROLD, Esther, Union of American Hebrew Congregations, Cincinnati. 2 acts, 40 min., 7 m, 2 f, extras, (adults). A farce with music.

NEWMAN, LOUIS I., The Miracle of the Scroll or Purim of Saragossa, Bloch Publishing Co., New York. 3 acts, 1 hour, 15 m, 2 f, (14–16). Based on an historical event.

PERL, ARNOLD, An Ordinary Megillah, Jewish Theological Seminary of America, New York. A radio dramatization, 25 min., 5 m, 2 f, (adults). The wanderings of a *Megillah* during World War II.

SEGAL, SAMUEL M., Mr. Haman Objects, Behrman House, New York. 3 scenes, 30 min., 10 m, 2 f, extras, (10–14). Action takes place in department store show-window where Purim robots are displayed.

SIMON, BEATRICE, Purim's Children, Union of American Hebrew Congregations, Cincinnati. 1 act, 20 min., 5 m, 9 f, (9–12). Haman seeks to determine the day for destroying the Jews.

SNYDER, SARA, Election in Foodland, Bloch Publishing Co., New York. 1 act, 20 min., 1 m, 1 f, extras, (10–12). Scene is laid in a food market and the extras portray various kinds of food.

SOIFER, MARGARET K., Downfall of Haman, Furrow Press, Brooklyn, New York. 10 min., 7 m, 2 f, extras, (10–16). A ballad which retells the Purim story.

———, Up Haman's Sleeve, Furrow Press, Brooklyn, New York. 9 scenes, 30 min., 3 m, 4 f, extras, (12–16). In the style of *Alice in Wonderland*, an American girl enters into the Purim story.

———, A Merry Good Purim, Furrow Press, Brooklyn, New York. 5 scenes, 40 min., 3 m, 3 f, extras, (13–18). An operetta of the Esther story with Gilbert and Sullivan tunes.

———, Mordecai Rides Again, Furrow Press, Brooklyn, New York. 3 scenes, 30 min., 4 m, 3 f, extras, (14–18). A comedy with songs to popular American tunes.

STANLEY, FRANCES, Plum Jam Purim, Jewish Education Committee of New York. A radio dramatization, 25 min., 8 m, 2 f, extras, (adults). Based on the special Purim of David Brandeis.

STEINBERG, JUDAH, "The Rose of Jacob," in *Purim Portfolio,* Jewish National Fund Youth Department, New York. 5 acts, 40 min., 11 m, 1 f, extras, (13–16). A comedy based on the Purim story.

WEILERSTEIN, SADIE ROSE, The Tiny Masqueraders, Bloch Publishing Co., New York. 20 min., 3 m, 1 f, extras, (5–8). A playlet in rhyme, song, and dance.

WISHENGRAD, MORTON, The Great Purim Scandal, Jewish Theological Seminary of America, New York. A radio dramatization, 25 min., 7 m, 2 f, (adults). Based on Maurice Samuel's *The World of Sholom Aleichem.*

———, Emma Lazarus — The Story of a Modern Esther, Jewish Theological Seminary of America, New York. A radio dramatization, 25 min., 8 m, 1 f, (adults). The life of Emma Lazarus.

———, Esther, The Queen, Jewish Theological Seminary of America, New York. A radio dramatization, 25 min., 9 m, 4 f, (adults). An adaptation of the Book of Esther.

Woolf, Henry, A Merry Purim, Union of American Hebrew Congregations, Cincinnati. 2 acts, 20 min., 8 m, 2 f, extras, (8–12). The Purim story with poems to the tunes of Mother Goose rhymes.

———, The Purim Tale, Union of American Hebrew Congregations, Cincinnati. 1 act, 30 min., 5 m, 1 f, extras, (8–12). The Purim story with dialogue in rhyme and song.

A Two Fold Celebration, Hadassah, New York. 1 act, 15 min., 4 f, extras, (adults). The anniversary of the founding of Hadassah and the observance of Purim are celebrated on the same day.

The Story of Purim, Jewish Education Committee of New York. A radio dramatization, 25 min., 5 m, 1 f, (adults).

KINDERGARTEN

Bearman, Jane, Purim Parade, Union of American Hebrew Congregations, Cincinnati, 1947.

Bernstein, Leah, Purim Pictures to Color, Minneapolis, 1945.

Egelson, Gussie E., "Purim Handwork," in Kindergarten Handwork for the Holidays, Union of American Hebrew Congregations, Cincinnati.

Gezari, Temima N., Jewish Festival Crafts, National Jewish Welfare Board, New York, 1946, pp: 23–26.

Golub, Rose W., "Purim," in Festival Course for Primary Grades, Bureau of Jewish Education, Cincinnati.

Goodman, Hannah Grad, Pupil's Activity Book for Days and Ways, Union of American Hebrew Congregations, Cincinnati, 1942, pp. 44–56.

Harris, Hannah, Leiderman, Lillian T., and Peikes, Annette, Hebrew Kindergarten Manual, Mizrachi National Education Committee, New York, 1946, pp. 79–85.

Landman, Eva, Kindergarten Manual, Union of American Hebrew Congregations, Cincinnati, 1918, pp. 148–155.

Pessin, Deborah, and Gezari, Temima N., The Jewish Kindergarten, Union of American Hebrew Congregations, Cincinnati, 1944, pp. 220–248.

Rosenzweig, Efraim and Marion J., Now We Begin, Union of American Hebrew Congregations, Cincinnati, 1937, pp. 61–72, 81.

Purim, Jewish Home Institute Series, Bureau of Jewish Education, New York, 1927–28.

Purim Artcraft Curriculum, Board of Jewish Education, Chicago.

510　THE PURIM ANTHOLOGY

XV. PURIM PRANKS

ABRAHAMS, ISRAEL, "Lost Purim Joys," in *The Book of Delight*, The Jewish Publication Society of America, Philadelphia, 1912, pp. 266–272.

LEWINSKI, YOM-TOB, Haman-Smiting in the Diaspora (Hebrew), Yeda-Am, Series I, Tel Aviv, 1947.

XVI. THE HISTORY OF PURIM PARODY IN JEWISH LITERATURE

ABRAHAMS, ISRAEL, "Purim Parodies," in *Festival Studie:*, Julius H. Greenstone, Philadelphia, 1934, pp. 32–39.

DAVIDSON, ISRAEL, Parody in Jewish Literature, Columbia University Press, New York, 1907.

STEINSCHNEIDER, MORITZ, "Purim und Parodie," in *Monatsschrift fur Geschichte und Wissenschaft des Judenthums*, Breslau, 1902–1904.

XVII. THE HISTORY OF PURIM PLAYS

ABRAHAMS, ISRAEL, "Queen Esther on the English Stage" and "Hans Sachs' Esther," in *Festival Studies*, Julius H. Greenstone, Philadelphia, 1906, pp. 124–138.

SAISSET, PASCALE, "La Litterature dramatique de Pourim," in *Pourim*, E. I. F., Paris, 1946, pp. 101–120.

SHATZKY, JACOB, "A History of Yiddish Theatre," in *Yiddish Encyclopedia*, vol. II (Yidn), CYCO, Paris, 1940, pp. 389–415. (Includes an exhaustive bibliography).

———, editor, Archives for the History of Jewish Stage and Drama (Yiddish), YIVO, Wilna, 1930, vol. I.

SHIPPER, ISAAC, Geshikhte fun Yidisher Teater-Kunst un Drame, Kultur-Liga, Warsaw, 1923–1926, three volumes.

WALDMAN, MARK, "Esther Drama," in *Goethe and the Jews*, G. P. Putnam's Sons, New York, 1934, pp. 128–138.

WEINRYB, B., "Zur Geschichte des alteren jüdischen Theaters," in *Monatsschrift fur Geschichte und Wissenschaft des Judentums*, Berlin, 1936, pp. 415–424.

ZOLLER, I., L'arte drammatica presso gli Ebrei in Italia, Lares, 1932, pp. 11–18.

ZYLBERCWEIG, ZALMAN, "Purim Spiel," in *Theatre Leaves* (Yiddish), Hebrew Actors Union of America, New York, 1944, pp. 1697–1756.

XIX. PURIM WIT AND HUMOR

DROUIANOFF, A., Sefer ha-Bedihah veha-Hidud, Dvir, Tel Aviv, 1935.

LIPSON, M., Midor Dor, Dorot, Tel Aviv and New York, 1938, vol. III, pp. 181-190.

———, Moed, Omanut, Tel Aviv, 1945.

MENDELSOHN, S. FELIX, The Jew Laughs, L. M. Stein, Chicago, 1935, pp. 57, 158.
———, Let Laughter Ring, The Jewish Publication Society of America, Phila-
delphia, 1942, pp. 11, 62, 110–111.
MEYER, MABEL and KLEIN, EDWARD E., It Happened in Chelm, New York, pp.
38–43.
NECHES, SOLOMON MICHAEL, Humorcus Tales cf Latter Day Rabbis, Western
Jewish Institute, Los Angeles, 1945, pp. 86–87.
NEWMAN, LOUIS I., The Hasidic Anthology, Bloch Publishing Co., New Yoik,
1944, pp. 82, 129–130, 161, 360–363, 471.
PERSKY, DANIEL, "Likbod Purim," in Zemanim Tobim, Pardes, New York, 5704,
pp. 135–174; "Purim," in Matamim le-Hag, Pardes, New York, 1939, pp.
139–152; and "Le-Purim" in Likbod ha-Regel, the author, New York, 5707,
pp. 118–211.
RICHMAN, JACOB, Laughs from Jewish Lore, Behrman House, New York, 1926,
pp. 300–301.

XX. PURIM PARTIES AND PROGRAMS

GEZARI, TEMIMA N., Masks for Purim, Jewish Education Committee of New York.
STERN, CAROLYN H. and JACQUES, "A Purim Carnival," in Jewish Teacher, vol.
II, no. 2 (January 1934).
Authentic Costumes for Jewish School Plays, Purim Series, Jewish Education
Committee of New York, 1947.
Games of all Kinds for the Jewish Club, National Jewish Welfare Board, New
York, p. 11.
Purim Carnival, Board of Jewish Education, Chicago.
Purim Carnival, Jewish Education Committee of New York, 1946.
Quiet Games for Jewish Youth Clubs, Board of Jewish Education, Chicago, p. 7.

XXI. PURIM DANCES

LAPSON, DVORA, Purim Dances, Jewish Education Committee of New York, 1946.

XXII. PURIM DELICACIES

ELZET, YEHUDAH, Yiddishe Maakalim, pp. 46–49.
GREENBAUM, FLORENCE KREISLER, Jewish Cook Book, Bloch Publishing Co.,
New York, 1918, pp. 20, 74, 221–223, 235, 239–240, 287, 293.

XXIII. PURIM IN THE SYNAGOGUE

BRILLIANT, NATHAN, and BRAVERMAN, LIBBIE L., Purim Children's Service, Euclid Ave. Temple, Cleveland.

DEMBITZ, LEWIS N., Jewish Services in Synagogue and Home, The Jewish Publication Society of America, Philadelphia, 1898, pp. 125, 256, 284–287, 345, 417–418.

IDELSOHN, A. Z., Jewish Liturgy, Henry Holt and Co., New York, 1932, pp. 163–164, 321–322, 367.

Hanukkah and Purim Service, reprinted from The Sabbath School Hymnal, by Isaac S. Moses, Bloch Publishing Co., New York, 1913.

Megillah Ritual, Central Conference of American Rabbis, Cincinnati, 1939.

Seder Purim, a prayer book for the festival, Prag, 1835.

Seder Yozrot im Kerobez le-Purim, Hebrew Publishing Co., New York, 1927.

Sefer Purim, a collection of all the prayers and piyyutim for this day, Redelheim, 1887.

Union Hymnal, Central Conference of American Rabbis, Cincinnati, Third Edition, 1940, pp. 541–543.

Union Prayer Book, I, Central Conference of American Rabbis, Cincinnati, 1940, pp. 83, 136–137, 298, 395.

NOTES TO CHAPTER I

THE ORIGIN OF PURIM

[1] Megillah 7a.

[2] Graetz, Heinrich, *Geschichte der Juden*, 3rd edition, vol. II, part II, pp. 305–6, 315.

[3] Lewy, Julius, "The Feast of the 14th Day of Adar," in *Hebrew Union College Annual*, XIV (1939), pp. 127–151.

[4] II Maccabees xv. 36.

[5] I Maccabees vii. 43, 49.

[6] Hoschander, Jacob, *The Book of Esther in the Light of History*, Philadelphia, 1923, p. 5, n. 9. Cf. the additions to the Book of Esther in the Apocrypha, 11.1.

[7] Megillah 3a, 3b.

[8] Tosefta, Megillah II, 5.

[9] Megillah 7a, b.

[10] See n. 6 above.

[11] Tal. Jerus. Megillah ci., p. 9, W: "Eighty-five elders . . . . were very sad about this affair . . . They said: Moses has told us: No prophet should add anything from now and henceforth; and yet Mordecai and Esther desire to appoint a new institution! But they did not cease to ponder over it, until God opened their eyes and they found (a justification for it) written in the law, and in the prophets, and in the writings."

[12] These details are argued at length in the treatise Megillah of the Babylonian Talmud.

[13] Cf. Hoschander, ibid., pp. 283, n. 57.

NOTES TO CHAPTER II

SPECIAL PURIMS

[1] *The Jewish Encyclopedia*, Funk and Wagnalls Company, New York, 1905, vol. X, p. 282.

[2] Courtesy of Rabbi L. Rabinowitz, Johannesburg, South Africa.

[3] Fishman, Judah Leb ha-Kohen, *Hagim u-Moadim*, Mosad Harab Kuk Publishing Co., Jerusalem, 1944, p. 165. Translated from the Hebrew by Jacob Sloan.

[4] Roth, Cecil, *A Jewish Book of Days*, Edward Goldston Ltd., London, 1931, pp. 184–185.

[5] Philipson, David, *Old European Jewries*, The Jewish Publication Society of America, Philadelphia, 1894, pp. 66–69. An indication of the economic background leading to the Fettmilch insurrection will be found in *Frankfort* by A. Freimann and F. Kracauer (translated by Bertha Szold Levin), The Jewish Publication Society of America, Philadelphia, pp. 73–107.

[6] *The Jewish Encyclopedia*, Funk and Wagnalls Company, New York, 1905, vol. X, p. 281.

[7] Greenstone, Julius H., *Jewish Feasts and Fasts*, Philadelphia, 1945, pp. 169–170.

[8] Roth, Cecil, *A Jewish Book of Days*, Edward Goldston Ltd., London, 1931, pp. 201–202.

[9] Dangoor, Hakam Ezra Reuben, *Megillat Paras*, in "The History of the Jews in Basra" by David S. Sassoon in *Jewish Quarterly Review*, New Series, vol. XVII, no. 4 (April, 1927), pp. 433–436.

[10] Roth, Cecil, *A Jewish Book of Days*, Edward Goldston Ltd., London, 1931, pp. 248–249.

[11] *Hadoar — Musaf la-Kore ha-Zair*, New York, vol. 25, no. 16, p. 290. Translated from the Hebrew by Jacob Sloan.

[12] Roth, Cecil, "Some Revolutionary Purims (1790–1801)" in *Hebrew Union College Annual*, Cincinnati, vol. X (1935), pp. 458–460.

[13] *The Jewish Encyclopedia*, Funk and Wagnalls Company, New York, 1905, vol. X, p. 283.

[14] Adler, Elkan Nathan, *Jews in Many Lands*, The Jewish Publication Society of America, Philadelphia, 1905, pp. 108–109.

[15] Meyuhas, Joseph, *Yerushalaim*, vol. IX (1911), p. 325. English translation from *Programme for Purim*, Jewish National Fund, Jerusalem, n. d.

NOTES TO CHAPTER III

PURIM IN MANY LANDS

[1] Pool, David de Sola, "Gershon Seixas Letters, 1813–1815," in *American Jewish Historical Society Publications*, no. 35 (1939), pp. 195–196.

[2] Zangwill, Israel, *Children of the Ghetto*, The Jewish Publication Society of America, Philadelphia, 1892, pp. xvi–xvii.

[3] *The American Hebrew*, vol. 92, no. 21 (March 21, 1913), p. 577.

[4] Mosenson, Moshe, *Letters from the Desert* (trans. from the Hebrew by Hilda Auerbach), Sharon Books, Inc., New York, 1945, pp. 184–186.

[5] *The American Hebrew*, vol. 50, no. 6 (March 11, 1892), p. 105.

[6] Mendele Moker Sefarim, *Ba-Yamim ha-Hem*, Dvir, Tel Aviv, 1929, pp. 90–92. Translated from the Hebrew by Jacob Sloan.

[7] Sachs, A. S., *Worlds That Passed*, The Jewish Publication Society of America, Philadelphia, 1928, pp. 232–234.

[8] Persky, Daniel, *Likbod ha-Regel*, New York, 5707, pp. 187–188. Translated from the Hebrew by Jacob Sloan.

[9] Chagall, Bella, *Burning Lights*, Schocken Books, Inc., New York, 1946, pp. 162–174.

[10] Levin, Shmarya, *Childhood in Exile* (trans. by Maurice Samuel), Harcourt, Brace and Co., New York, 1929, excerpts from pp. 137–160.

[11] Ben Joseph, Samuel, *Nahlat Joseph*. English translation from *Programme for Purim*, Jewish National Fund, Jerusalem, n. d.

[12] "The Memoir of Gabriel Brotier," in *Chinese Jews*, by William Charles White, University of Toronto Press, Toronto, 1942, Part I, pp. 61–62.

[13] *Young Israel*, vol. 30, no. 7 (March, 1938), p. 7.

[14] *The Reconstructionist*, vol. XII, no. 3 (March 22, 1946), pp. 14–18.

NOTES TO CHAPTER IV

PURIM IN THE BIBLE

[1] *The Holy Scriptures*, The Jewish Publication Society of America, Philadelphia, 1917, pp. 997–1006.

NOTES TO CHAPTER V

PURIM IN POST-BIBLICAL WRITINGS

[1] *The Apocrypha*, an American translation by Edgar J. Goodspeed, The University of Chicago Press, Chicago, 1938, pp. 167–175.

[2] The Additions to the Book of Esther are translated in the order in which they are found in the Greek (Septuagint) version of Esther, although the chapter numbers of the English Apocrypha are used.

[3] The following selections are culled from *Josephus*, with an English translation by Ralph Marcus, in The Loeb Classical Library, Harvard University Press, Cambridge, 1937.

NOTES TO CHAPTER VI

PURIM IN TALMUD AND MIDRASH

The citations in the text are those of the original sources; these do not always correspond with the sources of the translations. Both are given, in this way, to facilitate comparison.

The translations, in some cases abbreviated and occasionally adapted, have been taken from the following works:

"Megillah," by Maurice Simon in The Babylonian Talmud, *Seder Mo'ed*, translated into English with notes, under the editorship of Rabbi Dr. I. Epstein, London, Soncino Press, 1938.

"Esther," translated by Maurice Simon, in *Midrash Rabbah*, translated under the editorship of Rabbi Dr. H. Freedman and Maurice Simon, London, Soncino Press, 1939.

Pirke de-Rabbi Eliezer, translated and annotated with introduction and indices, by Gerald Friedlander, London, Kegan Paul, Trench, Trubner and Co., Ltd.; New York, Bloch Publishing Co., 1916.

II Targum, from *An Explanatory Commentary on Esther*, by Paulus Cassel, translated by Aaron Bernstein, Edinburgh, T. and T. Clark, 1888.

"Abba Gorion," "Midrash Tehillim to Ps. 22," "I Targum," "II Panim Aherim" and "Aggadat Esther," from *The Legends of the Jews*, by Louis Ginzberg, Philadelphia, The Jewish Publication Society of America, 1913.

NOTES TO CHAPTER VII

PURIM IN JEWISH LAW

[1] *The Mishnah*, translated from the Hebrew by Herbert Danby, Clarendon Press, Oxford, 1933, pp. 201–206.

[2] Moses ben Maimon, *Mishneh Torah, Hilkot Megillah*, chs. 1.1; 3.13; 2.11–18.

[3] Caro, Joseph, *Orah Hayyim*, "Laws of the Scroll," 692.2. Translated by Jacob R. Marcus in his *The Jew in the Medieval World*, Union of American Hebrew Congregations, Cincinnati, 1938, pp. 200–201.

[4] Ganzfried, Solomon, *Code of Jewish Law* (*Kizur Shulhan Aruk*), translated by Hyman E. Goldin, Hebrew Publishing Co., New York, 1927, vol. III, pp. 115–121.

NOTES TO CHAPTER VIII

PURIM IN MODERN PROSE

[1] Leeser, Isaac, *Discourses on the Jewish Religion*, Sherman and Co., Philadelphia, 5627, vol. I, pp. 190–192.

[2] Stanley, Arthur P., *History of the Jewish Church*, Scribner, Armstrong and Co., New York, 1877, Third Series, pp. 200–202.

[3] Aguilar, Grace, *The Women of Israel*, Groombridge and Sons, London, 1872, pp. 363–364, 367.

[4] Hoschander, Jacob, *The Book of Esther in the Light of History*, The Dropsie College for Hebrew and Cognate Learning, Philadelphia, 1923, pp. 298–299.

[5] *Jüdische Rundschau — The Jewish Review*, published by and for liberated

Jews in Germany, Marburg-Lahn, March, 1946, p. 3. Translated from the German by Jacob Sloan.

⁶ *Purim 5700*, Tenth year, Tel Aviv, p. 11. Translated from the Hebrew by Jacob Sloan.

⁷ *The Jewish Tribune and the Hebrew Standard*, vol. 8, no. 9 (March 2, 1923), p. 11.

NOTES TO CHAPTER IX

PURIM IN THE SHORT STORY

¹ Sholom Aleichem, *The Old Country* (trans. from the Yiddish by Julius and Frances Butwin), Crown Publishers, New York, 1946, pp. 51–66.

² Samuel, Maurice, *The World of Sholom Aleichem*, Alfred A. Knopf, New York, 1943, pp. 90–101.

³ Agnon, Samuel J., *The Bridal Canopy* (trans. from the Hebrew by I. M. Lask), The Literary Guild of America, New York, 1937, pp. 329–332, 344–346.

NOTES TO CHAPTER X

PURIM IN POETRY

¹ Pool, David de Sola, *Book of Prayers*, Union of Sephardic Congregations, New York, 1941, pp. 378–380. Translated from the Hebrew by David de Sola Pool.

² Fleg, Edmond, *The Jewish Anthology*, Behrman's Jewish Book House, New York, 1933, p. 222. Translated by Maurice Samuel. This and the following two poems are considered Wine Songs written in honor of Purim.

³ Friedlander, Joseph, *The Standard Book of Jewish Verse*, Dodd, Mead and Co., New York, 1917, pp. 773–776. Translated by Solomon Solis-Cohen.

⁴ Doniach, N. S., *Purim, or the Feast of Esther*, The Jewish Publication Society of America, Philadelphia, 1933, p. 243.

⁵ Klein, A. M., *Hath Not A Jew*, Behrman's Jewish Book House, New York, 1940, pp. 15–16.

⁶ Kohut, George Alexander, *A Hebrew Anthology*, S. Bacharach, Cincinnati, 1913, vol. I, p. 270.

⁷ Raskin, Philip M., *Songs of a Wanderer*, The Jewish Publication Society of America, Philadelphia, 1917, pp. 83–84.

⁸ *The Reconstructionist*, vol. VII, no. 2 (March 7, 1941), p. 6.

NOTES TO CHAPTER XI

PURIM IN MUSIC

[1] See musical illustration no. 1.

[2] *The Jewish Encyclopedia*, Funk and Wagnalls Co., New York, 1905, vol. X, p. 276.

[3] Idelsohn, A. Z., *Jewish Music*, Henry Holt and Co., New York, 1929, p. 65.

[4] See musical illustration no. 2.

[5] Beimel, Jacob, "Mesorot Zimratiyot bi-Kri'at ha-Megillah," *Hadoar*, New York, March 3, 1929.

[6] Idelsohn, A. Z., *Jewish Music*, Henry Holt and Co., New York, 1929, p. 65.

[7] Abrahams, Israel, *Jewish Life In The Middle Ages*, Goldston, London, 1896, p. 47.

[8] See musical illustration no. 4.

[9] Roth, Cecil, "Down With Haman," in *American Hebrew*, Feb. 19, 1937.

[10] Sachs, Curt, *History of Musical Instruments*, W. W. Norton, New York, 1940, p. 41.

[11] We still make noise on New Year's Eve, at the outgoing and incoming of the year. The *grogger* is one of the principal noisemaking instruments used at such festivities.

[12] Schauss, Hayyim, *Dos Yom Tob Buch*, New York, 1933, p. 212.

[13] See p. 323.

[14] This ms. was to be found in the Municipal Library of Frankfort on-the-Main before World War II. Included in his *Torah Or*, Amsterdam, 1857.

[15] See the wine songs on pp. 201–204.

[16] See pp. 355–356.

[17] Low, Leopold, *Die Lebensalter In Der Jüdischen Literatur*, Szegedin, 1865, p. 313. Rabbi Judah Starkes (1640) justified the use of a Polish melody in the synagogue. On setting new Hebrew poetry to popular songs of the day, see Preface to *The Ancient Melodies of the Spanish and Portuguese Jews*, by David de Sola, London, 1857.

[18] This collection is in mss. in the Bodleiana, Oxford. See Neubauer *Catalogue of Hebrew Manuscripts*, no. 2420. See also Shipper, Isaac, *Geshikhte Fun Yidisher Teater-Kunst*, Kultur-Liga, Warsaw, 1927, p. 53.

[19] Shatzky, Jacob "Di Ershte Geshikhte Fun Yidishen Teater," in *Philologishe Shriften*, YIVO, Wilna, 1928, vol. II, p. 239.

[20] Cf. Shipper p. 250. Cf. Shatzky for disagreement with Shipper as to whether *Acta Esther* was to be considered an opera.

[21] Cf. Shatzky, p. 255.

[22] Shatzky, Jacob, "Purim Spieler un Lezim in der Amsterdamer Getto" in *YIVO Bletter*, vol. 19, no. 2 (1942), pp. 212–220.

[23] For an interesting discussion on *Klezmer*, their music, organization, etc., see M. Beregowski, *Yiddishe Instrumentale Folks Musik*, Verlag fun Wissenshaft Academie, Kiev, USSR, 1937.

[24] Kamal, R. F., *Die Yuden in der Bukowina*, Globus, 1905, p. 158.

[25] See "An Ahashverosh Spiel in Prag Mit 100 Yohr Zurik," by Jacob Shatzky in *Arkhiv far der Geshikhte fun Yiddisher Teater un Drame*, YIVO, Wilna, 1930, vol. I, p. 162.

[26] For Judeo-German songs see Elijah Kirchan, *Simhat ha-Nefesh*, Fürth, 1727. Newly edited by Jacob Shatzky, Maisel, New York, 1926.

[27] Cf. Schauss, p. 212.

[28] Shatzky, Jacob, "Purim Spieler un Lezim in der Amsterdamer Getto" in *YIVO Bletter*, vol. 19, no. 2 (1942), pp. 212–220.

[29] Geshuri, M., *Zemirot Purim Ezel ha-Hasidim*, Haaretz, Tel Aviv.

[30] Davidson, Israel, *Parody in Jewish Literature*, Columbia University Press New York, 1907.

[31] Cf. note 18.

[32] Cf. note 26.

[33] See musical illustration no. 19.

[34] See musical illustration no. 21.

[35] See musical illustration no. 20.

[36] *Heint Iz Purim* has been translated into English by A. M. Dushkin, and *Pur Pur Purim* by Mabel H. Meyer.

[37] Binder, A. W., *The Jewish Year in Song*, G. Schirmer, New York, 1928, "I Love the Day of Purim," p. 16.

[38] *Union Hymnal*, Central Conference of American Rabbis, Cincinnati, Third Edition, 1940, Hymns 95, 123.

[39] See musical illustrations no. 34–38.

[40] Bloch Publishing Co., New York, 1937.

[41] See Bibliography, pp. 502–504.

NOTES TO CHAPTER XII

THE ESTHER STORY IN ART

[1] Rachel Wischnitzer, *The Messianic Theme in the Paintings of the Dura Synagogue*, University of Chicago Press, 1948, pp. 29–34; 71–73.

[2] *Targum Sheni* to Esther, M. David (editor), Berlin, 1898, p. 4.

[3] Herrade de Landsberg, *Hortus Deliciarum*, A. Straub and G. Keller (ed.), Strasbourg, 1901, vol. I, plate XVIII, fol. 60.

[4] L. Ginzberg, *The Legends of the Jews*, Philadelphia, The Jewish Publication Society of America, IV, 1942, p. 443; VI, 1946, p. 479, note 184.

[5] Z. Ameisenowa, *Biblja Hebrajska* XIVgo wieku, Cracow, 1929, p. 38, plate VI.

[6] L. Ginzberg, op. cit. IV, 439; VI, 476, note 170.

[7] Ibid., IV, 440; VI, 477, note 173.

[8] Yalkut Simeoni, II, 1057, cited in I. Katzenellenbogen, *Das Buch Esther in der Aggada*, Wuerzburg, 1933, p. 16.

[9] *Biblia (Antiguo Testamento)* traducida del Hebreo al Castellano por Rabi Mose Arragel de Guadalajara (1422–1433?) y publicada por el duque de Berwick y de Alba, Madrid, Imprenta artistica, 1920–22.

[10] Max Golde, in his articles in the *Jahrbuch fuer juedische Geschichte und Literatur*, Berlin, 1926, p. 9 f. and in *Menorah*, Vienna, V. 10 (October, 1927). 571 f., only touched upon the subject.

[11] I. Katzenellenbogen, op. cit. p. 5.

[12] Ginzberg, op. cit., IV, 375; 379.

[13] Ibid., IV, 378.

[14] Ibid., IV, 434; VI, 476, note 168.

[15] Illustrated in auction catalogue, *Die Judaica Sammlung. S. Kirschstein, Berlin*, Munich, Hugo Helbing, 1932, plate VII.

[16] H. Frauberger, "Verzierte Hebraeische Schrift und juedischer Buchschmuck," *Mitteilungen der Gesellschaft zur Erforschung juedischer Kunstdenkmaeler*, Frankfurt a. M., 1909, VI, fig. 17.

[17] In 1560 a set of parchment *Megillot* was produced with printed text in Riva di Trento. The innovation was not approved and the scrolls were destroyed. See A. Marx, "Ein verschollener Pergament-Druck Riva di Trento," 1560, *Festschrift for Aaron Freimann*, 1935, p. 83 f.

[18] Cecil Roth, "Among my Megillahs," in *American Hebrew*, March 2, 1934.

[19] Ida Posen in *Notizblatt der Gesellschaft zur Erforschung Juedischer Kunstdenkmaeler*, Nr. 28 (1931), p. 11. This scroll is apparently identical with the one mentioned by A. Wolf; see R. Wischnitzer-Bernstein, *Monatsschrift f. Geschichte und Wissenschaft des Judentums* (Sept.-Oct. 1932), p. 523.

[20] Discussed in R. Wischnitzer-Bernstein, "Der Estherstoff in der juedischen Illustration," *Monatsschrift f. Geschichte und Wissenschaft des Judentums*, 9-10 (Sep.-Oct. 1930), p. 388.

[21] The A. de Chaves *Megillah* has been published by L. Pinkhof in *De Vrijdagavond*, IX (August 26, 1932), p. 345; he gives the name as Abraham de Chaves. F. Landsberger believes that the author misread Aaron for Abraham, since drawings by an Aaron de Chaves are known (F. Landsberger in *Hebrew Union College Annual*, XVIII (1944), p. 305). Although a mistake is possible, there may have existed two designers by the name of Chaves in Amsterdam.

[22] R. Wischnitzer-Bernstein, "Von der Holbeinbibel zur Amsterdamer Haggadah," *Monatsschrift f. Geschichte und Wissenschaft des Judentums*, LXXV 7-8 (1931), 1–18.

[23] P. Schubring, *Cassoni*, Leipzig, 1923, 2nd ed., p. 66.

[24] Published in E. Munkacsi, *Miniaturmuveszet Italia Konyvtaraiban*, Budapest, Jewish Museum, n. d., p. 43, plates XIII–XIV.

[25] *Die Judaica Sammlung S. Kirschstein, Berlin*, Munich, Hugo Helbing, 1932, p. 11, Nr. 193.

[26] F. Landsberger, "Jewish Artists before the period of Emancipation," *Hebrew Union College Annual*, XVI (1941), p. 363.

[27] E. Namenyi, "Ein ungarisch-juedischer Kupferstecher der Biedermeierzeit," *Jubilee-Volume in honor of Prof. Bernhardt Heller*, Budapest, 1941, 3 ff.

²⁸ M. Goldstein and K. Dresdner, *Kultura i Sztuka Ludu Zydowskiego na Ziemiach Polskich*, Lwow, 1935, p. 115 f.

²⁹ Illustrated in M. Narkiss, "Celebrating the Purim Festival," *The New Palestine*, XVI (March 22, 1929).

³⁰ *Philo Lexikon*, Berlin, 1937, 4th ed., fig. on col. 589.

³¹ R. Hallo, "Judaica," in *Religioese Kunst aus Hessen und Nassau*, Marburg, 1932, p. 37, Nr. 112.

³² Ibid., Nr. 113.

NOTES TO CHAPTER XIII

STORIES FOR PURIM

¹ Edidin, Ben M., "The Festival of Purim," in *Jewish Life and Customs*, Unit Six, Jewish Education Committee of New York, 1943, pp. 3–11.

² Weilerstein, Sadie Rose, *The Adventures of K'tonton*, The Women's League of the United Synagogue of America, New York, 1935, pp. 42–48.

³ Braverman, Libbie L., *Children of the Emek*, Furrow Press, New York, 1937, pp. 60–61, 76–84.

⁴ Edidin, Ben M., "The Festival of Purim," in *Jewish Life and Customs*, Unit Six, Jewish Education Committee of New York, 1934, pp. 15–20.

⁵ Schwab, Hermann, *Dreams of Childhood* (trans. by Joseph Leftwich), The National Council for Jewish Religious Education, London, 5705, pp. 21–23.

⁶ Gaer, Joseph, *The Magic Flight, Jewish Tales and Legends*, Frank-Maurice, Inc., New York, 1926, pp. 49–57.

⁷ *Opinion*, vol. XVI, no. 5 (March, 1946), pp. 6–7.

⁸ Von Sacher Masoch, Leopold, *Jewish Tales* (trans. from the French by Harriet Lieber Cohen), A. C. McClurg and Co., Chicago, 1894, pp. 192–203.

⁹ *The Jewish Child*, vol. III, no. 8 (Feb. 26, 1915), pp. 1–2. Translated from the German by L. Kornfeld.

NOTES TO CHAPTER XIV

POEMS FOR PURIM

¹ Levy, Sara G., *Mother Goose Rhymes for Jewish Children*, Bloch Publishing Co., New York, 1945, pp. 35–36.

² Edidin, Ben M., "The Festival of Purim," in *Jewish Life and Customs*, Unit Six, Jewish Education Committee of New York, 1943, pp. 12–13. Trans. by Deborah Pessin.

³ Weilerstein, Sadie Rose, *The Singing Way*, League Press, New York, 1946, p. 37.

⁴ Levinger, Elma Ehrlich, *Jewish Festivals in the Religious School*, Union of American Hebrew Congregations, Cincinnati, 1923, pp. 139–140.

⁵ *Recitation Series No. I*, The Circle of Jewish Children of America, n. d.

⁶ *The Young Judaean*, vol. XXI, no. 5 (March, 1933), p. 8.

⁷ Sampter, Jessie E., *Around the Year in Rhymes for the Jewish Child*, Bloch Publishing Co., New York, 1920, p. 48.

⁸ *The Young Judaean*, vol. XIV, no. 2 (March, 1924), p. 2.

⁹ *Gems of Hebrew Verse* (trans. by Harry H. Fein), Bruce Humphries, Inc., Boston, 1940, pp. 29–30.

¹⁰ Levinger, Elma Ehrlich, *Jewish Festivals in the Religious School*, Union of American Hebrew Congregations, Cincinnati, 1923, p. 146.

¹¹ *The Jewish Exponent*, vol. 46, no. 22 (March 13, 1908).

¹² Aguilar, Grace, *The Spirit of Judaism* (edited by Isaac Leeser), Sherman and Co., Philadelphia, 5633, pp. 242–243.

NOTES TO CHAPTER XV

PURIM PRANKS

¹ Greenstone, Julius H., *Jewish Feasts and Fasts*, Philadelphia, 1945, p. 166.

² Deut. 25.19.

³ Prov. 10.7.

⁴ Deut. 25.2.

⁵ *Minhage Maharil*, no. 77.

⁶ *'Aruk*, s. v. "Shevar."

⁷ Ginzberg, Louis, *Geonica*, Jewish Theological Seminary, New York, 1909, vol. II, pp. 1–2.

⁸ Davidson, Israel, *Parody in Jewish Literature*, Columbia University Press, New York, 1907, p. 21.

⁹ Abrahams, Israel, *The Book of Delight*, The Jewish Publication Society of America, Philadelphia, 1912, pp. 226–272.

¹⁰ Sanh. 64 b.

¹¹ Ibid.

¹² Davidson, Israel, *Parody in Jewish Literature*, Columbia University Press, New York, 1907, p. 21.

¹³ Abrahams, Israel, *Jewish Life in the Middle Ages*, Edward Goldston, Ltd., London, 1932, p. 402.

¹⁴ Schudt, Johann Jakob, *Jüdische Merkwürdigkeiten*, Frankfort-on-the-Main, 1714, Part 2, p. 309.

¹⁵ Davidson, Israel, *Parody in Jewish Literature*, Columbia University Press, New York, 1907, p. 21.

¹⁶ Chorny, Joseph Judah, *Sefer ha-Masa'ot*, St. Petersburg, 1844, pp. 191–192.

¹⁷ *Rama*, in *Shulhan 'Aruk, Orah Hayyim*, "Hilkot Megillah" 680. 17.

¹⁸ Modena, Leon de, *The Ceremonies and Religious Customs of Various Nations of the Known World*, London, 1733, vol. I, p. 69.

[19] Doniach, N. S., *Purim*, The Jewish Publication Society of America, Phila. delphia, 1933, p. 71.

[20] Raphael Aaron ben Shimon, *Nahar Mizraim*, "Hilkot Purim" 10.

[21] Reifmann, Jacob, "Minhag Hakot Haman be-Purim" in *Hamagid*, Lyck, 1858, fo. V. 2, no. 11, p. 43.

[22] See *An English Purim*, by Gabriel Acosta, pp. 39–43.

[23] Zarchin, Michael M., *Jews in the Province of Posen*, Dropsie College, Philadelphia, 1939, p. 74.

[24] Deut. 22.5.

[25] Fishman, Judah Leb ha-Kohen, *Hagim u-Moadim*, Mosad Harab Kuk, Jerusalem, 5704, pp. 121–123.

[26] Hulin 139 b.

[27] Marcus, Jacob R., *The Jew in the Medieval World*, Union of American Hebrew Congregations, Cincinnati, 1938, pp. 84, 94, 95.

[28] Ibid., 212–213, 220.

[29] Philipson, David, *The Reform Movement in Judaism*, Macmillan Company, New York, 1931, p. 35.

[30] Esther 6.9.

[31] Raphael Aaron ben Shimon, *Nahar Mizraim*, "Hilkot Purim," 11.

[32] *Terumot ha-Deshen*, no. 106.

[33] Abrahams, Israel, *The Book of Delight*, The Jewish Publication Society of America, Philadelphia, 1912, pp. 266–272.

NOTES TO CHAPTER XVI

THE HISTORY OF PURIM PARODY
IN JEWISH LITERATURE

[1] Abstracted from *Parody in Jewish Literature*, by Israel Davidson, Columbia University Press, New York, 1907.

NOTES TO CHAPTER XVIII

PURIM CURIOSITIES

[1] II Maccabees 15.36.

[2] Katsh, Abraham I., *Hebrew in American Higher Education*, New York University Book Store, New York, 1941, pp. 62–63.

[3] Mashiof, S., "Purim b-Hodu," in *Ha-Zofeh*, II Adar 14, 5698, p. 2.

[4] Benjamin the Second, *Masay Yisroel*, Lik, 1859, p. 63.

[5] Isaacs, I. S., "Myer S. Isaacs," in *American Jewish Historical Society Publications*, no. 13 (1905), p. 146.

[6] *Purim Gazette*, Purim Association, New York, March 15, 1883, p. 5.

[7] *American Hebrew*, vol. 26, no. 2 (February 19, 1886), p. 24.

[8] Ibid., vol. 66, no. 13 (February 2, 1900), p. 413.

[9] Ibid., vol. 14, no. 5 (March 16, 1883), p. 59.

[10] Ibid., vol. 14, no. 3 (March 2, 1883), p. 35.

[11] Lowenthal, Marvin, *Henrietta Szold — Life and Letters*, The Viking Press, New York, 1942, pp. 76–77.

[12] Jewish Telegraphic Agency despatch from Zurich, March 14, 1941.

[13] Jewish Telegraphic Agency despatch from London, March 14, 1941.

[14] *The Purim Book*, Habonim, London, p. 14.

[15] JPS — Palcor despatch from Jerusalem, March 6, 1942.

[16] *New York Times*, January 31, 1944, p. 4.

[17] *New York Post*, October 16, 1946, p. 38.

[18] Pes. 117 a.

[19] Vogelstein, Herman, *Rome*, The Jewish Publication Society of America, Philadelphia, 1940, pp. 381, 391.

[20] Kohler, K., *Studies, Addresses, and Personal Papers*, The Alumni Association of the Hebrew Union College, Cincinnati, 1931, pp. 402–403.

[21] Mills, John, *Three Months Residence at Nablus and an Account of the Modern Samaritans*, John Murray, London, 1864, pp. 266–267.

NOTES TO CHAPTER XIX

PURIM WIT AND HUMOR

[1] Drouianoff, A., *Sefer ha-Bedihah veha-Hidud*, Dvir, Tel Aviv, 1936, vol. 2, pp. 289–290 (no. 1750).

[2] Rokotz, J. K. K., *Siach Sarfei Kodesh*, Lodz, 1929, vol. II, p. 46. This and the following three selections from hasidic literature have been culled from *The Hasidic Anthology*, selected, compiled and arranged by Louis I. Newman in collaboration with Samuel Spitz, Bloch Publishing Co., New York, 1934.

[3] Kleinman, M. S., *Or Yesharim*, Piotrkov, 1924, p. 134.

[4] Rokotz, J. K. K., *Siach Sarfei Kodesh*, Lodz, 1929, vol. II, p. 17.

[5] Megillah 7 a.

[6] Yellin, A., *Derek Zaddikim*, Warsaw, 1912, p. 32.

[7] Buber, Martin, *For the Sake of Heaven*, The Jewish Publication Society of America, Philadelphia, 1945, p. 258.

[8] Drouianoff, A., *Sefer ha-Bedihah veha-Hidud*, Dvir, Tel Aviv, 1936, vol. I, pp. 314–315 (no. 812).

[9] Ashkenazi, Izhak, *Ozros fun Yiddisher Humor*, 1929, p. 25.

[10] Lipson, M., *Midor Dor*, Dorot, Tel Aviv and New York, 1938, vol. III, p. 184.

[11] Ibid., p. 190.

[12] Ibid., p. 185.

[13] Adapted from *It Happened in Chelm*, by Edward E. Klein and Mabel H. Meyer.

NOTES TO CHAPTER XX

PURIM PARTIES AND PROGRAMS

[1] Brilliant, Nathan and Braverman, Libbie L., *Religious Pageants*, Union of American Hebrew Congregations, Cincinnati, 1941, pp. 76–87.

NOTES TO CHAPTER XXII

PURIM DELICACIES

[1] Elzat, Y., "Mi-Minhage Yisrael," in *Reshumot*, I, p. 343.
[2] Greenberg, Betty D., and Silverman, Althea O., *The Jewish Home Beautiful*, The Women's League of the United Synagogue of America, New York, 1941, pp. 103–107.

NOTES TO CHAPTER XXIII

PURIM IN THE SYNAGOGUE

[1] Jer. Meg. p. 25.
[2] Josephus, *Antiquities of the Jews*, Book XI, 6.5.
[3] Levinski, Yom Tob, "Ha-Shabatot ha-Meyuhasot b-Minhage Yisrael," pp. 109–111 in *Reshumot*, New Series, vol. I, Dvir, Tel Aviv, 5706.
[4] Sofrim 17.4.
[5] I Maccabees 7.49.
[6] Sofrim 17.4.
[7] Jer. Meg. p. 24.
[8] Mishnah Shekalim 1.1.
[9] Sofrim 20.8.
[10] Meg. 4 a.
[11] Meg. 21 b.
[12] Sofrim 14.6; Jer. Meg. 3.7.
[13] Fishman, Judah Leb ha-Kohen, *Hagim u-Moadim*, Mosad ha-Rab Kuk, Jerusalem, 5704, p. 143.
[14] Mishnah Meg. 3.6.
[15] Meg. 21 b.
[16] *Union Prayer Book*, Central Conference of American Rabbis, 1940, p. 83.
[17] Ibid., pp. 136–137.
[18] *Megillah Ritual*, Central Conference of American Rabbis, 1939.
[19] *Text of the Union Megillah*, prepared by the Committee on Ceremonies, Central Conference of American Rabbis, 1942.
[20] Mishnah Meg. 1.1.